Middle East Air Power in the 21st Century

This book is dedicated to Fergus and Joseph Ripley –
aspiring pilots for the twenty-first century!

Middle East Air Power in the 21st Century

Tim Ripley

Pen & Sword
AVIATION

First published in Great Britain in 2010 by
Pen & Sword Aviation
An imprint of
Pen & Sword Books Ltd
47 Church Street
Barnsley
South Yorkshire
S70 2AS

ISBN 978 1 84884 099 7

A CIP catalogue record for this book is
available from the British Library

Typeset in 10pt Palatino by Mac Style, Beverley, East Yorkshire
Printed and bound by Kyodo Nation Printing Service, Thailand

Pen & Sword Books Ltd incorporates the Imprints of Pen & Sword Aviation,
Pen & Sword Maritime, Pen & Sword Military, Wharncliffe Local History, Pen &
Sword Select, Pen & Sword Military Classics, Leo Cooper, Seaforth Publishing and
Frontline Publishing

For a complete list of Pen & Sword titles please contact
PEN & SWORD BOOKS LIMITED
47 Church Street, Barnsley, South Yorkshire, S70 2AS, England
E-mail: enquiries@pen-and-sword.co.uk
Website: www.pen-and-sword.co.uk

Contents

Preface

Dateline: September 2006

Location: Al Udeid airbase, Qatar

Even in the hot morning haze of the Arabian Gulf, the menacing shape of the giant Rockwell B-1B Lancer bombers was unmistakable. Five of the US Air Force bombers were parked up with ground crew around them loading bombs, pumping in fuel and checking for faults. An aircrew had arrived and were taking over the aircraft from a crew chief. A little over an hour later, the B-1Bs could be on combat air patrol duty over central Iraq on call to deliver satellite-guided joint direct attack munitions against insurgents threatening US and Coalition troops.

Along the massive flight line at Al Udeid, dozens of giant Boeing KC-135 Stratotanker air-to-air refuelling tankers, RC-135 Rivet Joint intelligence-gathering aircraft and E-8A Joint STARS ground surveillance aircraft were waiting to launch

Coalition air power over the Middle East. *(USAF)*

missions across the Middle East. On the transport ramp, thousands of tons of cargo were being unloaded from giant McDonnell Douglas C-17 Globemasters and chartered civilian cargo aircraft. Dozens of Lockheed C-130 Hercules transports were parked on the other side of the huge cargo-handling area waiting to take on board pallets of cargo for delivery to remote bases in Iraq and Afghanistan.

Taking shelter beneath sunshades was a squadron of McDonnell Douglas F-15E Strike Eagles on ground alert to scramble to support US and Coalition troops under attack. Outside hardened aircraft shelters, a pair of Lockheed Martin F-16C Fighting Falcons had just returned from a mission over Iraq and were being rearmed. On the other side of the hardened shelters, Royal Air Force Panavia Tornado GR4s were being prepared for a night-time patrol over Iraq.

In a heavily guarded compound on the edge of the airfield complex, hundreds of US, British and allied officers were choreographing Coalition air operations throughout the Middle East in a hi-tech 'war room'. Dubbed the Combined Air Operations Centre, or CAOC, the command post featured large computer displays showing the position of every aircraft flying over the Middle East, along with the location of friendly and hostile ground and naval forces. Live video feeds from unmanned aerial vehicles and other reconnaissance aircraft were projected onto the screens, giving senior commanders an unprecedented situational awareness of what was happening on the ground in Iraq, Afghanistan and elsewhere. This allowed split-second decisions to be made to authorise weapon release.

The location of the base, a few miles outside Doha, the capital city of the tiny Gulf state of Qatar, meant few of the country's population did not know their government had allowed Al Udeid to become the largest US airbase in the Middle East. Around the clock the sound of bombers, fighter jets, tankers and transport aircraft launching from Al Udeid was a very audible reminder of the base's presence in Qatar.

For the government of Qatar, the presence of the base was part of a delicate political balancing act. As well as being home to Al Udeid and the regional headquarters of US Central Command, Qatar also owned the Al Jazeera television station. This station had become famous for its reports from the front lines in Iraq and Afghanistan. Former US President George W. Bush was constantly critical of the station's coverage, which he claimed was overtly anti-American and deliberately fanning the flames of the Iraqi insurgency. In April 2004, he became so exasperated at Al Jazeera's reports of fighting in the Iraqi city of Fallujah that he even considered launching an airstrike on the TV station's headquarters in Doha city. The British Prime Minister, Tony Blair, talked Bush out of unleashing his air force on the station, but the incident illustrated the precarious nature of the Emirate's alliance with the USA.

The first decade of the twenty-first century has seen air power used on an unprecedented scale in the Middle East. The full spectrum of air operations from strategic air campaigns to support for ground troops engaged in counter-insurgency operations and humanitarian aid missions have been undertaken since the turn of the century.

Air operations from desert bases are now routine for US and British airmen. *(Author)*

This books aims to profile the current state of Middle East air forces and international air units deployed in the region. The condition of the region's aviation industry, which is growing in global importance, is also assessed. The book will then look at the main air campaigns of the past decade, including the conflicts in Iraq, Lebanon, the West Bank and Gaza. The role that air power based in the region has played in the Afghan conflict and in countering Somali pirates will also be assessed.

Continuing political, economic, religious and ethnic tensions in the region mean the Middle East will be afflicted by conflict and tension for many years to come. The fact that fifty-eight per cent of the world crude oil reserves lie under the Middle East mean that international powers, principally the USA and UK, will continue to take a close interest in shaping events in the region.

For these reasons, regional nations and international powers are undoubtedly going to rely on air power to protect their interests.

Armed and dangerous. An RAF Tornado GR4 ready for action at Al Udeid airbase in 2006. (*Author*)

The heart of this book is based on more than a decade of travel throughout the Middle East visiting airbases, Coalition headquarters, warships and conflict zones in Bahrain, Israel, Iraq, Kuwait, Qatar, Oman, Turkey and the UAE. The availability of commercial satellite imagery, including the huge amounts of imagery posted on the Google Earth website, has provided an unprecedented 'window' on parts of the Middle East that are still closed to outside observers, including Iran, Syria and parts of Saudi Arabia.

Many people have helped me over the years during the preparation of this book. For obvious reasons, many wish to remain anonymous. I hope this book opens a 'window' on the state of air power in the Middle East reason. It can only ever be a 'snapshot' in time, as events are always fast moving in the region.

Tim Ripley on HMAS *Anzac* off the coast of Iraq waiting to fly on a US Navy Sea Hawk helicopter. *(Author)*

Acknowledgements

With thanks to …

2003 Iraq War

US Navy
5th Fleet Public Affairs, Bahrain, Cdr Jeff Alderson, Lt Garret Kasper,Capt Roxi Merritt, Lt Cdr Steiner and Lt Cdr Dave Werner, Lt Billy Ray Davis, Lt Cdr Jeff Carer, USCG.

USS **Abraham Lincoln**
Capt Kendall L. Card, CAG Capt 'KC' Albright, Capt Buzby, Lt Cdr Jeff Bender, Lt Steve Wallburn, Cdr Dale Horan, Master Chief (AVCM) Farrel Briggs, Cdr Rich Simon, Cdr Paul Hass, Cdr George Falok, Lt Cdr Brad Kidwell, Ensign Bonnie Tanner, JOCS(SA / AW) John Barnett.

USAF
Ahmed Al Jaber AB, LTC Jennifer Cassidy USAF PAO, LTC Tom Bergy, 524th Fighter Squadron, LTC 'Skeeter' Gus Kohntopp, 190th FS, Boise, Idaho ANG, Ali Al Salem PAO, Capt John Sheets, Tsgt Neely; LTC Gary Fabricius, 15th Expeditionary Reconnaissance Squadron, Camp Doha ACCC.
Maj Gen Dan Leaf, Maj Dan Snyder, executive officer.

USMC Ahmed Al Jaber
Maj T.V. Johnson, 3 MAW PAO, LTC Ed Hebert 3 MAW staff, Maj Mark Butler VMA 214, Maj Bruce Laughlin, 3 MAW staff, Maj Jim Wolfe, 3 MAW ground liaison officer.

UK MoD
Simon Wren, Paul Bernard.

RAF
DCC(RAF); Wg Cdr Ian Tolfts, PIC Qatar, Gp Capt Al Lockwood, RAF PIC Kuwait, Spokesman Gp Capt John Fynes, Wg Cdr Mike Cairns and Steve Dargan, Ali Al Salem AB.

Gp Capt Andy Pulford, JHF, Wg Cdr Paul Lyall, 33 Sqn, Wg Cdr David Prowse, 18 Sqn, Wg Cdr Dave Robertson, 617 Sqn.
Ahmed Al Jaber AB.
Gp Capt Mike Harwood, Flt Lt John Gunther.

British Army
PIC Kuwait, Lt Col Rob Partridge; PIC Qatar, Maj Will MacKinnley.
PIC Kuwait, Maj Ray Tonner.

Royal Navy Bahrain
Cdr Nick Chatwin, Lt Cdr Steve Tatam, Lt Cdr Ken Sprowles RNR, Lt Cdr 'Mac' Mackenzie, CO of 849 Naval Air Sqn.

The Media
The Scotsman, Andrew McLeod, Tim Cornwall, James Hall, Gethin Chamberlain; *Daily Telegraph*, Michael Smith, Jack Fairweather, Neil Tweedie; *Sky News*, Tim Marshall, Francis Tusa, Geoff Mead, James Forlong; *DPL*; Dave Reynolds, Dil Bannerjee, Andrew Gilligan, *BBC Radio 4 Today Programme*, Michael Voss, *BBC Radio*, Paul Adams, Defence Correspondence, Nick Gowing; *BBC News 24*, Bhasker Solanki; Peter Graff, John Chalmers, Reuters; Alan Warnes, *Air Forces Monthly*; Richard Norton-Taylor, *The Guardian*; Davis Chartes, *The Times*; Gary Dimmock; *Financial Times*, Roula Khalaf, Emma Jacobs, Gwen Robinson, Victor Mallet; Stewart Penny, *Flight International*; Tony Holmes; Chris Pocock; *Jane's Defence Weekly*, Cliff Beale, Ian Kemp, Craig Hoyle, Marion Childs, Peter Felstead; *Jane's Intelligence Review*, Chris Aaron; Keith Gladdis, *News of the World*; Nick Allen, Press Association; Rosie Laydon, BFBS; Tim Shipman, *Sunday Express*; Christopher Cooper, *Wall Street Journal*.

2006 to 2009

RAF
CAS ACM Sir Glenn Torpy, Wg Cdr Jon Agar.

RAF Strike Command
Gp Capt Ian Tolfts, Wg Cdr Ailsa Gough, Sqn Ldr Karl Mahan.
Al Udeid AB, Qatar.
UK PIO Flt Lt Ian Heath, UK PIO, Sqn Ldr Andy Arnold and WO Sam McMillan 31 Squadron, C130 Det Command, Sqn Ldr Rich Waller, XXIV Sqn, Wg Cdr Nick Laird, 230 Sqn Air Cdre Clive Bairsto, AOC 83 EAG and UK Air Component Commander Op Telic and Op Herrick. Air Cdre Bryan Collins, NATO/ISAF LO TO CAOC.

US Navy Bahrain
Lt Paul Macapagal USN (PAO Expeditionary Strike Group 2/DESRON 50).

USAF Al Udeid
Col Charlie Catoe, Deputy Commander 379th Operations Group, Lt Col Sam Bellia, Director Operations 328th Tactical Airlift Squadron, Chief Master Sergeant Stanley Walker, of 379th Expeditionary Logistic Readiness Squadron.
CAOC Al Udeid.
CAOC Director Maj Gen Dutch Holland USAF, CAOC Deputy Director BG Tony Haires USAF, Capt Bill Reavey, USN, Wg Cdr Mason Fenlon, SO1 Senior UK Representative, RAF.

CDISS
Dr Martin Edmonds, Pauline Elliott, Richard Connaughton.

The following provided invaluable help researching photographs: Marc Boulton of BAE Systems, Tom Cooper, Francis Tusa, Peter Foster.

The individual country maps were provided by the US Central Intelligence Agency.

Abbreviations

AAC	Army Air Corps (British Army)
AB	Airbase
AC	Air Component Coordination Element (USAF)
ACW	Air Control Wing (USAF)
AEW	Air Expeditionary Wing (USAF)
AEG	Air Expeditionary Group (USAF)
AG	Air Group (USAF)
AMW	Air Mobility Wing (USAF)
ARG	Air Refuelling (USAF)
ARS	Air Refuelling Squadron (USAF)
ARW	Air Refuelling Wing (USAF)
AS	Airlift Squadron (USAF)
Avn	Aviation (US Army)
AW	Airlift Wing (USAF)
AWACS	Airborne Warning and Control System
Bn	Battalion
BS	Bombardment Squadron (USAF)
BW	Bombardment Wing (USAF)
CAOC	Combined Air Operations Center (USAF)
CFACC	Coalition Forces Air Component Commanders
CFLCC	Coalition Forces Land Component Commanders
CRG	Contingency Response Group (USAF)
CSAR	Combat Search and Rescue
Det	Detachment
EBS	Expeditionary Bombardment Squadron (USAF)
ECS	Electronic Combat Squadron (USAF)
EFS	Expeditionary Fighter Squadron (USAF)
EAS	Expeditionary Airlift Squadron (USAF)
ERS	Expeditionary Reconnaissance Squadron (USAF)
ERQS	Expeditionary Rescue Squadron (USAF
EBS	Expeditionary Bomber Squadron (USAF
EACCS	Expeditionary Airborne Command and Control Squadron (USAF)
ELINT	Electronic Intelligence
ERS	Expeditionary Reconnaissance Squadron (USAF)
FAC	Forward Air Controller

FARP	Forward Arming and Refuelling Point
Flt	Flight
FG	Fighter Group (USAF)
FS	Fighter Squadron (USAF)
FW	Fighter Wing (USAF)
GBU	Guided Bomb Unit
HARM	High Speed Anti-Radiation Missile
HC	US Navy Helicopter Support Squadron
HCS	US Navy Helicopter Combat Support Squadron
HMLA	US Marine Helicopter Attack Squadron, Light
HMH	US Marine Helicopter Squadron, Heavy
HMM	US Marine Helicopter Squadron, Medium
HS	US Navy Helicopter Anti-submarine Squadron
HVM	High-Velocity Missile (UK SAM)
IAEA	International Atomic Energy Agency
IADS	Integrated Air Defence System
IAAF	Iraqi Army Air Corps
IASF	Israel Air and Space Force
IQAF	Iraqi Air Force
IRIAA	Islamic Republic of Iran Army Aviation (IRIAA)
IRIAF	Islamic Republic of Iran Air Force
IRINA	Islamic Republic of Iran Navy Aviation (IRINA)
IRGC	Islamic Revolutionary Guard Corps (IRGC)
IRGCAF	Iranian Revolutionary Guard Corps Air Force (Pasdaran-e Inqilab)
JTAC	Joint Terminal Attack Controller (US)
LTW	Lynham Transport Wing (RAF)
MAW	Marine Air Wing (USMC)
MEB	Marine Expeditionary Brigade
MEF	Marine Expeditionary Force (USMC)
MEU	Marine Expeditionary Unit (USMC)
MODA	Ministry of Defence and Aviation
MOI	Ministry of the Interior (Saudi Arabia)
NAEWF	NATO Airborne Early Warning Force
NATO	North Atlantic Treaty Organisation
NAS	Naval Air Squadron (UK)
NSA	National Security Agency (US)
RA	Royal Artillery
RAF	Royal Air Force (UK)
RAAF	Royal Australian Air Force
RAFO	Royal Air Force of Oman
RSAF	Royal Saudi Air Force
RSLF	Royal Saudi Land Forces
SAFMS	Saudi Armed Forces Medical Services

RSNF	Royal Saudi Naval Forces
RSADF	Royal Saudi Air Defence Forces
Regt	Regiment
RS	Reconnaissance Squadron (USAF)
RW	Reconnaissance Wing (USAF)
RQS	Rescue Squadron (USAF)
RQW	Rescue Wing (USAF)
SAM	Surface-to-Air Missile
SANG	Saudi Arabian National Guard
SAS	Special Air Service (UK and Australia)
SEAD	Suppression of Enemy Air Defence
SLAM	Stand-off Land Attack Missile
SOAR	Special Operation Aviation Regiment (US Army)
SOG	Special Operations Group (USAF)
SOS	Special Operations Squadron (USAF)
SOW	Special Operations Wing (USAF)
Sqn	Squadron
TACP	Tactical Air Control Party
TDY	Temporary Duty (US military term)
TF	Task Force
TLAM	Tomahawk Land Attack Missile
USAF	US Air Force
USMC	US Marine Corps
USN	US Navy
UN	United Nations
UNSCOM	UN Special Commission
UNMOVIC	UN's Monitoring, Verification and Inspection Commission
USAF	United States Air Force
USS	United States Ship
VA	US Navy Attack Squadron
VAQ	US Navy Tactical Electronic Warfare Squadron
VAW	US Navy Carrier Airborne Early Warning Squadron
VF	US Navy Fighter Squadron
VFA	US Navy Strike Fighter Squadron
VMA	US Marine Attack Squadron
VMAQ	US Marine Tactical Electronic Warfare Squadron
VFMA(AW)	US Marine All-Weather Fighter Attack Squadron
VFMA	US Marine Fighter Attack Squadron
VMGR	US Marine Refuelling Squadron
VMU	US Marine Unmanned Aerial Vehicle Unit
VP	US Navy Patrol Squadron
VS	US Navy Anti-submarine Squadron
VQ	US Navy Fleet Reconnaissance Squadron

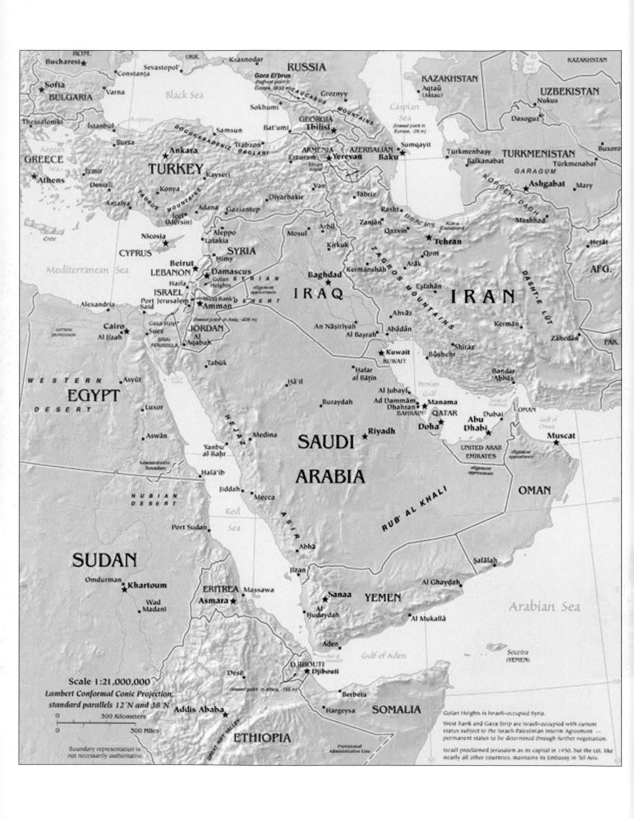

PART ONE

Introduction

Conflict in Iraq has dominated US and UK air operations in the Middle East for most of the first decade of the twenty-first century. *(USAF)*

CHAPTER ONE

Introduction to Air Power in the Middle East

The aim of this study is provide a snapshot of air power in the Middle East in the first decade of the twenty-first century. Over the past sixty years air power has played a major role in all conflicts in the region, and Middle Eastern countries continue to invest heavily in air warfare hardware.

Military power plays a significant role in Middle Eastern affairs because of the continuing political instability caused by the Israeli–Palestinian conflict and the growing influence of radical Islam. The region's considerable oil reserves mean that the major Western powers – Britain, France and the United States – remain committed to military involvement in the hope of maintaining economic access to the region.

Recognising that air power is judged not just by the type and number of airframes in an air force's inventory, it is also necessary to look at other key components in a state's air warfare capability, such as electronic warfare, air crew training, air defence systems, command and control.

There is considerable concern about the proliferation of weapons of mass destruction (WMD) in the Middle East. Combat aircraft represent one of the principal delivery systems for these weapons. So improvements to a nation's offensive air warfare capability can have serious implications for counter-proliferation.

A word of explanation is necessary for the definition of the 'Middle East' used in this book. I have centred my study on the states of the Arabian peninsula, the Levant and the adjoining states. These include the significant Middle Eastern military powers – Iran, Israel, Egypt and Turkey. Some might consider the inclusion of Turkey as unusual because it is rarely considered in military surveys of the Middle East. Indeed the authoritative International Institute for Strategic Studies (ISSS) *Military Balance* year book includes it in the NATO – not Middle East and North African – section. Turkey's escalating war with the Kurdish PKK guerrillas, regular incursions into northern Iraq, military co-operation with Israel and growing confrontation with Syria have now made the NATO member a 'player' in the Middle East military equation.

I have also deliberately played down states' political allegiance in this study. Given the rapidly fluctuating situation in the Middle East, these can and have changed, literally overnight. In the past, political realignments have been quickly followed by rapid arms transfers between states which previously had been at

A British Tornado GR4 pops flares during a mission over Iraq. *(USAF)*

daggers drawn. In 1991, Syria was in the anti-Iraq Coalition, but it is now closely aligned with Iran. While Jordan was the Iraqi leader Saddam Hussein's closest ally, it is now a close ally of the USA. During the 1980s, Israel and US supplied Iran with weapons to fight Iraq. Who knows where the political wind will blow over the next decade? This makes it very difficult to line up Middle Eastern states against one another for any length of time, and gives great concern to Western policy makers when they ponder the sale of advanced weaponry to the region.

A word of caution must also be mentioned about the number of airframes and weapons currently in service in Middle Eastern air forces. States of the region are notoriously secretive, and there is no arms control regime to ensure transparency, as is the case within Europe, with the Organisation for Security and Co-operation in Europe (OSCE). While the identifying type of airframes and weapons delivered is relatively straightforward to assess, the numbers in front-line service are less clear. The figures we provide should only really be taken as a guide, based on a variety of sources, rather than the last word on the subject.

Why air power?

Outside the United States of America and western Europe, the states of the Middle East are the greatest buyers of air warfare hardware in the world. There are valid military reasons for air power being considered the dominant form of warfare in the Middle East, but the region's unique political structures and culture also account for the great interest in air power.

The geography of the Middle East with its concentration of population centres into a few narrow coastal strips or fertile river valleys separated by vast expanses of barren desert makes air power decisive. Whoever commands the air can inflict decisive damage on any land army advancing across the featureless desert. This lesson was learnt the hard way by Rommel's *Afrika Korps* in the Second World War, the Egyptians in 1967 and the Iraqis in 1991. In the 1980–88 Iran–Iraq war, neither side could achieve air supremacy, so stalemate resulted. This lesson was reinforced during the 2003 US-led invasion of Iraq, when overwhelming US air supremacy led to the collapse of Saddam Hussein's government in less than a month of combat.

The Middle East is one of the world's oldest trading centres, and the majority of that trade is conducted by sea in two narrow confined waterways. Who has air supremacy over the Straits of Hormuz and the Red Sea controls the vast majority of the world's oil and other high-value trade.

Air power appeals to many political leaders in the Middle East because it offers the prospect of projecting power without relying on large land forces. This can either be due to a state's small population (e.g. Israel) or an unwillingness to arm and train the population (e.g. the Gulf states) for fear of insurrection or a *coup d'état*. In a region where political power is almost exclusively concentrated in the hands of a small political élite, the idea of near 'surgical air strikes' against a rival state's rulers also has attractions.

The role of air power in naval operations throughout the Middle East has been highlighted by the upsurge in piracy off the coast of Somalia during 2008. *(Author)*

The economic development brought by the region's oil wealth is a fairly recent phenomenon over the last half-century, and many political élites in the Middle East are keen to acquire symbols of 'modernisation' or 'westernisation' as 'hi-tech' virility symbols. The mere possession of the same type of aircraft as the USAF or Western air forces is meant to bring almost superpower prestige – at least it is perceived that way in some Middle East states.

For the smaller Gulf states, buying expensive Western hardware is also a deliberate policy act to try and tie the supplier militarily and diplomatically to the receiving state.

If a supplier is still owed significant amounts of money then it will be unwilling to allow the receiving state to be invaded and the debt never to be paid, or so goes the argument. The weaponry itself also becomes a 'hostage', requiring outside 'protection'. Some US Congressmen have argued against supplying the latest hi-tech weaponry to Gulf states because they lack the manpower and moral ability to defend themselves, so in effect 'giving' the weapons to Iran – a state implacably hostile to the United States.

Whatever the reasons, and they vary from state to state, the Middle East continues be one of the largest markets for air warfare hardware. Its inherent political instability means it also remains the most likely place on earth that air power will be used in anger on a large scale.

Asymmetric warfare

The lessons of the Arab–Israeli wars and the US-led wars against Iraq have not been lost on a number of countries and insurgent groups in the Middle East. The past decade has seen the development of so-called asymmetric strategies and tactics to try to neutralise US, British and Israeli air supremacy. These tactics centre around using urban guerrilla tactics to hide among civilian populations inside cities. This makes it difficult to use air power to its full potential because of the danger of inflicting casualties and damage on civilian populations and infrastructure. The Lebanese Hizbullah guerrilla group has become the master of camouflage and concealment, and Iraq's insurgents have made life very difficult for the US-led occupation forces for several years.

To counter asymmetric warfare, US, British and Israeli air forces have invested heavily in intelligence-gathering technology, such as unmanned aerial vehicles, and precision-guided munitions. They have also decentralised the control of air power to front-line ground commanders. This has caused some *Angst* among air power purists who believe that air power is best applied under centralised control, but the unique circumstances of counter-insurgency warfare dictate that air power must be used in a very precise and delicate way.

Israeli's war against the Hizbullah guerilla army in Lebanon in 2006 showed the limitations of modern air power. *(IDF Spokesman)*

Coalition air power operates from numerous bases across the Middle East. *(USAF)*

Air power effects

Air power in the Middle East has been used for three main purposes – killing people, destroying objects and influencing people. In the modern jargon of the US and British air forces, the former two roles are referred to as kinetic effects and the latter is known as non-kinetic effects. The buzzword 'effect' is now in widespread usage, but it also really means the military purpose or utility of air power. This term came into widespread usage during the Iraq occupation as US and British commanders sought means to influence events in a confused and congested battlefield. It really has its origin, however, in the doctrine of 'effects-based warfare' which the US and British armed forces developed in the 1990s to codify the use of force in the post-Cold War world. Many nations of the Middle East have adopted elements of the effects-based approach to warfare or already had similar air warfare concepts incorporated in their military doctrine. Effects-based warfare is centred around changing an opponent's behaviour, not physically destroying his armed forces or defence industry.

Kinetic effects are designed to destroy key elements of an opponent's military machine or infrastructure, known as centres of gravity. The destruction of these will result in him losing the will to continue fighting. Non-kinetic effects are more nebulous and are aimed at influencing an opponent's behaviour. All these effects can be employed at a strategic or tactical level.

For air forces, kinetic effects involve the use of a wide range of weapons. The air-to-ground weapons contain a mix of high explosive and shrapnel. A 500 lb air-dropped bomb will kill or seriously injury people in the open up to 500 metres from the impact point, through a mix of blast, hot flash and small pieces of hot shrapnel from the bomb casing. These pieces of hot shrapnel are propelled at high velocity hundreds of metres from the bomb detonation, causing grievous wounds for anyone caught by them. Bigger 1,000 lb or 2,000 lb bombs have even more impact, and if aimed at key parts of large buildings, such as supporting walls, can cause them to collapse.

During the Cold War, many nations developed so-called cluster munitions to allow attacks against area targets, such as large groups of infantry in the open or convoys of supply trucks. These used dispenser units to distribute small bomblets over several hundred square metres of ground. These small bomblets then detonated, creating a large area of destruction. High failure rates in bomblets led to them effectively creating 'minefields', and they became the subject of international treaties banning land mines. These weapons remain in several Middle East air forces' inventories.

The destruction of armoured vehicles requires the use of specialist warheads, such as High Explosive Anti-Tank (HEAT), which punch a hot jet of molten metal through armour and kill the vehicle's occupants. Defeating underground bunkers requires special warheads tipped with high-density steel, which use the momentum of the bomb to smash through their concrete roofs. Once a penetration is made, the explosive is detonated by a delayed-action fuse, and it unleashes carnage inside the structure.

Air-to-air missiles are designed to explode near to hostile aircraft or inside their engines. They then spread lethal shrapnel into the target aircraft, ripping apart key

Israel's air force is the most powerful in the Middle East. (*Author*)

Unmanned aerial vehicles like the USAF's MQ-9 Reaper have seen increasing use in Middle East conflicts. *(USAF)*

components and structures. Anti-radar missiles work on similar principles and are designed to rip apart hostile radar antennae.

Most jet combat aircraft and attack helicopters retain cannon and heavy machine-guns. These fire heavy metal shells or small high explosives at high velocity, which literally rip apart people, vehicles or buildings hit by them.

The non-kinetic effects of air power are equally important in the Middle East in both peace and war. Many nations use their air forces to send signals to neighbours and rivals. Air force deployments to airbases near crisis zones or by flying patrols along tense borders are regular crisis management tactics.

At a tactical level fast-jet combat aircraft can make low passes over hostile forces to intimidate them and reassure friendly forces that help is close by.

An increasingly important non-kinetic air power effect is intelligence, surveillance, targeting and reconnaissance (ISTAR) support to air, land and naval forces. These effects can be generated by specialist ISTAR aircraft, space satellite or even the crews of non-specialist aircraft just reporting what they see on the ground.

By giving commanders at all levels, from battlefield infantry commanders to national command authorities, an understanding of what is happening on the battlefield, they can better target enemy forces and protect their own troops from attack. Moving and supplying troops by air can be an important effect, if air transport protects them from attack.

Significant political effects can also achieved by using air power, particularly transport aircraft and helicopters, to deliver humanitarian aid to the victims of natural disasters. This can alter perceptions of a nation and its armed forces.

The important qualification for air power effects is that by their very nature they are temporary. All aircraft need to return to base to refuel, rearm and change their crews. To prolong these effects, a continuous stream of aircraft needs to be generated to maintain combat air patrols over battlefields. The exception to this are unmanned aerial vehicles that can remain on station for periods far in excess of manned aircraft. The longest-lasting effects are generated by space satellites parked in stationary orbits over particular points of the earth.

Combat aircraft

The most basic measure of a state's air power is the number and type of airframes in its inventory. There are several thousand fast-jet air frames in the Middle East, but only a few hundred could be considered to have 'top-of-the-range' capabilities. In this study I have defined combat aircraft as front-line fighter, attack or multi-role single- or two-seat jets. Training aircraft which may have a limited combat capability are covered elsewhere. I have assessed each air force by the percentage of aircraft that could be considered 1st-, 2nd-, 3rd- or 4th-generation combat aircraft.

This is a somewhat arbitrary categorisation, but it has some merits. For my purposes I have defined them as follows:

1st generation: 1950s-vintage subsonic fighters such as the Mikoyan MiG-15, MiG-17 and Hawker Hunter.

2nd generation: Supersonic fighters from the 1960s, such as the Mikoyan MiG-21, English Electric Lightning, Dassault Mirage III, Northrop F-5 Freedom Fighter, McDonnell Douglas F-4 Phantom and A-4 Skyhawk

The Royal Saudi Air Force has been investing in modern combat aircraft since the 1960s, when it bought English Electric Lightning fighters from the UK. *(BAE Systems)*

Modern F-15S Eagles are now in front-line service with the RSAF. *(USAF)*

The United Arab Emirates have an advanced version of the F-16 Fighting Falcon in service. *(Lockheed Martin)*

3rd generation: 1970s- and 1980s-era fighters that took advantage of modern computer technology to allow the use of so-called 'smart' weapons, such as the Panavia Tornado, SEPECAT Jaguar, Lockheed Martin F-16 Fighting Falcon, Boeing F-15 Eagle, Boeing F/A-18 Hornet, Dassault Mirage 2000, Mikoyan MiG-29 'Fulcrum', Sukhoi Su-24 'Fencer' and Su-27 'Flanker'. Russian sources, however, claim their most modern fighters are really 4th generation, though this is verging on a semantic argument.

4th generation: These are the new-generation aircraft which utilise so-called 'fly-by-wire', fully computer-driven 'agile' flight control and combat systems, which give high manoeuvrability and quicker weapon employment. Lockheed Martin argues that its later Block 50/60 versions of the F-16 has many 4th-generation features. The Lockheed Martin F-22 Raptor, Eurofighter Typhoon, Dassault Rafale and later versions of the Sukhoi 'Flanker' are all true 4th generation.

The Eurofighter Typhoon is transforming the capabilities of Middle East air power after deliveries began to be made to the RSAF in 2009. *(BAE Systems)*

Table 1. Combat Aircraft in the Middle East.

	Total No. Airframes	1st	2nd	3rd	4th
			Generation		
Bahrain	33		12	21	
Egypt	351		129	222	
Iran	211		96	115	
Israel	450		25	300	125
Jordan	118		24	46	48
Kuwait	39			39	
Oman	45			35	10
Qatar	12			12	
Saudi Arabia	245			245	
Syria	605		355	250	
Turkey	441		204	197	30
UAE	140			61	79
Yemen	61		43	18	
USAF	84			44	36
USN	48			24	24
USMC	24			24	
RAF	8			8	
France				6	

Notes:
1. Western air force units are those based in theatre, mainly in Iraq and Qatar. In a crisis reinforcements can be on hand in a short period, with the force possibly doubling in a week. During the 1994 Operation Vigilant Warrior deployment, some 450 additional aircraft were moved to the Middle East within thirty days.
2. The US Navy figures are based on the basis of a single aircraft carrier air wing, with fifty Boeing F/A-18 Hornets
3. The 4th-generation USAF, Israeli, Turkish and UAE aircraft are Block 50 F-16s.

Air-to-air missiles

Air-to-air weapons come currently come in two main varieties – infra-red guided or 'heat seeking' for close-range encounters, known as 'dog fighting', and radar frequency guided for beyond-visual-range (BVR) engagements at long range.

Technological advances in heat-seeking missiles means that the capabilities of different version of popular missiles, such as the AIM-9 Sidewinder, can vary considerably. The greater the sensitivity of the missile's seeker or guidance unit, the greater the capability to detect targets at longer ranges and off-bore sight, i.e. to the side of the firer's aircraft or even at an oncoming target. The early

Table 2. Heat-seeking air-to-air missiles in the Middle East.

	IR	IIR
Bahrain	x	
Egypt	x	
Iran	x	
Iraq	x	
Israel	x	x
Jordan	x	
Kuwait	x	
Oman	x	
Qatar	x	x
Saudi Arabia	x	x
Syria	x	
Turkey	x	x
UAE		x
Yemen	x	
USAF	x	x
USN	x	x
RAF	x	x
France	x	x

infra-red (IR) heat seekers were best employed directly behind the hot 'exhaust' of an opponent's jet. Modern imaging infra-red (IIR) seeker units, such as those fitted to the American AIM-9R or French MICA missiles, offer longer ranges and better off-bore sight capability. These new missiles also have high agility, which prevents an opponent out-manoeuvring a heat-seeking missile.

Advances in BVR missile technology offer 'decisive' advantages to air forces. The ability to engage and destroy an opponent before he can 'mix-it' in a dog fight and hope for lucky hit with a heat-seeking missile has proved a war winner in the 1982 Lebanon and 1991 Gulf Wars.

Radar-guided missiles of 1960s vintage, such as early versions of the AIM-7 Sparrow, were plagued by failures, due to unreliable systems and reliance of radar guidance from the launch aircraft.

These so-called semi-active missiles have now been superseded by missiles such as the AIM-120 AMRAAM, which rely only on their on-board or 'active' guidance, making them 'fire-or-forget', with ranges out to around a hundred miles. In combat in the Middle East and Bosnia the AMRAAM has developed a reputation as a 'one missile – one kill' weapon.

Table 3. Beyond-visual-range radar-guided missiles in the Middle East.

	Semi-Active Missile	Active Missile
Bahrain	x	x
Egypt	x	x
Iran	x	
Iraq	x	
Israel	x	x
Jordan	x	x
Kuwait	x	
Oman		x
Qatar	x	x
Saudi Arabia	x	x
Syria	x	
Turkey	x	x
UAE	x	x
Yemen	x	
USAF	x	x
USN	x	x
France	x	x

Long-range bombers

Once considered of great significance, the large long-range bomber is now seen as obsolete by many observers due to the effectiveness of modern air defences. The success of USAF B-52s in the Gulf illustrated that large bombers can deliver huge quantities of ordnance if enemy air defences are neutralised.

To ensure an 'acceptable' degree of survivability in the face of active air defences requires long-range precision-guided munitions, the employment of 'stealth' technology or low-level capability.

Table 4. Long-range bombers in the Middle East.

	Total	Unguided bombs	PGM	Stealth	Requirement
Iran					x
USAF	178	x	x	x	

The long-range Storm Shadow cruise missile was used with devastating effect during the 2003 invasion of Iraq. *(Author)*

Strike aircraft

Offensive air operations are a key component of air power. Time and again in the Middle East strike aircraft have delivered crushing blows against opponents' high-value assets or strategic 'centres of gravity'. The ability to conduct such operations is considered the 'holy grail' of air forces throughout the Middle East. Few air forces in the region have yet to attain a full operational capability in this area, even though they may nominally possess the required hardware. Only the Israeli air force, and perhaps the Saudis and UAE, have any true long-range strike capability.

Single- or two-seat strike aircraft, such as the F-16, F/A-18, Tornado, F-15E/S/I, Su-24 and Mirage 2000, have varying capabilities, ranges, precision-guided weapons (PGM) and survivability.

Table 5. Capabilities of strike aircraft in the Middle East.

Unrefuelled range	500 km	1,000 km	1,500 km Stealth	PGM (over 10 km range)
Bahrain	x			
Egypt	x	x	x	
Iran	x	x		x
Iraq				
Israel	x	x	x	x
Jordan	x			
Kuwait	x	x		
Oman		x	x	x
Qatar	x	x	x	
Saudi Arabia	x	x	x	x
Syria	x	x	x	
Turkey	x	x	x	x
UAE	x	x	x	x
Yemen	x			
USAF	x	x	x	x
USN	x	x	x	x
RAF	x	x	x	x
France	x	x	x	x

Table 6. Close air support capabilities in the Middle East.

	Total	Dumb bomb	PGM (under 10 km range)
Bahrain	24	x	x
Egypt	200	x	x
Iran	97	x	x
Iraq	46	x	x
Israel	495	x	x
Jordan	67	x	x
Kuwait	40	x	x
Oman	19	x	x
Qatar	12	x	x
Saudi Arabia	123	x	x
Syria	160	x	x
Turkey	455	x	x
UAE	25	x	x
Yemen	28	x	
USAF	36	x	x
USN	50	x	x
RAF	8	x	x
France	6	x	x

Close air support aircraft

The ability to safely provide air support for friendly troops engaged in combat with enemy ground forces is a highly skilled and demanding air warfare capability.

For fast jets to find small targets on a battlefield is very difficult unless assisted by ground or airborne controllers who guide them to their target. Very few Middle East air forces have demonstrated any consistent track record in this capability.

Precision-guided munitions

The introduction of guided munitions that can deliver ordnance to targets at long-range has dramatically transformed Middle East air warfare, making many air defence systems obsolete. The ability of US and British aircraft to attack targets from outside the envelopes of Iraqi air defences during the 2003 US-led invasion was instrumental in the low Coalition losses. For the later four decades of the twentieth century, laser and television guidance was the predominant method of directing precision-guided munitions. Just over a decade ago, satellite guidance introduced a new dimension to air warfare, allowing weapons to be directed with pin-point accuracy in bad weather and at night.

Table 7. Precision-guided munition capabilities in the Middle East.

Range up to	20 km	50 km	100 km	150 km	400 km	3,000 km	Penetrating warhead	Satellite guidance
Bahrain	x							
Egypt	x							
Iran	x	x	x					
Iraq	x							
Israel	x	x	x	x	x		x	x
Jordan	x							
Kuwait	x							
Oman	x							
Qatar	x							
Saudi Arabia	x			x	x			x
Syria	x							
Turkey	x							x
UAE	x				x		?	x
Yemen								
USAF	x	x				x	x	x
USN	x			x			x	x
RAF	x			x			x	x
France	x			x				x

Note: British and French 150 km range weapons are Apache/Storm Shadow variants.

USAF B-1B Lancer bombers operate across Iraq and Afghanistan in the close air support role with precision-guided munitions. *(USAF)*

Non-guided ordnance

Non-guided weaponry is still important in the Middle East, and provides some useful capabilities. Cluster weapons, for example, are very useful during attacks on ground forces and for interrupting operations on enemy airbases. There is, however, a question mark over the legality of cluster weapons with anti-personnel sub-munitions in the light of recent international moves to ban land mines.

Table 8. Non-guided ordnance capabilities in the Middle East.

	Iron bombs	Cluster weapons
Bahrain	x	
Egypt	x	x
Iran	x	x
Iraq	x	x
Israel	x	x
Jordan	x	
Kuwait	x	
Oman	x	x
Qatar	x	
Saudi Arabia	x	x
Syria	x	x
Turkey	x	x
UAE	x	x
Yemen	x	
USAF	x	x
USN	x	x
RAF	x	
France	x	x

Precision-guided weapons are now the 'weapons of choice' for Middle East air forces. *(US Navy)*

Table 9. Airborne early warning capabilities in the Middle East.

	E-2C	AWACS	Other AEW
Bahrain			
Egypt	x		
Iran			x
Iraq			
Israel	x		x
Jordan			
Kuwait			
Oman			
Qatar			
Saudi Arabia		x	
Syria			x
Turkey		x (NATO)	
UAE			
Yemen			
USAF		x	
USN	x		
RAF		x	
France	x	x	

Airborne early warning (AEW)

The elevation of radar surveillance systems to allow them to 'see' over the curve in the earth is an essential capability in the Middle East, given the vast distances over which air operations are conducted in the region. For countries such as Iran, Egypt and Saudi Arabia, their large land masses make it prohibitively expensive and technically difficult to provide full radar coverage from traditional terrestrially based radar.

Some airborne early warning aircraft also provide 'battle management' capabilities to allow air commanders to choreograph defensive and offensive air operations with a high degree of precision. The US Boeing E-3 Sentry AWACS-type aircraft have large battle staffs to conduct sophisticated operations, but the smaller Northrop Grumman E-2C Hawkeye and other systems are less capable in this area. Iranian and Syrian AEW capabilities are very problematical and are in no way yet equivalent to Western systems.

Electronic warfare

Dominance of the electromagnetic spectrum is now recognised as a decisive factor in air warfare, allowing key enemy targets to be identified and hiding one's own assets. Electronic warfare (EW) is divided into distinct categories: defensive measures aimed at collecting intelligence on the enemy's electronic 'order of battle', signals

Table 10. Electronic warfare capabilities in the Middle East.

	Defensive			Offensive
	SIGINT/COMINT	ELINT	JAMMING	ARM/SEAD WEAPONS
Bahrain				
Egypt	x	x	x	x
Iran	x	x	x	?
Iraq	x	x		?
Israel	x	x	x	x
Jordan				
Kuwait				x
Oman				x
Qatar				
Saudi Arabia	x	x	x	
Syria	x	x	x	x
Turkey	x	x	x	x
UAE				x
Yemen				
USAF	x	x		x
USN	x	x	x	x
RAF	x	x		x
France	x	x		x

intelligence (Sigint) or communications intelligence (Comint), which is aimed at locating and monitoring enemy communications traffic; electronic intelligence (Elint) is aimed at monitoring enemy radar and other sensor emissions.

Offensive EW is aimed at disrupting enemy communications and radars, either by jamming them with very powerful signals or physically destroying them with bombs or missiles that home in or electronic emissions, so-called anti-radiation missiles (ARM). Weapons and operations specifically aimed at air defence assets are sometimes termed suppression of enemy air defence (SEAD). Air forces that have the ability to conduct all these types of operation have a significant advantage over their opponents.

Air-to-air refuelling

Air-to-air refuelling (AAR) allows aircraft to conduct operations over almost unlimited ranges or to remain on station for very long periods of time. This latter capability is very significant for airborne early warning aircraft and air defence fighters.

Table 11. Air-to-air refuelling capabilities in the Middle East.

	Own AAR	AAR trained
Bahrain		x
Egypt		x
Iran	x	
Iraq		
Israel	x	
Jordan		
Kuwait		
Oman		x
Qatar		
Saudi Arabia	x	
Syria		
Turkey	x	
UAE		x
Yemen		
USAF	x	
USN	x	
RAF	x	
France	x	

Reconnaissance capabilities

The ability to accurately locate targets deep in hostile territory is a key capability for any air forces. Most Middle Eastern countries possess traditional style 'wet film' photographic reconnaissance aircraft, but they are vulnerable to enemy air defences and cannot rely on their images in 'real time'.

Satellites, ground surveillance radar aircraft and digital data-links to photo-reconnaissance aircraft or unmanned aerial vehicles (UAV) allow air commanders to 'look deep' into hostile territory and rapidly send strike aircraft to destroy them

Training

The standard of aircrew and ground personnel training is often the 'missing link' in Middle East air forces. Indigenous air forces are almost all desperately short of trained air crews, and many rely on foreign personnel or sources of training.

Many Middle East air forces have indigenous training programmes for basic or primary flight training. Some have advanced training facilities, involving weapons employment and individual air combat skills. Most Middle East air forces also assign their training aircraft fleets secondary ground attack roles for counter-insurgency or internal security operations.

Table 12. Reconnaissance capabilities in the Middle East.

	Photo-recce aircraft	Satellite	Ground surveillance radar	Unmanned aerial vehicle
Bahrain				
Egypt	x			x
Iran	x			x
Iraq	x			
Israel	x	x	x	x
Jordan	x			
Kuwait				
Oman	x			
Qatar				
Saudi Arabia	x			
Syria	x			
Turkey	x	x		x
UAE	x	x		x
Yemen	x			
USAF	x	x	x	x
USN	x	x	x	
RAF	x	x	x	x
France	x	x		x

Training aircraft, such as the BAE Systems Hawk, are used extensively by Middle East air forces. *(BAE Systems)*

Table 13. Air training aircraft in the Middle East.

	Number of aircraft	Primary	Advanced	Continuation/ high level of skills
Bahrain	9		x	
Egypt	445	x	x	
Iran	140	x	x	?
Iraq	28	x	x	
Israel	86	x	x	x
Jordan	32	x	x	
Kuwait	25	x	x	
Oman	23	x	x	x
Qatar	6	x	x	
Saudi Arabia	96	x	x	
Syria	238	x	x	
Turkey	271	x	x	x
UAE	101	x	x	x
Yemen	41	x	x	
USAF		x	x	x
USN		x	x	x
RAF		x	x	x
France		x	x	x

Except in conjunction with Western forces, it is currently very difficult for Middle East air forces to conduct continuation training, such as air tactics on a large scale, the employment of advanced electronic warfare tactics or the use of precision-guided munitions.

The exception to this is the Israeli air force. Although the Iranian air force has recently conducted a number of large-scale exercises, some in co-operation with the Syrians, it is not clear if these have involved advanced air warfare training.

Our assessments of the skill levels are based on recent combat performance, patterns of training and anecdotal evidence from foreign observers who have worked with the air forces in question. It also takes into account the resources available to fund training, and so the Jordanian air force, which was once very highly skilled, has slipped because of defence budget cuts since 1990.

Maritime aircraft and helicopters

This is very much a 'Cinderella' branch of air warfare in the Middle East. Both Iran and Iraq waged a violent naval air campaign against merchant shipping in the Gulf during the 1980s, but other Middle Eastern states have been slow to take up maritime air operations. This situation seems to be changing as the build-up of Iranian naval forces gathers momentum. The upsurge of piracy off the Somali coast in 2007 has reinforced the need for maritime airpower.

Table 14. Maritime aviation in the Middle East.

	Fixed wing aircraft	Helicopter	Anti-submarine capability	Anti-ship missile capability
Bahrain				
Egypt		x	x	x
Iran	x	x		x
Iraq		x		x
Israel	x	x		x
Jordan				
Kuwait		x		x
Oman				x
Qatar		x		x
Saudi Arabia		x	x	x
Syria		x	x	x
Turkey		x	x	x
UAE	x			x
Yemen				
USAF				x
USN	x	x	x	x
RAF	x		x	
RN		x	x	
France	x	x		
Spain	x			
Canada		x		
Australia		x		
Germany	x			

Combat helicopters

Rotary-wing aircraft play an important role in most Middle East armed forces. Israel and Syria were the pioneers of using attack and armed helicopters in action during the 1982 Lebanon War. Iraq and Iran also made extensive use of them in the 1980–88 Gulf War The Iraqi insurgency has seen extensive use of attack helicopters by US and Polish land forces.

Attack helicopters are purpose-designed weapon platforms, while armed helicopters are transport or liaison helicopters fitted with external weaponry. Support helicopters are transport, liaison and medical evacuation machines.

Table 15. Combat helicopter capabilities in the Middle East.

	Attack	*Armed*	*Support*
Bahrain	x		x
Egypt	x	x	x
Iran	x	x	x
Iraq	x	x	x
Israel	x	x	x
Jordan	x	x	x
Lebanon		x	x
Kuwait	x	x	x
Oman			x
Qatar		x	x
Saudi Arabia	x	x	x
Syria	x	x	x
Turkey	x	x	x
UAE	x	x	x
Yemen	x	x	x
USAF		x	x
USN			x
USMC	x	x	x
US Army	x	x	x
UK		x	x

Command and control

The command and control of air power is often the key to its successful employment. A number of models have been tried by Middle Eastern countries during the various conflicts that have plagued the region over the past fifty years.

The 'Western', or NATO-style, command structures which allow for centralised planning and decentralised execution of orders by subordinate commanders has been used successfully by the Israelis, Turks, Iranians, British, French and US forces during their operations in the region.

However, due to the political culture of the region, with the proliferation of dictatorships, Soviet-style, centralised tactical control has found favour with many Middle East air forces. This, however, makes them extremely vulnerable to electronic warfare attacks on their communications, which can lead to paralysis when tactical forces are cut off from higher headquarters.

Very few Middle East air forces also have experience of offensive strike planning, selecting targets or assigning weaponry.

Table 16. Air warfare planning and command capabilities in the Middle East.

	Western-style planning	Soviet centralised planning	Offensive air campaign planning	SATCOM
Bahrain	x			
Egypt	x			x?
Iran	x		x	
Iraq	x			x
Israel	x		x	
Jordan	x			
Kuwait	x			
Oman	x			
Qatar	x			
Saudi Arabia	x		x?	x
Syria		x		
Turkey	x		x	x
UAE	x		x?	x
Yemen		x		
USAF	x		x	x
USN	x		x	x
RAF	x		x	x
France	x		x	x

Increasing satellite communications are coming into their own as a command and control tool for air commanders. It allows long-range operations to be conducted and high volumes of traffic to be carried. Commercial satellite feeds are now possible, breaking the monopoly of the Western powers in this important field.

Air defence systems

The need to protect key high-value assets from air attack has led most Middle Eastern countries to invest heavily in air defence systems. There are a variety of capabilities currently in operation.

A number of pro-Western countries have NATO-style air defence systems, which link together all air and air defence assets in 'total' systems, sharing information and decentralising control.

In a throw-back to the days when Soviet influence was strong in the region, some Middle East countries still field old Soviet-style air and air defence forces, which assign fighters and surface-to-air missiles (SAM) defences to a single command and distinct command structure. These Soviet Integrated Air Defence Systems (IADS) are very vulnerable to electronic warfare. Some of the smaller Gulf Co-operation

Table 17. Air defence systems in the Middle East.

	Western style	Soviet IADS	Point defence	Tactical (Army)	BMD/EADS capability
Bahrain	x		x		
Egypt		x	x	x	
Iran		x	x	x	
Iraq					
Israel	x		x	x	x
Jordan	x		x	x	
Kuwait	x		x		x
Oman	x		x		
Qatar	x		x		
Saudi Arabia	x		x		
Syria		x	x	x	x
Turkey	x		x		
UAE	x		x	x	
Yemen		x	x		
USAF					
USN	x				x
US Army	x		x		x
RAF	x		x		
France	x				

Council (GCC) countries have opted out of air defence almost totally, relying on Saudi and US protection, except for short-range, shoulder-launched, heat-seeking SAMs used by land and naval forces.

Iran has recently invested heavily in new Russian air defence missile and radar systems, but has been unable to establish a country-wide IADS due to the large area of coverage needed. It has therefore created a series of localised area or point air defence networks around the capital Tehran, the Gulf coast and the Iraqi border. The only solution to this problem is some sort of airborne early warning capability.

The 1980–88 and 1991 Gulf Wars highlighted the emerging threat from ballistic missiles. Some Middle East states have begun to invest in ballistic missile defence (BMD), or so-called extended air defence capabilities.

PART TWO

Air Force Profiles

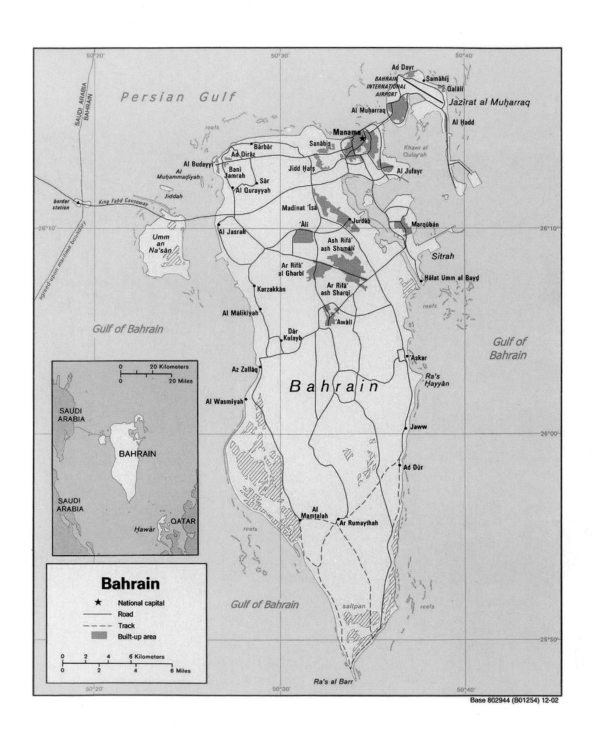

Persian Gulf

SAUDI ARABIA
BAHRAIN

Ad Dayr
BAHRAIN
INTERNATIONAL
AIRPORT
Samâhij
Qalâli
Jazîrat al Muḥarraq
Al Muḥarraq
Al Ḥadd

Manama
Khawr al
Qulay'ah
Bârbâr
Sanâbis
Ad Dirâz
Al Jufayr
Al Budayyi'
Al Muḥammadîyah
Banî Jamrah
Jidd Ḥafş
Sâr
Jiddah
Al Qurayyah

border station
King Fahd Causeway
Madînat 'Îsâ
Marqûbân

Al Jasrah
'Alî
Jurdâb

Umm an Na'sân
Ash Rifâ' ash Shamâlî
Sitrah

Ar Rifâ' al Gharbî
Ḥâlat Umm al Bayḍ

Karzakkân
reefs

Al Mâlikîyah
Ar Rifâ' ash Sharqî

Gulf of Bahrain
Dâr Kulayb
'Awâlî

Az Zallâq
Askar
Ra's Ḥayyân
Gulf of Bahrain

B a h r a i n

Al Wasmîyah

Jaww

Ad Dûr

Al Mamṭalah
Ar Rumaythah
reefs

Gulf of Bahrain
saltpan
reefs

Ra's al Barr

INSET MAP

0   20 Kilometers
0   20 Miles

SAUDI ARABIA

BAHRAIN

SAUDI ARABIA

Ḥawâr
QATAR

Bahrain

★ National capital
— Road
--- Track
▨ Built-up area

0   2   4   6 Kilometers
0   2   4   6 Miles

Base 802944 (B01254) 12-02

CHAPTER TWO

Bahrain

Population	727,755
Military / paramilitary aircraft	93
Air Force personnel	6,000

Royal Bahraini Air Force (RBAF)

History

The small island state of Bahrain achieved its independence from Britain in 1971, but did not form an air arm for six years. Initially it was equipped only with helicopters; it did not acquire fast jets until the mid-1980s, in the shape of F-5s. From 1991 onwards, these were augmented by US F-16s and Cobra attack helicopters. Originally titled the Bahrain Amiri Air Force, it was renamed in 2002.

Bahrain has invested considerably in aircrew training with a fleet of Slingsby Firefly aircraft. *(BAE Systems)*

Bahrain Air Arms Order of Battle as at 1 May 2009.

Airbase	Location	Wing/Base Designation	Squadron	Aircraft Type	Role
Royal Bahrain Air Force					
Shaikh Isa	25° 55′ N 50° 35′ E	Tactical Fighter Wing	1 Fighter	F-16C/D	Air defence/CAS
			2 Fighter	F-16C/F	Air defence/CAS
			6 Fighter	F-5E/F	CAS
			5	Hawk Mk 128	Training/ Air defence
			4	T67M260	Training
Muharraq International	26° 16′ N 50° 38′ E	Baharin Amiri Royal Flight		B727-2M7, B767-440ER, Bell 430, BAE146, Gulfstream II/IV	VIP transport
Rifa'a	26° 06′ N 50° 34′ E	Helicopter Wing	3	AB212	Troop transport
			7	Bo 105C	Liaison
			8	AH-1E	Attack
			9	UH-60A/L	Troop transport
Bahrain Amiri Navy					
Rifa'a	26° 06′ N 50° 34′ E			Bo105CBS	Naval support
Bahrain Public Security Force					
Rifa'a	26° 06′ N 50° 34′ E	Bahrain Public Security Flying Wing		Bell 412, Bell 412SP, Bell 427	Internal security

Structure
The RBAF reports direct to the Bahrain Ministry of Defence. The fast jets are grouped in the Tactical Fighter Wing, and rotary-wing assets are under the control of the Helicopter Wing. The Amiri Flight flies members of the royal family and government.

Air power doctrine and strategy
Bahrain's air force is committed to defensive operations of Bahrain island and the neighbouring states of the Gulf Co-operation Council.

Operational activity
Bahraini troops and naval forces deployed to Kuwait in the run-up to the US invasion of Iraq in March 2003, under the terms of the Peninsula Shield agreement

Bahrain Inventory as at 20 February 2008.

Type	Active	Stored	Ordered	Required
Bahrain Amiri Air Force				
COMBAT AIRCRAFT				
F-16C/F-16D	17:04			
F-5E/F-5F Tiger II	08:04			
TRANSPORT				
RJ-85	2			
RJ-1000	1			
COMBAT HELICOPTER				
AH-1E/TAH-1P	12:06			
BO105C	3			
UH-60A/L	01:01			
AB212	2			
UH-60M			9	
Bell 412SP				6
TRAINING AIRCRAFT				
T67M260 Firefly	3			
Hawk 129	6			6
Bahrain Amiri Naval Air Arm				
Bo105CBS	2			
Bahrain Amiri Flight				
TRANSPORT				
767-400ER	3			
Gulfstream II/IV	01:01			
727	1			
BAe 146	1			
Dell 430	1			
Bahrain Public Security Force				
AB412SP	4			
Bell 212	9			

for mutual defence of Gulf states. They have now returned home. Limited co-operation with other Gulf Co-operation Council air forces, particularly the Saudis, on air defence matters takes place with some sharing of radar information and other intelligence. The RBAF possess no air transport, air-to-air refuelling or other

BAE Systems Hawk Mk 129

The latest derivative of the best-selling Hawk is Bahrain's lead-in fighter trainer. Kuwait, Oman, Saudi Arabia and the UAE also use earlier variants of the Hawk in training and light attack roles.

Crew: 2 (student, instructor)
Length: 40 ft 9 in. (12.43 m)
Wingspan: 32 ft 7 in. (9.94 m)
Height: 13 ft 1 in. (3.98 m)
Maximum take-off weight: 20,000 lb (9,100 kg)
Powerplant: One Rolls-Royce Adour Mk 951 turbofan with FADEC, 6,500 lbf (29 kN)
Maximum speed: .84 Mach (638 mph, 1,028 km/h) at altitude
Range: 1,360 nm (1,565 miles, 2,520 km)

Armament
Note: all armament is optional
1 × 30 mm ADEN cannon, in centre-line pod

Up to 6,800 lb (3,085 kg) of weapons on five hardpoints, including:
4 × AIM-9 Sidewinder or ASRAAM on wing pylons and wingtip rails
1,500 lb (680 kg), limited to one centre-line and two wing pylons (Hawk T.1)

expeditionary capabilities to allow it to undertake sustained operations away from its home bases. To date the RBAF has not taken part in any combat operations. It has hosted major Gulf Co-operation Council air defence exercises at Shaikh Isa airbase, including Initial Link 08 in May 2008. This bi-annual event aims to practise large-scale air defence operations, utilising air-to-air refuelling, AWACS support and suppression of enemy air defence tactics. The last exercises featured Bahraini, USAF, US Navy, Kuwaiti, Qatari, Saudi and UAE aircraft operating from Shaikh Isa and their home bases. The exercise is to be expanded to include close air support training in 2010.

Airbase infrastructure
Shaikh Isa airbase on the southern end of Bahrain island is the main fast-jet base of the RBAF. It has been extensively hardened with aircraft shelters and other facilities. The air force and navy helicopter force operate out of a purpose-built base at Rifa'a to the south of Bahrain city.

Bahrain International Airport (formerly RAF Muharraq) on Muharraq island is available for use in an emergency.

Aircraft ordnance
The F-5s and F-16s have limited air-to-ground capabilities beyond iron bombs and AGM-65 Maverick TV/IR-guided air-launched missiles. AIM-9P Sidewinder heat-seeking and AIM-9F semi-active radar-guided missiles are operated by the F-16s. AIM-120 AMRAAMs were purchased in 1999. The Cobra attack helicopters have TOW wire-guided anti-tank missiles at Shaikh Isa airbase.

Strategic weapons
Bahrain has no strategic weapons.

Procurement
To help train pilots, Bahrain signed deals in 2002 with BAE Systems to establish a pilot academy, to use three Firefly and around six Hawk 129 trainers. Deliveries began in October 2006 and were complete by February 2007. The Hawks were be delivered in 2006 and additional Hawks could replace some F-5s. It began to seek an upgrade for its AH-1s in early 2001. At least one of the VIP Boeing 747s is to receive BAE's Nemesis defensive aids equipment. Two RJ85s have recently been sold off. In June 2007, Bahrain ordered nine UH-60s from Sikorsky helicopters in a deal worth $30.42 million. Bahrain requested approval for the sale from the USA of six Bell 412 helicopters in August 2007. A VIP transport version of the Sikorsky S-92 was ordered in November 2007.

Other air arms
The naval arm was formed in 1987. It is separate from the air force, and operates two BO105CBS helicopters. The Bahrain Public Security Force (BPS) reports to the

Ministry of the Interior and is responsible for internal security-type operations in support of the police.

Presence of foreign forces

After British forces departed in 1971, the USA moved quickly to establish a presence, and since then American links to Bahrain's military have grown considerably. After the 1991 Gulf War, the US Navy established the shore headquarters of its 5th Fleet on the island. Several thousand US service personnel are now permanently based on Bahrain. Muharraq International airport is also a key hub for US Navy aviation activity in the Middle East. A squadron of US Navy P-3 Orion maritime patrol aircraft and a detachment of EP-3 Aries III electronic-intelligence-gathering aircraft were based at Muharraq until 2005/6 before they relocated to Al Udeid airbase in Qatar to free up ramp space for civilian developments at Bahrain's main civil airport. The airport also serves as an air transport hub for US Navy and USAF air transport aircraft. Helicopters of the HC-2 'Desert Ducks' operate from the base, resupplying US Navy and Coalition warships in the Arabian Gulf. The RAF maintained air-to-air refuelling tankers at Muharraq from 1993 until 2006 to support no-fly operations over Iraq and the subsequent occupation of that country. The VC-10s of 10 Squadron then moved to Al Udeid as part of a concentration of UK air assets in the region. A BAe 146 and HS125s of 32 (The Royal) Squadron replaced the departing VC-10s.

Shaikh Isa airbase was used by USAF and USMC aircraft during 2003, and both services continue to have access to the base. Pre-positioned USAF equipment stocks are maintained there.

USAF flying instructors are detached to serve with RBAF F-16 and F-5 squadrons, and the US Army supports the RBAF helicopter units with flying instructors and ground personnel. Contractor logistic support personnel also operate at RBAF bases. This presence is expected to grow once BAE Systems gets its flying school activity up and running.

Assessment

The Bahraini Air Force is a competent but small force. Its personnel have a high level of training and access to relatively modern equipment. Question marks remain over the air force's ability to defend against a prolonged attack on Bahrain without Allied help.

CHAPTER THREE

Egypt

Population	83 million
Military/paramilitary aircraft	1,174
Air Force personnel	35,000
Air defence personnel	80,000

Al Quwwat al Jawwiya Il Misriya (Arab Republic of Egypt Air Force)

History

Egypt has one of the oldest air forces in the Arab world, with its first air units being formed in 1930, some two years after King Fuad asked for volunteers to begin flying training. Until the end of the Second World War, Egypt was firmly under British influence and its air forces used surplus RAF equipment.

The newly expanded Egyptian air force fought against the recently founded Israeli air force during the 1948 war in Palestine that led to the foundation of the Jewish state. The 1950s and 1960s saw many Arab countries come into the grip of Arab nationalism, and Egypt was at the centre of this movement. Western support for Israel forced Egypt to turn to the Soviet Union for arms. After the 1956 conflict with Israel, Britain and France, the Egyptians began to receive accelerated supplies of Soviet weaponry, including a large number of MiG fighters to boost the strength of their air force.

Defeat in the 1967 War saw Egypt receive even more weaponry from Moscow, and these deliveries included large numbers of radar-guided surface-to-air missiles (SAM). The revamped Egyptian armed forces, particularly their air defences, initially performed well against the Israelis in the 1973 War, but soon they were out-manoeuvred by Israeli tank columns.

The cost of maintaining the Arab world's largest armed forces was too much to bear, and by the end of the 1970s, the Egyptians had signed a peace accord with Israel. This opened the way for US military aid, but it lost the country the support of the rich Gulf states, which undermined several ambitious projects to develop an aerospace industry.

In the 1980s, the first US weapons, including General Dynamics F-16 Fighting Falcons, arrived in Egypt. The USA also began to stage its series of Bright Star exercises with the Egyptians.

This decade also saw the Egyptians give strong support to the Iraqi leader Saddam Hussein in his war against Iran. Egyptian pilots and military advisers helped the

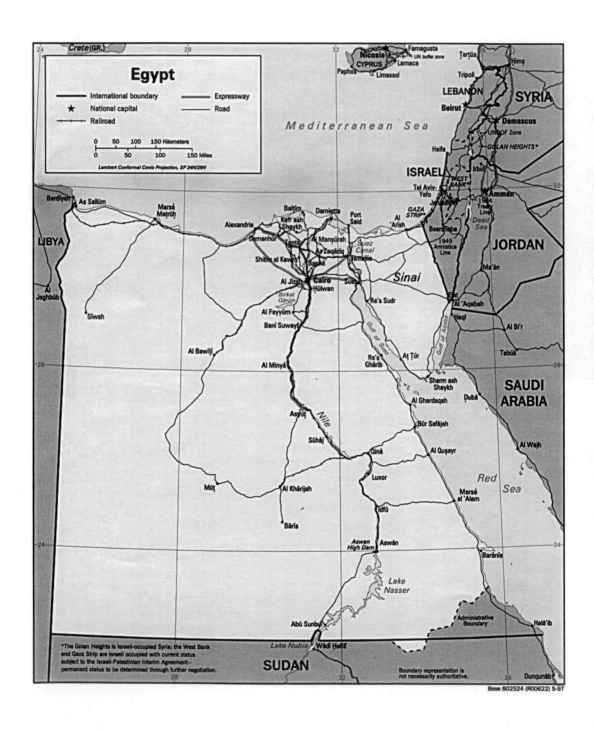

Egypt

- International boundary
- ★ National capital
- Railroad
- Expressway
- Road

0 50 100 150 Kilometers
0   50   100   150 Miles

Lambert Conformal Conic Projection, SP 24N/29N

*The Golan Heights is Israeli-occupied Syria; the West Bank and Gaza Strip are Israeli occupied with current status subject to the Israeli-Palestinian Interim Agreement— permanent status to be determined through further negotiation.

Boundary representation is not necessarily authoritative.

Base 802524 (R00622) 5-97

US-supplied F-16 Fighting Falcons are the Egyptian air forces' main front-line fighter. *(USAF)*

Many of Egypt's F-16s were assembled in Turkey. *(Lockheed Martin)*

Egyptian Air Arms Order of Battle as at 1 May 2009.

Airbase	Location	Wing/Base Designation	Squadron	Aircraft Type	Role
Mersa Matruh	30° 57′ N 31° 25′ E	102 Fighter Brigade	26	F-7, FT-7	Air defence
			82 det.	Mirage2000BM, Mirage2000EM	Air defence
Al Mansurah	30° 57′ N 31° 25′ E	104 Fighter Brigade	22	F-7/TF-7	Air defence
			45	MiG-21MF/U	Air defence
			49	MiG-21MF/U	Air defence
Fayid	30° 19′ N 32° 16′ E	102 Fighter Brigade	40	F-16C, F-16D	Air defence/Strike
			64	F-16C, F-16D	Air defence/Strike
Assouan	23° 57′ N 32° 49′ E	?? Fighter Brigade ??		MiG-21MF	Air defence
Cairo-West	30° 06′ N 30° 54′ E	601 AEW Brigade	87	E-2C	
			76	F-4E	Air defence/Strike
			78	F-4E	Air defence/Strike
Kom Ashwin	29° 33′ N 30° 53′ E	?? ECM Brigade	??	IL-28	EW
			??	KT-107	EW
		53. Helicopter Brigade	7	Mi-8	Troop transport
			18	CH-47D	Troop transport
Jiyanklis	30° 49′ N 30° 11′ E	211 FGA Brigade	20	F-6, FT-6	Air defence
			21	F-6, FT-6	Air defence
		272 Tact Fighter Brigade	75	F-16C/D Block 40 (TUAS)	Air defence/Strike
			77	F-16C/D Block 40 (TUAS)	Air defence/Strike
Inshas	30° 19′ N 31° 26′ E	232 Tact Fighter Brigade	72	F-16A/B Block 42 (ex15)	Air defence
			74	F-16A/B Block 42 (ex15)	Air defence
		601 ECM Brigade	81	Beech 1900C-1 (ELINT)	EW
Birma/Tanta	30° 50′ N 30° 56′ E	236 FGA Brigade	69	Mirage 5SDE/SDD/SDR	Air defence/Strike/Recce

Airbase	Location	Wing/Base Designation	Squadron	Aircraft Type	Role
			73	Mirage 5SDE /5SDD	Air defence/ Strike/Recce
Gebel Al Basur	30° 32′ N 30° 33′ E		71	Mirage 5SDE, Mirage 5SDD, Mirage 5SDR	
			82	Mirage 2000BM, Mirage 2000EM	
Beni Suef	29° 11′ N 31° 01′ E	242 Tact Fighter Brigade	68	F-16C/D Block 32	Air defence/ Strike
			70	F-16C/D Block 32	Air defence/ Strike
Abu Suwayr	30° 34′ N 32° 05′ E	262 Tact Fighter Brigade	60	F-16C Block 40, F-16D Block 40	Air defence/ Strike
Cairo-East/ Almaza	30° 05′ N 31° 21′ E	?? CAS Brigade	57	Alpha Jet MS2	CAS
			58	Alpha Jet MS2	CAS
		516 Brigade	??	Mi-8	Troop transport
		533 Brigade	??	Mi-8	Troop transport
Wadi al Jandali (Al Qatamiyah)	30° 03′ N 31° 50′ E		Flying Training Air	Ghoumhouriya	Training
		550 Attack Heli Brigade	51	AH-64D	Attack
Az Zaqaziq (also known as Abu Hamad)	30° 35′ N 31° 39′ E	550 Attack Heli Brigade	52	AH-64D	Attack
Hurghada	27° 11′ N 33° 47′ E	53. Helicopter Brigade	??	Mi-8	Troop transport
			??	Mi-8	Troop transport
			sq (det)	MiG-21	Air defence
Cairo International	30° 07′ N 31° 24′ E	??? Transport Brigade	4	C-130H	Transport
			16	C-130H, C-130VC, EC-130H	Transport/EW
			??	AS-61, King Air, Boeing 707&737, Sea King, G.1159-III,	VIP transport

Airbase	Location	Wing/Base Designation	Squadron	Aircraft Type	Role
				G.1159-IV, S-70A, UH-60L	
			40	SA-342 (VIP)	VIP transport
		516 Transport Brigade	2	DHC-5D,	Transport
			??	Z-526	Transport
			??	Z-526	Transport
Alexandriya – Borg el Arab	31° 11′ N 29° 56′ E	5th Tactical Helicopter Wing	7	Sea King Mk47	Troop transport
			11	SA-342L	Naval support
			37 (Navy)	SH-2G(E)	Naval support
Air Force Academy					
Bilbeis	30° 23′ N 31° 36′ E	117 Primary Training Brigade	??	Grob 115EG	Training
			??	Grob 115EG	Training
			83	EMB312	Training
			84	EMB312	Training
			85	EMB312	Training
			86	EMB312	Training
		Air Navigation School	??	DHC-5	Training
		?? OCU	??	F-6, FT-6	
El Minya	28° 05′ N 30° 43′ E	?? Weapon Training Brigade	201	Alpha Jet MS2, Alpha Jet MS1	Training
		?? Flying Training Brigade	88	L-39ZO, L-59E	Training
			??	K-8E	Training
		?? Heli Training Brigade	??	SA-342L/L	Training

Iraqis, and in return large orders were placed with Cairo's defence industry. This all came to an end with the Iraqi invasion of Kuwait, when Egypt joined the US-led Coalition to free the oil-rich Gulf state. Egyptian ground troops were sent to fight alongside the Coalition, but apart from some air lifts no Egyptian combat aircraft participated in Operation Desert Storm.

The aftermath of the 1991 Gulf War was not good for the Egyptian military. Much of its 1970s-era Soviet-supplied hardware was nearing the end of its operational life, and US military aid was not sufficient to allow one-for-one replacement. Egypt's economy was also in a poor condition, so there was little prospect of cash purchases of new equipment for countries apart from the USA. Some barter deals were done with the Chinese for fighter and trainer aircraft, but not in major quantities.

The delivery of US equipment and the near obsolescence of Soviet-era equipment has led to a gradual adoption of Western-style air warfare tactics and procedures.

In the 1980s, the Egyptians managed to acquire US Scarab and Skyeye unmanned aerial vehicles, but it has not had the money to buy more modern unmanned systems.

Structure

Egyptian air power still has a largely Soviet-era structure, with the air force controller of aircraft and the Air Defence Command being responsible for ground-based radars and anti-aircraft weapons.

All Egyptian military aircraft and helicopters, except for a handful of helicopters in the navy, are controlled by the air force. Egypt's ten Super Seasprites have been

Soviet-era surface-to-air missiles, such as the V-75 Davina (SA-2 Guideline), are still in front-line service with the Egyptian air defence command. *(US DoD)*

Egypt Inventory as at 1 May 2009.

Type	Active	Stored	Ordered	Required
Al Quwwat al Jawwiya Il Misriya (Arab Republic of Egypt Air Force)				
COMBAT AIRCRAFT				
F-16A/F-16B	30:-6			
F-16C/F-16D	135/32		12:12	
Mirage 2000EM/B	15:-4			
Chengdu F-7A		53		
MiG-21PF/PM/R/U	42	10/20/2010		
Mirage 5E2/DE/SDR/SDD	12/6/31/6			
F-4E Phantom	32			
F-6/FT-6		40/5		
ISTAR/SPECIAL MISSION				
E-2C Hawkeye/2000	4:02		2	
Beech 1900C	8			
C-130H	2			
An-24 MPA	3			
TRANSPORT				
King Air	1			
C-130H/H-30	20:03		3	
VC-130H	2:-1			
DHC-5D Buffalo	9			
A340	1			
Il-14	23		11	
707	1			
737	1			
An-74TK	3		6	
An-12		10		
COMBAT HELICOPTER				
AH-64D Apache	35			
SA342L/M Gazelle	40	39		
Mi-8/Mi-17	42/20			
Mi-6		9		
CH-47D Chinook	19			
AS-61 SEA KING	2			
UH-60A/UH-60L	4		18	
S-70A2-21	2			
Commando Mk1/Mk2/E	5/17/2			
TRAINING AIRCRAFT/HELICOPTERS				
Alpha Jet MS1/MS2	15/13			
L-59E	48			

Type	Active	Stored	Ordered	Required
EMB-312 Tucano	46			
Hiller UH-12E	17			
K-8 Karakorum	61		19	
Grob G115EG	73			
L29	112			
L39	12			
Zlin 242	48			
UNMANNED AIR VEHICLES				
Scarab	32			
R4E Skyeye	23			
Egyptian Navy				
COMBAT HELICOPTER				
Super Seasprite	12		1	
Sea King Mk47		5		
SA342L Gazelle	12			
Government of the Arab Republic of Egypt				
TRANSPORT				
Falcon 20	3			
Gulfstream III/IV	2:04			
An-72T-200A	1			
A340	1			
Sea King Mk2B	4			
VC-130H	1			
King Air	4			
Boeing 707	1			
Boeing 737	4			

remanufactured from US Navy stocks, and are the only SH-2s to be equipped with dipping sonar. First deliveries were in 1997, and an upgrade programme is under way for completion by 2011. The Egyptian navy deploys the SH-2s aboard four frigates.

The Egyptian government operates it own fleet of VIP transport aircraft independent of the air force.

Some 35,000 personnel serve in the Egyptian air force, with the majority of aircrew being long-term professionals.

Air power is an effective way for the Egyptian military to defend the country's long borders and coastline. *(USAF)*

Operational context

As well as being a major Middle East power, Egypt is also in a key strategic position in the eastern Mediterranean and North Africa. This means that its air power is deployed to meet these challenges.

   Peace with Israel means that the Egyptian air force has had to pull back from the Sinai peninsula, which has largely been demilitarised. The main day-to-day activity of the air force is having fighter aircraft on alert to deal with any hostile incursion into Egyptian air space.

Since the 1991 Gulf War, Egyptian forces have not participated in live operations, so its pool of personnel with combat experience is diminishing rapidly. This puts a premium on training, and Cubic Worldwide Technical Services continues to run the Egyptian air combat manoeuvring instrumented (ACMI) range. It was originally installed in 1989 at Beni Suef (main base) and Cairo West. Since then, three sites have been added, at Anchas, Abu Suer and Gianaclese.

Air power doctrine and strategy

Egyptian air power doctrine and strategy has had to evolve considerably since the 1970s when it closely mirrored the Soviet model. The main task of Egyptian air power is to protect the country's air space and support the land forces. It concentrates most of its activity on air defence and supporting internal security forces.

Egypt does not have the resources or ambitions to have an expeditionary strategy, so the role of its air force is very much focused on operations from its home bases.

Operational activity

Egypt continues to open its airspace to US and UK aircraft operating in the Middle East, reinforcing the country's strong ties with Washington.

The Egyptian air force and navy have assisted in US-UK maritime security patrols around the approaches to the Suez Canal since 2001. US aircraft stage through several Egyptian airbases. Mirage units have exercised with French air force counterparts. The Bright Star series of US-led multinational exercises in Egypt resumed in the autumn of 2005, and they continued in 2007. Egyptian Sea Kings returned the body of Palestinian leader Yassir Arafat for burial in the West Bank in 2004.

Airbase infrastructure

Egypt airbases mostly date from the 1960s when the Soviets oversaw a huge expansion, including the building of hardened aircraft shelters and other facilities.

Some facilities to accommodate US-sourced equipment has since been built, but the Egyptian air force's infrastructure is largely unchanged since the 1970s.

US forces conduct regular training exercises with the Egyptian air force, including the air-to-air refuelling operation. (USAF)

The main operating bases are Cairo West (F-4E/C-130/E-2C/F-6), An Shaf (F-16), Abu Suwayr (F-16), Genaklis (F-16), Beni Suef (F-16), Genachi (Mirage 2000), Bilbeis (AlphaJet).

Aircraft ordnance
The weaponry used by Egypt's aircraft has evolved considerably from the 1970s when Soviet ordnance was to the fore. Now a mix of Soviet, French and US weapons are in service.

Precision-Guided Munitions
AGM-65 Maverick TV/IR-guided air-launched missile (3-20km)
AS-12 wire-guided anti-tank missile
AS-30 air-launched missile (10km)
AS-30L air-launched laser-guided missile (10km)
HOT wire-guided anti-tank missile
Paveway GBU-10, -12, -16 and -24
AGM-114 Hellfire

Suppression-of-Enemy-Air-Defence Weapons
Armat anti-radiation missile
AGM-84 HARM

Anti-Ship Missiles
AM-39 Exocet

Air-to-Air Missiles
R-13/AA-2 'Atoll' heat-seeking missile
AIM-7E/F/M Sparrow semi-active radar-guided missile
AIM-9F/L/P Sidewinder heat-seeking missile
R-530 semi-active radar-guided missile
R-550 Magic heat-seeking missile
AIM-120 AMRAAM active heat-seeking missile

Strategic weapons
Egypt does not possess long-range strategic missiles or nuclear weapons. In the 1960s and 1970s, the country launched an effort to bulk-manufacture chemical weapons, and residual capability in this area is likely to exist, including air-dropped dispenser weapons.

During the 1980s Egypt co-operated with Iraqi efforts to develop long-range ballistic missiles, but these collapsed after international arms sanctions were imposed on Baghdad in 1990. Egypt retains some twenty-four Scud ballistic missile launchers and around a hundred missiles, as well as twelve FROG-7 tactical missile launchers. These weapons are controlled by the Egyptian land forces.

Procurement

Egypt receives some $1.3 billion annually in military aid from the USA, which represents eighty per cent of Egypt's annual defence budget, according to some sources. The US law requires that the procurement element of this aid be only spent on US products, so Egypt's air force has by default had to focus its procurement on US aircraft and weapons.

Egypt is moving towards making the F-16 its only front-line type, and is considering the Block 60 as an F-4 replacement. It is also looking to acquire a reconnaissance pod from the USA. Egypt's air defence fighters are supported by six E-2C AEW aircraft. Two E-2Cs have been upgraded to Hawkeye 2000 standard, and work on a third is under way.

Egypt signed a deal to upgrade its AH-64Ds, and deliveries started in late 2003, before being completed in January 2007. The export of surplus USAF KC-135R tankers was approved in mid-2004 but has not yet taken place. Sixteen CH-47s were upgraded to the D standard, with the USA approving three more upgrades in 2006. The purchase of the CH-47F is now being considered.

Consideration is being given to upgrading the Scarab UAV.

Egypt selected the Chinese K-8 to replace its L-29s, and its first of eighty flew in mid-2000, with deliveries complete by 2004. A further forty are on order in what is believed to be a barter deal involving local production in Egypt.

Egypt also has an advanced trainer requirement to replace L-59s and Alpha Jets for which the Hawk and L-159 are being considered. Egypt expressed interest in four to six C-130Js, but has instead opted to buy three ex-Danish C-130Hs. Three An-72TKs are on order out of a possible requirement for eighteen, with one delivered in September 2005. SIAC is upgrading the country's two instrumented helicopter and air defence training ranges.

The serviceability of the older fighter types is in doubt, and much of the Soviet- and Chinese-supplied inventory is up for sale. Two squadrons still operate versions of the MiG-21.

Egypt's ageing fighter fleet is in urgent need of replacement, particularly the MiG-21s and F-4Es. Attempts to buy US F-15E Strike Eagles and F-16 Block 60s have so far not come to success due to objections from Israel. Chinese/Pakistani JF-17s seem a strong option if finance can be arranged. Another option, of a return to the purchase of Russian MiG-29 SMTs or Sukhoi Su-35s, is also under consideration, but this would pose major integration products with US-sourced equipment.

The Egyptians are also keen to acquire more advanced airborne weapons, such as the Raytheon AIM-120 AMRAAM beyond-visual-range missile and satellite-guided Boeing joint direct attack munition (JDAM).

Presence of foreign forces

Egypt does not host any major US bases but plays a key element in US strategy in the Middle East. US Navy vessels are granted priority passage through the Suez

Canal, and according to US figures, Egypt granted air space access to 36,553 US military aircraft between 2001 and 2005. US Navy C-2 Greyhound COD aircraft and CH-53E Sea Stallion helicopters regularly provide logistic support to US Navy carrier battle groups operating in the Red Sea from the civil/military airfield at Hurghada.

The other major element of the Egypt–USA alliance is the Bright Star series of exercises. These were temporarily halted in 2003 because of the Iraq War, but restarted in 2005. US Central Command's Army, Air Force, Navy, Marine Corps and special operations forces components, along with military forces from Egypt and twelve other nations, participated in Bright Star 2005/6, a joint combined training exercise in Egypt. This exercise is an important part of US Central Command's theatre engagement strategy and is designed to improve readiness and interoperability and strengthen the military and professional relationships among US Egyptian and participating forces.

Although the focus on Bright Star is mainly on land forces, USAF and US Marine Corps aviation units were strongly involved. The 2007 exercise involved a counter-insurgency scenario, and USAF C-17 and C-130s conducted parachute-drop training. This exercise involved 7,400 troops from thirteen countries, including the USA, France, Britain, Greece, Germany, Italy, the Netherlands, Jordan and Kuwait. Pakistan, Turkey and Yemen participated for the first time.

The Sinai peninsula also hosts the Multinational Force and Observer Mission, which is tasked with monitoring the demilitarisation of the Sinai under the Israel–Egypt peace treaty. Ten nations contribute troops, including the USA, which provides a company of US Army UH-60 Blackhawk helicopters for troop transport and liaison.

Air defence command

Egypt's air defence has suffered from poor funding for more than two decades, and a serous question mark hung over its combat capability until US-made Raytheon Patriot missile systems were supplied earlier this century. Some seven batteries of the Patriot system, which has an anti-ballistic missile capability, have so far been delivered. Commercial satellite imagery shows that the vast majority of its surface-to-air missile (SAM) sites have been vacated for several years. It has some 80,000 personnel, of whom the majority are conscripts.

The bulk of the command's SAMs are 1960s-vintage Soviet-era S-75 Dvina (SA-2 Guideline) and S-125 Pechora (SA-3 Goa) weapons, with some seventy batteries in its order of battle. An effort was made in the 1990s to update them to make them compatible with US-supplied radars and communications systems, but the progress of this effort is thought to have been slow, with large parts of the SAM inventory remaining unmodified.

In 2006, Russia's Oboronitelniye Sistemy had started implementing the second stage of a contract to upgrade Egypt's S-125 Pechoras to Pechora-2M standard. Under the contract, some thirty battalions of Egyptian Air Defence Command

Pechora S-125 systems will be upgraded in three stages. The first stage, which calls for the upgrade and delivery of ten Pechora-2M systems, was completed by 2006, with the second stage providing for the upgrade of the next ten battalions.

US-supplied Raytheon I-Hawk and French Crotale SAMs have not replaced the Soviet weapons on a one-for-one basis, with only some twelve batteries of each system in service.

Tactical air defence for the army is controlled by the land forces. It has responsibility for some fourteen Kub or SA-6 Gainful batteries, which were once considered Egypt's best SAMs. They have since been augmented by US-supplied Avenger gun systems.

Assessment

From once being the Arab world's leading air force, in terms of both capability and combat experience, the Egyptian air force has fallen behind its regional rivals considerably. It lacks a full spectrum of modern airborne weapons, its aircraft are not the most modern and its pilots lack relevant combat experience. While the pilots and aircrew whom Egypt does have are relatively skilful, the commanders and senior officers of the country's air force have not been exposed to a high-intensity war for more than twenty years. This is a major problem for the Egyptian air force.

Egypt has economic problems – the country has no major oil reserves – and unless it receives a major injection of foreign aid this situation is not going to be reversed in the near term. One possibility is if Egypt opens dialogue with the new F-16 users in the Gulf, Oman, UAE and Bahrain to help them with training both air and ground crew. This would give the Egyptians exposure to the latest version of the US-made jet and give the Gulf states the benefit of the Egyptians' twenty-eight years of experience operating the aircraft.

Wider integration of the Egyptians into Arab military co-operation is unlikely until there is a change of regime in Cairo. Egypt's air force is likely to remain on the edge of Arab air force developments.

CHAPTER FOUR

Islamic Republic of Iran

Population	66 million
Military/paramilitary aircraft	970
Air Force personnel	18,000
Air defence personnel	12,000

IRIAF – Islamic Republic of Iran Air Force

History

Military aviation in Iran can trace its history back to the mid-1920s when the then Shah formed the first Persian air force. British influence was strong until the mid-1960s, when the regime of the Shah turned to the USA to help build up the Iranian armed forces to give it a 'regional policing or superpower' role. Some 500 combat aircraft were bought from the USA, along with more than 900 helicopters to build up an army aviation corps. By the time of the 1979 Islamic revolution, the Iranian air force boasted more than 100,000 personnel.

The turmoil of the revolution split the air force, with many of the conscripts and non-commissioned officers backing the overthrow of the Shah's regime and the service's senior officers siding with the old order. Purges and the execution of the Shah's supporters caused chaos in the air force, perhaps to a greater degree than did the withdrawal of US advisers and logistic support.

Iraq's invasion of Iran in 1980 threw the Iranian air force into an eight-year war that would transform its fortunes. Its pilots become battle hardened and the country's aviation industry developed a considerable self-sufficiency to produce weapons and spare parts, and in some cases to develop the capability to build complete aircraft and helicopters.

Some of the 100–120 aircraft flown to Iran by Iraqi air crew during the 1991 Gulf War were put into service by the air force, including the Il-76-based Adnan AWACS, Su-25s.

During the 1980s and 1990s, Iran purchased aircraft and other military equipment from Russia, China, North Korea and Ukraine. The reliability of this equipment was very low, and so the Iranians decided to continue to upgrade and enhance their existing inventory of US-supplied aircraft.

Structure

Iran has two 'pillars of armed forces'. The regular armed forces are configured for conventional operations, and the Islamic Revolutionary Guard Corps (IRGC) is the country's rapid reaction/intervention force. It also has a role in mobilising the patriotic masses if necessary.

The air force used to control the air defence arm, but in December 2009 a new unified Iranian armed force air defence force was formed. This brought together the air defence weapons and early warning radar assets for the air force, armed forces and IRGC into a single unitary command.

The air force organisation follows the six-district or 'territory-of-operation' structure of the Iranian armed forces. Each district has its own unified command to control all regular and IRGC units in its area of operation.

Operational activity

Since the end of the war with Iraq in 1988, the Iranian armed forces have been involved regularly in operations against drug smugglers from Afghanistan and Pakistan, as well mounting raids on MEK/MKO insurgent camps in Iraq. Iran also participated in several operations in Afghanistan during the 1990s. Earthquake relief operations after the city of Bam was devastated in 2003 involved air force air transport and helicopter assets on a large scale.

Surveillance operations were intensified during US offensive operations against Iraq in 1999, Afghanistan in 2001 and Iraq in 2003, but Iran was not drawn into these conflicts. During the 2003 conflict, Iranian aircraft maintained constant dawn-to-dusk combat air patrols along the country's western border. Subsequently in 2004, the Iranians and US Central Command concluded an arrangement to reduce tension and ensure their respective air and naval forces remained at safe distances to prevent accidents and incidents.

Iran has staged major air, land and sea exercises on an annual basis since 2002, which often involve the showcasing of new aircraft and missiles to the international media.

It is almost twenty years since the end of the Iran–Iraq war, so the generation of aircrew who gained considerable combat experience during that conflict are now in senior command appointments. The vast majority of Shah-era US-trained pilots have retired. Training a new generation of aircrew and fine-tuning their combat skills is a high priority for the Iranians. For much of the 1990s, Iranian pilots only averaged some 150–60 flight hours a year, but as tension has grown with the USA in recent years flight training has increased. Now each fighter wing participates in at least five major exercises a year. A review of flight training has been ordered to improve safety and operational effectiveness. This has resulted in an increase in the number of qualified aircrew, with some fifty F-14 crew members being declared combat ready

Although a significant number of F-14, F-4E and F-5 jets remain in service in significant numbers, the more recently supplied Russian MiG-29s and Su-24s have

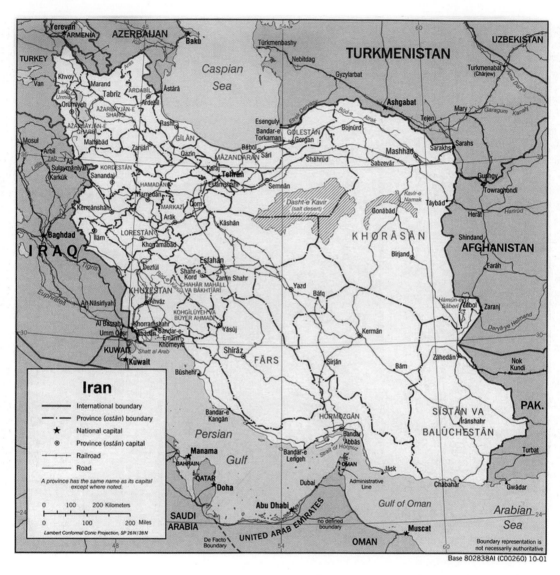

taken on an increasing number of roles. The air force is dispersed around fifty airfields to protect it from any US or Israeli pre-emptive strike.

Airbase infrastructure

The Shah's military expansion programme during the 1970s involved a major airfield building component. Iranian main operating bases were provided with air defence missile batteries, 3,000-metre-long runways, hardened aircraft shelters and revetments, underground command posts, maintenance facilities, fuel stores and ammunition bunkers. The bases at Esfahan (Khatami airbase), Hamadan (Shahroki airbase), Dezful (Vahdati airbase), Shiraz, Bushehr and Ahvaz (Omidiyeh) were all built to this high standard to support combat aircraft operations.

The veteran F-4E is still in the front line of Iranian air power. *(IRIAF via Tom Cooper)*

Mehrabad airport in Tehran was the main operating base for transport and tanker aircraft, and the military facilities were adjacent to the capital's main international airport. The air force headquarters is at Doshan Tapeh airbase in Tehran, and it also boasts a hardened underground command bunker,

Other major military airbases include Chan Bahar, Ghaleh Morghi (Tehran), Mashhad, Tabriz, Zahedan, Masjed Suleyman (Shahid Asyaee), Aghajari, Kerman, Khorramshahr, Khark Island, Nou Shahr (Noshahr), Abamusa Island, Badr (Sepah airbase) and Bandar Beheshti. Bandar Abbas in the south is shared with the navy, and the two services have a joint hardened command bunker to control air/naval operations in the strategic Straits of Hormuz.

Iran Air Arms Order of Battle, as at 1 May 2009.

Islamic Republic of Iran Air Force
Western Area Command

Airbase	Location	Wing/Base Designation	HAS Shelters	Squadron	Aircraft Type	Role
Tehran Mehrabad Int'l A31 1st Tactical	35° 41' N 51° 18' E	1st Tactical Fighter Wing / Transport Wing	Nil	11 TFS	MiG-29A/C, MiG-29UB	Air defence
				14 TFS	Su-24MK	Strike
				11 TAS	C-130E, C-130H	Transport
				12 TAS	C-130E, C-130H	Transport
				Transport	B707, B747	Transport/AAR
				Support	Falcon 20/20F; F27-400M/600	VIP transport
				VIP	Falcon 50, L-1329	VIP transport
				Recce	RC-707, RC-130	EW
				11 Helicopter	CH-47C	Troop transport
				Base flight/SAR	AB214A	SAR
Tabriz 2nd Tactical	38° 07' N 46° 14' E	22nd Tactical Fighter Wing	25	21 TFS	F-5E, F-5F	CAS
				23 TFS	MiG-29A/C, MiG-29UB	Air defence
				Base flight/SAR	Beech F33C, AB212, AB214A	SAR
Nozheh (Hamadan, Shahrokhi) 3rd Tactical	35° 11' N 48° 39' E	31st Tactical Fighter Wing	11	31 TRS	RF-4E	Reconnaissance
				31 TFS	F-4E	Air defence/Strike
				?? TFS	Su-24MK	Strike
				Base flight/SAR	Beech F33C, AB212	SAR
Vahdati (Dezful) 4th Tactical	32° 26' N 48° 23' E	14th Tactical Fighter Wing		41 TFS	F-5E, F-5F	CAS
				43 TFS	F-5E, F-5F	CAS
				Base flight/SAR	Beech F33C, AB212	SAR

Base	Coordinates	Wing	Strength	Squadron	Aircraft	Role
Omidiyeh (Omidieh/Umidiyeh) 5th Tactical	30° 50' N 49° 32' E	51st Tactical Fighter Wing	27	51 TFS	F-7M, FT-7	Air defence
				52 TFS F	F-7M, FT-7	Air defence
				53 TFS	F-7M, FT-7	Air defence
				Base flight/SAR	Misc.	SAR
Shiraz Shahid Dastghaib Int'l (Siraãz) 7th Tactical	29° 32' N 52° 35' E	71st Tactical Fighter Wing	18	72 TFS	Su-24MK	Strike
				83 TFS det.	F-14A	Air defence
				Training	PC-6	Training
				Base flight/SAR	Beech F33C	SAR
		Transport Wing		71 TAS	C-130E, C-130H	Transport
				72 TAS	C-130E, C-130H	Transport
				73 TAS	Il-76TD	Transport
				71 ASW	P-3F	MPA
Esfahãn/Shahid Beheshti Int'l (formerly Khatami) 8th Tactical	32° 45' N 51° 51' E	81st Tactical Fighter Wing	44	81 TFS	F-14A	Air defence
				82 TFS	F-14A	Air defence
				?? TFS det.	Su-24MK	Strike
				Base flight/SAR	AB212	SAR
Badr (aka Sepah)	32° 37' N 51° 41' E	??th Tactical Air Base			?? MFI-17 Mushshak	Training
Tehran-Doshan/Tappeh	35° 42' N 51° 27' E	12th? Tactical Air Base		VIP/Support	AS-61A-4	VIP transport
Southern Area Command Bushehr 6th Tactical	28° 56' N 50° 50' E	61st Tactical Fighter Wing	44	61 TFS	F-4E	Air defence/Strike
				62 TFS	F-4E	Air defence/Strike
				82 TFS det.	F-14A	Air defence
				??	Falcon 20	VIP transport
				Base flight/SAR	Beech F33C, AB212,AB214A	SAR
Bandar Abbas Int'l A27 9th Tactical	27° 13' N 56° 22' E	91st Tactical Fighter Wing	24	91 TFS	F-4E	Air defence/Strike
				92 TFS	F-4E	Air defence/Strike
				91 SAR Flt.	Beech F33C, AB212, AB214A	SAR

Airbase	Location	Wing/Base Designation	HAS Shelters	Squadron	Aircraft Type	Role
Chah Bahar (Chabahar) 10th Tactical	25° 26' N 60° 22' E	101st Tactical Fighter Wing	22	101 TFS	F-4D	Air defence/Strike
				?? TFS det.	Su-24MK	Strike
				Base flight/SAR	AB212, AB214A	SAR
Eastern Area Command						
Ghale-Morghi 11th Tactical?	35° 38' N 51° 22' E			?? Tactical Training	Beech F33C,EMB312, PC-7	Training
				?? Tactical Training	MFI-17 Mushshak (?)	Training
Birjand/Gayem al-Mohammad 13th Tactical	32° 53' N 59° 17' E					FOB
Zahedan 11th Tactical	29° 28' N 60° 54' E					
Mashhad 14th Tactical	36° 14' N 59° 38' E	140th Tactical Fighter Wing	4	141 TFS	Mirage F-1EQ, Mirage F-1BQ	Air Defence/CAS
				?? TFS	F-5E, F-5F	CAS
Kooshk-e-Nosrat/Kushke Nosrat/Manzariyeh	34° 59' N 50° 48' E				T-33	Training
Islamic Republic of Iran Army Aviation (IRIAA)						
Tehran Mehrabad Int'l	35° 41' N 51° 17' E			Transport	AC690 , F-27, Falcon 20	Transport
Ghale-Morghi	35° 38' N 51° 22' E			Helicopter	AB214	
Esfahān (aka Badr AFB)	32° 37' N 51° 41' E	Training Wing			AH-1J, AB205, AB206, CH-47C	Training

Location	Coordinates	Unit	Role	Aircraft	Role
Shahid Vatanpour (aka Esfahān Helifield)	32° 34' N 51° 41' E	Helicopter Training School		? AB212 AB205, AB206, ?? CH-47C	Training Training
Ghale-Morghi	35° 38' N 51° 22' E			?? AB205, AB206, Bell 214A/B, AC690	Training
Zahedan	29° 28' N 60° 54' E	Prov Support & Assault Group	Assault Attack Reconnaissance	Bell 214A/B AH-1J, AH-1J(TOW), AB205A, AB206B AB206	Troop transport Attack Reconnaissance
Mashhad	36° 14' N 59° 38' E	5 Support & Assault Group	Assault Assault Attack Reconnaissance	Bell 214A/B Bell 214A/B AH-1J, AH-1J(TOW), AB205A, AB206B AB206	Troop transport Troop transport Attack Reconnaissance
Masjed Suleyman aka Shahid Asyaee	32° 00' N 49° 16' E	2 Support & Assault Group	Assault Assault Attack Reconnaissance	Bell 214A/B Bell 214A/B AH-1J, AH-1J(TOW), AB205A, AB206B AB206	Troop transport Troop transport Attack Reconnaissance
Bakhtaran (Shahid Ashrafi Esfahani aka Kermanshah)	34° 20' N 47° 09' E	1 Support & Assault Group	Assault Assault Attack Reconnaissance	Bell 214A/B Bell 214A/B AH-1J, AH-1J(TOW), AB205A, AB206B AB206	Troop transport Troop transport Attack Reconnaissance
Kerman	30° 15' N 56° 57' E	3 Support & Assault Group	Assault Assault Attack Reconnaissance	Bell 214A/B Bell 214A/B AH-1J, AH-1J(TOW), AB205A, AB206B AB206	Troop transport Troop transport Attack Reconnaissance

Airbase	Location	Wing/Base Designation	HAS Shelters	Squadron	Aircraft Type	Role
Islamic Republic of Iranian Navy Aviation (IRINA)						
Bandar Abbas navy field 400M	27° 09' N 56° 09' E	Navy Helicopter Wing		2	Navy Patrol	Falcon 20E, F27-MPA
Bandar Abbas Heliport				1 ASW	SH-3D, Mi-171, AB212ASW	Naval support
				Liaison	AB205A, AB206A	Naval support
				?? ASW	SH-3D, AB212ASW	Naval support
				??	RH-53D	Mine clearing
Bushehr Heliport	28° 54' N 50° 51' E			Liaison	AB205A, AB206A	Naval support
Iranian Revolutionary Guard Corps Air Force (IRGCAF)						
Tehran Mehrabad Int'l (OIII)	35° 41' N 51° 18' E			Transport	An-74T(K)-200, An-14	Transport
				Attack	? Su-25K	CAS
				VIP	Falcon 20E	VIP
				Support	Y-12-II	Transport
Qom?		Training Academy		Training	Training	EMB312 Tucano
Badr (aka Sepah)	51° 37' N 51° 41' E				EMB312 Tucano/0-2	CAS/Training
						CAS/Training
Bandar Abbas Int'l	27° 13' N 56° 22' E			Support	Y-12-II	Transport
Ahwaz	31° 20' N 48° 45' E			Helicopter	Mi-17	Troop transport
Mashhad	36° 14' N 59° 38' E			Transpprt	Il-76MD/TD, An-74T/TK	Transport
Shiraz Shahid Dastghaib Int'l (Siraãz)	29° 32' N 52° 35' E			Support	Y-12-II	Transport
				Attack	Su-25	CAS
				AEW unit	Il-76AEW	AWACS
				Support	Y-12-II	Transport
				Helicopter	Mi-17	Troop transport

Location	Coordinates		Aircraft	Role
Bushehr	28° 56′ N 50° 50′ E	Support	Y-12-II	Transport
Fath / Faraj	35° 42′ N 50° 56′ E	Helicopter	Mi-17	Troop transport
		Attack	AH-1	Attack
		Training	AB206	Training

Iranian Revolutionary Guard Corps Navy (IRGCN)

Location	Coordinates		Aircraft	Role
Bandar Abbas navy field	27° 09′ N 56° 09′ E		?? Mi-17	Naval support

Islamic Republic of Iran Police Aviation

Location	Coordinates
Tehran Mehrabad Int'l	35° 41′ N 51° 18′ E
Ghale-Morghi	35° 38′ N 51° 22′ E
Firuzabad / Aseman Rei	35° 31′ N 51° 30′ E

Iran is now the sole military user of the F-14 Tomcat. *(Mohammad Razzazan)*

IRIAF long-range strike power depends on the Su-24MK 3. *(Mohammad Razzazan)*

Boeing 747 tankers are unique to the IRIAF and are an impressive force multiplier. *(Mohammad Razzazan)*

In time of crisis the Iranian military has access to the country's twenty-six civilian airports, which include six international airports, and six airfields for the National Iranian Oil Company. Another eight airports are being built in various parts of Iran by private investors. The international airports are Tehran Mehrabad airport, Efahan, Shiraz, Mashad, Tabriz, Bandar Abbas. Others are in Bushehr, Bandar Lengeh, Kish Island, Kerman, Rasht, Chahbahar, Ahvaz, Urumieh, Baakhtaran, Birjand, Zabol, Iranshahr, Laar, Khorramabad, Hamedan, Sanandaj, Raamsar and Noshahr.

The Air Defence Command operates fourteen major radar surveillance sites, including Dowshan Tappeh, Karaj, Tabriz, Babolsar, Mashhad, Shahr Abad, Hamedan, Bushehr, Esfahan, Bandar Abbas, Jask, Kish Island, Lengeh Island. A battery of the newest S-200/SA-5 surface-to-air missiles is based near the Bushehr nuclear reactor, which was nearly complete in early 2009

Aircraft ordnance

During the 1970s, the Iranians received a range of precision-guided munitions from the Americans. These included AIM-9 Sidewinder heat-seeking, AIM-7 Sparrow semi-active radar-guided and AIM-54 Phoenix active radar-guided air-to-air missiles, as well as AGM-65 Maverick television-guided air-to-ground missiles. Over the past twenty-five years the Iranians have reverse-engineered most components of these weapons, although some elements of the AIM-54s could not be copied. The Iranians then modified HAWK surface-to-air missiles for use from their F-14 Tomcats, with

Iran Inventory as at 15 March 2009.

Type	Active	Stored	Ordered	Required
Islamic Republic of Iran Air Force (IRIAF)				
COMBAT AIRCRAFT				
MiG-29A/MiG-29UB	35/5		48?	
F-14A	44	13		
Su-24MK	31			
F-4D/E/RF-4E	14	15		
F-4D	14			
F-5E/B/F Tiger II	29?	15	30?	
F-5E Saeghe	?			
F-7N/FT-7	13:-4	36		
Mirage F1EQ/BQ	18-22	13		
Su-20/Su-22		4:40		
ISTAR/SPECIAL MISSION				
Il-76 AEW	2	1		
P-3F Orion	3	2		
RC-130H	2			
Dornier 228	5			
707-3J9C	1			
TANKER				
707-3J9C	8			
747F-200	4			
TRANSPORT				
707	5			
An-74/T260			12	
747F-131	5			
An-140TC			45	
F27-400M/600	10	4		
Y-12	8			
Il-76	6			
Falcon 20	1			
Jetstar 8	2			
Commander 690	4			
C-130E/H	22	20		
747	10			
AN-140TC	?			
PC-6/B	15			
COMBAT HELICOPTER				
AB212/AB214A/C	5:20			
Mi-171/Mi-171Sh	21/30		30	

Type	Active	Stored	Ordered	Required
CH-47C Chinook	5			
AB206B JetRanger	2			
TRAINING AIRCRAFT				
T-33	5			
F33 Bonanza	26			
EMB-312 Tucano	25			
K-8			25?	
PC-7/S-68	35			
MFI-17B Mushshak	25			
Super Mushshak	1			
JT2-2	0			

Islamic Republic of Iran Navy Aviation (IRINA)

TRANSPORT

Fokker 27	4			
Falcon 20E	4			
Commander 500/690	1:07			

COMBAT HELICOPTER

RH-53D	2			
SH-3D Sea King	10			
AB212AS	6			
AB205A	5			
AB206B JetRanger	10			
Mi-17	??			

Islamic Republic of Iran Army Aviation (IRIAA)

TRANSPORTS

Falcon 20E	2			
Commander 690	5			
Cessna 185	10			
Fokker 27	2			

COMBAT HELICOPTER

AH-1J Cobra	70			
CH-47C Chinook	19			
AB214A/C	100			
AB212	20			
AB205A-1	10			
AB206A/B	39			

Type	Active	Stored	Ordered	Required
Government of the Islamic Republic of Iran				
Fajr-22 (Dept of Environment)	2			
An-140 (Police)	1			
An-140 (Border Guard)			20	
Civil Aviation Organisation of the Islamic Republic of Iran				
TRANSPORT				
BN Islander	1			
Islamic Revolutionary Guards Corps Air Force				
COMBAT AIRCRAFT				
Su-25T/UBT	3:03		7	
EMB-312 Tucano	23			
COMBAT HELICOPTER				
Mi-8AMTSH	20			
TRANSPORT				
An-74	10			
Shahed-5 (212)	20			
Falcon 20E	1			
Il-76	5			
Y-12(II)	7			
Boeing 737	1			
Boeing 727		2		
F-28	1			
Commander 681	1			
Commander 690	2			
A321	1			
UNMANNED AIR VEHICLES				
Ababil 1/2/3	?			
Mohajer III/IV	?			
Saeghe I/II	?			
Islamic Revolutionary Guards Corps Navy				
TRANSPORT				
Fokker 27				

Bell AH-1 Cobra gunships played an important role in the Iran–Iraq war, and the Iranian army still relies heavily on them. *(Sharam Sharimi)*

Iraqi pilots fled to Iran during the 1991 Gulf War in almost a hundred aircraft, and many, including this Mirage F.1BQ, have since been incorporated into the IRIAF. *(Mohammad Razzuzan)*

the missiles being dubbed AIM-23C. An air-to-ground version known as 'Yasser' has also been developed, but has not entered service. A factory was built in Iran by the Americans for Maverick assembly, and this is believed to still be operational. British-supplied BL-755 cluster bombs, as well as US CBU-71 cluster bombs, are also believed to have been re-engineered by the Iranians. They, however have been largely replaced by the Kite 200 dispenser. The USA supplied some twenty GBU-8/9 laser-guided bomb kits, and they were developed and enhanced by the Iranians.

The purchase in the late 1980s of Chinese aircraft resulted in a number of precision-guided munitions being supplied by Peking, including PL-7 and PL-9 Chinese heat-seeking air-to-air missiles and C-802K air-launched air-to-ground missiles. A Chinese attempt to modify the launch rails of their F-4s, F-5s and MiG-29s to take the PL-7 was stopped in favour of a local evolution of the AIM-9P, dubbed the Fatter, which features a locally developed seeker. The Fatter has been mounted on all major Iranian aircraft types. A large batch of French-made Magic heat-seeking air-to-air missiles was reportedly purchased from Libya in 1997.

When the first MiG-29s were delivered in the 1990s, a package of weapons was supplied that included R-60 (AA-8 'Aphid') heat-seeking, R-33 (AA-9 'Amos') semi-active radar-guided, R-27R/T (AA-10 'Alamo') semi-active or heat-seeking guided and R-73 (AA-11 'Archer') heat-seeking guided air-to-air missiles. A number of precision-guided air-to-ground weapons were believed to have been delivered, including Kh-25 (AS-10 'Karen') laser/radio-guided, Kh-29 (AS-14 'Kedge') laser/IR/TV-guided missiles, Kite 'smart' munitions dispensers and Raad laser-guided bombs and Kh-58 (AS-11 'Kitter') anti-radar missiles.

Procurement

In the 1990s, the USA thwarted attempts to buy second-hand equipment from former Soviet republics, forcing Iran to turn to China. The purchase of Xian FB-7 and Shenyang F-8IIM strike aircraft was discussed, but none were ordered. Up to twenty-one Mi-171s were delivered to Iran from Russia in 2000/01, while thirty Mi-171SH armed helicopters were delivered in early 2003. Iran has kept its fleet of US-supplied aircraft flying by the local production of spares, as well as black market purchases of spares, which resulted in eighteen US companies being investigated for breaching US export controls in mid-2003. Russian-supplied Su-24s have been fitted with US-style air-to-air refuelling probes to make them compatible with Iranian tanker aircraft.

Presence of foreign forces

No foreign military forces are present in Iran. A small number of Russian and Ukrainian technical representatives are working at aerospace industry sites in Esfahan and on airbases to support products supplied by their companies.

The Islamic Republic of Iran Army Aviation (IRIAA)

History
During the 1970s, the Army air arm expanded greatly with the acquisition of over 300 Bell 214As and 200+ Bell AH-1J Cobras, together with approximately 185 Italian-built Agusta-Bell 206s, approximately a hundred AB205s and sixty-six CH-47C Chinooks that were built by Agusta-Meridionali. The fixed-wing force consisted of Cessna O-2s, Cessna-185s, Cessna 310s, Dassault Falcon 20Es, Rockwell AC690 Aero Commanders and Fokker F27s, from which the Fokkers and the Falcons are currently operational.

Operational activity
The IRIAA was one of the most effective air arms during the 1980–88 war with Iraq. Iran's helicopter pilots developed innovative tactics to counter Iraqi armoured forces. Iran's aviation industry has also proved itself very adept at reverse-engineering spare parts for the IRIAA's helicopters, and so it is still expected to be able to put a sizeable force of attack and transport helicopters into the field. It regularly conducts large-scale training exercises.

Aircraft ordnance
The locally manufactured version of the US-designed TOW missile remains the main anti-armour weapon of the IRIAA. Many weapons have been sources via non-US sources since the 1980s. Locally produced Maverick missiles have also been seen mounted on Iranian AH-1s.

The Islamic Republic of Iran Navy Aviation (IRINA)

History
The principal attack and ASW role of the IRINA was executed by its twenty or so SH-3D Sea Kings, supported by a number of AB212ASWs. It also purchased some heavy-lift RH-53Ds, and for liaison purposes it had Agusta-built AB205As and AB206As. The Navy Patrol Squadron is equipped with Dassault Falcon 20Fs and Fokker F27-400Ms.

Operational activity
The small naval air arm is considered one of most professional in the Iranian armed forces. It regularly conducts training exercises with naval surface units in the Straits of Hormuz. Surveillance missions are also flown on a daily basis to track US naval forces operating off Iran's coast.

IRGCAF – Iranian Revolutionary Guard Corps Air Force (Pasdaran-e Inqilab)

History
The Islamic Revolutionary Guards Corps was formed out of the paramilitary groups that spearheaded the overthrow of the Shah's regime in 1979. During the war with Iraq in the 1980s, the Revolutionary Guards were expanded considerably. This eventually grew to include a small air arm, equipped with helicopters and jet fighter aircraft. During the 1980s, its air arm shrank, and a formal division of activity with the air force was put in place. There is, however, still great rivalry between the two organisations, which is not helped by the continuing existence of a separate procurement system for the Revolutionary Guards.

Structure
The IRGC is currently commanded by General Yahya Rahin Safavi, the IRGCAF is led by General Hossein Salami and the deputy naval commander of the IRGC is Ali Fadavi. There is also an air defence force, which is entrusted with the defence of strategic high-value targets. In all its branches the IRGC musters some 125,000 men.

Operational activity
The IRGCAF is now focused on providing helicopter and close air support for the guards' combat divisions. It has its own air training organisation and a small number of VIP transports. During early April 2005, the IRGC participated in a major air/naval exercise in the Straits of Hormuz, dubbed Great Prophet.

Strategic weapons
Iran began to develop a number of strategic weapon systems to counter Iraq missile attacks on its cities and chemical weapon attacks on its troops during the 1980s. Today Iran has continued to co-operate with North Korea and China to build and improve a number of ballistic missiles, derived from the basic Russian Scud design.

UAV operation
Iran procured a number of US and British target drones in the 1970s to train its aircrews and air defence missile batteries, including US Ryan BGM-34 Firebees. These formed the basis of Iranian attempts to field functioning UAVs during the 1980s and 1990s. The most numerous locally produced UAV is the Mohajer. The IRGCAF is in the forefront of these efforts, and during the Iran–Iraq War it managed to field operationally Mohajers armed with unguided rocket-propelled grenades.

In recent years the Hizbullah units have been active in southern Lebanon, flying Mohajer UAVs over Lebanon. The most recent incursion over Israel was during March 2006. The USAF claimed that one of its fighters shot down an Ababil 3 UAV on 25 February 2009 some sixty miles north-east of Baghdad in mysterious circumstances.

Assessment

The status of Iran's air power is of great international significance. The level of resistance it would be able to put up in the face of a US or Israeli air onslaught plays an important part in any calculations by Washington and Tel Aviv to strike at Iran's nuclear facilities.

Few outside observers have had recent access to the Iranian air arms to make an objective assessment easy. Some factors must come into play:

- The airworthiness of the Iranian aircraft fleet is open to question due to its age, despite the ingenuity of Iran's aviation industry
- The lack of modern airborne weapons, particularly beyond visual range weapons, could be a major weakness
- The level of combat experience and training of Iranian aircrew is an unknown quantity.

On the positive side, the Iranians have the benefit of:

- Mass (the sheer size of the Iranian air force and its airbase infrastructure means it would take a significant campaign to neutralise it)
- The size of the country, which would present even the USA with a major challenge for any air space dominance effort.

The biggest question mark is over the command and control of Iran's air power. The Iranians do not seem to have a hi-tech real-time command system as employed by the Israelis and USA. However, the degree to which the Iranians could absorb a US or Israeli first strike and keep on fighting would determine if a surgical strike against Iran's nuclear facilities was a one-off or the precursor for a regional war. If it was the latter, then the Iranian air force could be said to be an effective deterrent against a US or Israeli attack.

CHAPTER FIVE

Iraq

Population	28 million
Military/paramilitary aircraft	86
Air Force personnel	1,600

Al Quwwat al Jawwiya al Iraqiya (Iraqi Air Force/IQAF)

History

The Iraqi air force can trace its lineage back to the air units formed by the British authorities in 1931 during the occupation of the country under the League of Nations mandate. During the 1940s and 1950s, Iraq was a hotbed of Arab nationalism, and eventually the British abandoned the country after the royal family was deposed in 1958. British traditions were strong in the Iraqi air force during the 1950s and early 1960s until Soviet aircraft were purchased in large numbers. French influence grew in the 1980s when the Iraqis started to buy Mirages, missiles and helicopters from Paris for use during the Iran–Iraq War.

Pre-2003 war

The disastrous war with the USA and its allies following the 1990 invasion of Kuwait resulted in more than half the IQAF's inventory being lost and most of the country's airbase infrastructure being badly damaged. The 1990s were a lean period for the IQAF. UN sanctions cut it off from sources of replacement aircraft and new technology. No-fly zones imposed by the Americans and British meant it was reduced to flying in a small area in the centre of the country. It lost a MiG-25 and MiG-29 to US fighters in late 1992 and early 1993, and after that it did not even dare to engage Coalition fighters. This, on top of its failure to stop US air raids during the Gulf War, seriously undermined the IQAF's reputation in the eyes of Iraq's president. Particularly damaging to the IQAF usefulness to Saddam Hussein was the loss of almost all of the prized Su-24 deep-strike fleet, which the Iranians refused to return after they fled there during the 1991 Gulf War.

Although there were rumours of the IQAF importing black-market spares from eastern Europe in a bid to boost its lamentable serviceability rates, this was not reflected in any upsurge in air activity, with reports in early 2003 suggesting that it had fewer than 100 serviceable airframes.

Air activity has been concentrated at eight main operating bases around Baghdad, Mosul and Kirkuk, as well as a handful of dispersal bases. These bases had largely

Table 1. Iraqi Air Force equipment and personnel, summer 2002.

Personnel: 30,000–35,000
300+ airframes in inventory
69–93 operational combat aircraft, including:
   13 Mirage F.1s (multi-role fighter)
   15–25 Mikoyan MiG-21s (fighter-bomber)
   15–20 MiG-23s (multi-role fighter)
   4 MiG-25s (long-range interceptor)
   5–10 Sukhoi Su-25s (close air support)
   15–18 Su-22s (ground attack)
   1 MiG-29 (long-range interceptor)
   1 Su-24 (long-range bomber)
   1 Il-76s (transport)
   ? Al Yammah-As (reconnaissance drone)
   ? Marakubs (based on Mirach 100 target drone)
   ? Sarab-Bs (version of Banshee target drone)
   ? L-29 drones (based on Czech jet trainer)

Table 2. IQAF main operating bases, summer 2002.

* Al-Rashid
Republican Guard Sqn (PA-34 and An-2), Special Transport Sqn (Bell 214ST)
* Al Habbaniyah / Al Taqaddum
MiG-29 (6 Sqn), MiG-21 (14 Sqn), MiG-23 (73 Sqn), Su-25 (109 Sqn), Su-22 (44 Sqn)
* Al Bakr (Tikrit)
MiG-23 (49?, 63? and 93 Sqns), Su-24 (8 Sqn), Su-22 (5 Sqn), An-24 and An-26 (3 Sqn),
   Il-76 and PA-34 (33 Sqn)
* Al Qadisiya (Al Asad)
MiG-21 (combat training wing)
MiG-21 (17, 47 and 57 Sqns) and MiG-25 (96 Sqn)
* Al-Hurriya (Kirkuk)
Su-22 (69 Sqn)
* Al Quayara (Mosul)
Mirage F.1 (79? and 89? Sqns) and MiG-21 (9 Sqn)
* Abu Gharid, Baghdad
Air Force Academy, three squadrons of EMB-312 and L-39
* Dhuloya, Baghdad
unmanned aerial vehicles

Table 3. Iraqi Army Air Corps equipment, summer 2002.

Total 500 helicopters, including 120 armed helicopters
(estimated 250+ operational)
Mil Mi-8/17s 'Hip' (transport)
Mi-25s 'Hind' (gunship)
MBB Bo-105s (liaison/attack)
Bell 212STs (transport)
Aerospatiale SA-342 Gazelles (liaison/armed)
SA-316 Alouettes (liaison/armed)
Hughes 500s (liaison/attack)
Pilatus PC-7 and PC-9 fixed-wing turbo-prop
armed training aircraft

---

been renovated but the IQAF did not have the resources to completely rebuild all
the hardened shelters and runways destroyed by US and British bombing during
Operation Desert Storm.

Bolstered by its key role in crushing the 1991 rebellions, the Iraqi Army Air Corps
enjoyed a more prosperous decade, particularly officers and units with links to the
Republican Guard Forces Command (RGFC). A number of special squadrons were
formed to support the RGFC in both the IAAC and IQAF.

Most of Saddam Hussein's air force was buried in the desert before the 2003 war with the US-led
Coalition. *(USAF)*

Table 4. IAAC main bases, summer 2002.

---

* Al-Jadida, Baghdad
HQ Military Aviation,
* Kirkuk, 1st Wing
PC-9 (83 Sqn), Mi-17 (4 Sqn), Mi-8 (2 Sqn), SA-316 (30 Sqn), Hughes 500D and SA-342(84 Sqn)
* Taji, Baghdad, 2nd Wing
Mi-25 (66 Sqn), Mi-17 (55 sqn), Bo-105 (106 Sqn), SA-342 (22 Sqn)
* Kut, 3rd/4th Wing
SA-342 (88 Sqn), Mi-17 (15 and 99 Sqn)
* Al-Swenta, 5th Wing
PC-7 (107 Sqn), Mi-6, Mk-117, SA-342, Mi-8/17, Bell 214ST (Special Sqn)
* Iskandceria, Baghdad, 7th/9th Wing
(2 Sqn?, 8 Independent Sqn, 77 Special Purpose Sqn)
* Al-Suwaira, Military Aviation School
Bell 214ST, Hughes 500D/F

Saddam Hussein's air force proved a paper tiger in the 2003 war. It did not fly a single combat sortie during the whole war. US forces later discovered that many of its aircraft had been buried on airbases to hide them from Coalition intelligence. The Iraqi air force was formally disbanded by the US occupation forces in April 2003.

Iraq's air defences

The brunt of the effort to defend Iraq from US and British no-fly-zone patrols fell on the Air Defence Command, which had some 17,000 men under its control in early 2003, based throughout the country. The Iraqis relied on a mix of SAM and AAA systems bought largely during the 1970s and 1980s from the then Soviet Union and France. Some Western systems were captured from Kuwait in 1990 and others had been smuggled into the country after the 1991 Gulf War in violation of the UN arms embargo.

The mainstay of the Iraqi SAM force was some 20–30 batteries of Soviet V-75 Dvina (NATO codename: SA-2 'Guideline'), 25–50 batteries of S-125 Neva (SA-3 'Goa') and 36–55 batteries of 9M9 Kub (SA-6 'Gainful') radar-guided SAMs. The exact number of launchers operational in early 2003 was unclear, but it was probably in the region of a hundred or so of each type of systems. The Iraqis established local repair facilities for all these systems and limited production facilities to manufacture replacement missiles. In 1983, the Iraqis bought Roland SAM launchers and 300 missiles from France, and some of these were still operational in early 2003. All these weapon systems were dependent on radar surveillance and guidance, and the Iraqis possessed an abundance of radars organic to them. For area surveillance the Iraqis had a number of radars, including Soviet P-14 'Tall King' and French made Thomson-CSF Volex III.

To fill out their defences, the Iraqis possessed some 4,000 AAA guns, ranging from 12.7 mm up to 23 mm, 37 mm and 57 mm calibre weapons. Thousands of short-range radar and heat-seeking guided SAMs, including Strela-2 (SA-7 'Grail'), Romb (SA-8 'Gecko'), Strela-1 (SA-9 'Gaskin') and Igla-1 (SA-16 'Gimlet') were also in Iraqi hands, and they were used to provide local protection of the bigger radar-guided SAMs or army units.

The nerve centre of the Air Defence Command was a large underground bunker complex at Al Muthanna airfield in central Baghdad. Iraq was split into four air defence zones, each with its own sector operating centre (SOC) to control specific engagements. The 1st SOC at the Al Taji complex outside Baghdad controlled the defence of the airspace in the centre of the country. It had command of the bulk of the SAM assets to provide protection of the capital and other sensitive locations, such as Saddam's palaces and weapons-of-mass-destruction factories. Its order of battle included at least two missile brigades with sixteen SA-2 and SA-3 batteries, as well as scores of independent SA-6 and Roland batteries.

Western Iraq was controlled by the 2nd SOC at Al-Waleed (H-3) airbase, with some ten SAM batteries at its disposal. The job of challenging US and British aircraft in the southern no-fly zone was left to the 3rd SOC near Tallil airbase, north-west of Basra. It had at least one SAM brigade and scores of AAA batteries. The 4th SOC at Al-Hurriya airbase, outside Kirkuk, was tasked with engaging Western aircraft over the northern no-fly zone. It had at least half a dozen SA-2 and SA-6 batteries. Supporting the SOCs were dozens of radar and electronic warfare detachments. Missile crews and radar operators were trained at the Air Defence Institute at Al Taji. New equipment in 2001 and 2002 included mobile SA-3 launcher vehicles that saw action in southern Iraq. Extra fuel cells were installed on SA-2 missiles to allow them to engage high-flying U-2s.

Iraq's missile forces
Saddam Hussein's interest in long-range missiles developed in the 1980s after his air force showed that it was not able to penetrate Iran's air defences. His ambitious plans to field strategic missiles forces are well documented, and a determined effort was made by the United Nations Special Commission (UNSCOM) in the 1990s to dismantle Iraq's missiles with a range of more than 150 kilometres. Imported and home-manufactured versions of the Soviet R.1 (Scud SS-1) missiles were the core of this force, and just under a hundred Al Hussein versions were destroyed by UNSCOM in the early 1990s.

Long-range tactical surface-to-surface ballistic missiles (SSM) were on the Iraqi shopping list in the 1980s, and Baghdad was also keen to develop indigenous production capabilities. The Iraqis were supplied with Luna-M (FROG 7) missiles by the Soviets, and they later extended their range from 40 to 90 kilometres. Some 260 ASTROS multiple rocket launchers were purchased from Brazil, which had a range

US-supplied UH-1H Hueys are to form the core of the new Iraqi air force's helicopter force. *(USAF)*

of between 30 and 90 kilometres. This weapon was dubbed the Sajeel by the Iraqis. A co-operation agreement was reached with the Yugoslavs to co-develop a multiple rocket launcher known as the Ababil-50 by the Iraqis and the M-87 Orkan by the Yugoslavs. It had a range of around 50 kilometres. Co-operation between Baghdad and Belgrade came to a halt after the 1991 Iraq War and the collapse of Yugoslavia in 1992. Some intelligence sources suggested that the co-operation restarted in the late 1990s. The Ababil-100 was a scaled-up version of the Ababil-50 that boasted four 100 mm launch tubes, which could fire high-explosive or sub-munition warheads. An Ababil-100 missile was shown in the UK government's September 2002 dossier on Iraq's weapons of mass destruction, mounted on what appeared to be a V-75 Dvina (SA-2 Guideline) surface-to-air missile launcher.

Comp Air 7L were some of the first aircraft to operate after the Iraqi air force was re-formed in 2004. *(USAF)*

The Jordanian-made Seabird SB7L Seeker was the first aircraft to enter service with the new Iraqi air force for surveillance missions. *(USAF)*

The Iraqis went to great lengths to ensure the loyalty of the SSM force's commanders and personnel, rewarding them with extra pay and privileges. Like all other aspects of Iraq's missile programme, the SSM brigades were heavily infiltrated with Iraqi intelligence operatives to ensure they did not give away any information to UN weapons inspectors.

The 1991 Gulf War and the subsequent imposition of the UNSCOM inspection regime crippled Iraq's missile programmes during the 1990s, with many of the scientists and technicians devoting most of their efforts to avoiding UNSCOM inspectors. Iraq was also bankrupted by the UN oil embargo, so there was little money to fund work on new weapon programmes. This situation changed after the withdrawal of the UNSCOM inspectors in 1998, and the Iraqis started to ramp up work on tactical missiles, particularly the Al Samoud II. This was another Scud derivative that was powered by converted V-75 missile engines. The Iraqis claimed it was legal under the UN arms control restrictions, although UNSCOM's successor, United Nations Monitoring, Verification and Inspection Commission (UNMOVIC) later determined it had flown some 183 kilometres in test. The Iraqis ramped up production of the Al Samoud II considerably in 2001 and 2002, having some seventy-five ready for operation in late 2002 according to their declarations to UNMOVIC. In the weeks before the US-led invasion of Iraq, UN inspectors oversaw the destruction of fifty Al Samoud IIs.

The Iraqi navy was also involved in tactical missile efforts, and oversaw the deployment of locally produced versions of the Chinese HY-2 Silkworm anti-ship missiles in the land attack role. These weapons were dubbed Seersuckers by the Pentagon.

The demise of the Iraqi long-range missile force and atrophying of the Iraqi air force as an effective fighting force during the 1990s meant that the importance of the tactical SSM grew considerably. It was one of the few weapons the Iraqis had that could strike at US bases in Kuwait and deep into the Kurdish enclaves in northern Iraq. This gave them a strategic importance in the coming confrontation with the US, and meant American intelligence agencies put them under intense surveillance. US intelligence believed the tactical SSM force would be in the forefront of any chemical or biological weapon strike on US and allied forces massing on Iraq's borders.

The Iraqis organised their tactical SSM forces into four operational brigades, an independent battalion and a technical support battalion to prepare missiles for launch. They were all placed under the direct control of the Armed Forces General Staff Headquarters (GHQ), but several elements of the SSM force were placed in direct support of tactical commanders, including elements of the RGFC.

Iraq's Taji industrial complex and military barracks was the centre of all Iraqi missile operations. Not only did it contain the main missile production facilities but it was also home to the 226th and 227th SSM Brigades, the 228th Technical Support Battalion and the Al Samoud II battalion. Training and repair operations all took place at Taji. Two other missile brigades were forward deployed, with the 224th Brigade based to the south of Mosul and the 225th Brigade operating in the south. The 224th, 225th and 227th Brigades had a FROG-7 battalion, an Ababil-100 battalion and a ASTROS battalion, although the 227th Brigade had two ASTROS battalions. Ababil-50 battalions were assigned to the 224th and 227th Brigades.

The brigade in the north had the mission of supporting the three Iraqi army corps that were deployed to contain the Kurdish enclave. In the south, the 225th Brigade was deployed between the cities of Basra and Al Amara to support Iraqi troop positions along the Iranian and Kuwaiti borders. Also in the south was a detachment of between two and five Seersucker missile launchers, which was based at Al Zubayr heliport south of Basra in a facility built by French engineers in the late 1980s. The US assessed that some eighty-eight missiles were available to the Iraqi coastal defence forces.

The Al Samoud IIs were Iraq's most potent missile force, and they were based around Baghdad. The three FROG-7 battalions of the 226th Brigade operated in direct support of the RGFC.

The exact number of launchers and missiles in service with the Iraqis in early 2003 is still unclear. According to the 32nd Army Air Missile Defence Command (AAMDC), the Iraqis had more than eleven Al Samoud II launchers and 200 missiles, more than fifteen Ababil-100 launchers and 200 missiles, and forty-six FROG-7 launchers and 600 missiles. US intelligence claimed that the Iraqis had some ten Al Hussein launchers and forty missiles hidden from UN inspectors. This later proved not to be the case.

The new Iraqi Air Force, June 2004

The re-emergence of nominally independent Iraqi armed forces in June 2004 was quickly followed by the re-formation of the IQAF. Many former members of the old air force were recruited to provide a cadre of experienced personnel. Initial planning for the new Iraqi air force envisaged surplus US, Jordanian and UAE equipment as being its mainstay. By late 2008, the Iraqi and US governments had agreed a status of forces agreement to eventually see the full withdrawal of US combat forces. The incoming administration of US President Barack Obama confirmed these agreements, which will see the ending of US combat operations by the middle of 2011. These accords included provision for the gradual handing over control of Iraqi air space to the new IQAF.

Structure

As part of the new Iraqi armed forces, the IQAF reports to the military high command in Baghdad and then to the country's new Ministry of Defence. The Ministry of Defence formally assumed control of the air force on 7 September 2006. It was to have 3,285 personnel by the end of 2007, but in June of that year it mustered only around 900 personnel.

Operational activity

During day-to-day operations the IQAF closely co-ordinates its activities with US and Coalition military authorities. Iraqi air space is still under the control of the

Iraq Air Arms Order of Battle as at 1 May 2009.

Airbase	Location	Squadron	Aircraft Type	Role
Al Quwwat al Jawwiya al Iraqiya (Iraqi Air Force)				
Baghdad IAP (ORBI) / Al Muthana	33° 15′ N 44° 14′ E	23	C-130E	Transport
			Cessna 208B	Observation
		70	SAMA CH2000	Observation
Al Basrah (ORMM)	30° 32′ N 47° 39′ E	70	SBL-360 Seeker	Observation
			SAMA CH2000	Observation
Kirkuk (ORKK)	35° 28′ N 44° 20′ E	3	SAMA CH2000	Observation
			Comp Air 7SL	Observation
		Flight School	Cessna 172	Training
		2	Bell 206B, OH-58	Training
Al Taji	33° 31′ N 44° 15′ E	2 Helicopter	Huey II	Troop Transport
		15 Helicopter	Mi-17, W3	Troop Transport
		4 Helicopter	Mi-17CT	Troop Transport

Mil Mi-17 (NATO: HIP)

The Mi-17 and its derivatives are in widespread service around the Middle East, thanks to its rugged construction and performance in 'hot and high' conditions. Originally supplied only to Soviet allies during the Cold War, it has since been widely available on the open market at very competitive prices.

Crew: 3 (2 pilots, 1 engineer)
Capacity: 32 passengers or 8,800 lb (4,000 kg) on internal, and 10,250 lb (4,500 kg) external hardpoints
Length: 60 ft 5 in. (18.42 m)
Rotor diameter: 69 ft 10 in. (21.35 m)
Height: 15 ft 7 in. (4.76 m)
Disc area: 3,830 ft² (356 m²)
Maximum take-off weight: 28,700 lb (13,000 kg)
Powerplant: Two Klimov TV3-117VM turboshafts, 2,225 shp (1,450 kW) each
Maximum speed: 156 mph (250 km/h)
Range: 594 miles (950 km)

Armament
Up to 3,300 lb (1,500 kg) of disposable stores on six hardpoints, including bombs, rockets and gunpods

US-led Combined Air Operations Centre (CAOC) in Qatar, and all flights by IQAF aircraft must be approved as part of the air tasking order formulation process. US aircraft are responsible for all air defence activity over Iraq and the policing of the country's air space.

USAF special forces personnel are assisting with in-country training as part of the Multinational Security Transition Command.

The IQAF is organised and equipped for counter-insurgency operations. Intelligence, Surveillance and Reconnaissance (ISR) units perform daily operational missions over Baghdad and key national infrastructure locations, supplying actionable intelligence for both Iraqi and Coalition ground forces. The intelligence gathered during these flights has provided timely evidence of Baghdad perimeter security breaches and infiltration by insurgent forces. Iraqi crews have passed this information to deployed Iraqi ground forces for interdiction.

The establishment of a Flight Training School at Kirkuk airbase is at the heart of Iraqi plans to rebuild its air force.

Airbase infrastructure

Almost all of the old IQAF airbase infrastructure was destroyed by US bombing between 1991 and 2003, and by looting in the chaotic aftermath of the US-led occupation in April 2003. While runways and hardened shelters generally survived this period, little else did, so the new IQAF has had to start from scratch.

C-130E Hercules provide transport support to the Iraqi ground forces. *(USAF)*

Initial operations were conducted from US- and British-occupied airfields at Tallil, Kirkuk, Basra and Baghdad International. A construction programme was launched to establish a purpose-built IQAF base on the military side of Baghdad International, known as Al Muthana. This became operational in early 2006 when the Hercules unit took up residence. The first UH-1Bs are operating from Taji, north of Baghdad, and the SB7L-360s have flown missions from Basra International airport.

The helicopter force is operating from Taji north of Baghdad. Al Muthana airbase in Baghdad is being rebuilt as the new operational hub for fixed-wing aircraft.

Aircraft ordnance

Beyond door machine-guns for helicopters, the IQAF has no aircraft weapons. The delivery of Cessna 208B Caravans armed with Hellfire missiles has given the IQAF its first air-to-ground capability.

Strategic weapons

Iraq now has no strategic weapons.

Procurement

Iraqi aircraft procurement has been organised by both the Baghdad government and the US military assistance organisation in Iraq. The latter procurement efforts have proved far more than successful than the former.

A December 2004 deal to buy helicopters from Poland, including thirty new W-3s and twenty-four surplus Mi-17s from Russian and Ukrainian stocks, evolved into a contract to purchase ten new Mi-8MTV-5/17V5s, which were delivered in February 2006. The vendor could not deliver the W-3s on time, so these were replaced by the delivery of two surplus aircraft from the Polish army contingent in Iraq and three more Mi-17V5s.

The first ten Iraqi-procured Mi-17 helicopters were not operationally employed after delivery due to defensive system shortfalls. The IQAF addressed this need with a US$6 million defensive system contract, with a scheduled delivery of the first system suites ninety days after payment. The IQAF has ordered a total of twenty-eight Mi-17s, with final delivery scheduled for December 2007.

The USA is now looking to expand the air force's capabilities to include light-attack aircraft, attack helicopters and possibly UAVs. Poland has indicated that it might also donate surplus Mi-24s. Some sixteen UH-1Hs donated by Jordan were being upgraded to Huey II standard by US Helicopter Inc. of Alabama.

A $500 million FMS sale request was made to the USA in 2006 for the purchase of twenty Mi-17s, twenty-four King Air 350ERs for ISTAR and a similar number for transport, although this requirement might be met with PZL M-28s. Some $200 million in logistic support was also requested. In January 2007, the US government approved the sale of six King Air 350s for ISTAR and one for light transport duties under a $123 million contract with Raytheon. The aircraft were due for delivery in 2008. Each ISR aircraft will be fitted with a Lynx IIE SAR/GMTI radar, MX-15i

Electro-optical/Infra-red (EO/IR) camera system, CLAW software, and a high-bandwidth data-link system. Iraq's capabilities to conduct airborne ISR are being further enhanced with additional procurements of interim and advanced platforms. The first of three Cessna 208B Caravan interim ISR aircraft arrived in December 2008, giving the IQAF an enhanced day-and-night capability, once initial and mission qualification training is completed. The ATK company in the USA is integrating Hellfire missiles onto these aircraft. A further three were scheduled for delivery by the end of 2009.

The USAF concluded accident investigation of the cause of a Comp Air SB-7L crash in May 2005 and then oversaw the return to flight of the rest of fleet. Deliveries

Iraq Inventory as at 15 March 2009.

Type	Active	Stored	Ordered	Required
Al Quwwat al Jawwiya al Iraqiya (Iraqi Air Force)				
ISTAR/SPECIAL MISSION				
SB7L-360	5			9
CH2000	8		17	
Air 7SL	5			
King Air 350	4		4	19
Cessna 208B	3		2	
TRANSPORT				
C-130E	3			3
King Air 350	1		1	23
PZL M-28				24?
TRAINER				
Cessna 172	8		10	10
Bell 206B	5		5	
Cessna 208B	5			2
OH-58	10			
COMBAT HELICOPTER				
PZL W-2	2			
Mi-17	9		10?	20?
Huey II	16		48	
Mi-171	4		4	
Bell 407			24	
EC635			24	
Mi-17T			22	

Armed Mil Mi-17 Hip assault helicopters bring firepower to Iraqi aviation operations. (USAF)

of Jordanian Aircraft Industries SAMA CH2000s continued during 2007, and an additional order for aircraft for the new Flight School was placed.

In May 2007, the USAF Aeronautical Systems Centre issued a requirement document for eight COIN aircraft on behalf of the Iraqi air force, to be delivered between November 2008 and April 2009. This eventually resulted in 2008 in the Iraqis requesting the purchase of twenty Hawker T-6A Texan trainers and thirty-six AT-6B Texan attack aircraft in a package worth $366 million. At the same time the Iraqis also requested the sale of twenty-six armed Bell 407 scout/attack helicopters worth $366 million.

The IQAF has requested an additional three surplus US C- 130s to bring its transport squadron size to a more optimal six aircraft.

In August 2007, the USAF Material Command awarded Cessna a $10.56 million contract for the purchase of eighteen Cessna 172 Skyhawk aircraft, with an option for a further ten aircraft. The first aircraft were delivered to Iraq in October 2007 to help establish the IQAF's Flight Training School at Kirkuk airbase. All the aircraft were to be delivered during 2008. The final establishment of the school is expected to include twelve Cessna 172s, five Cessna 208Bs, seventeen CH2000s, twelve Bell 206s, ten Huey IIs and nine Mi-17s. The first Cessna 172s were delivered in October 2007. Westar Aerospace and Defence, along with the VSE Corporation, has been contracted to run the Iraqi Flight School under a $62 million contract.

In a surprise move in December 2007, the Iraqis ordered twenty UTVA Lasta 95 trainers from Serbia for $230 million.

In August 2007 the US Congress was notified of a prospective upgrade of another sixteen Huey II aircraft by ARINC Corporation of Maryland in a deal worth $150 million, although it is unclear where the airframes are to be sourced from. This was followed by another notification to Congress in September 2007 of the possibility of upgrading another thirty-two Huey II helicopters. The ambition is to have sixty-four Huey IIs in service.

In November 2007 Cessna won another contract to supply five more 208B Caravan aircraft for training, with an option for two more, in a deal conducted via the USAF Material Command. An additional five King Air 350s were ordered in September 2008 for $10.5 million.

The most recent Iraqi purchases are some twenty-four Bell 407 armed helicopters to give the IQAF an attack helicopter capability. France has also reportedly secured a deal to sell twenty-four EC635 search-and-rescue helicopters after a visit to

Cessna 172s are central to the Iraqi air force training effort. *(USAF)*

Baghdad by the French President, Nicolas Sarkozy, in 2008. A further deal to buy twenty-two Mi-17CT transport helicopters from Russia was announced in March 2009, and this also involved their modernisation in the USA.

Presence of foreign forces

The 180,000-strong US-led occupation forces currently run several major airbases in Iraq, including Tallil (now renamed Ali), Basra International, Baghdad airport, Taji, Balad, Al Asad, Kirkuk and Mosul. There are also scores of forward operating bases for use by helicopters and improvised landing strips for C-130 tactical transports. These include Al Qaim in western Iraq, Tikrit, Ramadi, Taqqadom, Habbanya and Samara in the infamous Sunni Triangle around Baghdad.

Plans to withdraw large numbers of occupation forces are being developed, but it will be several years before a full withdrawal is possible. It is expected that the increasingly US-led forces will withdraw to large airbases outside Iraq's large cities, ahead of any final exit from the country.

Assessment

Iraq's air force has gone through a tumultuous decade. From being one of the Arab world's largest air force it has been reduced to a rump force, capable only of limited counter-insurgency operations. It will be several decades before the IQAF is a major regional force again.

CHAPTER SIX

Israel

Population	7 million
Military/paramilitary aircraft	827
Air Force personnel	35,000

Tsvah Haganah le Israel – *Zroa HaAvir VeHa alal* (Israeli Defence Force – Air and Space Force)

History

Israel's air force has played a pivotal role in the Jewish state wars since its establishment in May 1948. Its formation predated the formal establishment of the State of Israel by several months, when the underground Jewish militia, the Haganah, established its air wing, dubbed the Sherut Avir. Its personnel were mainly veterans of the British RAF or US Army Air Corps, and their first work involved the covert purchase of surplus warplanes around Europe. These airmen and aircraft played an important role in Israel's war of independence.

Over the next two decades, Israel's air power grew in strength and capabilities as conflict intensified with its Arab neighbours. It emerged victorious against Egyptian, Syrian, Jordanian and Iraqi air forces in open war in 1956 and 1967, as well as in border skirmishes up to the 1970s. The Israeli air force's surprise attack in the opening hours of the 1967 Six-Day War proved decisive and changed the military balance of power in the Middle East. Israel's airpower was put severely to the test in the 1973 Yom Kippur War, but it eventually mastered Egypt and Syria's Soviet-supplied surface-to-air missile defences with electronic warfare technology provided by the USA.

During the 1980s, Israel brought on line more domestically developed advanced suppression of enemy air defence technology and unmanned aerial vehicles (UAVs). These proved decisive during the 1982 conflict with Syria in Lebanon. The Israeli air force started to bring large numbers of US-supplied F-16 and F-15 fighters into service, which dramatically enhanced its capabilities.

Israel's occupation of southern Lebanon and uprisings among the Palestinian population of the occupied territories in the late 1980s and 1990s forced the Jewish state's air force to become involved in low-intensity operations against insurgent fighters. This trend continued in the twenty-first century when the so-called 'Al Asqa Intifada' broke out in 2000, when the Israeli air force found itself fighting in a seemingly unending guerilla war.

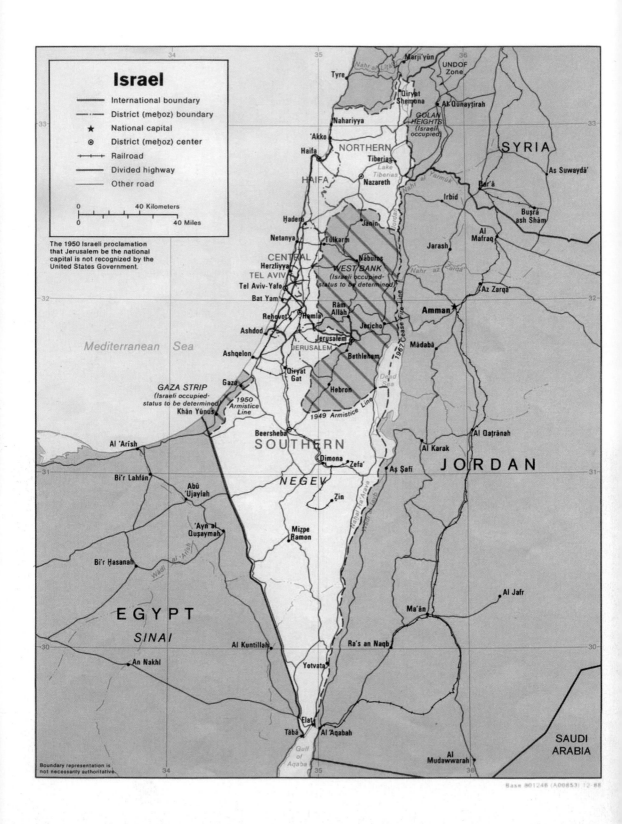

The 2006 Lebanon War saw the full strength of the Israeli air force committed against the Hizbullah guerilla groups for little apparent return. The lessons of this war were applied in December 2008 and January 2009 as the Israeli military launched a punitive offensive against the Hamas government in Gaza.

At the same time, the Israeli military has begun to focus on preparing for a confrontation with a resurgent Iran, whose hard-line Islamic government has become increasing hostile to the Jewish state. The Israeli military has found itself pulled in three directions – preparing for conventional war to deter Syria, conducting counter-insurgency operations in the occupied territories and building up long-range strategic strike capabilities to counter Iran. At the same time, the country's population has become less willing to fund high levels of military expenditure, resulting in several governments launching a series of economy drives.

Until the 2006 Lebanon War, Israel's armed forces suffered from several budget cuts as a result of economic problems and the continued Palestinian guerrilla campaign against the Jewish state's occupation of the West Bank and Gaza Strip. Defence budget cuts of twenty per cent during the 1990s forced the air force to concentrate on a few core types, and many older types of aircraft are being phased out of service as part of the rationalisation. The focus of the air force became a long-range strike to counter the Iranian military build-up. To reflect its expanding role in space and missile defence, the service was retitled Israel Air and Space Force (IASF) on 1 June 2005.

The F-16 is the core of Israeli air power, with more than 200 in front-line service. *(USAF)*

Isreali Air Arms Order of Battle, as at 1 May 2009.

Airbase	Location	Wing/Base Designation	Squadron	Name	Aircraft Type	Role
Tsvah Haganah Le Israel – Zroa Haavir Veha Alal, (Israeli Defence Force – Air And Space Force)						
Hatzerim	31° 14' N 34° 39' E	6th Airbase	69	The Hammers Squadron	F-15I	Strike
			102	The Flying Tiger Squadron	TA/A-4N, Bell 206, G-120A-1, Tzukit, AH-1E	Training
			123	Desert Birds	S-70a	Troop transport
			107	Orange Tail Knights	F-16I	Strike
			5707		UH-60A, S-70A	Troop transport / Special Forces
Hatzor	31° 45' N 34° 43' E	4th Air Wing	101	The First Fighter Squadron	F-16C Block 40	Air defence / Strike
			105	The Scorpion Squadron	F-16D Block 40	Air defence / Strike
Nevatim	31° 12' N 35° 00' E	28th Airbase	116	Defenders of the South Squadron	F-16A/B	Advanced OCU
			140	The Golden Eagle Squadron	F-16A/B	Air defence / Strike
			103	The Elephants Squadron	C-130E, K/C-130H	Transport
			120	International Squadron	B707 variants	Intelligence
			122	Nahshon Squadron	G550	AEW/SIGINT
			131	The Yellow Bird Squadron	C-130E, K/C-130H	Transport
Ovda	29° 56' N 34° 56' E	10th Airbase	115	Flying Dragon Squadron	F-16A/B	Aggressor
Palmachim	31° 53' N 34° 41' E	30th Airbase	124	The Rolling Sword Squadron	UH-60A, S-70A	Troop transport
			160	Fighting Family Squadron	AH-1E/F	Attack
			161	The First Attack Squadron	AH-1E/F	Attack
			200	1st UAV Squadron	Eitan, Shoval	Intelligence
			166	2nd UAV Squadron	Hermes 450, Searcher 2	Intelligence

Airbase	Location	Wing/Base Designation	Squadron	Name	Aircraft Type	Role
			151	Missile Test Squadron		Test
			5101			Foreward air control/Special Forces
Ramat David	32° 39′ N 35° 10′ E	1st Air Wing	109	The Valley Squadron	F-16D Block 30	Air defence/Strike
			110	The Knights of the North	F-16D Block 30	Air defence/Strike
			117	The First Jet Squadron	F-16D Block 30	Air defence/Strike
			193	Defenders of the West Squadron	AS565MA	Naval support
Ramon	30° 46′ N 34° 40′ E	25th Air Wing	113	The Hornet	AH-64D	Attack
			119	The Bat Squadron	F-16I	Strike
			190	The Magic Touch Squadron	AH-64A	Attack
			201	The One Squadron	F-16I	Strike
			252	Negev Squadron	F-16I	Strike
Sde Dov	32° 06′ N 34° 46′ E	15th Air Wing	100	The Flying Camel Squadron	Beech 200	liaison
			125	The Light Helicopters Squadron	Bell 206B, OH-58B	liaison
			135	Kings of the Air Squadron	Beech 200, BeA36 Cochit, Beech 35	liaison
			191		RC-12D/K	Intelligence
Tel Nof	31° 50′ N 34° 49′ E	3rd Airbase	106	The Point of the Spear Squadron	F-15B/C/D	Air defence/Strike
			114	Nighte Guides Squadron	CH-53-2000	Troop transport
			118	Night Owls Squadron	CH-53-2000	Troop transport
			133	The Knights of the Twin Tail Squadron	F-15B/C/D	Air defence/Strike

Airbase	Location	Wing/Base Designation	Squadron	Name	Aircraft Type	Role
			601/FTC	Flight Test Centre	F-15I F-16A/B/C/D	Test
			669		CH-53-2000, UH-60	SAR/Special Forces
Sodt Mcha		2nd Air Wing	150		Jericho Ballistic Missile	Nuclear missile
			199		Jericho Ballistic Missile	Nuclear missile
			248		Jericho Ballistic Missile	Nuclear missile
Biraneet						FOB
Bezet						FOB
Haifa	32° 35′ N 35° 13′ E	21st Airbase				FOB
Israeli Police Helicoper Unit						
Sde Dov			Unit 55		Bell 206	Liaison/Observation

Structure

The IASF role in Israeli military policy and planning is complex. The service is part of the unified Israeli Defence Forces (IDF), and it reports direct to the IDF Chief of Staff. This is unlike most Western air forces, which are separate services and directly report to civilian ministries of defence. Israel does not have individual service chiefs for its army, navy and air forces who are of equal status, so the IASF does not have an independent voice within the Israeli defence structure. A high degree of political control is exercised over IASF operations, particularly high-profile missions in the occupied territories or against targets in neighbouring Arab countries, by the Jewish state's government. It is not unusual for the prime minister and defence minister to personally supervise details of IASF raids on strategic missions.

IASF headquarters in Tel Aviv contains a high-tech operations centre to allow the service's senior leadership to monitor in real-time air operations in and around Israeli air space. As the service's new name implies, this also includes managing operations in space and ballistic missile defence.

The IASF also has well-established procedures for delegating control of tactical air support to IDF regional ground forces' headquarters for specific operations – particularly attack helicopter and UAV missions in the occupied territories. The headquarters of the Northern, Central and Southern Commands are responsible respectively for the Lebanese/Golan, West Bank and Gaza fronts. Their command posts contain the necessary communications and video down-links to allow senior army commanders to monitor in real-time the progress of air operations, via imagery from UAVs.

There are three main air-control centres at Mount Meron, Baal-Hazor Hill and Mitzpe Ranon, which monitor air space with radar and provide air traffic control services for military aircraft.

The peacetime strength of the IASF is around 35,000, of which some 15,000 serve in the Air Defence Command. Most of this latter organisation's personnel are conscripts, whereas the majority of personnel in flying units are career professionals. Some 55,000 reservists can be mobilised in time of crisis. Airline personnel and professionals from the Israeli defence industry, including UAV specialists, are among IASF reservists who regularly augment flying units carrying out missions in support of on-going operations in Lebanon and the occupied territories.

The F-15I provides Israel with a long-range, deep-strike capability. *(USAF)*

The IASF has exclusive control of all Israeli military aircraft, with the exception of small, hand-held UAVs owned by the IDF ground forces. A single squadron of maritime helicopters is jointly controlled by the IASF and the Israeli navy.

Air power doctrine and strategy

Since its formation, the IASF has been torn between the needs of supporting army troops in contact with enemy forces on the battlefield and the desire to launch strategic air strikes against the heart of Arab nations.

From the 1960s to 1980s, the strategic priority for the then IAF was to achieve air supremacy, to allow the army to operate with impunity on the battlefield. Israeli national strategy at this time never envisaged the air force operating on its own. The collapse of the Arab military threat in the 1990s and changes in Israeli society during this period made the idea of large-scale land combat, with the resulting heavy casualties, less appealing to the Israeli public. This, combined with the need to build up long-range capabilities to meet the emerging threat from Iran, meant the air force assumed a more central role in Israeli defence planning.

Senior Israeli air force officers watched with great interest US and UK air campaigns in the Balkans, Afghanistan and Iraq, which seemed to demonstrate that air power alone could coerce opponents by hitting their strategic centres of gravity with precision-guided munitions. The use of so-called effects-based strategies was at the heart of Israeli war planning for the 2006 Lebanon War. This coincided with the appointment of the first ever air force officer, Lieutenant-General Dan Halutz, as IDF Chief of Staff. Halutz devised the strategy for the Lebanon War, which envisaged using air power to hit strategic targets in Lebanon to force the country's government to act against the Hizbullah guerilla group. The failure of the strategy had far-reaching implications for the IASF. Halutz resigned from his post and was replaced by an army officer. The army received an enhanced budget, and IASF operations again became closely integrated with those of the land and naval forces.

Operational activity

Continuing Palestinian guerrilla activity in the occupied territories, instability in Lebanon and the state of war with Syria means that the Israeli air force maintains a significant part of its forces on a high state of alert. Fighter and airborne early warning aircraft fly nearly continuous combat air patrols to deal with any hostile air threats. Strike aircraft are held on ground alert if army units need air support in the occupied territories. Casualty evacuation and rescue helicopters are also on alert to recover isolated IDF personnel.

UAVs, including air vehicles operated by the contractor Aeronautics Defense Systems, are on 24/7 patrol over the occupied territories. Attack helicopters are rotated from their home bases to stand alert at forward operating bases close to the occupied territories to allow immediate close air support missions to be launched.

The need to cycle forces through these ongoing commitments means that senior commanders have to juggle their forces considerably to free up units and aircraft in order to participate in major training exercises to hone skills for higher-intensity operations.

The IASF is keen to participate in international exercises to gain experience of new air warfare tactics and procedures. In 2005, the Israeli naval helicopters participated in a joint SAR exercise, dubbed Reliant Mermaid 7, with US and Turkish naval units. USAF F-15 Eagles and E-3C Sentry AWACS conducted a joint exercise at Nevatim airbase in 2006.

NATO E-3A AWACS aircraft visited Israel in February 2006 for a joint training exercise. Israeli aircraft have participated in training exercises on the Decimomannu Ranges in Italy, the most recent visit being in September 2008. Visits to Exercise Red Flag in the USA and Maple Flag in Canada are also growing in regularity. Large contingents of Israeli aircraft have also participated in the Turkish Anatolian Eagle series of exercises.

The skills needed to launch pin-point long strikes, such as the 2007 strike on the suspected Syrian nuclear reactor, require extensive training and preparation. The IASF makes use of the Mediterranean Sea to practise such missions, as its fighter aircraft often adopt the transponder 'persona' of commercial air traffic so that they do not attract attention.

Airbase infrastructure

All of Israel's main military airbases are hardened to varying degrees. All fighter aircraft, ammunition storage and command post facilities on airbases are hardened but it is more difficult to protect large aircraft and maintenance facilities.

A major programme is under way to rationalise the air force's base infrastructure to cut costs and reduce manpower. The large transport and ISTAR fleet has moved from the country's main civilian airport at Ben Gurion in Tel Aviv to purpose-built facilities at Nevatin airbase. Significant numbers of F-4s, Kfirs, A-4Es, C-130s and helicopters remain in storage and are up for sale.

Main operating bases are Tel Nof (F-15, CH-53), Hatzor (F-16), Hatzerim (F-16, F-15, S-70), Nevetim (F-16, large transport/EW), Ramat David (F-16, AH-64), Palmachin (transport helo, AH-1, UAV), Sde Dov (light comms aircraft), Ramon (F-16, AH-64).

Aircraft ordnance

The IASF has developed its own requirements for aircraft ordnance. It is known to have bought or fielded a range of precision-guided munitions, including:

Air-to-ground weapons

- AGM-62B Walleye TV-guided, air-launched weapon (16 km)
- Gabriel I/II/III air-launched missile (40 km)
- Popeye I/II TV-guided, air-launched weapon (92 km)
- Lockheed Martin Hellfire II laser and Longbow anti-tank missiles

- TOW / I-TOW wire-guided, anti-tank missile
- GBU-12 Paveway laser-guided bomb
- Elbit Opher laser-guided bomb
- Guillotine / Pyramid laser-guided bomb
- Runway Attack Munition (RAM)
- Rafael SPICE satellite-guided bomb
- Elbit Systems' Lizard 3 advanced Laser-Guided Bomb (LGB)

Suppression of enemy air defence weapons

- AGM-45A / B Shrike
- AGM-45D Shrike
- AGM-78A / B / CD Standard / Purple Fist
- AGM-88 HARM

Anti-ship missiles

- Gabriel

Early versions of the F-15 Eagle still serve in air supremacy roles, and many have been modified to allow them to conduct strike missions. *(Author)*

Lockheed Martin F-16I Sufa (Storm)

The Israeli variant of the F-16 Block 50 was designed to meet the demanding requirements of the Israeli Air and Space Force. It incorporates a large quantity of Israeli-made weapons and electronic warfare equipment. The F-16Is first saw service in the 2006 Lebanon War.

Weight: 12.8 tons (empty), 23.5 tons (maximum)

Dimensions
Length: 48 ft 10 in. (14.93 m)
Wingspan: 31 ft (9.45 m)
Height: 16 ft 8 in. (5.1 m)
Propulsion: Pratt & Whitney F100-PW-229
Performance: High altitude: >Mach 2
                 Low altitude: 895 mph (1,440 km/h)
Radius of action: 1,305 miles (2,100 km)
Combat systems missiles: Rafael Python 5, AMRAM (AIM-120) JDAMs bombs

Israel Inventory as at 15 March 2009.

Type	Active	Stored	Ordered	Required
Tsvah Haganah Le Israel – Zroa Haavir Veha Alal, (Israeli Defence Force – Air and Space Force)				
JSF F-35A			25	50
F-16A/F-16B Netz	88/16			
F-16C Barak/F-16D	77/50			
F-16I Suefa	101			
F-15A/F-15B Baz	38/6			
F-15C/F-15D Akef	16:-9			
F-15I Ra'am	24			
Kfir C7/TC7		120		
F-4E/F-4E-2000/RF-4E		100/53/17		
A-4N Ahit	25	123		
ISTAR/SPECIAL MISSION				
707-320	6			
Gulfstream 550 CAEW	3			
Gulfstream 550 Sigint	3			
IAI-201 Arava		6		
EC-130E	2			
RC-12D/K	7			
TANKER				
707-320	4			
KC-130E	3	1		
TRANSPORT				
707-320	3			
C-130E/H	8	12		
King Air B200CT	27			
U-21A/RU-21A		4		
C-130J				3 to 5
COMBAT HELICOPTER				
AH-64A	28			
AH-64D	17			
AH-1F Tsefa	54			
CH-53-2000 Yas'ur	29	9		
AS565SA Atalef/HH-65	8:-1			
Bell 212 Anafa		7		
UH-60A/UH-60L	48			
JetRanger/Longranger		17:06		
AS.565M Panther	7			
Dhruv	1			

Type	Active	Stored	Ordered	Required
TRAINING AIRCRAFT/HELICOPTERS				
Dornier 28 Agur		12		
AH-1E	14			
CM170 Zukit	12	30		
PA-18 Super Cub		35		
Queen Air B80		4		
Grob 120 Snonit	27			
Beech A36	18		6	
TR20 Trinidad		21		
Bell 206 Jet Rangers	10			
T-6A Texan II	5		10	
UNMANNED AIR VEHICLES				
Searcher II	?/20			
Hermes 450	?/12			
Aerostar	??			
Eitan HALE	??			
Eitan+A23 (Heron) HALE	??			
Israeli Police				
HELICOPTERS				
Bell 206L-3	2			

Air-to-air missiles

- AIM-7F/M semi-active radar-guided missile
- AIM-9J/L/M/P heat-seeking guided missile
- R-530 semi-active radar-guided missile
- Shafrir I/II heat-seeking guided missile
- Python III, IV heat-seeking guided missile
- AIM-120 AMRAAM active guided missile

The IASF has started to move from laser over to satellite-guided weapons as its weapon of choice, and has launched several procurement efforts to buy large numbers of these weapons from the USA. The JDAM is essentially a low-cost guidance kit which, aided by a combined inertial navigation system and global positioning system, creates accurately guided smart weapons, which may be released from as far away as fifteen miles from their target. The bombs, which

UH-60 Blackhawks provide the main front-line combat support roles, including casualty evacuation and special forces tasks. *(IDF Spokesman)*

are produced by Boeing, are used by specially adapted F-15s and F-16s, and are considered the most advanced of their type in the world.

Over the past decade, the IASF has become a major purchaser of US guided weapons. Heavy usage in the 2006 Lebanon War also prompted a drive to restock its bomb dumps. Major purchases that have emerged in public are as follows:

1997
45 AGM-142D Popeye air-to-ground missiles, containers, spares

1998
64 AIM-120B AMRAAMs

1999
700 Joint Direct Attack Munitions (JDAM) tail kits for 2,000 lb bombs

2000
41 AGM-142D Popeye medium-range air-to-surface missiles and associated equipment

Two-seat versions of the F-16 are popular with Israelis, who modify them to conduct suppression of enemy air defence and complex strike missions. *(Lockheed Martin)*

2001
48 AIM-120C-5 AMRAAM

2002
1,000 Joint Direct Attack Munitions (JDAM) tail kits for 2,000 lb bombs

2005
100 Guided Bomb Units (GBU-28) that include BLU-113A/B penetration warheads; 5,000 Joint Direct Attack Munitions (JDAM) tail kits (which include 2,500 GBU-31 for Mk 84, 500 GBU-31 for BLU-109, 500 GBU-32 for Mk 83, and 1,500 GBU-30 for Mk 82 bombs); 2,500 Mk 84 live bombs; 1,500 Mk 82 live bombs; 500 BLU-109 live bombs; 500 Mk 83 live bombs. Elements of this package were rushed to Israel in an emergency airlift in July 2006 during the Lebanon War.

2006

As a result of heavy usage of munitions in the 2006 Lebanon conflict, the IASF ordered a $1.2 billion new package of air-launched weapons, including 10,000 JDAM tail kits, 2,000 Paveway II LGB kits, 11,500 Mk 82 and Mk 84 bombs, 2,000 BLU-109 bombs, 50 GBU-28 LGBs, 500 AIM-9M Sidewinders, 200 AIM-120C-7 AMRAAMs and 20,000 live fuses.

2007

3,500 Mk 84 general-purpose 2,000 lb bombs
2,000 radio frequency (RF) TOW 2A missiles
14 RF TOW 2A fly-to-buy missiles
1,000 AGM-114K3 HELLFIRE II missiles
200 AGM-114L3 HELLFIRE II Longbow missiles
500 AGM-114M3 HELLFIRE II missiles
100 PATRIOT Guidance Enhanced Missile Plus (GEM+)

2009

1,000 GBU-39 small-diameter bombs

As part of its effort to restock supplies of precision munitions following the depletion of stocks during the 2006 war in Lebanon, Elbit Systems was awarded a $15 million contract for several hundred Lizard 3 kits. Introduced in 2003, the Lizard 3 has an accuracy of 1 m circular error probable, and can be used against targets moving at up to 150 km/h.

Procurement

The IASF is effectively locked into buying US combat aircraft and other large air warfare systems because of Israel's reliance of US military aid. Currently this is running at around $2.4 billion annually, but comes with the important caveat that the majority of it must be spent on US-sourced products. The IASF, however, insists that large amounts of locally produced systems, such as electronic warfare devices and Litening targeting pods, are fitted to US-produced aircraft.

The centre-piece of IASF procurement over the past decade has been a $2.5 billion deal for fifty two-seat F-16Is, which was signed in 2000, and this remains the centre-piece of Israeli air force procurement plans. Israel exercised fifty-two options the following year. Initial F-16Is were delivered in 2003, with almost all being delivered by early 2009 to allow four squadrons to be formed.

Older F-15A/B/C/Ds have been upgraded to given them a strike capability, and consideration is being given to an F-15I follow-on, dubbed the F-15SX.

In August 2003, US contractor Gulfstream Aerospace announced that it had been awarded a contract to supply the Israeli Ministry of Defence with three Gulfstream jet aircraft, with an option for two additional aircraft for the air force, for signal intelligence (SIGINT) purposes. The ministry awarded a contract to Elta, a wholly owned subsidiary of Israel Aircraft Industries (IAI) to provide the new generation of airborne SIGINT systems to be installed on the Gulfstreams. The systems comprise Elta's new generation of electronic intelligence (ELINT), communication intelligence (COMINT), communications, and command and control subsystems.

In June 2005, the IAF took delivery of its first Gulfstream 550 (G550) long-endurance special electronic mission aircraft (SEMA), dubbed Nashshon Shavit (Comet). The second and third SEMA aircraft arrived during 2006. The first aircraft took part in the 2006 Lebanon War even though it was still undergoing experimental testing.

A total of six aircraft, three in SEMA configuration and three in Compact Airborne Early Warning (CAEW) configuration, are scheduled to replace the IASF's current fleet of Boeing 707 SIGINT/AEW in a contract estimated at $473 million, which is partly financed by US foreign military funding (FMF). The first CAEW aircraft, dubbed Nashshon Eitam (Fish Eagle) arrived in Israel to be fitted with their mission equipment in May 2006, and they began flight testing in June 2007. The second airframe was flown to Israel in March 2007.

A-4s are being upgraded to allow them to continue as lead-in trainers for the F-16 and F-15, and to support air-combat training using a newly formed aggressor unit.

The IASF is acquiring two variants of the IAI Heron medium-altitude, long-endurance (MALE) UAVs. The first eight of these, known as the Shoval, were delivered in March 2007 in a $50 million project. These vehicles have a tactical or battlefield role. In October 2007, the IASF unveiled the Eitan variant of the Heron, which is to be used for long-endurance strategic surveillance and targeting missions, via satellite control. This system is obviously aimed at strategic targets in Iran and Syria. The project is said to be worth an estimated $60–80 million.

The Elbit Hermes 450 is to be the main tactical UAV, with three batches of air vehicles being ordered since 1999. A second batch worth $47 million was ordered in 2003, and a new batch worth $30 million was ordered in 2007.

A CH-53 service life extension project was launched in late 2005 to be completed by the IASF's Aircraft Maintenance Unit, under a project known as Yasour 2025. This is being run by IASF personnel rather than an industry prime contracting team. The project involves improvements to survivability, avionics, night vision, radar, communications, airframe and dynamic system. The Apache fleet is to receive the M-TADS night vision upgrade from 2008 onwards.

The Elbit subsidiary Cyclone was contracted in 2004 to run the IASF Flying School's helicopters. In March 2007, Elbit was awarded a ten-year PFI contract to run a simulation centre for special mission crews of King Air B200 aircraft. Some fifteen Hawker Beachcraft T-6A Texan II trainers are in the process of being delivered.

The Teffen 2012 defence plan includes provision for the first purchases of nine C-130J aircraft to augment the fleet of C-130E/Hs.

It was announced in January 2002 that Israel's Ministry of Defence contracted Israel Aircraft Industries (IAI) to upgrade three of its air force Boeing KC-707-300 refuelling aircraft. Under the terms of the deal, IAI's Bedek Aviation Group undertook to modernise the aircraft with advanced avionics, a flight safety system and a communication and navigation system. In February 2001, Bedek completed a

The Israelis have converted Gulfstream G550 executive jets to be their main airborne early warning and electronic intelligence-gathering platforms. *(Author)*

Israel leads the world in many areas of unmanned aerial vehicle operations. *(IDF Spokesman)*

project to install a new refuelling system on one of the air force's KC-707s. Further upgrades are planned after the 2007 defence plan did not approve the purchase of a replacement aircraft. In 2008, the Israel government sought permission to buy Boeing 767 tanker aircraft, but the US government refused the request, fearing it would raise speculation of an Israeli attack on Iran's nuclear facilities

The C-130E/H fleet is being progressively upgraded under the Karnaf Avionics Upgrade Programme. This includes the fitting of a Rafael Toplite FLIR turret under the nose and other electronic/avionic improvements. The 2007 commitment to buy C-130Js means there is a question mark over whether all the C-130 inventory will be upgraded.

Israel participated in the JSF concept demonstration phase, but has been frozen out of the project for over a year because of US objections to Israel's defence deals with China. These differences appeared to be resolved in 2008 when the Israeli government was given permission to buy up to seventy-five Lockheed Martin F-35 Lightning II Joint Strike Fighters (JSF). Some twenty-five F-35A conventional take-off-and-landing variants will be procured initially, with the potential of an additional fifty F-35B short-take-off-and-landing variants in the next work plan. Some of these aircraft could be deployed on the Israeli navy's future amphibious landing ship. The IASF is expected to begin payments for the JSF in 2009 in order to receive the first aircraft by 2014, but the $15 billion price tag for the aircraft has raised some concern in Israel. The IASF is also reportedly unhappy that the USA is not offering Israeli engineers access to the JSF's computer software codes to allow Israeli-made electronic warfare equipment and weapons to be integrated onto the new aircraft.

The USA does not yet permit the export of the Lockheed Martin F-22 Raptor air superiority fighter, which is the IASF-preferred aircraft to replace its ageing F-15s. These issues means that the IASF is unlikely to buy any new combat aircraft during the first half of the next decade.

Strategic weapons

Israel has possessed nuclear weapons since the 1960s, when a co-operation programme with France allowed the Jewish state to acquire the ultimate guarantee of its existence. The IASF has played a key part in the Jewish state nuclear weapon programme, and its McDonnell Douglas F-4 Phantoms were the service's main airborne nuclear delivery platform for many years. This mission has now reportedly passed to the F-16s force.

The core of Israel's nuclear capability is the Jericho ballistic missile force based at Sdot Mchha. Three ISAF squadrons (150th, 199th and 248th) operate the missiles from a series of underground shelters at the base. The main nuclear armed missile in service is the Jericho II, which has a range of 1,300 kilometres.

The Jericho III is currently replacing the older missile. It is believed to have a three-stage solid propellant and a payload of 1,000–1,300 kg. It is possible for the missile to be equipped with a single 750 kg nuclear warhead or two or three low-yield multiple re-entry warheads. It is estimated that it will have a range of 4,800–7,000 km (2,982–4,350 miles), bringing all of the Middle East within range of Israel's nuclear missiles. On 17 January 2008, Israel test-fired a multi-stage ballistic missile believed to be of the Jericho III type reportedly capable of carrying 'special warheads'.

Space systems

As part of its emphasis on intelligence and early warning, and on maintaining a qualitative edge in military capability over states regarded as a threat to its security, Israel has put a considerable emphasis on its military space programme. The escalation of tension with Iran over its alleged nuclear weapons policy has led to an increased emphasis on remote sensing satellites by the Israeli government during 2007.

Israel's military space efforts are overseen by the Ministry of Defence (MoD), which has a special section with its own budget dealing with the space programme. Also relevant is the civilian Israel Space Agency (ISA), which has broad responsibilities for both civil and military technologies, and liaises closely with other government agencies. The IASF became the IDF lead service for space operations in 2003. Its interest in space is to provide earth-sensing imagery and signals intelligence coverage of threat nations around Israel, to provide advanced communications support to military operations and to provide navigation support. This latter area is taking on greater importance, and to provide an alternative to the US-run GPS navigation system Israel has joined the rival European Galileo system.

The Israel also uses the EROS-A, an Israeli commercial electro-optical satellite launched in 2000, for imagery. In addition, the Israelis have access to US intelligence imagery.

Israel does not have a dedicated military communications satellite capability but leases capacity on the Spacecom's AMOS-1 and 2 space vehicles. Spacecom is a joint venture of Eurocom, Israel Aircraft Industries, General Satellite Services Co. (GSSC) and Mer Services Group Ltd.

There was considerable relief in the IASF in June 2007 when an improved Shavit launcher successfully placed Ofeq-7 in orbit to replace the in-service Ofeq-5 electro-optical remote sensing or photo-reconnaissance satellite. This is expected to be followed by at least two more Ofeq satellites, dubbed Ofeq-8 and Ofeq-Next, by 2011. An innovative satellite boasting synthetic aperture radar (SAR), dubbed TechSAR, was scheduled to be launched in India aboard the Polar Satellite Launch Vehicle in October 2007, but this was delayed until December 2007.

Other space projects on the near horizon include the civilian/military AMOS-3 twin band, AMOS-4 multi-band communications satellite.

Air and missile defence

The IASF has devoted an increasing quantity of resources to developing and deploying systems to defeat hostile missile threats, including short-, medium- and long-range threats. A major-general controls the Air Defence Command, which also has extensive links to the civil defence organisation to provide warnings of missile attacks to the population.

In co-operating with the US it has developed the Arrow ballistic missile defence system, which is designed to defeat Syrian and Iranian missile attacks at long ranges in the high atmosphere or upper tier. The US Army deployed an X-band radar to Israel in 2008 to enhance the long-range radar coverage of the system. Two batteries are deployed at Palmachin airbase, and a third system is deployed near Haifa. Turkey and South Korea are considering buying the Arrow system.

US Army Patriot PAC-3 missile batteries regularly deploy to Israel from bases in Germany to expand coverage of the IASF's own three batteries of the missile system. The IASF requested the purchase from the USA of 1,000 GEM+ Patriot missiles in 2007, and the following year looked to upgrade its Patriot fire units to REP standard.

Other layers of defence are provided by six batteries of I-HAWK surface-to-air missiles (SAMs), twelve battery Chapparal vehicle-mounted heat-seeking SAMs and hundreds of anti-aircraft guns positioned around key points. These forces are assigned to three air defence regiments, supporting the land force's northern, central and southern commands.

In May 2006, the Israeli Missile Defence Organisation (IMDO) and the US Missile Defence Agency (MDA) moved to address Israel's middle-tier short-range ballistic missile defence requirement for threats of 70–400 km, selecting a joint tender by Rafael, teamed with Raytheon of the USA, to build the Stunner system. In Israeli service, this will be launched from existing IASF PAC-2 transported launchers, with sixteen interceptors per launcher. The system is scheduled for operational deployment by 2011, and will be networked with established ground missile defence assets.

A programme to develop an effective solution against the shorter-range threats in the 4–70 km envelope (Qassam/Katyusha-class rockets) was initiated in 2004, although the Israeli Ministry of Defence subsequently fast-tracked the procedure in the wake of the 2006 Lebanon War. Some fourteen different proposals were tendered, and nine were formally assessed, with three down-selected for final consideration in February. As yet technical problems have not allowed the successful deployment of an interceptor missile able to counter threats from ranges of 2–250 km.

Presence of foreign forces
Israel has a close alliance with the USA. Since the 1980s, it has allowed US equipment to be pre-positioned in Israel. This is now thought to include elements of Patriot missile defence systems. US Army Patriot units deployed to Israel in 1991 to defend the Jewish state against Iraqi Scud missile attacks. This deployment was repeated in 2003 during the US-led invasion of Iraq.

The USA is watching Iranian missile and nuclear developments closely, and there is considerable co-operation between the US Ballistic Missile Agency and its Israeli counterparts. The US Army deployed an X-band radar system to Israel in 2008 to provide early warning of Iranian missile attacks.

Assessment

Israel's air force is undoubtedly the most powerful in the Middle East. It possesses the full spectrum of air power capabilities, from nuclear strike to air defence and close air support. It has modern aircraft, helicopters and airborne weapons that outclass anything possessed by its potential opponents.

If the IASF has any weaknesses, it is in two areas. The first is its power projection capabilities, particularly airlift and air-to-air refuelling, which make the prospects for an extended air campaign against nuclear targets in Iran difficult to contemplate. A one-off strike could be possible, but anything requiring sustained operations would severely strain IASF.

Secondly, the Israeli government is beginning to regard the IASF as a hammer to pummel its opponents into submission, rather than as a precision strike force. The Lebanon War and Gaza operations in December 2008 and January 2009 saw overwhelming force applied against the government and civilian infrastructure of Israel's opponents. This has certainly sent a warning to Israel's neighbours, that a military confrontation will result in the devastation of their countries. The long-term sustainability of this strategy is questionable, and certainly Hizbullah was not defeated by Israel's iron fist approach. It also risks undermining the international support, particularly in the USA, that Israel relies on for its survival.

Close air support for army units is a major role of Israeli attack helicopter units. *(IDF Spokesman)*

IASF Aircraft Designations

Atalef: Bat:	Eurocopter AS565 Panther
Ayit: Eagle:	McDonnell Douglas A-4 Skyhawk
Barak: Lightning:	Lockheed F-16C/D Fighting Falcon
Baz: Falcon:	McDonnell Douglas F-15 Eagle
Chofit: Stint:	Beech A36 Bonanza
Eitan: Steadfast:	Heron MALE UAV
Eitam: Fish Eagle:	Gulfstream G550 CAEW
Karnaf: Rhinoceros:	Lockheed C-130 Hercules
Nachshon: Pioneer:	Gulfstream G550
Netz: Hawk:	Lockheed F-16A/B Fighting Falcon
Ra'am: Thunder:	Boeing F-15I
Re'em: Oryx:	Boeing 707
Saifan: Avocet:	Bell 206 Jet Ranger
Saifanit: Gladiolus:	Bell 206L Long Ranger
Saraf: Serpent:	Boeing AH-64A Apache
Shahaf: Seagull:	IAI Seascan
Shavit: Comet:	Gulfstream G550 SIGINT version
Shoval: Trail:	Heron tactical UAV
Soufa: Storm:	Lockheed F-16I Fighting Falcon
Tzefa: Viper:	Bell AH-1 Huey Cobra
Tzufit: Honeydew:	Beechcraft B200 King Air
Tzukit: Cliff:	IAI Tzukit
Yanshuf: Owl:	Sikorsky UH-60 Black Hawk
Yas'ur: Petrel:	Sikorsky CH-53

The Israeli air and space force has considerable assets in orbit to monitor potential enemies of the Jewish state. *(IAI)*

US-supplied CH-53 helicopters are being extensively upgraded to extend the service until 2030. *(Author)*

CHAPTER SEVEN

Jordan

Population	6.3 million
Military/paramilitary aircraft	295
Air Force personnel	8,500

Al Quwwat al Jawwiya al Malakiya al Urduniya (Royal Jordanian Air Force)

History

The RJAF can trace its history back to the early 1920s, when British rule was established after the First World War and the RAF set up two airbases in what was termed a League of Nations Mandate Territory. Although not officially a colony, the British effectively ran the country until immediately after the Second World War. Its locally recruited but British-officered armed forces, the Arab Legion, soon established an air arm for liaison and transport work.

The Arab Legion fought to protect the Arab population of Palestine after the declaration of the State of Israel in 1948. Its air arm had no combat aircraft, and so could not join the fight in the air, and it was not until 1955 that the Arab Legion air arm was transformed into RJAF and plans were laid to acquire modern fighter aircraft. British Vampire aircraft were purchased and efforts made to train Jordanians to take over more tasks from British personnel. An Arab commander of the RJAF was appointed in 1956 and the RAF evacuated all its bases in Jordan the following year.

The RJAF suffered heavily at the hands of the Israelis in the 1967 war, when a large number of its aircraft were knocked out on the ground in IDF pre-emptive strike that opened the conflict. Subsequently the RJAF was heavily engaged against Palestinian guerilla forces in 1970 and their Syrian allies. The Jordanians did not directly operate against the Israelis in the 1973 Yom Kippur War, but aircraft were sent to fight alongside the Egyptians and Syrians.

In the 1980s, the Jordanians were closely allied with the Iraqis against the Iranians, and RJAF bases hosted Iraqi aircraft that were evacuated westwards to escape Iranian attacks on their bases.

During the 1990s, the Jordanians signed a peace deal with the Israelis and moved overtly into the pro-USA camp. This opened the way for the resumption of US military aid and deliveries of military equipment that had been cut off after Jordan supported Iraq in the 1990/91 Kuwait crisis.

Structure

The RJAF is the sole operator of military aircraft for the Royal Jordanian armed forces. It has established a wing structure, with its main types grouped together for training and maintenance. Many of the helicopters are assigned to a new joint services Jordanian special operations command, although the personnel and aircraft remain under RJAF control for routine matters. The air force also operates three BO105CBSs and four EC635s acquired in 1989 on behalf of the police.

Operational activity

The mission of the RJAF is to protect and defend the sovereignty and the integrity of the Hashemite Kingdom of Jordan. Its primary task is to defend the Jordanian airspace against any potential air threat. Its secondary role is to support the country's land forces in any armed conflict with any external power. In addition it has the tasks of maintaining internal security, anti-smuggling and border security operations.

The Royal Jordanian Air Force has not made any contributions of combat forces to multinational peace support operations. RJAF C-130s have flown all over the world to participate in UN peace-keeping operations, support relief operations in various disaster areas, and evacuation of citizens from conflict areas. The RJAF supported all Jordanian Army units serving with UNPROFOR in the former Yugoslavia by transporting troops in C-130s. The RJAF has participated in humanitarian aid missions in Malaysia, Japan, Turkey, Iran, Sudan, Bangladesh, Yemen, Bosnia and Chechnya.

Since 2003, internal security operations to counter Islamic fundamentalists have been the main activity of the air force, particularly involving helicopter units.

The serviceability of the Mirage and F-5 fleets has been questionable since the early 1990s, when Gulf states cut off financial assistance as punishment for Jordan's support for Iraq during the 1991 war. Only the resumption of US military aid in the late 1990s allowed the RJAF to return its operations to meaningful levels. The delivery of the first batch of sixteen ex-USAF F-16A/Bs in 1997 was a major milestone in this effort.

The small size of the RJAF combat force compared to its neighbours – Israel, Syria and Saudi Arabia – means it would have difficulty challenging any major incursion into its air space without US support.

The focus of the helicopter force is on internal security and border patrol as part of the newly formed Special Operations Command. RJAF pilots have trained with the USAF's 6th Special Operations Squadron (6th SOS) in Florida in counter-insurgency operations.

In May and June 2007, the newly formed RJAF F-16 squadrons participated in a joint exercise, dubbed Falcon Meet, with USAF, Turkish and Belgian F-16 units at Azraq airbase. The following year, French air force Mirage F.1 units deployed to Azraq for Exercise Desert Mirage. RAF units are also regular visitors to Jordan for joint exercises.

Beirut
Baabda
Zahlé
Sirghâyâ
Sab' Âbâr

Sidon
LEBANON
Dûmâ
Qumayr
At Tanf

Mediterranean
Sea
Nabatîye
et Tahta
Marjayoûn
Qatana
Damascus

Tyre
UNDOF
Zone
Al Kiswah

Bent Jbail
Al-Qunayṭirah
Burrâq

SYRIA

IRAQ

Naharîyya
GOLAN
HEIGHTS
(Israeli
occupied)
Az Zalaf
Ṭirbîl

Akko
Zefat
Shaykh
Miskîn
Shahbâ'

Haifa
Lake
Tiberias
alignment
approximate

Nazareth
Tiberias
Zayzûn

ISRAEL
'Atula
Dar'â
As Suwaydâ'

Hadera
Irbid
Ar
Ramthâ
Buṣrâ
ash Shâm
Ṣalkhad
Ar Ruwayshid

Netanya
Janin

Tel
Aviv-
Yafo
Kefar
Sava
Ṭûlkarm
'Ajlûn
Jarash
Aş Şafâwî

Qalqilya
Nablus

West
Bank*
As
Salt
Suwaylih
Az Zarqâ'
track

Petah
Tiqwa
Ramallah
Wâdî
as Sîr
Ar-Ruşayfah
Azraq ash Shîshân

Rishon
LeZiyyon
Jericho
Amman

Jerusalem
Sahâb

Bet Shemesh
Bethlehem
Al Jizah
Al
'Umarî
Ṭurayf

Qiryat
Gat
Mâdabâ
Dead
Sea

Hebron
Kâf

1949 Armistice Line
Al Quṭrânah
Al Qurayyât

Beersheba
'Arad
SAUDI ARABIA

Dimona
Zefa'
Al Karak

Zin
Aş Şâfî
Al 'Īsâwîyah

Mizpe Ramon
Aṭ
Ṭafîlah
Al Ḥasâ

ISRAEL
Jurf ad Darâwîsh
Bâ'ir

Ash
Shawbak

Petra

Ma'ân
Al Jafr

Ra's an Naqb

Yotvata

Jordan

—— International boundary

—·—·— Governorate (muḥâfaẓah) boundary

★ National capital

◉ Governorate (muḥâfaẓah) capital

+++++ Railroad

——— Expressway

——— Road

A governorate has the same name
as its capital except where noted.

| 0 | 25 | 50 Kilometers |
| 0 | 25 | 50 Miles |

EGYPT
Elat
Ṭâbâ
Al 'Aqabah

Gulf
of
Aqaba
Haql

Al
Mudawwarah

SAUDI
ARABIA

*Israeli occupied with current status subject to the
Israeli-Palestinian Interim Agreement—permanent
status to be determined through further negotiation.

Israel proclaimed Jerusalem as its capital in 1950,
but the US, like nearly all other countries, maintains
its embassy in Tel Aviv.

Boundary representation is not necessarily authoritative.

Al Bî'r

Lambert Conformal Conic Projection, SP 29°41'N/33°05'N

Base 803050AI (C00697) 4-04

The delivery of F-16 Fighting Falcons has transformed the capabilities of Jordan's air force. (*Lockheed Martin*)

Airbase infrastructure

The main fighter bases at El Jahr, H-5 and Azraq have hardened aircraft shelters to protect the RJAF's command aircraft from a surprise attack. The other bases have limited protection beyond air defence gun and missile batteries.

Aircraft ordnance

The RJAF's main air-to-ground armaments are iron or dumb bombs. The Mirage fighters have French-supplied R-530 semi-active radar-guided missiles and R-550 Magic heat-seeking guided missiles, while the F-5s and F-16s have US-supplied AIM-9 heat-seeking guided missiles. A batch of fifty AIM-120 AMRAAMs was ordered in November 2004 for use on the second batch of F-16s, which will significantly boost the air-to-air capabilities of the RJAF.

TOW wire-guided anti-tank missile are operated by the AH-1 Cobra fleet.

Strategic weapons

Jordan has no strategic weapons.

Jordanian Air Arms Order of Battle as at 1 May 2009.

Airbase	Location	Squadron	Aircraft Type	Hardened Shelters	Role
Main Operating Bases					
King Abdullah/ Amman-Marka	31° 58′ N 35° 59′ E	3	C-130H, CASA 212M-100, CN235 on loan		Transport
		7	AS332M-1		Troop transport
		8	UH-1H		Troop transport
		14	EC-635T1, UH-1H, Sweizer SA 2-37		Training
		Royal Flight	G.1159B, CL-604, L-1011,S-70A		VIP transport
		Police	Bo105		Observation
King Abdullah II (heli-port)	31° 59′ N 36° 13′ E	10	AH-1F/S		Attack
		12	AH-1F/S		Attack
Al Azraq/As Shaheed Muwaffaq Salti	31° 49′ N 36° 47′ E	1	Mirage F1BJ, Mirage F1CJ, Mirage F1EJ	30, 3 small, 4 QRF	Air defence/CAS
		2	F-16A/B ADF		Air defence/CAS
		6	F-16A/B ADF		Air defence/CAS
		Det 8	UH-1H		SAR
H5/Prince Hassan	32° 09′ N 37° 08′ E	17	F-5E/F	29	Air defence/CAS
King Feisal bin Abdul Aziz/ Al Jafr	30° 20′ N 36° 08′ E	9	F-5E/F	36, 8 QRF	Air defence/CAS
Dispersal Airfields					
H-4				8	FOB
Zarqa					FOB
Al Aqabab					FOB

Procurement

Jordan is increasingly dependent on the USA for the supply of combat aircraft, and a second batch of seventeen F-16A/Bs was delivered in 2003. It placed an $87 million contract to upgrade these to the MLU standard and for structural upgrades to take place in Jordan and Turkey from 2006 to 2009. Some twelve aircraft are to be upgraded at TAI in Turkey, and the remaining five in Jordan. The first aircraft was delivered back to the RJAF in October 2007.

In November 2005, Jordan signed an agreement to acquire three F-16BMs from the Netherlands for operational training, pending availability of additional upgraded aircraft. In the following April, it was announced that Jordan was to obtain an additional twenty-two surplus F-16AM and F-16BM fighters – eight from the Netherlands, comprising five F-16AMs and three F-16BMs, and fourteen from Belgium (twelve F-16AMs and two F-16BMs). In 2007, these requirements were finalised in contracts for twenty F-16AM/BMs, including six F-16BMs from the Netherlands and twelve F-16AMs and two F-16BMs from Belgium. These are all MLU-standard aircraft that began entering RJAF service in 2008, all being fully upgraded to MLU standard. When deliveries and upgrade work are completed, Jordan's air force should possess close to sixty F-16 aircraft, of which forty are of MLU standard. Eight additional aircraft were purchased from Belgium in 2009.

The RJAF is in the process of withdrawing its Northrop F-5 Freedom Fighters from service, and in 2007 agreed to sell twelve F-5Es and three F-5Fs to Kenya. Jordanian Aeronautical Systems (JAS) at Marka airbase is to overhaul the aircraft before delivery.

Surplus aircraft have been purchased to maintain the force structure, including three Dutch F-16s and two Spanish F-1DDAs. A further twenty surplus Dutch and Belgian F-16s are being sought. The EC635 fleet was augmented in January 2006 with an order for four more, leaving three options left to be exercised. Two CN-235s have been leased from Turkey. Eight new UH-60Ls were ordered in July 2004 for delivery in 2006. A request for two more UH-60ls for VIP duties was made to the USA in September 2006. Russian aircraft being considered include Mi-17s, Mi-28s and Su-30s. Ex-UAE AS350Bs have been acquired to replace the Hughes 500Ms, and four ex-Libyan CH-47Cs might be acquired, also via the UAE. Six CH2000 observation aircraft are being purchased, the first of which were delivered in September 2006.

In August 2005, Jordan was to buy two Russian-built Ilyushin Il-76MF strategic transport aircraft equipped with Russian-made PS-90A-76 turbofan engines. It was subsequently reported in December 2005 that Jordan held an option for two more Il-76MFs and was considering the purchase of two Sukhoi Su-80 utility transport aircraft in a customised lightweight tactical airlifter configuration. However, despite the reported existence of a preliminary agreement, no contract has yet been placed for the Su-80. The US$100 million contract for two Il-76s was eventually signed in July 2007. It also emerged in December 2007 that an Antonov An-32 was being prepared for delivery to the RJAF in Ukraine. It is unclear if any additional An-32s are on order. The US government is trying to sell Jordan Alenia C-27J as part of its Joint Cargo Aircraft programme for the US Army.

AH-1F/S Cobra gunships give a tremendous close air support capability to the RJAF. *(Peter Foster)*

Veteran F-5E/F Freedom Fighters are being progressively withdrawn from service. *(Peter Foster)*

Jordanian Hercules aircraft regularly travel overseas to support the country's troop contingents on UN duty. (*Author*)

French-supplied Mirage F-1B/C/Es will still serve in strength until more F-16s can be acquired. (*Peter Foster*)

Jordan Inventory as at 19 March 2009.

Type	Active	Stored	Ordered	Required
Al Quwwat al Jawwiya al Malakiya al Urduniya (Royal Jordanian Air Force)				
F-16A/F-16B	16			
F-16A/B MLU	48			
Mirage F1B/C/E	30			
F-5E/F Tiger	24			
SPECIAL MISSION				
CH2000	1		5	
TRANSPORT				
C-130H	4			
C-130B		2		
Il-76			2	2
CN-235	2			
C-295	2			
A340	1			
737	1			
An-32			1	
TriStar 500	1			
Challenger 604	2			
Gulfstream IV	1			
SA 2-37	1			
Su-80			2	
COMBAT HELICOPTER				
AH-1F/S Cobra	9:22			
S-70/UH-60L	11			2
SA316C	1			
TB-20	1			
UH-1H/UH-1L	35/18			
AS332M-1	12			
EC-635	5		4	3
Bell 212	2			
CH-47C				4
TRAINING AIRCRAFT/HELICOPTERS				
C101CC Aviojet	11			
T67 Firefly	16			
Hughes 500D		7		
Extra 300	5			
AS350B			??	

Type	Active	Stored	Ordered	Required
POLICE				
BO105	3			
EC6325	4			
Government of Hashemite Kingdom of Jordan				
CL-604 Challenger	3			
737	1			
A340	1			
Gulfstream G450	1			

In 2003, Jordan requested the supply of eight Sikorsky UH-60L Black Hawk helicopters through a US Foreign Military Sales (FMS) agreement. Congressional approval was received, and in July 2004 it was confirmed that an agreement had been signed between Sikorsky and the US government to build the helicopters for the RJAF. Delivery of these helicopters was due to begin in June 2006, with all eight handed over by November 2007. They are being used extensively by the RJSF.

Presence of foreign forces

Jordanian agreement to allow US, British and Australian troops to invade Iraq from its territory during March 2003 has brought accelerated deliveries of US defence equipment. Azraq airbase in the eastern desert was the main focus from the US, British and Australian deployment, which included USAF F-16s, RAF Harrier GR7s and Canberra PR9s, as well as special-forces helicopters from all three nations. US Patriot missile batteries also protected the Coalition deployment. USAF ground equipment is believed to have been pre-positioned in Jordan for activation in time of crisis. Since the overthrow of Saddam Hussein's regime Jordan offered training facilities for the reformed Iraqi armed forces and police, including the training of Iraqi air force personnel. US aircraft also stage through Jordanian bases *en route* to Iraq.

British and US ground units regularly use desert training areas in Jordan. British air assets supporting these exercises include RAF C-130s and Bell 212 Griffins from Cyprus.

Assessment

Jordan's air force is completely orientated to support the kingdom's land forces, particularly in counter-insurgency operations. Although its pilots are well trained and motivated, they do not have the equipment or resources to take on the Israelis in a stand-up fight. The RJAF would be better able to take on the Syrians in any defensive battle on their border.

The isolation of Jordan in the early 1990s did irreparable harm to the RJAF. It will be many years before it is restored to its former glory.

CHAPTER EIGHT

Kuwait

Population	2.6 million
Military/paramilitary aircraft	122
Air Force personnel	2,500

Al Quwwat al Jawwiya al Kuwaitiya (Kuwait Air Force)

History

The Kuwaiti air force was formed with British assistance in 1961 after the small emirate at the north of the Gulf achieved its independence. Relations with Iraq have always been strained, which has made the country and population genuinely grateful for US and British military support. This makes Kuwait one of the few Middle Eastern countries to openly welcome the presence of Western forces. During the 1960s, Britain was the main source of aircraft. This changed in the 1970s when French Mirage fighters and Gazelle armed helicopters were ordered, along with US Skyhawk fighter bombers.

In the 1980s, Kuwait allied itself with Saddam Hussein against Iran, and Iraqi aircraft made use of Kuwaiti airbases during the Iran–Iraq War. The Kuwaiti air forces put up spirited resistance to the Iraqi invasion in August 1990, but when their bases were threatened with being overrun the flyable aircraft were evacuated to Saudi Arabia.

Free Kuwaiti air force units joined allied forces to strike back against the Iraqis during Operation Desert Storm. When the Kuwaitis returned to their airbases, it was discovered that they had all been extensively damaged and would require major work to get them back in operational condition. In the early 1990s, a major effort to revamp the air force's air defence and strike capability was launched with an order for 40 McDonnell Douglas F/A-18C/D Hornets.

Structure

The Kuwaiti air force reports to the Ministry of Defence. A number of helicopters have been transferred to the recently formed Police Air Wing

Operational activity

During 1998/9, the then British Aerospace returned the Hawk fleet to airworthiness, and the Tucanos have also returned to the air, marking the resumption of Kuwait's flying training programme.

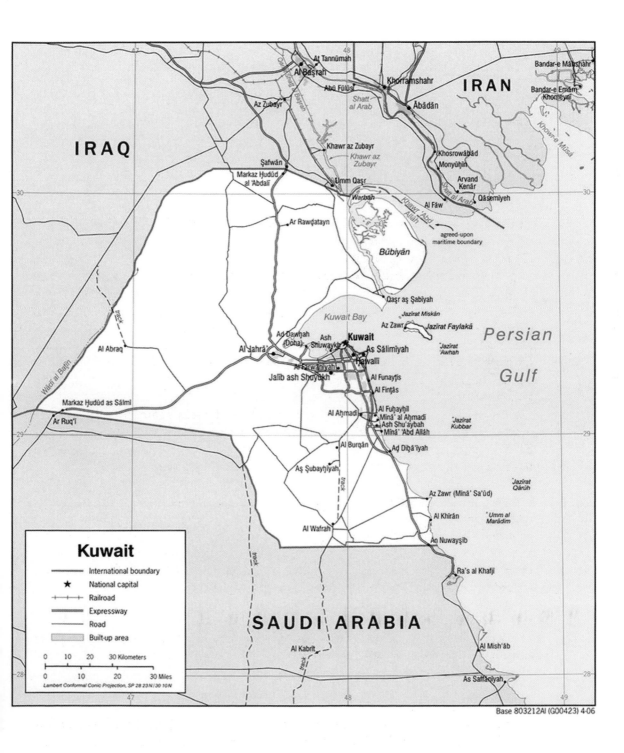

Kuwait

——— International boundary
★ National capital
+++++ Railroad
■■■ Expressway
——— Road
▒ Built-up area

0 10 20 30 Kilometers
0 10 20 30 Miles
Lambert Conformal Conic Projection, SP 28 23 N / 30 10 N

Base 803212AI (G00423) 4-06

Kuwaiti Air Arms Order of Battle, as at 15 May 2009.

Airbase	Locations	Wing/Base Designation	Squadron	Aircraft Type	Role
Kuwait Air Force (KAF) – al-Quwwat al-Jawwiya al-Kuwaitiya					
Ahmed al Jaber	28° 56′ N 47° 47′ E		9 Fighter	F/A-18C/D	Air defence/CAS
			25 Attack	F/A-18C/D	Air defence/CAS
Ali al Salem	29° 20′ N 47° 31′ E		32 Helicopter	SA330H	Troop transport
			33 Helicopter	SA342K	Liaison
			62 Helicopter	AS332M, AS532SC	Troop transport
			88 Helicopter	AH-64D	Attack
		Flight Training Centre	12 Training	Hawk T64	Training
			19 Training	Tucano T.52	Training
			41 Transport	L-100-30	Transport
Fort Hood, Texas			Training Detachment	AH-64D	Training
Kuwait Government					
Kuwait IAP	29° 13′ N 47° 58′ E		VIP Transport Flight	A300C4-620, A310-308, G-IV, G-V	VIP transport
Kuwait Police Kuwait IAP	29° 13′ N 47° 58′ E	Police Helicopter Wing		SA330H, SA342K, EC135T1, AS365N3	Observation and transport

Since the large-scale deployment of USAF forces in the mid-1990s to counter the threat of Iraqi attack, the Kuwaiti air force scaled back its air operations and allowed the USA to take the lead in air defence operations. During the run-up to the 2003 invasion of Iraq, the Kuwait air force was effectively grounded to clear the air space for US and British operations.

In the aftermath of the 2003 war and departure of US and British combat aircraft, the Kuwaitis have been required to increase their air defence operations. In 2008, Kuwaiti Hornets took part in Exercise Initial Look 08, run by the Bahraini air force.

Airbase infrastructure
Both of Kuwait's main air force bases, Ahmed Al Jaber and Ali Al Salem, were extensively damaged during 1991. Initially the returning Kuwaiti air force units

Kuwait Inventory as at 15 March 2009.

Type	Active	Stored	Ordered	Required
Al Quwwat al Jawwiya al Kuwaitiya (Kuwait Air Force)				
COMBAT AIRCRAFT				
F/A-18C/D	31:08:00			
Mirage F1BK/CK		3:08		
TRANSPORT				
L-100-30 Hercules	3			
C-130J/KC-130J				4:-2
DC-9/MD-83		2		
COMBAT HELICOPTER				
AH-64D	16			
AS532AF Cougar	3			
SA330H Puma	6			
SA342K Gazelle	12			
TRAINING AIRCRAFT				
Hawk 64	11			
Shorts Tucano	16			
Government of the State of Kuwait				
TRANSPORT				
747	1			
Gulfstream V/IV	3			
A300C	1			
A310	1			
A320	1			
Kuwait Police Air Wing				
HELICOPTERS				
EC-135T1	2			
SA-330H	1			
SA-342K Gazelle	4			
AS-365N3	2			

operated from Kuwait International airport until the late 1990s, when the airbases were operational again.

The hardened aircraft shelters at both airbases were all destroyed by USAF air strikes during the war, and they have not been repaired and put back into use. Ahmed Al Jaber remains the main fighter base, with training aircraft and helicopters

The F/A-18C/Ds delivered in the early 1990s are the core of Kuwait's air defence. (*Kuwaiti Air Force*)

The famous 'Free-Kuwait' A-4 Skyhawks were retired after the 1991 Gulf War. (*US DoD*)

based at Ali Al Salem. Kuwait International is the home of the air transport and VIP fleet.

Aircraft ordnance

The purchase of the Hornet was also accompanied with a package of precision-guided muntions, including AGM-65G Maverick TV/IR-guided air-launched missile, AGM-88 HARM anti-radar weapons, AGM-84 Harpoon anti-ship missiles, and AIM-9L heat-seeking and AIM-7F radar-guided air-to-air missiles.

Some guided weapons were purchased for the Mirage F.1 fleet in the 1970s and 1980s, including Magic air-to-air missiles and Amrat anti-radar missiles, but few are considered to be operational. A number of HOT wire-guided anti-tank missiles are available for the Gazelle helicopters.

Some 384 Lockheed Martin HELLFIRE missiles (including twenty-four training and fifty dummy missiles) were purchased for the Apache force.

In 2002, the USA approved the sale of eighty AIM-120C AMRAAMs, sixty AIM-120C Launch Rails, two Captive Air Training Missiles, flight test instrumentation, AMRAAM operational and training devices, missile containers, spare and repair parts, support and test equipment, publications and technical documentation, maintenance, pilot training, and other logistical support elements.

Strategic weapons

Kuwait has no offensive strategic weapons. It has taken delivery of four batteries of Raytheon Patriot anti-ballistic missile batteries in the 1990s, and discussions began with the USA in 2007 to purchase enhancements.

Procurement

Kuwait is targeted as an F/A-18E/F customer, and is expected to take twenty aircraft to replace half its fleet of C/Ds. The remainder would also receive a modest upgrade. Kuwait selected the AH-64D in late 1997, and the country signed a contract in October 2003 for sixteen aircraft and eight Longbow radars. The first aircraft was handed over in July 2005 and remained in the USA until early 2007 for trials and training activities. In February 2007, the first six AH-64Ds were delivered, and a further six were due for delivery during 2008. Four are expected to remain at Fort Hood in Texas for crew training purposes. The Mirage F1s are grounded awaiting sale. Kuwait was expected to sign a deal for four to six C-130Js, but has instead expressed interest in acquiring Russian transports or putting the three L-100-30s through an AMP process, and requested export approval for this from the USA in October 2007 in a deal potentially worth $250 million. Airborne early warning has been improved by the purchase of aerostats from the USA.

Presence of foreign forces

The US military still has a significant presence at Ali Al Salem airbase to provide logistic support for its occupation force in Iraq. This base is now an air transport hub for US C-130 transports and chartered civilian airliners bringing troops into the Middle East from bases in Europe and continental USA, before transloading into tactical transports for flights into Iraq. USAF Special Operations Command helicopters and AC-130 Spectre gunships continue to operate from the base. Kuwait International is also used by US flights, and the British also stage some flights through the airport. The 200 or so US and British tactical fighters that occupied Ahmed Al Jaber during Operation Iraqi Freedom were withdrawn during the summer of 2003, and the base is now used almost exclusively by the Kuwaitis.

US Army helicopter units continue to operate from a series of field bases in the north of Kuwait, around the Udairi range complex. Units arriving in the Middle East ahead of deployment to Iraq use the Kuwait facilities to assemble the helicopters and then conduct 'shake-down' training. A number of US Army helicopter units are also based in Kuwait with US Central Command's reserve brigade, ready to deploy into Iraq in time of crisis.

A small number of personnel from Boeing, Raytheon, Eurocopter and BAE Systems remain in Kuwait to help maintain their products in service with the country's air force.

Assessment

The Kuwaiti air force has limited combat capability because of its small size and vulnerable geography. Surrounded by large neighbours, little Kuwait's air force would soon be overwhelmed in a major war unless allied forces could quickly deploy to its assistance. This did not happen in 1990, with disastrous results. Nothing has really changed since then, so the Kuwaitis have remained firm allies of the USA and allowed American forces to remain based in their country.

CHAPTER NINE

Lebanon

Population	4 million
Military/paramilitary aircraft	41
Air Force personnel	1,000

Force Aerienne Libanaise/al Quwwat al Jawwiya al Lubananiya (Lebanese Air Force)

History

As a League of Nations mandate territory under French control, the Lebanon has a long history of co-operation with the French military. The Lebanese air force was formed in 1949 out of air units formed to support the French military command in the Levant. During the 1950s and 1960s, the Lebanese bought military aircraft from both France and Britain. In the 1970s, the fate of the small country appeared doomed as its larger neighbours – Syria and Israel – seemed destined to use Lebanon as a battlefield. From the mid-1970s through to 1990, the country was convulsed by civil war, followed by Israeli and Syrian intervention. The Lebanese armed forces split along religious and ethnic grounds, and for most of this period the air force was moribund.

Lebanon's years of strife are reflected in its combat fleet, delivered before the civil war erupted in the mid-1970s. Other equipment, predominately French helicopters, was received during the civil war, but this is now thought to be non-operational. As peace returned in the 1990s, the USA began military aid and donated twenty-four UH-1Hs in 2000, but relations became frosty soon afterwards and further US aid dried up. The stored Mirage IIIs were sold to Pakistan in 2000.

Lebanon's air force put up no resistance to Israeli attacks in 2006, and much of its airbase infrastructure was destroyed in air strikes. Israeli forces continue to operate in the country's airspace. Hizbullah guerrillas launched UAV missions over Israel during the fighting in July and August 2006.

Structure

The Lebanese air force reports to the Ministry of Defence. It consists of five squadrons, being the 10th and the 11th at Beirut airbase operating the UH-1, the 12th at Rayak airbase, operating some UH-1Hs on loan from Beirut airbase, the 14th at Kleyate airbase, also operating the UH-1H on loan from Beirut airbase, and the 15th at Rayak airbase, operating the R44 Raven.

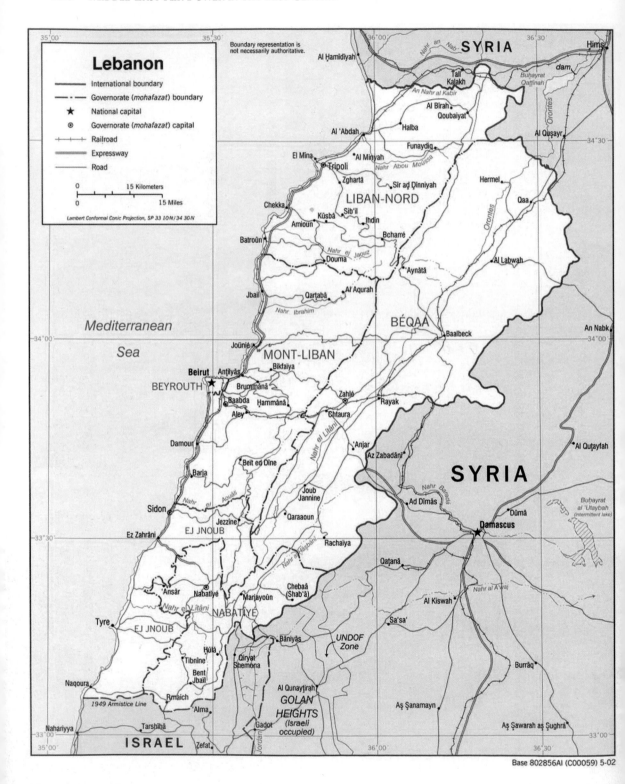

Base 802856AI (C00059) 5-02

Beirut International Airport *(Google Earth)*

Italian Army Bell 212s have served with UNIFIL on the Israeli border since the 1980s. *(UN Photo/John Isaac)*

Lebanese Air Arms Order of Battle, as at 1 May 2009.

Airbase	Location	Wing/Base Designation	Squadron	Aircraft Type	Role
Beirut International	33° 48′ N 35° 29′ E		10	UH-1H/AB212	Troop transport
			11	UH-1H/AB212	Troop transport
			??	Gazelle	Liaison/Gunship
Kleiat/Kleyate	34° 35′ N 36° 00′ E		14	UH-1H	Troop transport
Rayak	33° 51′ N 35° 59′ E		12	UH-1H	Troop Transport
			15	R-44	Training
Halat					
Foreign Forces					
Naqoura		UNIFIL	Italian Army Aviation Det	Bell 412?	Liaison/Medivac

Operational activity

The much reduced Lebanese air force is limited to SAR missions, as well as VIP transport. Syrian troops withdrew from Lebanon in March 2005. Israeli forces continue to operate in the country's airspace, mounting regular air strikes on bases claimed to be harbouring groups hostile to the Jewish state. The UH-1Hs received from the US Army have given good service but some have been cannibalised for spares after the USA restricted spares.

Much of Lebanon's infrastructure was devastated in Israeli air strikes during the summer of 2006. The country's main international airport was closed by Israeli bombing and an air exclusion zone enforced. A UN-brokered ceasefire will see a 15,000-strong international peacekeeping force deployed in the south of the country.

The ex-UAE Gazelle gunships were in use to support a Lebanese army operation against Palestinian militants in a refugee camp near the northern city of Tripoli in May and June 2007.

Airbase infrastructure

The former main operating base at Rayak in the Beka'a Valley is largely run down because it was in the heart of the Syrian occupation zone. Kleiat airport to the north of Beirut was the main operating base for the rump of the helicopter fleet during the 1980s. Following the peace agreements of the 1990s, Beirut International was rebuilt and has become the main operating base for the newly arrived Bell UH-1Hs.

Lebanon Inventory as at 1 May 2009.

Type	Active	Stored	Ordered	Required
Force Aérienne Libanaise/al Quwwat al Jawwiya al Lubananiya (Lebanese Air Force)				
COMBAT AIRCRAFT				
Hunter F70/T66C		5:2		
ISTAR				
Cessna 208			3	
RQ-11 UAV			3	
TRANSPORT				
Falcon 20	1			
COMBAT HELICOPTER				
UH-1H	23			
SA330L Puma		3	10	
SE3130 Alouette II		2		
SA316B Alouette III		6		
SA342L Gazelle	9	4		
AB212		7		
R-44	4			
TRAINING AIRCRAFT				
CM170 Magister		5		
Bulldog 126		5		
Government of Lebanon				
TRANSPORT				
HS 125	1			

Aircraft ordnance
Aircraft weaponry is limited to door-mounted machine-guns on some of the helicopter fleet.

Strategic weapons
Lebanon has no strategic weapons.

Procurement
Two R22s were purchased in January 2005, and two more were bought in December 2005. It is unclear how much of the air force's inventory survived the Israeli onslaught, but it means new procurement might be necessary to replace losses. To replace losses during the 2006 conflict, the UAE donated nine Gazelle light

helicopters. The UAE followed this in February 2009 with an offer of a further ten Pumas.

The most difficult procurement decision facing the Lebanese air force is the replacement of the Hunters. Three were returned to airworthiness in 2008, but their longer-term prospects are not good due to problems sourcing spares. Russia offered surplus MiG-29s; however, operating such a complex aircraft would be beyond the Lebanese air force's capabilities. It might also be considered provocative by the Israelis. Surplus UAE BAe Hawks are high on the wish list of Lebanese air force chiefs, and this might happen now that the UAE has selected new trainer aircraft. Italy is assisting in returning seven AB212s to service.

The USA agreed in early 2008 to supply three Aerovironment RQ-11 Raven UAVs and three ISTAR-equipped Cessna 208 Caravans.

German Navy Westland Sea King Mk 41s were a key element of the UN Maritime Task Force working off Lebanon in 2006. (*UN Photo/Jorge Aramburu*)

Presence of foreign forces

After the departure of the large Syrian military contingent during 2005, the only major overt foreign military force in the country is the United Nations Force in Lebanon (UNIFIL). The UN force has been in southern Lebanon since 1978, and boasts a small Italian Army Aviation unit, operating Agusta Bell 212 helicopters. In the aftermath of the Israeli onslaught of July and August 2006, an expanded UNIFIL force deployed, including French and Italian helicopter units.

Guerrilla forces

Hizbullah guerrilla fighters launched UAV missions over Israel in November 2004 and April 2005. The UAVs are believed to have been supplied by Iran. By early 2006, some eight Ababil UAVs had been deployed by Hizbullah in southern Lebanon.

Assessment

The Lebanese air force has faced crisis forces that would have destroyed many other air arms. It is clearly no match for the air power of neighbouring Syria and Israel. Through careful husbanding of aircraft, equipment and personnel, it has been able to rise again.

CHAPTER TEN

Oman

Population	3.4 million
Military/paramilitary aircraft	129
Air Force personnel	5,000

al Quwwat al Jawwiya al Sultanat Oman (Royal Air Force of Oman/RAFO)

History

Oman has a strategic position on the eastern fringe of the Arabian peninsula, dominating the southern side of the Straits of Hormuz and its vital oil tanker routes.

For most of the first half of the twentieth century the country was dominated by Britain, but gained its independence in 1959. British influence remained strong, and on 1 March 1959, the Sultanate of Muscat and Oman Air Force (SMOAF) was formed with British assistance. Its first aircraft were mainly for transport and liaison, and it did not gain combat aircraft until the late 1960s. In the 1970s it was renamed the Sultanate of Oman Air Force (SOAF), and two decades later become the Royal Air Force of Oman (RAFO).

In its first three decades, the Omani air force relied heavily on seconded British officers from the RAF or mercenary/contract personnel. The British company Airwork was heavily involved in keeping the SOAF's aircraft operational during the border war with Yemen in the early 1970s. British pilots flew combat missions during the conflict in Strikemaster attack jets, Skyvan transports and Bell 212 helicopters.

During the late 1970s, the Sultan of Oman began to increase his links with the USA as Cold War tension in the region increased after the Soviet invasion of Afghanistan in 1979. The USA was granted basing rights, and began to build up pre-positioned stocks of equipment and fund the improvement of airbase facilities. US aircraft and commandos used the Omani airbase on Masirah Island to launch their ill-fated rescue mission to Tehran in 1980. US and British aircraft operated from Omani bases during the Iran–Iraq War in the 1980s, the 1991 Gulf War, the invasion of Afghanistan in 2001 and Operation Iraqi Freedom in 2003.

Structure
The RAFO is a separate service, within the Omani armed services.

Operational activity

The RAFO air force has not been involved in major operational activity in recent years beyond routine air defence and search and rescue missions. It regularly participates in joint exercises with US, UK and French air forces. These have included Exercise Saif Sareea II (Swift Sword II) in 2001 and the annual Magic Carpet series of exercises with the RAF and UK naval aviation.

Co-operation with army units in the southern and western borders remain the main task of the helicopter force, along with search and rescue coverage.

The Jaguars have been brought up to the RAF's Jaguar 97 standard, and are expected to stay in service until the turn of the decade, suggesting that the F-16s will initially be for air defence only, alongside the Hawk 200s. Three of the Skyvans have been modified for coastal patrol and SAR duties.

Over the past twenty years a major programme of 'Omanisation' has been under way to recruit and train more Omani nationals to serve in the RAFO.

RAFO units and personnel joined relief efforts in June 2007 after Cyclone Guno struck Oman, causing widespread damage and the loss of more than thirty lives.

Airbase infrastructure

Oman's airbase infrastructure has been steadily improved over the past twenty-five years, thanks to extensive US support. Each base now boasts significant extra capability in terms of fuel storage, ramp space and taxi facilities to cope with a sudden influx of US or allied aircraft. As yet the RAFO has not hardened many of its facilities. The main transport hub for the RAFO is Seeb North airbase. The fighters operate from Masirah and Thumrait, while Salalah in the south is the main forward base for the helicopter force.

To enable the grow of civilian traffic to Seeb, the RAFO is building a new airbase 120 km west of the capital Muscat, called Al Musnana.

Only Masirah airbase is hardened, with six aircraft shelters.

Aircraft ordnance

The purchase of the Jaguars in the late 1970s resulted in the delivery of a small package of precision-guided munitions, including AS-30L laser-guided missiles, AM-39 Exocet anti-ship missiles and AIM-9P heat-seeking, guided air-to-air missiles. As a result of the upgrading of the Jaguars in the late 1990s, the RAFO was loaned a small number of GEC-Marconi Thermal Imaging and Laser Designation (TIALD) targeting pods by the RAF, and the first deliveries of Paveway laser-guided bombs took place. The USA donated 191 Mk 20 Rockeye cluster bombs in 1998.

The delivery of the F-16s is expected to see a quantum leap in the ordnance available to the RAFO. When the F-16 sale was announced in 2001, an application to Congress for export approval of a package of weapons was also made public. This included fourteen LANTIRN targeting pods, fourteen LANTIRN navigation pods with terrain-following radar, fifty AIM-120C AMRAAMs and ten AMRAAM training missiles, one hundred AIM-9M-8/9 Sidewinder missiles, ten Sidewinder training missiles, eighty AGM-65D/G

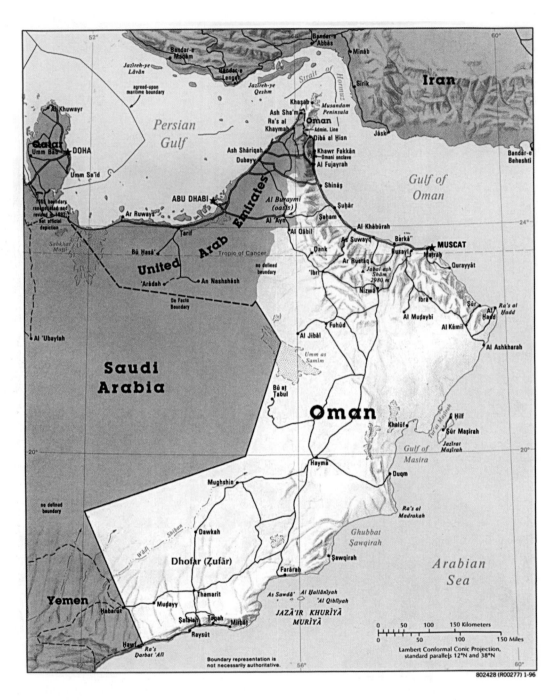

Maverick missiles, ten Maverick training missiles, twenty AGM-84D Harpoon air-launched anti-ship missiles, one hundred Enhanced GBU-10 and one hundred Enhanced GBU-12 Paveway II laser-guided bomb kits, eighty GBU 31/32 joint direct attack munitions, LANTIRN night-vision-goggle-compatible cockpits and associated support equipment

The following year an additional ordnance package was requested by the Omanis, including 50,000 20 mm high-explosive projectiles, 50,000 20 mm training projectiles, 300 Mk 82 500 lb general-purpose bombs, 200 Mk 83 1,000 lb general-purpose bombs, one hundred Enhanced GBU-12 Paveway II 500 lb laser-guided bomb kits, fifty GBU-31(v)3/B JDAMs, fifty CBU-97/105 sensor-fused weapons, 20,000 RR-170 self-protection chaff, 20,000 MJU-7B self-protection flares, support equipment, software development/integration, modification kits, spares and repair parts, flight test instrumentation, and technical support.

US-supplied F-16 Fighting Falcons have provided the RAFO with a true multi-role capability for the first time. *(Lockheed Martin)*

BAe Hawks have dual training and ground attack roles. *(BAE Systems)*

Oman Air Arms Order of Battle as at 1 May 2009.

Airbase	Location	Wing/Base Designation	Squadron	Aircraft Type	Role
Royal Air Force of Oman (RAFO) – al-Quwwat al-Jawwiya al-Sultanat Oman					
Masirah AFB (OOMA)	20° 40′ N 58° 53′ E	Sultan Qaboos Flying Academy	1	Super Mushshak, Scheibe SF-25 Motorfalke, PC-9(M)	Training
			6	Hawk 103, Hawk 203	Training/CAS
			15 Sqn SAR Det.	Lynx 300	Naval support/SAR
Seeb South AFB	23° 35′ N 58° 17′ E		2	SC7-3M-4022 (Skyvan & Seavan)	Transport
			4	BAC111-485GB, Airbus A320-214	VIP transport
			16	C-130H	Transport
Al Musanah	23° 38′ N 57° 28′ E		14	AB205, B212, HH-1H, AS332C, AS332L-1	Troop transport/SAR
			15	Lynx 300	Naval support/SAR
Salalah AFB	17° 02′ N 54° 05′ E		3	AB205, Bell 206B, Lynx 300	Troop transport/SAR
			5	SC7-3M-4022 (Skyvan)	Transport
Thumrayt AFB	17° 39′ N 54° 01′ E		8	Jaguar S/B	CAS/Strike
			20	Jaguar S/B	CAS/Strike
			18	F-16C/D	Air defence/ Strike
Khasab AFB (OOKB)	26° 10′ N 56° 14′ E		14 Sqn SAR Det.	HH-1H	SAR
Royal Oman Police – Directorate of Police Aviation					
Seeb	23° 35′ N 58° 17′ E				
Fixed wing Wing				CN235M-100, Do228-100	Transport
Helicopter Wing				Bell 205A-1, Bell 214ST, AW139	Transport/ Observation
Oman Royal Flight					
Seeb AFB (OOMS) Royal Flight				B747SP-27, G-IV, EC225, Puma	VIP transport

Oman Inventory as at 1 May 2009.

Type	Active	Stored	Ordered	Required
al Quwwat al Jawwiya al Sultanat Oman (Royal Air Force of Oman)				
COMBAT AIRCRAFT				
Eurofighter Typhoon				24
Jaguar S/Jaguar B	15:04	1		
Hawk 103/Hawk 203	4:11			
Hawk 115	1			
F-16C/D Blk 50	6:04	2		
TRANSPORT				
Skyvan 3M	7:-1	6		
One-Eleven 475	1	2		
C-130H	3			
A320 ACJ(VIP)	1	1		
COMBAT HELICOPTER				
Super Lynx 300	15			
Bell 212		2		
Bell 206B	3			
AB205A		13?		
NH90			20	
TRAINING AIRCRAFT				
PC-9M	12			
Super Mushshak	7			
AS202 Bravo	2			
Super Falke	2			
Oman Royal Flight				
TRANSPORT				
747SP	3			
Gulfstream IV	2			
AS330J Puma	3			
AS332C/L1	3			
ES225LP				
Royal Oman Police – Flight Operations				
TRANSPORT				
Dorner 228-100	1			
CN-235	2			
HELICOPTERS				
Bell 205A1	3			
Bell 206B	2			
Bell 214	4	4		
AB139	6		4	

SEPECAT Jaguar

Oman was the only Middle East country to purchase the Anglo-French Jaguar, and it has seen stalwart service with the RAFO. Since the UK and France retired their Jaguars from service, Oman and India are the remaining users of the multi-role combat aircraft. The RAFO is looking to replace the Jaguars with the Eurofighter Typhoon.

Crew: 1
Length: 55 ft 3 in. (16.83 m)
Wingspan: 28 ft 6 in. (8.69 m)
Height: 16 ft 1 in. (4.92 m)
Maximum take-off weight: 34,600 lb (15,700 kg)
Powerplant: Two Rolls-Royce/Turbomeca Adour Mk 102 turbofans, 7,305 lbf (32.5 kN) each
Maximum speed: Mach 1.6 (1,055 mph, 1,593 km/h)
Range: 335 miles combat, 2,190 miles ferry (535 km/3,525 km)

Armament
Guns: 2 × 30 mm (1.18 in.) ADEN cannon or DEFA cannon, 150 rounds/gun
Rockets: 8 × Matra rocket pods with 18 × SNEB 68 mm rockets each
Missiles: 2 × AIM-9 Sidewinders or Matra R550 Magics on overwing pylons (Jaguar International and RAF Jaguars only)
Bombs: 10,000 lb (4,540 kg) of payload on five external hardpoints, including a variety of bombs, reconnaissance pods (such as the Joint Reconnaissance-Pod), drop-tanks or the Anglo-French AS-37 Martel missiles

Twelve ALQ-211(V)4 Advanced Integrated Defense Electronic Warfare Systems for F-16s were ordered later in 2002 for $51 million, along with $42 million-worth of fifty smart bomb kits, one hundred GBU-12 Raytheon Paveway-series laser-guided bombs and fifty Textron Systems CBU-97 sensor-fused weapon anti-tank cluster bombs.

The Omanis also ordered two Goodrich DB-110, or two BAE Systems F-9120 pod reconnaissance systems for their F-16s. One Goodrich or one BAE Systems Exploitation ground station was also expected to be included in the package.

The veteran Jaguar is to be replaced by Eurofighter Typhoon aircraft. *(BAE Systems)*

Deliveries of NH-90 transport helicopters will transform the RAFO's rotary-wing force. *(EADS)*

Strategic weapons
Oman has no strategic weapons.

Procurement
In March 2001, it was announced that the air force would acquire twelve F-16C/Ds and sixteen armed Super Lynx 300s. The air force's first F-16 made its debut flight earlier in 2006, and deliveries are now complete under the $1.1 billion-plus deal. Super Lynx deliveries began in mid-2004. Oman ran a competition for up to fifty transport and SAR helicopters to replace its AB205s, AB212s and AB214s, and in 2004 selected twenty NH90s for delivery from 2008 after a first flight in 2007. Oman is viewed as a good prospect to become a C-130J customer.

The Skyvan and Hercules fleets will need to be replaced in the medium term. The RAFO has had talks with Alenia and Lockheed Martin to explore how their products could meet their airlift requirements.

The Omanis have a long-standing requirement to field a new generation of maritime patrol aircraft. It has looked at MPA variants of the CASA 295, ATR-72 and Dash-8. Cost factors have led the RAFO to look at a commercial service provider solution, that would involve Omani aircrew operating mission systems and sensors.

Details of contract negotiations over the sale of up to twenty-four surplus RAF Eurofighter Typhoon combat aircraft between the Omani and UK governments emerged in November 2008.

An initial agreement on the sale, worth up to £1.5 billion, was concluded in July 2008, and the Omanis are now moving to complete their internal approval processes, according to a senior UK defence industry source.

The aircraft are expected to be Tranche 1 aircraft Block 5 modified to conduct air-to-ground missions with precision-guided weapons, which will be transferred from the UK inventory early in the next decade.

The UK Ministry of Defence will in turn use the revenue from the sale of the aircraft to fund the purchase of Tranche 3 Typhoon aircraft.

It is unclear when the Omanis will receive their first aircraft, but it is not expected to be until the RAF starts to receive significant numbers of Tranche 2 aircraft in the 2011/12 period. A contingent of Omani pilots is expected to undergo training at RAF Coningsby in Lincolnshire ahead of the delivery.

The deal will be a 'government-to-government arrangements', and the newly formed defence export team in the UK Trade and Investment organisation have been representing the UK government. BAE Systems will be heavily involved in supporting the deal.

Presence of foreign forces
US aircraft made extensive use of Omani bases to support its invasion of Iraq during March and April 2003, reinforcing the Sultanate's defence links with Washington. US forces have recently scaled down their presence in the country.

Two Airbus A320s are replacing the ageing BAC 111s in the transport role. *(Airbus)*

Masirah Island is used extensively by US Navy P-3 Orion maritime patrol aircraft. Thumrait is used by British and US fast jets, including B-1B bombers, on training exercises because of close proximity to large bombing ranges. British Nimrod MR2 maritime patrol aircraft have operated from Seeb North airbase almost constantly since 1990, first to enforce UN trade sanctions against Iraq and then to support the US-led 'Global War on Terror' in the Middle East. In 2001 and on several occasions subsequently, RAF Canberra PR9s have operated out of Seeb to fly reconnaissance missions over Afghanistan. Royal Navy Agusta Westland Merlin HM.1 maritime patrol helicopters have operated from Seeb North airbase since the summer of 2006 to take over naval support roles from the RAF Nimrod force.

An upsurge in attacks against international shipping by Somali pirates in 2008 and into 2009 saw Oman's role as a logistic base for US, UK and international naval forces grow. Several navies positioned logistic support helicopters at Salalah airport to help sustain their naval forces operating off the Somali coast.

Assessment

Oman's small air force has the reputation of being the most highly trained and capable of Arab air forces. The Sultanate's strong links to the UK continue to this day, and the effort the Omanis put into keeping up to date with the latest tactical, technical and procedural developments is one of the main reason for its high level of expertise. The small size of the RAFO, however, means it has limited capability to participate in sustained operations without allied assistance.

Oman's strategic position along the south-eastern coast of the Arabian peninsula means it will continue to be courted by the USA and UK for many years. Airbases in Oman continue to play an important role in international operations in Iraq, Afghanistan and Somalia. For this reason, Oman is likely to have access to advanced combat aircraft and weapons from Western nations for many years to come.

CHAPTER ELEVEN

Qatar

Population	833,285
Military / paramilitary aircraft	39
Air Force personnel	1,500

Qatar Amiri Air Force

History

After gaining independence from Britain in 1971, this tiny Gulf state began building up its armed forces. It air force was formed in 1974 with British equipment, including Hawker Hunter jet fighters. As a result of increasing oil revenues during the 1980s, an expansion was undertaken, which included the purchase of British and French helicopters, followed by French Dassault Alpha Jet trainers and Mirage fighters.

Structure

The Qatar Amiri air force is a branch of the country's armed forces and reports direct to the Ministry of Defence.

The Qatari royal family and senior government leaders make use of the services of four VIP aircraft, including two AirbusA340s, an Airbus A320 and a Boeing 747SP. They are based at Doha IAP and are supported by the national airline. In 2003, the US government notified Congress that it wanted to sell one AN/AAQ-24(V) NEMESIS Directional Infra-red Countermeasures System. This was purchased for $61 million to protect the Amiri Flight's Boeing 747.

Operational activity

It now appears that the QAEF has decided to give up its air defence role and pass on responsibility of securing the country's air space to USAF units operating from Al Udeid airbase. This would result in the service concentrating on direct support for the army and navy with helicopters and light attack aircraft.

Air defence responsibilities have been taken over by US F-15E and F-16C/D aircraft based at Al Udeid. Beyond routine training flights, the Qatari fast jet fleet conducts little operational activity, and Qatari aircraft did not participate in Operation Desert Storm in 1991 or subsequent operations against Iraq. The helicopter and VIP transport fleets are in greater use for routine internal security and transport activities. The Alpha jets participated in an exercise in Oman in early 2007.

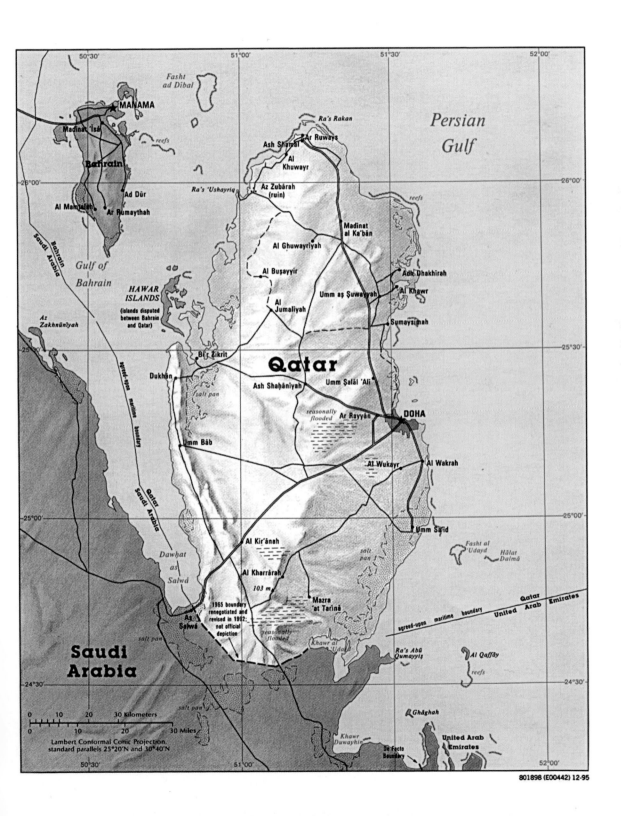

Qatari Air Arms Order of Battle as at 1 May 2009.

Airbase	Location	Wing/Base Designation	Squadron	Aircraft Type	Role	Hardened Shelters
Qatar Amiri Air Force						
Doha International	25° 15′ N 51° 33′ E	2nd Rotary Wing	6th Close Support	SA341L	Liaison/ Gunship	4
			8th Anti Surface Vessel	WS Commando 3	Naval support	
			9th Multirole	S Commando 2A, WS Commando 2C	Troop transport	
		Qatar Amiri Flight		B747SP-27, A310-304, A320-232, A319-133X, A340-211, B707-3P1C, B727-2P1, Falcon 900	VIP transport	
		1st Fighter Wing	7th Air Superiority	Mirage 2000-5DDA, Mirage 2000-5EDA	Air defence	
			11th Close Support	Alpha Jet	CAS	
Al Udeid airbase					Used by Coalition Forces	10
Al Ghariyeh airbase					FOB	

In early 2007, the Alpha Jet squadron participated in a Gulf Co-operation Council in Oman. The QAEF participated in air exercises with a US Navy carrier battlegroup in mid-2007.

Airbase infrastructure

All Qatari air units operate from Doha international airport. There is a small hardened shelter complex on the military side of the airport.

Maintenance activities are conducted from a hangar complex on the eastern side of the airport's main runway. A hardened aircraft shelter complex at the southern end of the main runway is occasionally used for quick-reaction-alert fighters. The rebuilding of Doha international airport is expected to force the QAEF to move out to Al Udeid. Al Udeid airbase has extensive infrastructure, including hardened aircraft shelters and command facilities. It was built in the late 1990s but was made available to the USA during the invasion of Afghanistan in 2001.

Qatar Inventory as at 1 May 2009.

Type	Active	Stored	Ordered	Required
Qarar Amiri Air Force				
COMBAT AIRCRAFT				
Mirage 2000-5EDA/DDA		10:1		
Alpha Jet	6			
COMBAT HELICOPTER				
Commando Mk3/2A/2C	8:3:1			
Gazelle	12			
NH-90				20
AW139			18	
TRANSPORT				
C-17			4	
C-130J-30			4	
Government of State of Qatar/Qatar Amiri Flight				
A340-200	2			
A319	1			
A320	1			
A310	1			
707-320	1			
727-200	1			
747SP	1			
Hawker 800XP	1			
Global Express	1			
Challenger 300	1			

Aircraft ordnance

The Mirage 2000 fleet was provided by France with a range of air-to-air missiles, including Matra R-530 heat-seeking guided missiles, R-550 Magic-2 radar-guided missiles and MICA-RF active guided missiles. AM-39 Exocet anti-ship missiles have also been purchased. There are reports that Qatar has also purchased MBDA Apache long-range cruise missiles and Amrat anti-radar missiles from France, but these have not been confirmed. The Gazelle helicopters are armed with HOT wire-guided anti-tank missiles.

Strategic weapons

Qatar has no strategic weapons.

Qatar's air force has long relied of French-supplied Mirages and Alpha Jets. After the 1991 Gulf War it replaced its Mirage F.1s with Mirage 2000EDA/DDAs. *(US DoD)*

In July 2008 Qatar ordered eighteen Agusta Westland AW139 utility helicopters. *(Agusta Westland)*

Qatar has ordered four C-17 Globemasters to boost the country's capability to conduct humanitarian operations. (*Author*)

The huge US presence at Al Udeid airbase in Qatar is clearly visible on commercial satellite imagery. (*Google Earth*)

Doha International airport is in the process of being redeveloped, which will result in the country's air forces having to relocate to Al Udeid airbase. The airport was used by US and Australian C-130s during the 2003 invasion of Iraq.

Procurement

Qatar is reviewing its training needs, and has further discussed a deal with BAE Systems – it previously selected the Hawk – although it could adopt a flying academy service agreement similar to that offered by BAE to Bahrain. The A340 of the Royal Flight is to receive BAE's Nemesis defensive aids system. Some twenty multi-role helicopters in the NH-90 class are reportedly required.

The Mirage fleet is grounded and up for sale. Pakistan and India are interested in buying the aircraft. The Alpha jets are also up for sale.

In 2008, the Qataris announced a major expansion of their airlift capability with the ordering of four Boeing C-17 Globemasters and four Lockheed Martin C-130J-30 Hercules. The latter deal is worth $393.6 million. The first C-17s are due to enter service in 2009, with the C-130Js later in the same year.

Presence of foreign forces

This small Gulf Emirate is home to a large US military presence of more than 10,000 personnel, including the forward headquarters of US Central Command (CENTCOM), which controls all US military activity in the Middle East, including the occupation of Iraq, as well as ongoing operations in Afghanistan and the Horn of Africa. The CENTCOM compound is a former industrial site on the outskirts of Doha city. Nearby is the Al Udeid airbase, which was built up by the USA after the start of the operation to topple the Taliban regime in Afghanistan in late 2001. This base has since been the home to a US Air Force air combat wing of around a hundred aircraft of various types. US, UK, Singapore and Australian air transport units use the base and Doha international airport was used as a hub to supply their troops in Iraq during 2003. British and US aircraft use Al Udeid for combat missions over Iraq and Afghanistan. The USAF's Middle East Combined Air Operations Centre (CAOC), which oversees all Coalition air operations in the region, is also at Al Udeid.

Assessment

The Qatari air force has very limited combat capability, and the Emirate's government seems to have little interest in making rapid changes to this situation. Support for international humanitarian operations is the main priority of Qatar defence policy.

CHAPTER TWELVE

Kingdom of Saudi Arabia

Population	28 million
Military/paramilitary aircraft	540
Air Force personnel	20,000
Air defence personnel	16,000

The Kingdom of Saudi Arabia is unique among Middle Eastern nations because it was never fully occupied by Turkish, British or French colonial forces during the first half of the twentieth century. As an absolute monarchy, political power resides in the Royal House of Saud, which has the distinction of being the 'Guardians' of Islam's holiest religious sites. Key members of the Saudi royal family lead the main government ministries, and as a result there are several ministries that have an interest in defence and internal security. Each of these 'power' ministries has control of its own military or paramilitary forces, and many of these are supported by their own air arms. This resulted in the Saudi air arms taking a very different course from those of other Arab air arms.

The Ministry of Defence and Aviation (MODA) is responsible for the Royal Saudi Air Force (RSAF), as well as the air arms of the Royal Saudi Land Forces (RSLF), Saudi Armed Forces Medical Services (SAFMS), Royal Saudi Naval Forces (RSNF) and the Royal Saudi Air Defence Forces (RSADF). This latter force is a separate military service, and it controls the country's surface-to-air missile batteries and ground radar network. The powerful Ministry of the Interior (MOI) controls police aviation and the Saudi Arabian National Guard, which has ambitions to develop a strong helicopter force. As befits an oil-rich kingdom, Saudi ministries all have their own VIP aircraft. Saudi Arabian Airlines VIP runs the Special Services Flight which flies senior government leaders and the royal family. The Ministry of Finance and Economy and the Saudi Embassy in Washington DC all have their own VIP flights.

Al Quwwat al Jawwioya as Sa'udiya (Royal Saudi Air Force)

History

The RSAF is one of the oldest Arab air forces and can trace its history back to 1950, when Britain helped train the first Saudi pilots. From 1952, US influence grew as the USAF established a large airbase at Dhahran, in eastern Saudi Arabia. During the 1960s, the RSAF began a major expansion programme as the kingdom's oil industry started to ramp up production. The first major deal for modern aircraft involved

Saudi Arabia

———	International boundary
———	Province (*minṭaqah*) boundary
★	National capital
◉	Province (*minṭaqah*) center
———	Railroad
———	Road
- - -	Track

0 100 200 300 Kilometers

0 100 200 300 Miles

Lambert Conformal Conic Projection, SP 14 N / 32 N

Base 802921AI (C00454) 1-03

Boundary representation is not necessarily authoritative.

the UK in the 1960s, which saw the delivery of English Electric Lightning and BAC Strikemaster jets. Large deals with the Americans followed in the 1960s and 1970s for the sale of Lockheed C-130 Hercules and Northrop F-5s.

The 1980s saw further deals with the Americans as Washington increasingly saw the kingdom as a bulwark against Iranian influence in the Gulf. During this period the US government overruled protests from the pro-Israeli lobby in Congress against selling Boeing E-3A Sentry AWACS radar aircraft and McDonnell Douglas F-15C Eagle fighters to allow the Saudis to protect their eastern oilfields from Iranian air attack. The Iran–Iraq War was at its height, and Saudi F-15s scored their first air-to-air kills against Iranian F-4s in mid-1980. The F-15 deal with the USA was followed by the Al Yamamah deal with the UK to supply the Panavia Tornado, BAe Hawk and Pilatus PC-9 trainer.

The 1990 Iraqi invasion of Kuwait prompted the Saudis to ask the USA, UK and other Coalition countries to deploy forces to protect their kingdom. RSAF aircraft participated in offensive operations against Iraq, with Tornados flying strike missions against Iraqi airbases. The F-15s again scored a number of air-to-air kills. In the immediate aftermath of the war, the Saudis ordered additional aircraft, missiles and other military equipment from the UK and USA.

Structure
The RSAF is deployed around the kingdom at seven main operating bases, each of which hosts a wing comprising several combat and support squadrons. The wing commanders are powerful figures in the service, and they are all senior members of the royal family. The main operational unit is the squadron. Central control of day-to-day operations is exercised from the MODA headquarters in Riyadh.

The 2007 deal to buy Eurofighter Typhoon aircraft from the UK will transform the RSAF's combat capabilities. The first Saudi Typhoon flew from BAE Systems' Warton plant on 20 October 2008. (*BAE Systems*)

Kingdom of Saudi Arabia Air Arms Order of Battle as at 1 May 2009.

Airbase	Location	Wing/Base Designation	Squadon	Aircraft Type	Role	Hardened Shelters
Royal Saudi Air Force						
King Khalid Military City	27° 54′ N 45° 31′ E	Wing 1			FOB	
Taif (King Fahd airbase)	21° 29′ N 40° 32′ E	Wing 2	No. 5	F-15C/D	Air defence	31
			No. 12 Det	AB212/412	SAR, Utility	
			No. 14	AB412/212	SAR, Utility	
			No. 17	F-5E/F, RF-5E	Ground attack, Recce	
			No. 34	F-15C/D	Air defence	
			No. 3	F-5A/B	Ground attack	
Dhahran (King Abdullah Aziz airbase)	26° 15′ N 50° 09′ E	Wing 3	No. 7	Tornado IDS	Strike	15
			No. 13	F-15C/D	Air defence	
			No. 75	Tornado IDS	Strike	
			No. 83+C39	Tornado IDS	Strike	
			No. 92	F-15S	Strike	
			No. 13	F-15C/D	Air defence	
			No. 44	AB412/212	SAR, Utility	
			No. 35	Jetstream	Training	
		Weapons & Tactics School	Test Squadron	??		
Riyadh AB port	24° 42′ N 46° 43′ E	Wing 4	No. 1 (Royal Flight)			VIP trans-
		King Faisal Air Academy	No. 8	Cessna 172	Training	
			No. 9	PC-9	Training	
			No. 22	PC-9	Training	
		Saudi Armed Forces Medical Services (SAFMS)				
Khamis Mushayt (King Khalid AB)	18° 18′ N 42° 48′ E	Wing 5	No. 6	F-15C/D	Air defence	20, 5 small
			No. 55	F-15S	Strike	
			No. 14 Det	AB412/212	SAR, Utility	
			No. 15	F-5E/F	Ground attack	
Al Karj (Prince Sultan AB)	24° 03′ N 47° 34′ E	Wing 6	No. 18	E-3A/KE-3A	AWACS, AAR	
			No. 19	RE-3A	RLINT	
			No. 32	KC-130H	AAR	
			No. 99	AS532A2	CSAR	

Airbase	Location	Wing/Base Designation	Squadon	Aircraft Type	Role	Hardened Shelters
Tabuk (King Faisal AB)	28° 21' N 36° 37' E	Wing 7	No. 2	F-15C/D? or F-5E/F?		15, 14 small
			No. 21	Hawk Mk65	Training	
			No. 79	Hawk Mk65	Training	
			No. 88	Hawk Mk65	Training	incorporates the "Saudi Hawks" (ex Green Falcons) Display Team.
Jeddah (Prince Abdullah AB)	21° 40' N 39° 09' E	Wing 8	No. 4	C-130E, C-130H, C-130H-30	Transport	
			No. 16	C-130E, C-130H	Transport	
King Khalid Military City – KKMC	27° 54' N 45° 31' E		No. 12	AB212/412EP+E69	SAR, Utility	5
Al Jouf						4
Nejran						12? Small
Hail						8

Royal Saudi Land Forces (RSLF)

Airbase	Location	Wing/Base Designation	Squadon	Aircraft Type	Role	Hardened Shelters
King Khalid Military City (KKMC) Hafr, Al Batin	27° 54' N 45° 31' E	RSLAF Aviation Command	1 Aviation Battalion	Bell 406CS, S-70A-1, VH-60L	Scout, Utility	
			2 Aviation Battalion	AH-64A	Attack	

Royal Saudi Naval Forces (RSNF)

Airbase	Location	Wing/Base Designation	Squadon	Aircraft Type	Role	Hardened Shelters
Jeddah - King Faisal naval base	21° 20' N 39° 10' E	RSNF Western Fleet	No. 62? No. 72?	SA365F AS332F-1		
Jubail - King Abdulaziz naval base	26° 56' N 49° 42' E	RSNF Eastern Fleet	??	SA365F		

Ministry of the Interior (MOI)/General Civil Defence/Administration

Airbase	Location	Wing/Base Designation	Squadon	Aircraft Type	Role	Hardened Shelters
Riyadh/ Dhahran/ Jeddah/ Adha		??	??	2 Dornier Do228-201 and 17 KV-107		

The RSAF has withdrawn its Tornado ADV air defence fighters from service ahead of the arrival of the first Typhoons in 2009. *(US DoD)*

A major upgrade of the RSAF Tornado IDS fleet will see it remain in service until *c.*2025. *(Author)*

The BAe Hawk remains the bedrock of the RSAF's training fleet. *(BAE Systems)*

The RSAF's F-15S fleet is in the process of receiving new engines. *(USAF)*

Operational context

The main task of the RSAF is to secure the kingdom's air space against foreign threats. At the Tauf, Khamis-Mushayt, Tabuk and Dhahran main operating bases, pairs of fighter aircraft are maintained around the clock on quick-reaction alert to intercept hostile or unidentified aircraft approaching the kingdom.

The security of the eastern oilfields is the RSAF's highest priority. The Dhahran airbase hosts two squadrons of F-15Cs and all the Tornado IDS strike force, as well as an F-15S squadron. Instability along the border with Yemen is a continuing worry to the Saudis, and strong forces are always deployed at Taif and Khamis Mushayt airbases in the south-west. Tabuk airbase in the north is a lower priority, and it only hosts a squadron of F-15C/D fighters and Hawk trainers. The AWACS, ELINT and tanker force is based at the former larger US airbase at Al Kharj, south-east of Riyadh.

The RSAF, which had not participated in combat operations since 1991, was sent into action to support the Saudi land incursion into Yemen in November and December 2009.

Operational activity

The air force has not been involved in ongoing counter-insurgency operations against Islamic rebels, with this task falling mainly to police and government helicopter units. F-15S aircraft participated in Red Flag exercises in the USA. A detachment of F-15s deployed to Tabuk in the north to deter the Iraqis during the 2003 US invasion of that country.

The F-15C fleet has been plagued by serviceability problems, which prompted a recent programme to repair and overhaul its engines. The F-5 fleet has largely been grounded since early 2004, and the Bell 206 fleet has also been retired. Both fleets are up for sale. Nine F-5E/Fs were sold to Brazil in a $24 million deal in December 2005. The Tornado ADV fleet was also withdrawn from service in 2006.

Air-to-air combat training is conducted on a Cubic-supplied Interim Training System Aid Combat Manoeuvering Instrumentation Range. This is used to support F-15 fighter pilot training, and the system's components include Cubic's GPS-based rangeless pods, ICADS debrief systems and test equipment.

Operational training is for the most part conducted within the Gulf region, but over the past decade the RSAF has staged a series of joint exercises with UK and US air forces. Eight Tornado IDS aircraft of No. 75 Squadron participated in the first major training exercise to take place outside the Middle East when they deployed to RAF Lossiemouth in the UK in August and September 2007. Hosted by No. 617 Squadron, RAF, this involved joint training with locally based Tornados, as well as Typhoons from No. 3 Squadron at Coningsby, and followed a visit made to Saudi Arabia by No. 617 Squadron in 2006.

RSAF F-15S squadrons have participated in Red Flag exercises in the United States on a number of occasions, including early in 2008. USAF F-15C squadrons have also visited the kingdom.

Saudi Arabia Inventory as at 22 February 2009.

Type	Active	Stored	Ordered	Required
Al Quwwat al-Jawwioya as Sa'udiya (Royal Saudi Air Force)				
COMBAT AIRCRAFT				
F-15C/D/S	61/30/70			
Tornado IDS/TSP	84			
Tornado ADV		22		
F-5E/B/F/RF-5E Tiger		32/17/21/14		
Typhoon			24	48
ISTAR/SPECIAL MISSION				
E-3A Sentry	5			
RE-3A	2			
TANKER				
KC-130H Hercules	7			
KE-3A	7			
A330-200			3	
TRANSPORT				
C-130E/H/H-30	7/28/2			
VC-130H	2:-1			
CN-235	4			
BAe 125-800	4			
Jetstar 8	2			
Learjet 25/35A	1:01			
Boeing 737	2:-1			
COMBAT HELICOPTER				
AB205	5			
AB212	24			
Bell 412TP/AB412TP	16			
AS532A2 Cougar MkII	12			20
AS61A	3			
TRAINING AIRCRAFT & HELICOPTER				
Hawk ADT				60
Hawk MK65/A	25/16			
PC-9	45			
Jetstream 31	1			
Cessna 172G/H/M		13		
Cessna 310	2	1		
Super Mushshak	7		13	
Fennec				30
AB206A JetRanger		21		

Type	Active	Stored	Ordered	Required
Royal Saudi Navy				
COMBAT HELICOPTER				
AS565SA Panther	20			12
AS532AL Cougar	12			
Royal Saudi Land Forces				
COMBAT HELICOPTER				
AH-64A	12			
AH-64D			12 upgrade	25
OH-58D	13			
UH-60	15			12 upgrade
UH-60L				24
Ministry Interior/Saudi Arabian National Guard (SANG)				
COMBAT HELICOPTERS				
S-92			16	
S-76			15	
Schweizer 434			9	
Saudi Arabian Airlines VIP/Special Services Flight				
TRANSPORT				
707	2:01			
747SP/747-3G1	3			
727	1			
MD-11	2			
TriStar	2			
L-100	4			
VC-130H	3			
Gulfstream II/III/IV	0:00			
Cessna Citation	2			
CL-604	1			
Saudi Government/Saudi Armed Forces Medical Services/General Civil Defence Administration				
TRANSPORT				
Gulfstream II/III/IV/V	1/5/1900			
Learjet	1			
C-212	2			
L100-30	3			
C-130H	4			
757-200	1			
DC-8	1			

Type	Active	Stored	Ordered	Required
HELICOPTER				
KV-107IIA	15			
SA365N	6			
S-70A	3			
Royal Embassy of Saudi Arabia				
TRANSPORT				
A340-200	1			
Ministry of Finance and Economy				
Boeing 737	1			

Airbase infrastructure

The Al Tauf, Khamis-Mushayt, Tabuk and Dhahran main operating bases are all fully hardened facilities with concrete-reinforced aircraft shelters, weapons stores and command posts. The RSAF's large aircraft are operated from Riyadh, Jiddah and Al Kharj, which have extensive support facilities.

A network of secondary bases has been built at Al Jouf, Ar'ar, Hafr Al Batin, As Sulayyil, Nejran and Hail to allow the dispersal of RSAF units away from their main bases in time of crisis and to host foreign forces. These bases have parking ramps, weapons stores and some hardened shelters.

Aircraft ordnance

The RSAF has a range of precision-guided ordnance for air-to-air and air-to-ground combat.

Air-to-air weapons include:

AIM-9J heat-seeking, guided missiles (F-15C/D/S, Tornado ADV/IDS, Hawk, F-5)

300 AIM-9M heat-seeking, guided missiles (F-15C/D/S, Tornado ADV/IDS, Hawk, F-5)

1,500 AIM-9L heat-seeking, guided missiles (F-15C/D/S, Tornado ADV/IDS, Hawk, F-5)

300 AIM-9S heat-seeking, guided missiles (F-15C/D/S, Tornado ADV/IDS, Hawk, F-5)

300 AIM-7F/M semi-active, radar-guided weapons (F-15C/D/S)

500 AIM-120C AMRAAM active, radar-guided weapons (F-15S)

Skyflash semi-active, radar-guided weapons (F-15 ADV)

Air-to-ground weapons include:

900 AGM-65D/G IR/TV guided, air-launched weapons (F-5, F-15S)
AGM-45 Shrike anti-radiation missiles (F-5, F-15S?)
700 GBI-10/12 Paveway laser-guided bombs (F-15S, Tornado IDS)
556 GBU-15 guided-bomb units (F-15S)
600 CBU-87 cluster-bomb units (F-15S)
JP-233 anti-runway weapons (Tornado IDS) (probably withdrawn from use)
ALARM anti-radar missiles (Tornado IDS)
Sea Eagles (Tornado IDS)

Some reports suggest the JP-233s were withdrawn from service in 1999 after the UK withdrew the weapon for use by the RAF. As a result the UK made a quantity of Paveway II LGBs available for use on the RSAF's Tornado IDS fleet. This would imply that the UK has sold Ferranti/BAE Systems' TIALD laser targeting pods to Saudi Arabia, although no public announcement of this sale has ever been made. It has also been reported that French-made targeting pods have been acquired for the Tornado force.

In 1992, the US sold LANTIRN target pods for the use of the F-15S fleet. This is the only publicly declared targeting pod in RSAF service. A sale of five Pathfinder/ Sharpshooter pods was requested in 1998 from the USA. A request was made to the US government in December 2007 to buy forty Lockheed Martin Sniper targeting pods worth $220 million.

The US Defence Security Co-operation Agency announced in January 2008 that Saudi Arabia had requested the sale of 900 satellite-guided Boeing Joint Attack Munitions worth $123 million, including 550 GBU-38 500 lb bombs, 250 GBU-31 2,000 lb bombs and 100 GBU-31 BLU-109 penetrator warhead variants. Later in 2008 the Saudis requested the purchase of 250 AIM-9X Sidewinders for $164 million.

Strategic weapons
Saudi Arabia has no nuclear or chemical weapons.

Procurement
The RSAF has ambitious plans to replace much of its equipment by the middle of the second decade of the century. Equipment that is not being replaced is to be upgraded and modernised.

The largest single air force procurement is expected to be the replacement of the F-5 and Tornado F3 fleets, with the Eurofighter Typhoon being selected in December 2005 under Project Rohan in co-operation with BAE Systems. Some seventy-two aircraft are envisaged being sold to the RSAF under the deal. A contract for the first twenty-four aircraft was signed in October 2007 under the newly named Project Salam. The initial phase of the contract for the first twenty-four aircraft, which are Tranche 2 standard, is thought to be worth some $3 billion. They are being diverted from the UK's order for Tranche 2 aircraft, and the first examples were delivered to Saudi Arabia in the summer of 2009. An initial cadre of pilots and ground crew are undergoing training in the UK to allow them to set up an operational conversion unit at Taif airbase. The follow-on phase of Project Salam envisages local assembly of the remaining forty-eight aircraft, possibly in partnership with the Alsalam Aircraft Company.

In July 2006, it emerged that France was also negotiating a €7 billion arms package that is focused on the procurement of some 140 helicopters, including 64 NH-90s (forty-two army, twelve Saudi Arabian National Guard, ten Navy), thirty Fennecs for the air force and twelve for the SANG, twenty Cougars for CSAR, twelve Panthers for naval SAR and twelve Tiger gunships for the SANG, with options for twenty-four to thirty-six more. This deal has yet to be concluded, and in 2008 it emerged that the Saudis had opened talks with Russian helicopter manufacturers on a package of Mil Mi-17 transport and Mi-35 attack helicopters worth more than $2 billion.

The RSAF has also been long interested in A330-200 tankers, and in October 2008 a contract was signed for three of the large aircraft. This is the first major contract with France for air force equipment, which had previously been a closed US and UK market. This defeated a bid by Boeing to sell tanker versions of 767 airliners. The Airbus tanker will be equipped with the EADS/CASA refuelling boom system to allow fuel to be passed to RSAF F-15 and E-3 aircraft, as well as under-wing hose-drogue refuelling pods. It is unclear when the aircraft will be delivered.

The European missile manufacturer MBDA is still negotiating the sale of a €1.5 billion plus order for weapons for the RSAF's Typhoon and Tornado fleets, including Meteor, Storm Shadow, Brimstone and ASRAAM missiles, and Paveway IV LGBs.

A mid-life upgrade or sustainment effort for the Tornado interdiction fleet, similar to the RAF's GR4 programme, is separate from the Project Salam deal, and three demonstrator aircraft began testing in the UK in April 2005 to kick off the Tornado Sustainment Programme (TSP). A further three aircraft arrived at Warton in December 2006. The establishment of an in-country deep depot-level maintenance facility for the Tornado fleet by BAE Systems and Alsalam Aircraft was seen as a precursor for the upgrade, which is to be complete in 2009. The first TSP aircraft began returning to Saudi Arabia from Warton in December 2007.

BAE Systems is prime contractor for the programme, with overall responsibility for delivering the entire contract, which includes aircraft, associated hardware, radar, communications, support, construction and manpower for the RSAF. In addition to direct in-country operational support, BAE Systems is also working on a sensor upgrade, which should result in Saudi Arabian Tornado IDS aircraft acquiring a target designator pod system such as LANTIRN or Sniper, as well as new weaponry, most probably including ASRAAMs, MBDA Storm Shadow stand-off missiles, Enhanced Paveway IV laser/GPS-guided bombs, and Brimstone air-to-surface missiles. Modification of aircraft is now under way, and the eight Tornado IDS aircraft that deployed to Lossiemouth for Exercise Saudi Green Flag in August and September 2007 had all been brought to TSP standard in Saudi Arabia.

Boeing and the USAF provide logistic support for the RSAF E-3A Sentry fleet, in co-operation with the Saudi aerospace industry. *(USAF)*

An additional project to conduct 'advanced maintenance' of the F-15 fleet is under way. The US Congress was notified in November 2006 that a $1.5 billion contract was being negotiated to replace the Pratt & Whitney F100-PW-229 engines of the F-15S fleet with a General Electric F1100-GE-129C engine. An initial $300 million contract for sixty-five engines was signed in October 2007 for delivery in 2008. In September 2008 an additional order was signed for ninety-one more engines. These two contracts, worth some $750 million, will allow the re-engining of all the F-15S fleet, but leaves a question mark over long-term serviceability of the F-15C/D fleet.

The capability of the E-3A AWACS fleet is being maintained after a $42 million contract was signed with Boeing in August 2008 to upgrade the RSAF aircraft's radars to the Radar System Improvement Programme (RSIP) standard. A $49.2 million contract was signed in September 2007 to install Link 16 data-links in the AWACS fleet. Some 165 Link 16 data-links are also to be purchased for the F-15s, to allow the fighters to automatically share information with the AWACS and ground-based command posts.

This site could also be used for work on AH-64s and C-130s. An $800 million AMP-style upgrade is being negotiated with the US government to modify fifty-four

Air-to-air refuelling of RSAF Cougar helicopters tasked for combat search and rescue. *(EADS)*

C-130E/Hs for the RSAF and other Saudi government agencies. Vector Aerospace's UK subsidiary, Sigma Aerospace, was named as preferred bidder in October 2006 to maintain the RSAF's C-130 fleet. Two Cessna 550s were delivered in October 2005 to replace Learjet 35s, and two more arrived in May 2006.

Saudi Arabia has a long pedigree of operating the Patriot missile system, so an upgrade of GEM- and PAC-3-class weapons must be a high priority for the RSADF, but as yet no indications have emerged of active negotiations with the US government or Raytheon.

Royal Saudi Land Forces (RSLF)

The Royal Saudi Land Forces control the army aviation element of the Saudi armed forces. They received their own aircraft in 1986 when the US Congress agreed the delivery of fifteen Bell 406CS Combat Scouts, which were eventually delivered in the second half of 1990. Earlier that same year the RSLAF received thirteen S-70A Black Hawks. The RSLF received twelve Boeing AH-64A Apaches in 1993.

The force is concentrated at King Khalid Military City in the north-east of the country. Some of the helicopters participated in the 1991 offensive to liberate

Kuwait from Iraqi forces. The 406CS are armed with TOW-II wire-guided anti-tank missiles, and the Apaches have Hellfire laser-guided anti-tank missiles and 2.75-inch rockets,

During 2006, US Congress had been notified of Saudi interest in upgrading twelve land-forces Apaches to D model under a $400 million project, with options of twenty-five new-build aircraft. Some twenty-four new UH-60Ls were requested at a cost of $350 million, and twelve UH-60As could be upgraded.

The RSLF was expected to receive some aircraft from the major helicopter package that was being negotiated with the French earlier this decade, but this seems to have fallen through. In September 2008, the Saudis made another request to Washington to upgrade their AH-64As to D Block II standard under a $598 million deal.

Saudi Armed Forces Medical Services (SAFMS)

A portion of the C-130 fleet is allocated to the SAFMS, configured as air ambulances. It also has its own fleet of ambulance helicopters.

Royal Saudi Naval Forces (RSNF)

The Saudi naval forces have a small helicopter contingent that is assigned to operate from frigates or conduct anti-surface operations from shore bases. It operates from Jubail on the east coast and Jiddah on the Red Sea. The first of twenty-four anti-submarine ASW-equipped SA365F Dauphins were delivered in 1985. These were augmented in the early 1990s by twelve AS332F-1 Super Pumas. The navy is looking to buy up a fleet of fixed-wing MPAs and twelve Panthers for naval SAR (as part of the large package of helicopters being negotiated with France mentioned above). The RSNF's current helicopters are armed with AS-15 and AS-30L air-launched missiles The twenty AS33s were upgraded with new navigation equipment between 2005-07 at Marignane in France and Jeddah naval base.

Royal Saudi Air Defence Force (RSADF)

History

The RSADF was formed in 1984 to oversee all of Saudi Arabia's ground-based air defence infrastructure and weapons, which include gun systems, self-propelled short-range missile systems, and medium- and high-altitude missile systems. The purchase of Patriot missile systems from the USA in 1990 gave the RASDF a strategic defence mission against Iraqi, Iranian and Israeli ballistic missile systems and long-range cruise missile threats.

Structure

To support this complex array of weapons, the RSADF has an Air Defense Operations Center (ADOC) located in each of the six group commands, which is in turn linked to the main air defence command centre in Riyadh. The estimated strength of the RSADF is 16,000 personnel.

The gun systems within the RSADF are used in support of manoeuvre units and other air defence operations as deemed necessary. Close-in, as well as medium-range, systems can be found within all group commands.

The RSADF deploys sixteen batteries with I-Hawk III SAMs (128 launchers), and it is also equipped with the French Crotale SAM system, possessing sixteen acquisition units and forty-eight firing units. In addition, the RSADF deploys Anti-Aircraft Artillery (AAA) pieces. Raytheon Patriot SAMs form part of the kingdom's theatre anti-ballistic-missile defences, although the exact numbers in service are unclear.

One of the most important elements in the Saudi air defence network is the $8.4 billion 'Peace Shield' system. Completed in 1995, it comprises seventeen AN/FPS-117(V)3 long-range, 3-D radar systems linked to AN/TPS-43 and AN/TPS-72 short- and medium-range radars. Each major airbase has a sector operations centre, and the system integrates the RSAF's E-3A Sentry AWACS aircraft, as well as air defence fighters, SAM batteries and some AAA pieces.

Until 2004, the RSADF shared its headquarters with the RSLF. However, a modern headquarters facility was built in Riyadh, and this allowed it to move out. The Air Defense Operations Center underwent modifications in 2002/3 that will allow it to integrate all air defence assets under one command and control system. Completion of this effort was achieved during 2003 after final certification and acceptance tests were successfully completed.

There are six major RSADF operational group commands:

- 1st Group in Riyadh
- 2nd Group in Jeddah
- 3rd Group in Tabuk
- 4th Group in Khamis Mushayt
- 5th Group in Dhahran
- 6th Group at Hafar Al-Batin (King Khalid Military City)

The bulk of the Patriot force is deployed with the 5th Group to protect oil infrastructure in the Eastern Province and with the 1st Group to protect the capital.

Activity
The RASDF has not yet fired any weapons in anger. It conducts regular training with US forces and local Gulf Co-operation Council allies.

Training and support
The RSADF has several vital locations and facilities that are instrumental in providing training and education for all their soldiers and officers who successfully make it into the ranks of the Royal Saudi Air Defence Forces. The headquarters, located in Riyadh, provides the operational and logistical planning and co-ordination support for the six group commands, which are similarly aligned with the air defence

The Royal Saudi Land Forces have their own fleet of armed attack and scout helicopters, including OH-58Ds. *(US DoD)*

sectors that are in the kingdom. It is also the location of the staff college that trains field-grade officers in staff operations. Jeddah is the home of the Air Defence Forces Institute (ADFI), the Maintenance and Technical Support Depot, and the location for all RSADF initial entrance and weapon systems training. It is at the ADFI that the officer basic course and the officer advance course are taught to the company-grade officers. The ADFI is also the location of the RSADF military college. The college opened in 2002.

The Maintenance and Technical Support Depot is a multi-million-dollar high- to medium- range air defence (HIMAD) missile inspection facility that enables the RSADF to inspect Patriot missiles in the kingdom, precluding the requirement to send them back to the USA. This offers a tremendous saving of millions of dollars to the RSADF.

Strategic weapons
The RSADF is also understood to control the strategic CSS-2 surface-to-surface ballistic missiles that were obtained from China in the 1980s. These missiles are based at remote desert sites at As Sulayyil and Al Jouffer, south of Riydadh. The current operational status of these weapons is unclear.

Procurement
The Saudis bought two batches of Patriot equipment and missiles. The first batch was ordered in September 1990 just after Iraqi forces invaded Kuwait. The export application to Congress included the purchase of forty-eight launchers and 384 missiles in a package worth some $984 million, although some reports suggest only eight launchers, or two batteries' worth, were actually delivered. In December 1992, a second order for a further thirteen launcher units and 761 PAC-2 missiles was placed for $1.03 billion. This would suggest that the RSADF has the capability to establish Patriot firing sites to protect between ten and twelve locations. Commercial satellite imagery from 2007 located two Saudi Patriot battery sites near Riyadh and six in Eastern Province.

In June 2000, Raytheon was awarded a $300 million training and support contract for the Saudi Patriot force, followed in October 2007 by a $100 million support contract. From 1991 through to 2003, the US Army maintained a Patriot task force in Saudi Arabia, and the US Army and RSADF continue to maintain close links, via a training and advisory team that remains in the kingdom. An upgrade of the Saudi Patriot systems to GEM and PAC-3 standard has long been on the agenda, but so far little has appeared in the public domain about the progress of discussions between the kingdom and the USA over air defence upgrade.

Ministry of the Interior (MOI)

Saudi Arabian National Guard (SANG)
The SANG is the premier internal security/paramilitary force in the kingdom. It operates independently of the military. It has ambitions to build up its own fleet, including twelve NH-90 troop transport helicopters, twelve Tiger gunships for the SANG, with options for twenty-four to thirty-six more. This is part of the large package of helicopters being negotiated with France mentioned above. In November 2007, the MOI placed orders with Sikorsky for sixteen S-92 medium-lift and fifteen S-76 light utility/observation helicopters, as well as nine Schweizer 434 light helicopters. These helicopters are to be used for medical evacuation, emergency/ disaster response and traffic surveillance.

Saudi Police/General Civil Defence Administration
The Saudi police use a number of surveillance and liaison helicopters. These have been used extensively in operations against Islamic extremists. KV-107IIAs were used in 2004 to fly élite counter-terrorist teams to assault compounds in Dhahran that had been seized by extremists.

Saudi Arabian Airlines VIP/Special Services Flight

The state-owned airline, Saudia, has a specialised division that operates VIP aircraft on behalf of the royal family and government ministries. Three of its Boeing 747s are to receive BAE's Nemesis defensive aids system under a $20 million deal authorised in 2003

The Ministry of Finance and Economy and the Saudi Embassy in Washington DC have their own VIP aircraft.

Presence of foreign forces

Saudi Arabia allowed US and British aircraft to operate from its bases during Operation Iraqi Freedom in March and April 2003. The USA and UK withdrew their air forces from the kingdom in the summer of 2003, but the USA left pre-positioned equipment behind when it relocated its forces from Al Kharj and Riyadh to Al Udeid in Qatar.

The USA has a United States Military Training Mission (USMTM), which maintains a headquarters at Eskan Village in Riyadh.

The main US, UK and French defence manufacturers maintain large support operations in the kingdom. BAE Systems has some 5,000 employees in the kingdom, of whom around half are expatriates. Lockheed Martin, Boeing and Raytheon all maintain teams in the kingdom to support their products.

Assessment

Saudi Arabian air power is a major factor in the military balance in the Middle East. The RSAF is one of the region's big five air forces, alongside the Egyptian, Israeli, Iranian, Turkish and UAE air forces, in terms of numbers, training and modern equipment.

Ambitious plans to build 4th-generation Eurofighter Typhoon aircraft and a package of modern airborne ordnance could transform the RSAF into the Arab world's most powerful air force.

The main problem facing oil-rich Saudi Arabia's military is the quality and quantity of its human resources. Only if sufficient personnel can be trained can the RSAF's plans achieve their full potential.

CHAPTER THIRTEEN

Syria

Population	20 million
Military/paramilitary aircraft	1,100
Air Force personnel	30,000
Air defence personnel	54,000

History

The Syrian Arab Republic once possessed one of the most powerful air forces in the Arab world. The Syrian air force was established in the years after World War Two when Syria gained its independence from France. Syrian air force units were in the forefront of wars with Israel in 1948, 1967 and 1973. Syria's air force has a history of political involvement in the country's government.

The confrontation in Lebanon in 1982 dealt a severe blow to the Syrian air force and Air Defence Command, with more than a hundred aircraft and scores of air defence missile batteries being lost. Political and economic isolation over the past twenty years have all weakened the country's armed forces, particularly its air and air defence forces.

Syria remains in a state of war with Israel. Although a ceasefire was agreed between the two countries after the 1973 October War, tension remains high, and the Syrian military is on a permanent war footing. It is one of the few Arab countries to continue to rely on conscription to provide manpower for its armed forces. Commercial satellite imagery of Syrian military bases, even ones deep in the interior of the country, show they are all ringed by defensive positions, bunkers and anti-aircraft gun pits, really to repel any Israeli raids.

The main bone of contention between Tel Aviv and Damascus is the status of the Golan Heights mountain range that provides a natural line of defence for whoever controls it. For the Israelis, holding the Golan prevents a surprise offensive against the Galilee region, while the Syrians see it as a barrier that could protect their capital, Damascus. Israel has annexed the Golan and built civilian farming settlements on it. This has enraged the Syrians, who see the Golan as occupied Arab territory. Since the late 1970s, the rivalry between the two Middle East military giants has been played out in Lebanon, with both sides using covert groups to try to gain influence in the country.

Several attempts to broker a peace deal between the Israelis and Syrians have yet to come to fruition.

al Quwwat al Jawwiya al Arabiya Assouriya (Syrian Arab Air Force)

Structure

Soviet-era influences remain strong in both the Syrian Arab Air Force and the Air Defence Command, reflecting the key role the Soviet armed forces played in their modernisation and expansion in the 1960s and 1970s. This Soviet-style centralised command structure remains in place today.

Air operations are closely controlled from the ground, and a great deal of effort is put into integrating them with anti-aircraft missile batteries.

A main air and air defence command post in the Damascus region is thought to be the nerve centre of Syrian air operations.

Operational context

The main emphasis of the air force is on air defence, in co-operation with the Air Defence Command. The Syrian air force has had little experience of offensive strike and close air support operations. Co-operation with land forces is the main preserve of the air force's helicopter units, and its armed Gazelle and Mi-24 helicopters are based in the Damascus region, ready to intervene if Israeli tanks start to move across the Golan.

Soviet-supplied MiG-23s are still in service with the Syrian air force in large numbers. *(IDF Spokesman)*

Syrian Air Arms Order of Battle as at 1 May 2009.

Airbase	Locations	Hardened Shelters	Squadron	Aircraft Type	Role
Syrian Air Force					
Tiyas	34° 31' N 37° 37' E	37	1 Squadron	MiG-25	Air defence
Tiyas	34° 31' N 37° 37' E		5 Squadron	MiG-25	Air defence
Shayrat	34° 29' N 36° 54' E	21?	7 Squadron	MiG-25	Air defence
Deir Zzor / Kameshli	35° 17' N 40° 10' E	1 × HAS Complex	8 Squadron	MiG-21	Air defence
Dumayr	33° 36' N 36° 44' E	24, 11 revetments	9 Squadron	MiG-25	Air defence
Dumayr	33° 36' N 36° 44' E		?? Squadron	MiG-23ML	Strike
Dumayr	33° 36' N 36° 44' E		?? Squadron	Su-22M-2	CAS
Jirah	36° 05' N 37° 56' E	9, 7 revetments	10 Squadron	MiG-21	Air defence
Jirah	36° 05' N 37° 56' E		?? Squadron	L-39	Training
Tabqa	35° 45' N 38° 34' E	2 × HAS complex	12 Squadron	MiG-21	Air defence
Tabqa	35° 45' N 38° 34' E		Base Flight 12 Bde	Mi-8	Troop transport
Marj Ruhayyil	33° 17' N 36° 27' E	16, tunnel complex with 4 x entrances	54 Squadron	MiG-23	Strike
Marj Ruhayyil	33° 17' N 36° 27' E		77 Squadron	MiG-23	Strike
Dimashq-Mezze	33° 28' N 36° 13' E	17	565 Squadron	Yak-40	VIP transport
Dimashq-Mezze	33° 28' N 36° 13' E		575 Squadron	Falcon 20	VIP transport
Dimashq-International	33° 24' N 36° 30' E	12	585 Squadron	Tu-134, Boeing 737	VIP transport
Shayrat	34° 29' N 36° 54' E		675 Squadron	MiG-23	Strike
Shayrat	34° 29' N 36° 54' E		677 Squadron	Su-22	CAS
Abu ad Duhor	35° 43' N 37° 06' E	13	678 Squadron	MiG-23	Strike
Hamah	35° 07' N 36° 42' E	2 HAS Complex	679 Squadron	MiG-21	Air defence
Hamah	35° 07' N 36° 42' E		680 Squadron	MiG-21	Air defence
Hamah	35° 07' N 36° 42' E		?? Sqn	MiG-29	Air defence
Shayrat	34° 29' N 36° 54' E		685 Squadron	Su-22	CAS
An Nasiriya	33° 55' N 36° 51' E	14	695 Squadron	MiG-23	Strike
Saiqal (Tsaykal)	33° 40' N 37° 12' E	3 or 4 HAS complex	697 Squadron	MiG-29	Air defence
Saiqal (Tsaykal)	33° 40' N 37° 12' E		698 Squadron??+ R[-22]C	MiG-29	Air defence
An Nasiriya	33° 55' N 36° 51' E		698 Squadron	MiG-23	Strike
Saiqal (Tsaykal)	33° 40' N 37° 12' E		699 Squadron	MiG-29	Air defence
Tiyas	34° 31' N 37° 37' E		819 Squadron	Su-24M-4	Strike
Al Qusayr	34° 34' N 36° 34' E	3 × HAS complex	825 Squadron	MiG-21	Air defence
Al Qusayr	34° 34' N 36° 34' E		826 Squadron	Su-27?	Air defence
Tiyas	34° 31' N 37° 37' E		827 Squadron	Su-24MK	Strike
Khalkhalah	33° 03' N 36° 33' E	2 HAS Complex	945 Squadron	MiG-21	Air defence

Airbase	Locations	Hardened Shelters	Squadron	Aircraft Type	Role
Khalkhalah	33° 03′ N 36° 33′ E		946 Squadron	MiG-21	Air defence
Minakh	36° 31′ N 37° 02′ E		4 FTS	Mi-8, Mi-2, MBB-233 Flamingo	Training
Alfis	35° 58′ N 36° 46′ E		253 Squadron	Mi-8	Troop transport
Alfis	35° 58′ N 36° 46′ E		255 Squadron	Mi-8	Troop transport
Marj As Sultan	33° 29′ N 36° 28′ E		525 Squadron	Mi-8	Troop transport
Marj As Sultan	33° 29′ N 36° 28′ E		537 Squadron	Mi-2/8	Troop transport
Qadr as Sitt	33° 30′ N 36° 28′ E		532 Squadron	Mi-8	Troop transport
Es Suweidaya	32° 42′ N 36° 24′ E	8	765 Squadron	Mi-24	Attack
Es Suweidaya	32° 42′ N 36° 24′ E		766 Squadron	Mi-24	Attack
Marj Ruhayyil	33° 17′ N 36° 27′ E		767 Squadron	Mi-24	Attack
Dimashq-Mezze	33° 28′ N 36° 13′ E		909 Squadron	Mi-8	Troop transport
Dimashq-Mezze	33° 28′ N 36° 13′ E		976 Squadron	Gazelle	Scout/Anti-Armour
Dimashq-Mezze	33° 28′ N 36° 13′ E		977 Squadron	Gazelle	Scout/Anti-Armour
Dimashq-Mezze	33° 28′ N 36° 13′ E		?? Squadron	Mi-8	Troop transport
Abu ad Duhor	35° 43′ N 37° 06′ E		2 Squadron	L-39OZ	Training
Abu ad Duhor	35° 43′ N 37° 06′ E		?? Sqn	L-39OZ	Training
Rasin el Aboud	36° 11′ N 37° 34′ E	2 HAS complex	3 FTS	L-39, MBB-233 Flamingo	Training
Dimashq-Mezze	33° 28′ N 36° 13′ E		522 Squadron	An-24/An-26/Il-76	Transport
Nayrab-Aleppo	36° 10′ N 37° 13′ E	7	?? Squadron	Mi-8	Troop transport
			?? Squadron	Mi-8	Troop transport
Tudmor/Palmyia		1 × HAS complex			

Syrian Navy

| Latakia | 35° 24′ N 35° 56′ E | | 618 Squadron | | |

The veteran MiG-17s are used for pilot training by the Syrians. *(IDF Spokesman)*

Israeli F-15 units boast numerous kill markings for Syrian aircraft claimed over sixty years of conflict. *(Author)*

Iranian air force personnel are now reported to be helping train the Syrian air force, and joint training exercises have been undertaken. A memorandum of understanding for defence co-operation was signed in Tehran on 16 June 2006 between Iran's Minister of Defence and Armed Forces Logistics, Sardar Sartiph Mostafa Mohammad Najjar, and his Syrian counterpart, Hassan Ali Turkmani. In a preliminary round of talks before the 16 June MoU, the Islamic Republic of Iran Air Force commander, General Karim Quami, and the Syrian Armed Forces Chief of Staff, General Ali Habib, also agreed on combined air exercises, including IRAIF pilots training in Syria on Syrian air force platforms to familiarise themselves with the regional topography.

Operational activity

Reports have emerged of Syrian pilots participating in training exercises in Iran, and this would allow them to benefit from the Iranians' experience, particularly in strike and close air support. Also, the Iranians closely monitor US air operations over Iraq and Afghanistan, and they are likely to pass on details of these operations to Damascus.

However, the Syrians are considered one of the most able operators of Soviet-era air defence systems, and they are reported to be very skilled at protecting their

The Israelis have seized a MiG-23 flown to the Jewish state by a defector from the Syrian air force. *(IDF spokesman)*

systems from Israeli attack. Strict emission control is one way for the Syrians to preserve their resources until absolutely necessary. This would account for them not being willing to engage small numbers of Israeli aircraft that penetrate their airspace, such as the group that bombed the alleged nuclear reactor in north-east Syria in September 2007. It was noteworthy that a Syrian Air Defence Command unit failed to destroy any of the Israeli aircraft carrying out a strike against an alleged terrorist camp in Syria on 5 October 2003. IAF F-16D Fighting Falcons, accompanied by four F-15 Eagle air superiority fighters, delivered an undisclosed number of precision-guided munitions at the Ein Saheb camp, fifteen kilometres north-west of Damascus, destroying ten buildings. The IAF aircraft launched stand-off munitions from Lebanese airspace without entering Syrian airspace. It is highly likely that the IAF used electronic warfare capabilities to jam the fire-control radars of Syrian missile batteries deployed in the area and rendered them inoperable.

Israeli media reports suggest that Syrian fighters and Mi-24s regularly patrol the Golan region. At least one MiG-21 crashed in this region in October 2007. The SAAF carries out regular training but shortage of spares means the pilot flight time is significantly less than in the 1980s.

Syria withdrew its integrated air defence system and early warning network from eastern Lebanon in the spring of 2005. Israeli aircraft overflew Syria ahead of the outbreak of fighting in Lebanon in July 2005, prompting return fire by the country's air defence network, but Syrian forces were not drawn into the conflict.

Lack of spares is believed to have resulted in widespread unserviceablity across the fleet.

Airbase infrastructure

Syrian airbases are all hardened against surprise attack, with extensive provision of hardened aircraft shelters, protected ammunition storage sites and underground command posts. Gun and missile anti-aircraft batteries are deployed at all airbases. Trenches and other field fortifications are common to defend against Israeli aircraft and heli-borne commando assaults. Main operating bases are at Aleppo, Palmiyra, Mansorah, Aabadani, Hama, Te Kuzek, Saikal, Damascus, Katana, Sanamin, Latakia and Tartus (naval helicopters).

Aircraft ordnance

The Soviet Union was the main source of all Syrian aircraft, and it also supplied a wide range of aircraft ordnance:

Precision-guided munitions

- 9M17 (AT-2 'Swatter') wire-guided anti-tank missiles
- Kh-23 (AS-7 'Kerry') radio-command-guided missiles (10 km)
- HOT wire-guided anti-tank missiles
- Kh-25ML (AS-10 'Karen') laser/radio-guided air-launched missiles (10 km)
- Kh-25MT (AS-12 'Kegler') TV-guided air-launched missiles (10 km)

Syrian Inventory 1 May 2009.

Type	Active	Stored	Ordered	Required
al Quwwat al Jawwiya al Arabiya Assouriya (Syrian Air Force)				
COMBAT AIRCRAFT				
MiG-23BN/UM	60/6			
MiG-23MF/ML/MS	80			
MiG-25PD/RB/PU	8/30/2002			
MiG-21PF/MF/bis/U/UM	159/20/40			
MiG-29A/UB	84			
Su-27	14			
Su-22M/U	90/6			
Su-24MK	20			
TRANSPORT				
An-26	7			
IL-76M/T	4			
Tu-134B-3	2			
Yak-40	6			
Falcon 20F	2			
Falcon 900	1			
COMBAT HELICOPTER				
SA342L Gazelle	55			
Mi-24	36			
Mi-8/17	100			
Mi-6	10+			
Mi-2	20			
TRAINING AIRCRAFT				
L-39ZA/ZO	43/55			
MiG-17F	30			
L-29	40			
MBB Flamingo	48			
MiG-15UTI	15			
Mushshak	6			
PA-31 Navajo	1			
Navy				
Mi-14		20		
Ka-25		5		

The MiG-23 has proved outclassed by the F-16s in Israeli service. *(IDF Spokesman)*

Suppression of enemy air defence weapons

- Kh-24 (AS-7 'Kerry')
- Kh-28 (AS-9 'Kyle')
- Kh-25MP (AS-12 'Kegler')

Air-to-air missiles

- R-13 (AA-2 'Atoll') heat-seeking guided missiles
- R-40 (AA-6 'Acrid') semi-active or heat-seeking guided missiles
- R-23/24 (AA-7 'Apex') semi-active guided missiles
- R-60 (AA-8 'Aphid') heat-seeking guided missiles
- R-27R/T (AA-10 'Alamo') semi-active or heat-seeking guided missiles

Strategic weapons

Syria is believed to have developed an advanced chemical weapon capability, which is held in strategic reserve to deter any Israeli nuclear or chemical strike. The main delivery means for these chemical weapons are long- and medium-range ballistic missiles.

Procurement

No major arms procurement has taken place since April 2000, when Syria closed a $2 billion deal for Russian military equipment, but it is unclear what was actually involved in the deal. The most recent reports, from May 2008, suggest that a major package of arms sales is under discussion between Damascus and Moscow, involving fifty MiG-29SMT multi-role combat aircraft, seventy-five Yak-130 trainers, Il-76 tankers, Iskanderr-E ballistic missiles, two diesel submarines and additional Pantsir-S1E air defence systems.

In early 2009 US reports suggested the Syrians had signed a deal with Russia to supply MiG-29M/M2 and MiG-31E aircraft.

Syria was involved in talks in late 2001 with the Czech company Aero Vodochody with regard to upgrading the fleet of about ninety L-39ZA/ZO Albatros armed trainers.

In mid-2006, Rosoboronexport and MiG put forward a proposal whereby surplus Russian MiG-31 'Foxhound' high-altitude interceptors could be reworked to

The remains of a Syrian MiG-17 lost in air-to-air combat with the Israeli air force. (*Author*)

MiG-31E configuration and made available for export in exchange for the MiG-25 'Foxbat'. Syria is one country that was suggested as a potential recipient. There have also been reports that second-hand Indian Sukhoi Su-30 fighters could be refurbished and sold to Syria by their Russian manufacturer. At the Paris Air Show in June 2007, Russian Aircraft Corporation MIG announced that it was in talks with a state 'in the Middle East' in relation to a possible upgrade programme. The company currently offers an extensive upgrade to MiG-29SMT standard, including integration of new weaponry – Zhuk ME radar, 'glass cockpit', new avionics and GPS navigation, which makes the aircraft truly multi-role according to officials. It seems likely that Syria would be chosen, given their pressing requirements and close relationship with the Russians.

There have been suggestions that the Syrians are looking to secure deals to have their aircraft, surface-to-air missiles and radar systems overhauled in Ukrainian and Belarus maintenance facilities.

Syria has long-standing requirements to replace its ageing MiG-17 and L-39 jet trainers, with the Yak-130 being the most likely candidate. In February 2006, it was reported that Syria was to receive six Russian aircraft simulators, according to defence industry sources. The sources said that Syria has ordered, among other things, three A-level integrated helicopter simulators, which were due to arrive in late 2008: two were for the Mil Mi-17 military transport helicopter and one for the Mi-24/25 strike helicopter. In addition, the Syrian air force will receive three Sukhoi Su-22/24 fighter-bomber simulators. The simulators will be built by RET Kronstadt.

Presence of foreign forces

In 2008 Syria reached an agreement with the Russian government to allow Russian naval forces to open a base at Tartus. This was a return to the old Cold War-era strategic alliance with Moscow. A number of Russian naval personnel are based at the facility, which Damascus sees as a counter-weight to continuing US military support for Israel.

Syria's Air Defence Command

History

To counter Israel's air power, Syria has long relied on its Soviet-supplied air defence network. This boasts more than 4,000 surface-to-air missile (SAM) launchers and anti-aircraft guns, backed by several hundred radar systems. The density of the defence systems around the Syrian capital, Damascus, is the thickest on the planet outside the Korean peninsula.

The relative strengths and capabilities of Israeli air power and Syrian air defences are central to the balance of power between Tel Aviv and Damascus. Syria's position on the eastern seaboard of the Mediterranean means its air defence network has strategic implications beyond the Arab–Israeli conflict. The strategic alliance between Syria, Lebanon's Hizbullah militia and Iran means that any conflict between the USA, Israel and Iran could easily spread to the eastern Mediterranean. Syrian SAM batteries are easily able to engage aircraft using UK bases on Cyprus, the US airbase at Incirlik in Turkey and airports around Amman, the Jordanian capital. Any Western military action against Iran, Syria and Hizbullah is highly likely to entail some sort of engagement with the Syrian Air Defence Command.

Structure

The Air Defence Command is a separate service in its own right, of equal status to the air force and distinct from the air defence branch of the land forces. This model of controlling air defence follows the Soviet model of organising radar and air defence weapon systems. The role of the command is to detect and warn of air attack from Israel or any other potential enemy, and to co-ordinate the response by interceptor fighters and SAM batteries. The Air Defence Command also liaises with anti-aircraft units of the land forces. Prior to the troop withdrawal from Lebanon in early 2005, Syria took advantage of its military presence to site radar installations at key locations in the country. The largest Syrian radar installation on Lebanese soil was at Dahr al-Baidar, a strategic 1,829 m (6,000 ft) high peak beside the Damascus highway, thirty-two kilometres east of Beirut. In April 2001, the station suffered heavy damage from strikes by Israeli aircraft, in retaliation for attacks on Israeli troops by the Syrian-supported Lebanese Islamic guerrilla group, Hizbullah. A major challenge for the Syrians was the repositioning of their air defence network inside their own borders after they were forced to withdraw from Lebanon in 2005.

Most are equipped with SA-2 'Guideline' and SA-3 'Goa' SAMs; eight batteries have SA-5 'Gammon' missiles. In addition, a significant number of SA-6 'Gainful' mobile launchers are deployed, as well as an estimated 4,000 anti-aircraft artillery pieces of up to 100 mm calibre.

Syria extensively reorganised its air defence network following the severe losses it sustained during the Israeli invasion of Lebanon in 1982. The network was restructured on the basis of a Soviet-supplied command and control system, with three computerised air defence centres co-ordinating activities of missile batteries and fighter interceptors. Major improvements were also made to radar systems, electronic warfare capabilities and the level of integration of air defence forces generally. Nevertheless, the system is considered to pose only a limited threat to Israeli air superiority, and would be vulnerable to the kind of sophisticated countermeasures possessed by Israel.

The Air Defence Command has an estimated strength of over 54,000 personnel, and controls two Anti-Aircraft Divisions (AADs), specifically the 24th and the 26th AAD, comprising a total of twenty-five air defence brigades and two SAM regiments operating an estimated 130 missile batteries.

Syria has given particular priority to the radar network covering Lebanon and Israel. There appear to be seven main Syrian SAM networks, covering the northern city of Aleppo and its weapons of mass destruction facilities, the coastal ports of Latikia and Tartus, the industrial city of Homs, Tiyas, the capital Damascus and the Golan front. The withdrawal from Lebanon in 2005 resulted in a major reorganisation of the Air Defence Command to ensure coverage of the border region and to plug 'gaps' in radar and SAM coverage.

Syrian airbases, such as Marj Ruhayyil, are extensively hardened, with aircraft shelters and tunnel complexes. (*Google Earth*)

Table 1. Syrian surface-to-air missile battery locations.

Type SAM	Location	Latitude and longitude
SA-3	Aleppo	36° 17′ N, 39° 09′ E
SA-3	Aleppo	37° 16′ N, 37° 05′ E
SA-2 empty	Aleppo	36° 08′ N, 36° 59′ E
SA-2	Aleppo	36° 14′ N, 37° 18′ E
SA-2	Al Safir	36° 03′ N, 37° 10′ E
SA-3	Al Safir	36° 11′ N, 37° 26′ E
SA-2	Al Safir	36° 03′ N, 37° 20′ E
SA-2	Al Safir	35° 57′ N, 37° 16′ E
SA-3	Al Safir	35° 58′ N, 37° 27′ E

Type SAM	Location	Latitude and longitude
SA-2	Latakia	35° 40′ N, 35° 47′ E
SA-3	Latakia	35° 38′ N, 35° 47′ E
SA-2	Latakia	35° 35′ N, 35° 52′ E
SA-2	Latakia	35° 33′ N, 35° 44′ E
SA-2 empty	Latakia	35° 31′ N, 35° 49′ E
SA-3	Latakia	35° 30′ N, 35° 49′ E
SA-3	Latakia	35° 28′ N, 35° 53′ E
SA-3	Latakia	35° 19′ N, 35° 55′ E
SA-2	Latakia	35° 24′ N, 35° 55′ E
SA-2 empty	Tartus	35° 15′ N 35° 56′ E
SA-3 empty	Tartus	35° 07′ N 35° 53′ E
SA-3	Tartus	35° 02′ N 35° 54′ E
SA-2 empty	Tartus	34° 57′ N 35° 56′ E
SA-3	Tartus	34° 54′ N 35° 53′ E
SA-2	Tartus	34° 49′ N 35° 55′ E
SA-5	Tartus	35° 09′ N 36° 14′ E
SA-5	Tartus	34° 56′ N 36° 15′ E
SA-2	Homs	34° 49′ N 36° 42′ E
SA-2 empty	Homs	34° 46′ N 36° 36′ E
SA-3	Homs	34° 42′ N 36° 48′ E
SA-2	Homs	34° 39′ N 36° 42′ E
SA-2	Homs	34° 39′ N 36° 44′ E
SA-5	Homs	34° 37′ N 36° 46′ E
SA-2 empty	Homs	34° 36′ N 36° 35′ E
SA-2	Homs	34° 36′ N 36° 40′ E
SA-2 empty	Homs	34° 35′ N 36° 41′ E
SA-6	Homs	34° 35′ N 36° 43′ E
SA-3	Homs	34° 32′ N 36° 37′ E
SA-3	Homs	34° 32′ N 36° 45′ E
SA-2 empty	Homs	34° 26′ N 36° 57′ E
SA-6	Homs	34° 26′ N 36° 57′ E
SA-3	Tiyas	34° 31′ N 37° 35′ E
SA-2 empty	Tiyas	34° 30′ N 37° 37′ E
SA-3 empty	Tiyas	34° 29′ N 37° 37′ E
SA-3	Tiyas	34° 28′ N 37° 38′ E
SA-3	Tiyas	34° 31′ N 37° 40′ E
SA-2 empty	Tiyas	34° 30′ N 37° 41′ E
SA-2 empty	Tiyas	34° 40′ N 37° 41′ E
SA-3 empty	Tiyas	34° 29′ N 37° 43′ E
SA-2	Tiyas	34° 26′ N 37° 40′ E

Type SAM	Location	Latitude and longitude
SA-2	Damascus	33° 37' N 36° 53' E
SA-2	Damascus	33° 32' N 36° 46' E
SA-5	Damascus	33° 32' N 36° 41' E
SA-2 empty	Damascus	33° 33' N 36° 40' E
SA-6	Damascus	33° 31' N 36° 36' E
SA-6	Damascus	33° 35' N 36° 34' E
SA-3	Damascus	33° 32' N 36° 27' E
SA-2 empty	Damascus	33° 29' N 36° 25' E
SA-2 empty	Damascus	33° 26' N 36° 25' E
SA-2	Damascus	33° 25' N 36° 31' E
SA-2 empty	Damascus	33° 20' N 36° 33' E
SA-3	Damascus	33° 33' N 36° 18' E
SA-2 empty	Damascus	33° 26' N 36° 19' E
SA-2 empty	Damascus	33° 33' N 36° 10' E
SA-3 empty	Damascus	33° 28' N 36° 07' E
SA-3	Damascus	33° 28' N 36° 07' E
SA-6	Damascus	33° 23' N 36° 09' E
SA-2	Damascus	33° 21' N 36° 07' E
SA-6	Damascus	33° 19' N 36° 14' E
SA-5	Golan	33° 10' N 36° 37' E
SA-6	Golan	33° 04' N 36° 14' E
SA-6	Golan	33° 03' N 36° 09' E
SA-2	Golan	33° 01' N 36° 13' E
SA-3	Golan	32° 59' N 36° 21' E
SA-3	Golan	32° 55' N 36° 12' E
SA-2 empty	Golan	32° 54' N 36° 23' E
SA-6	Golan	32° 51' N 36° 12' E
SA-2	Golan	32° 49' N 36° 14' E
SA-2	Golan	32° 47' N 36° 20' E
SA-5 empty	Golan	32° 47' N 36° 17' E
SA-3	Golan	32° 45' N 36° 10' E
SA-6	Golan	32° 47' N 36° 13' E
SA-6	Golan	32° 48' N 36° 07' E
SA-6	Golan	32° 46' N 36° 05' E
SA-2	Golan	32° 41' N 36° 16' E
SA-2	Golan	32° 35' N 36° 21' E
SA-3	Golan	32° 41' N 36° 23' E
SA-3	Golan	32° 35' N 36° 14' E
SA-2	Golan	32 34' N 36° 21' E
SA-6	Golan	33° 16' N 36° 09' E
SA-6	Golan	33° 20' N 36° 08' E

Activity
The 2007 Israeli strike on Syria's alleged nuclear reactor in the east of the country highlighted the relative weakness of the country's air defence network. While the Syrians claim to have detected and engaged the Israeli raiders, there is little evidence to suggest that the Syrians were in any way able to seriously disrupt the Israeli air operation.

Procurement
Modernisation of the ADC's equipment remains a high priority for the Syrian military command. The Syrian military took delivery of the first batches of the vehicle-mount variant of Russian Kolomna KBM Strelets ('Archer') multiple-launch units for use with the 9M39 Igla (SA-18 'Grouse') fire-and-forget surface-to-air missile (SAM) systems in 2003. In May 2007, Russia agreed to sell Damascus 'some fifty Pantsyr-S1E systems' for some $730 million, with initial deliveries set to begin in early 2008. Syria is understood to be receiving the Pantsyr-S1E equipped with the latest Roman I-Band fire-control radar. It is understood that ten of these units would be resold to Iran.

These two systems, while they improved the 'point defence' capability of the ADC, did not improve the command's area defensive capability. To achieve this aim the Syrians have long sought to buy the sophisticated Almaz S-300 (SA-10 'Grumble') air defence missile system from Russia, Ukraine or Belarus. It is likely that the primary role of the S-300 in Syrian hands would be to protect Damascus from air attack.

In December 2006, General Akhmad Al Ratyb, Syrian Air Defence Commander, visited Moscow to 'discuss aspects of development of bilateral co-operation of Russian Air Force and Syrian Air Defence'. According to media reports, while in Russia the Syrian delegation visited the Special Air Forces Command, Gagarin Air Force Academy, Zukovskiy Air Force Engineering Academy, Army Air Combat Employment Centre, Federal State Unitary Enterprise 'Rosoboronexport', Russian Aircraft Corporation 'Mig' and aircraft-repair bases. No details of any procurement deals or contracts to upgrade and overhaul Syrian air defence equipment were revealed.

Assessment
Syria's airpower has suffered twenty years of neglect. The country's poor economic position and the ending of Soviet military aid in 1990 has meant that military modernisation has effectively been on hold since the end of the Cold War.

For the Syrian air force and air defence this means having had no new equipment and hardly any spares for almost twenty years. As a result their combat capability has decreased considerably. At the same time, the number of experienced aircrew and missile operators in front-line service has declined considerably.

Syria's air force, however, has the benefit of still having a large number of airframes that would require a considerable air campaign to neutralise. The same could be said of the air defence command, but it would be expected to inflict heavy losses on any attacker.

The Syrian air force would face serious problems if it found itself in a major war with the Israelis.

CHAPTER FOURTEEN

Turkey

Population	76 million
Military/paramilitary aircraft	1,409
Air Force personnel	57,000

Turkish Air Force (Türk Hava Kuvvetleri)

History

Military aviation in Turkey dates back almost a century, to 1911, when the Ottoman imperial forces formed their first air unit. With the establishment of the Republic of Turkey in 1923, the modern Turkish air arm came into existence. Turkey's neutrality in the Second World War limited its exposure to advanced air warfare tactics and modern aircraft. This changed in the 1950s after Turkey joined NATO and became eligible for US military assistance. This opened the way for Turkey's airmen to fly supersonic fighter jets and participate in major multinational NATO exercises.

Although NATO's confrontation with the Soviet Union during the Cold War absorbed much of the Turkish military's attention until the late 1980s, the country had other strategic interests that it wanted to protect. The confrontation with Greece led to the Cyprus crisis in 1974, which culminated in Turkish forces invading and occupying the northern part of the island to protect the ethnic Turkish minority. Turkish air force combat aircraft flew attack missions during the invasion, which also involved large-scale parachute drops and army helicopter operations.

During the 1990s, the Turkish air force was active on several fronts. To support NATO in 1993 it deployed Lockheed F-16C Fighting Falcon combat jets to Italy to support no-fly-zone operations over Bosnia, and transport aircraft delivered humanitarian aid to besieged Sarajevo. Turkish F-16s flew strike missions against Serbian targets during Operation Allied Force in 1999.

The 1991 Gulf War saw the deployment of NATO air support and Patriot anti-ballistic-missile batteries to help defend Turkey against any Iraqi retaliation. A strike wing of USAF aircraft operating from Incirlik airbase in south-eastern Turkey flew attack missions against targets in northern Iraq during Operation Desert Storm. In the aftermath of the war, US, British and French air units began operating from Incirlik to protect the Kurdish 'safe haven' in northern Iraq. The political vacuum in northern Iraq was of great concern to the Turkish government in case it allowed Kurdish insurgents of the PKK to establish safe bases.

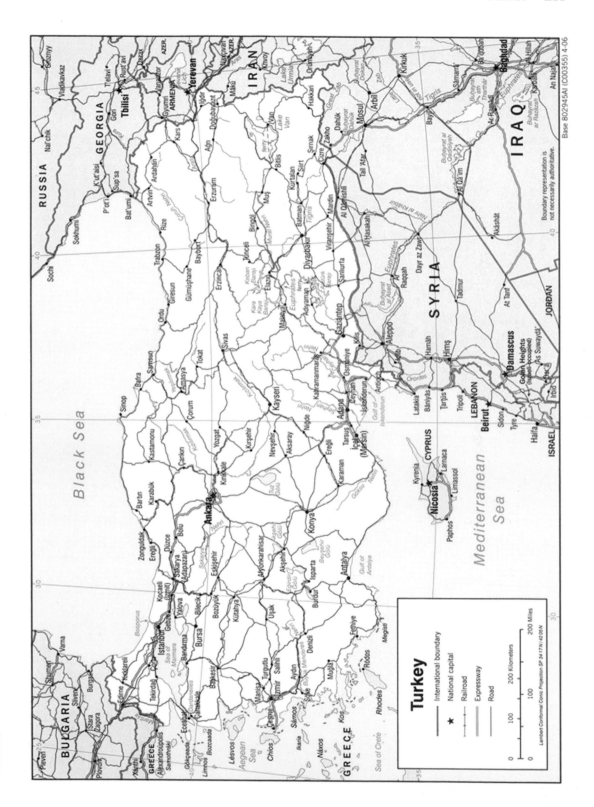

Turkey

—— International boundary
★ National capital
+++ Railroad
Expressway
Road

0   100   200 Kilometers
0   100   200 Miles

Lambert Conformal Conic Projection SP 34°17'N / 42°06'N

Base 802945AI (C00355) 4-06

Boundary representation is
not necessarily authoritative.

Turkish Air Arms Order of Battle, as at 1 May 2009.

Airbase	Location	Airbase Designation	Squadron	Aircraft Type	Role
Turkish Air Force (Türk Hava Kuvvetleri)					
Air Staff Division - HQ Erkilet					
Erkilet	38° 47′ N 35° 30′ E				
Incirlik	37° 00′ N 35° 26′ E	10 Airbase	101	KC-135R	AAR
Ankara – Etimesgut	39° 57′ N 32° 41′ E	11 Airbase	211	CN235-100, CN235EW	
			212	Ce550,Ce650, UH-1H, Gulfstream IV, CN235M-100	
Izmir – Kakliç	38° 31′ N 27° 01′ E	12 Airbase	221	C-160D	Transport
			222	C-130B, C-130E	Transport
			223	CN235M-100	Transport
1st Tactical Air Force Command - HQ Eskişehir					
Eskişehir	39° 47′ N 30° 35′ E	1 Airbase	111	F-4E 2020	Strike
			112	F-4E	Strike
			113	RF-4E	Reconnaissance
			201	CN-235M-100	Transport
Ankara – Akinci	40° 05′ N 32° 34′ E	4 Airbase	141	F-16C/D-30/40	Strike/Air defence
			142	F-16C/D-30/40	Strike/Air defence
			143	F-16C/D-30/40	Strike/Air defence
Bandirma	40° 19′ N 27° 59′ E	6 Airbase	161	F-16C/D-30/40 (LANTIRN)	Strike/Air defence
			162	F-16C/D-30/40	Strike/Air defence
			SAR Flight	UH-1H	SAR
Balikesir	39° 37′ N 27° 56′ E	9 Airbase	191	F-16C/D-50	Strike
			192	F-16C/D-50	Strike
			SAR Flight	UH-1H	SAR
2nd Tactical Air Command - HQ Diyarbakir					
Merzifon	40° 50′ N 35° 31′ E	5 Airbase	151	F-16C/D-50 (HARM/SEAD)	SEAD
			152	F-16C/D-50	Strike
			SAR Flight	UH-1H, AS532UL	SAR
Malatya – Erhaç	38° 26′ N 38° 06′ E	7 Airbase	171	F-4E 2020	Strike
			172	F-4E	Strike

Airbase	Location	Airbase Designation	Squadron	Aircraft Type	Role
			173	F-4E	OCU
			SAR Flight	UH-1H	SAR
Diyarbakir	37° 54′ N 40° 12′ E	8 Airbase	181	F-16C/D-30/40 (LANTIRN)	Strike
			182	F-16C/D-30/40	Strike/Air defence
			202	CN235-100, AS532AL/UL	CSAR

Air Training Command - HQ Gaziemir

Airbase	Location	Airbase Designation	Squadron	Aircraft Type	Role
Istanbul – Yeşilköy	40° 58′ N 28° 49′ E		1-5 Training Flights	T-41D	Training
			203	CN235M-100	Training
Izmir – Adnan Menderes	38° 18′ N 27° 09′ E				
Izmir – Çiğli	38° 30′ N 27° 01′ E	2 Airbase	121	T-38B	Training
			122	T-37B/T-37C	Training
			125	AS532AL, AS532UL, CN235M-100, UH-1H	Training
		2 Airbase	123 Flight	SF260D	
Kayseri – Erkilet	38° 47′ N 35° 30′ E				
Konya	37° 59′ N 32° 34′ E	3 Airbase	131	Boeing 737 AEW&C	AEW&C
			132	F-4E, F-4E-2020, F-16C/D-40	Training
			133	(N)F-5A-2000, (N)F-5B-2000	Training
			134 (Turkish Stars)	NF-5A, NF-5B	Air display
			SAR Flight	UH-1H	SAR
Yalova	40° 41′ N 29° 23′ E	Air Warfare School		SZD50-3 Puchacz	Training

Turkish Army Aviation (Türk Kara Kuvvetleri)

Airbase	Location	Airbase Designation	Squadron	Aircraft Type	Role
Ankara – Güvercinlik	39° 56 N 32° 45 E	Army Aviation School	Special Forces Air Group	S-70A, CN235M-100	SF
			Air Transport Group	BeB200, Ce421C, AB212, UH-1H, AS532UL	

Airbase	Location	Airbase Designation	Squadron	Aircraft Type	Role
			901 Maintenance and Overhaul Depot		
			1 Attack Helicopter Battalion	AH-1W, TAH-1P	Attack training
			Helicopter Battalion	UH-1H. S-70A	Training
			Basic Training Battalion	TH-300C, AB206R, T-41D, T-42A	Training
			Tactical Observation Battalion	AB204B, UH-1H, OH-58B, U-17B, CN235M	Training
Diyarbakir	37° 54′ N 40° 12′ E	7th Aviation Battalion	3 Attack Helicopter Sqn	AH-1P, AH-1W	Attack
			7th Company	S-70A, UH-1H, U-17B	Troop transport
Erzincan	39° 43′ N 39° 31′ E	3rd Aviation Regiment	1st Battalion	AB205, UH-1H	Troop transport
			2nd Battalion	AB205, UH-1H, S-70A	Troop transport
			Command Group	UH-1H, U-17B	Troop transport
Istanbul – Samandira	41° 00′ N 29° 13′ E	1st Aviation Regiment	1st Battalion	UH-1H, S-70A	Troop transport
			2nd Battalion	UH-1H, S-70A	Troop transport
			Command Group	UH-1H, U-17B	Troop transport
Izmir – Gaziemir		Agean Aviation Regiment	1st Battalion	AS532Al	Troop transport
			3rd Battalion	S-70A	Troop transport
			Command Group	UH-1H, U-17B	Troop transport
Keşan		2nd Aviation Battalion+C28+C56	1st Company	UH-1H/U-17	Troop transport
Malatya – Erhaç	38° 26′ N 38° 06′ E	2nd Aviation Regiment	1st Battalion	AB205, UH-1H	Troop transport
			2nd Battalion	AB205, UH-1H, S-70A	Troop transport
			Command Group	UH-1H, U-17B	Troop transport

Airbase	Location	Airbase Designation	Squadron	Aircraft Type	Role
Pinarbaşi, Cyprus		2nd Special Forces Air Group		UH-1H, U-17B	Troop transport

Turkish Navy (Türk Deniz Kuvvetleri)

Topel	40° 44′ N 30° 05′ E		301	TB-20, CN235M-100 MPA	Maritime patrol
			351	AB204B(AS), AB212AS, AB212AS(EW), S-70B-28	Naval support/ASW

Turkish Coastguard (Türk Sahil Güvenlik Komuntanliği)

Izmir – Adnan Menderes	38° 18′ N 27° 09′ E		MPA Helicopter	CN235M-100 (MPA) A109A-II, AB412EP	Maritime patrol Maritime patrol

Paramilitary Police (Türk Jandarma Havaçilik Komutanliği)

Ankara – Güvercinlik	39° 56′ N 32° 45′ E		Command Group	Ce182P, S-70A-17	Troop transport
			1 Helicopter	AB205, S-70A-17	Troop transport
			2 Helicopter	Mi-17-1V	Troop transport
Aydin – Çildir	37° 49′ N 27° 54′ E		Aydin Helicopter	AB205, S-70A	Troop transport
Diyarbakir	37° 54′ N 40° 12′ E		1 Helicopter	AB205	Troop transport
			2 Helicopter	S-70A	Troop transport
Van	38° 28′ N 43° 20′ E		Van Helicopter	AB205	Troop transport

Ministry of the Interior (Emniyet Teskilatii Genel Müdürlügü)
Police Aviation Unit

Adana – Sakirpasa	36° 58′ N 35° 16′ E				
Ankara-Gölbasi	40° 07′ N 33° 00′ E			SA318C, MD600N	Police observation
Diyarbakir – Ünal Arikan Heliport	40° 58′ N 28° 49′ E			S-70A-17	Police observation
Istanbul – Atatürk	40° 58′ N 28° 49′ E			SA318C, S-70A-17	Police observation

During the 1990s, Turkish army and paramilitary gendarmerie helicopters were heavily involved in operations against the PKK in eastern Turkey and northern Iraq. F-16 and F-4E jets often supported these operations.

Structure

The Turkish General Staff has direct control of all of the Republic's military forces, reporting to both the Prime Minister and the Minister of Defence.

The air force is the predominant air arm of the Turkish military, but the land and naval forces have strong air components. The paramilitary gendarmerie is controlled by the General Staff.

The air force is split between two main operational commands, covering the east and west of the country respectively, and a training command. Transport, reconnaissance and air-to-air refuelling units are controlled centrally. Airbases control squadrons for training and peacetime administration, but for operations the Turkish General Staff in Ankara exercises close control.

Anti-aircraft missile batteries and radar stations are controlled by the Turkish air force. The majority of the forty-eight Raytheon I-Hawk and BAe Dynamics Rapier surface-to-air missiles are deployed to defend airfields.

Air power doctrine and strategy

Turkey is closely integrated in NATO, and it is steeped in NATO tactics and operating procedures. Large numbers of senior Turkish air force officers and aircrew have served in NATO command appointments and participated in several complex alliance air operations. This has given the Turkish air force experience of air defence, strike, close air support and air transport operations in expeditionary missions.

Turkey, however, has developed its own national air power strategy, which is intrinsic to the country's defence strategy along its eastern and southern borders. The Turkish military has also established close defence ties with Israel to counter the influence of Syria. Ankara and Damascus have a number of disputes over the control of water sources along their common border. Ankara has a national intelligence-gathering strategy that involves high-flying Gnat 750 and I-Gnat unmanned aerial vehicles (UAVs) and photographic reconnaissance aircraft. Fast jets, and attack and transport helicopters, are also closely integrated into Turkish counter-insurgency warfare concepts. Offensive air support is used either in conjunction with ground operations or on stand-alone strikes against specific targets, such as PKK camps. Turkish intelligence operatives also conducted covert missions in foreign countries, with the famous example being the seizure of the PKK leader in Kenya in 1999.

In line with its national air power strategy, Turkey has ordered Boeing 737 airborne early warning and control to allow its air force to create its own recognised air picture, independent of the NATO air defence network and the alliance E-3A AWACS force.

Turkey uses the Anatolian Eagle series of air warfare exercises at Konya airbase to develop its own tactics and doctrine, as well as to build relationships with non-

NATO air forces, including Israel and Pakistan. Links have been established with F-16 users across the Middle East, including Egypt, Jordan and the UAE. Pilots from the UAE have trained in Turkey.

Operational activity

The main focus of Turkish air operations in the Middle East have been countering the PKK insurgency. In 2007 and 2008, the Turkish air force flew several air strikes against PKK bases in northern Iraq. From October 2007 to February 2008, some six major air raids were launched at PKK bases in northern Iraq. On 21 February 2008, the Turkish army launched Operation Sun to occupy and destroy PKK camps in northern Iraq. Backed by heavy air and attack helicopter support, the incursion lasted eight days. A Cobra gunship was lost to PKK ground fire. Some 272 air strikes were carried out during the operation. Two further raids took place in late April 2008, and on one occasion in May of that year both F-16s and F-4Es, using precision guided weapons, were involved.

Airbase infrastructure

Turkey benefited from extensive NATO infrastructure funding in the 1970s to improve its airbase infrastructure. All major fighter bases received hardened shelters, command posts and support structures. Several dispersal bases were also hardened facilities. Underground fuel lines were also built to major airbases from oil refineries and ports.

Aircraft ordnance

The Turkish air force does not have a significant inventory of modern precision-guided munitions, but is moving to rectify its shortcomings in this area.

In the 1980s and 1990s, it received a suite of weapons to equip its F-16s predominantly for air-supremacy missions, including 386 AIM-7 Sparrows, nearly 2,500 AIM-9B/L./M/S/P3 Sidewinders and latterly AIM-120 AMRAAM (176 A model and 138 B model) weapons from the USA. Some 1,200 GBU-10/12 Raytheon Paveway I and II laser-guided and 200 Rockwell GBU-8B HOBOS television bombs were purchased for air-to-ground missions in conjunction with 110 Lockheed Martin Low-Altitude Navigation and Targeting Infra-Red for Night (LANTIRN) pods, to supplement 500 lb, 1,000 lb and 2,000 lb iron or dumb bombs, as well as 523 Durandal anti-runway weapons. Some 158 F-16s have been converted to operate LANTIRN pods. A primary air-to-surface weapon is the Raytheon AGM-65 Maverick missile, of which some 820 have been purchased.

More than a hundred Israeli Rafael Popeye I & II stand-off cruise missiles were purchased for use from the F-4Es as part of their Israeli-managed upgrade. Some hundred Harpy anti-radar unmanned aerial vehicles have also been purchased from Israel, as well as Elbit Systems' LOROP photographic reconnaissance pods. Israeli Rafael Python 4 and Derby air-to-air missiles have also reportedly been sold to Turkey, along with Spice air-to-ground missiles.

The F-16 Fighting Falcon is the Turkish air force's primary combat aircraft. *(US DoD)*

The decision to standardise the Turkish air force fleet to Block 50+ standard has opened wider weapon options. Over the past four years orders for a range of advanced air-to-ground ordnance have been placed with US companies, including 457 AIM-9X Sidewinder air-to-air heat-seeking missiles, 107 AIM-120C-7 beyond-visual-range missiles, ninety-five AGM-88 HARMs suppression-of-enemy-air-defence missiles, fifty AGM-84H SLAM-E land attack missiles, fifty AGM-154A and 54 AGM-154C JSOW land attack missiles and 500 satellite-guided Boeing GBU-31/38/BLU-109 Joint Direct Attack Munitions (JDAM), fifty CBU-103 and 50 CBU-105 cluster bombs, and thirty Sniper advanced targeting pods.

Strategic weapons
Turkey has no offensive strategic weapons and no published plans to acquire them.

C160s have served in the Turkish air force since the 1970s. (*Author*)

Turkey's air force is a major player on NATO's southern flank. (*Author*)

Turkish Inventory, as at 1 May 2009.

Type	Active	Stored	Ordered	Required
Turkish Air Force (Türk Hava Kuvvetleri)				
COMBAT AIRCRAFT				
F/RF-4E	165			
F-5A/B	49			
F-16C/D Block 40	176/41			
F-16C/D Block 50			30	
F-35				100+
ISTAR				
737 AEW			4	
CN-235 (EW)	1			
CN-235 (MPA)	1			
TANKER				
KC-135R	7			
TRANSPORT				
A319	1			
A400M			10	
C160	17			
C-130E/H	13			
CN-235	41			
COMBAT HELICOPTER				
AS532	19			
UH-1H	62			
TRAINING AIRCRAFT				
KT-1			40	
NF-5A/B	38			
SF-260	37			
T-37	59			
T-38A	67			
Turkish Army Aviation (Türk Kara Kuvvetleri)				
ISTAR				
King Air	2			
TRANSPORT				
CN-235	2			
Cessna 421	37			
King Air	4			
U-17	20			
Do28D-2	2			

Type	Active	Stored	Ordered	Required
COMBAT HELICOPTER				
AB204	5			
AB205	69			
AB206	3			
Bell 212	8			
AH-1P/S/TAH-1	29			
AH-1W	8			
AS532	26			
OH-58B	3			
S-70A	54			
T129			50	
UI1-1I1	86			
TRAINING HELICOPTERS				
AB204	10			
AB206	22			
Hughes 269	21			
TRAINING AIRCRAFT				
T-41D	30			
T-42A	4			
Citation	15			

Turkish Navy (Türk Deniz Kuvvetleri)

Type	Active	Stored	Ordered	Required
ISTAR				
AB212 (AEW)	3			
ATR-72 (MPA)			10	
CN-235 (MPA)	6			
CN-235 (MPA)(Coast Guard)	3			
COMBAT HELICOPTER				
AB204	3			
AB212	10			
S-70A	7			
A109 (Coast Guard)	1			
Bell 412EP (Coast Guard)	14			

Paramilitary Police (Türk Jandarma Havaçilik Komutanliği)

Type	Active	Stored	Ordered	Required
TRANSPORT				
D-28D-2	3			

Type	Active	Stored	Ordered	Required
COMBAT HELICOPTERS				
Mi-171	19			
S-70A	33			
AB204	2			
AB205	19			
AB212	1			
Ministry of the Interior (Emniyet Teskilatii Genel Müdürlügü)				
HELICOPTERS				
S-92	2			
SA330 Puma	3			
MD600N	10			
S-70A	6			
SA31816	16			

Veteran F-4Es have been upgraded to extend their service life. *(IAI)*

General Dynamics F-16C Fighting Falcon Block 30

This variant of the best-selling F-16 was introduced in the 1980s, and was widely exported around the Middle East to Bahrain, Egypt, Israel and Turkey. It was the first F-16 capable of employing a wide range of 'smart' precision-guided weapons.

Crew: 1
Length: 49 ft 5 in. (14.8 m)
Wingspan: 32 ft 8 in. (9.8 m)
Height: 16 ft (4.8 m)
Maximum take-off weight: 42,300 lb (19,200 kg)
Powerplant: One F110-GE-100 afterburning turbofan

Maximum speed
At sea level: Mach 1.2 (915 mph, 1,470 km/h)
At altitude: Mach 2+ (1,500 mph, 2,414 km/h)
Combat radius: 295 nm (340 miles, 550 km) on a hi-lo-hi mission with six 1,000 lb (450 kg) bombs
Ferry range: 2,280 nm (2,620 miles, 4,220 km) with drop-tanks

Armament
Guns: 1 × 20 mm (0.787 in) M61 Vulcan Gatling gun, 580 rounds
Hardpoints: 2 × wingtip air-to-air missile launch rails, 6 × underwing and 3 × under-fuselage pylon stations holding up to 20,450 lb (9,276 kg) of payload
Air-to-air missiles: 8 × AIM-7 Sparrow or 12 × AIM-9 Sidewinder or 12 × IRIS-T or 12 × AIM-120 AMRAAM or 12 × Python-4
Air-to-ground missiles: 6 × AGM-45 Shrike or 12 × AGM-65 Maverick or 4 × AGM-88 HARM
Anti-ship missiles: 4 × AGM-84 Harpoon or 4 × AGM-119 Penguin
Bombs: 2 × CBU-87 Combined-Effects Munition, 2 × CBU-89 Gator mine, 2 × CBU-97 Sensor-Fused Weapon, Wind-Corrected Munitions Dispenser capable, 4 × GBU-10 Paveway II, 6 × GBU-12 Paveway II, 6 × Paveway-series laser-guided bombs, 4 × JDAM, 4 × Mark 84 general-purpose bombs, 8 × Mark 83 GP bombs, 12 × Mk 82 GP bombs, B61 nuclear bomb

The Turkish air force, however, will gain a strategic reconnaissance as a result of a planned $360 million project with Italy's Telespazio to purchase the long-delayed Göktürk electro-optical surveillance satellite, This is scheduled to be launched into orbit in 2012. The satellite is planned to have a resolution of up to 0.8 metre, which will give Turkish air planners the resolution needed to target precision-guided munitions.

Procurement

The Turkish air force has ambitious plans to modernise its F-16 fleet to bring it up to Block 50 standard, which involves major computer upgrades to allow multi-role smart weapon employment. In May 2007, a $1.78 billion deal with Lockheed Martin was signed for the delivery of fourteen F-16C variants and sixteen F-16Ds. The first F-16 aircraft is scheduled to be delivered to Turkey in mid-2011, with the remaining twenty-nine fighter aircraft set to follow by the end of 2012. Final assembly of the thirty aircraft – Block 50 F-16s – will be carried out at TAI facilities near Ankara under the 'Peace Onyx IV' programme.

This follows on from a deal signed in April 2005 for some 213 Turkish F-16s to be upgraded to CCIP or Block 50+ standard at a cost of $1.1 billion.

The ageing fleet of Cessna T-37s is being replaced as part of a 2007 deal between TAI and Korea Aerospace Industries (KAI), worth $330 million, for the production of forty KT-1 Woong-Bee aircraft under a deal signed in 2007. Under this programme the manufacturing, assembly, flight testing and delivery of the forty aircraft (plus an option for fifteen more) will be carried out by TAI. The first aircraft is due for delivery in 2009, with the rest following within two years.

The transport force is to be augmented by ten Airbus Military A400M aircraft, but their delivery is to be delayed for several years.

Boeing is building four B-737 airborne early warning and control (AEW&C) aircraft for Turkey at a cost of about $1 billion (with an option for another two), but this project has been delayed for almost three years due to problems that occurred during the completion of software source codes and radars.

Turkey has a strong interest in UAVs and made a formal request to the US government in December 2008 to purchase two new UAV systems – one armed and one unarmed. General Atomics' MQ-9 Reaper and MQ-1 Predator will replace the existing Gnat 750 system, which dates from the mid-1990s.

The first two of ten Israel Aerospace Industries Heron strategic UAVs were delivered to Turkey in November 2008. They are to feature upgraded engines to enable them to reach an altitude of 30,000 ft, and they will be fitted with a Turkish-made electro-optical sensor system.

In the long term the Turkish air force aims to buy one hundred Lockheed Martin F-35 Lightning II Joint Strike Fighters from 2015. The $10 billion project is the largest ever undertaken by Turkey and will make it the largest user of the stealth aircraft in the Middle East region.

Turkey is looking to build up its anti-ballistic defence capabilities, and in 2009 is to launch a new project to purchase a long-range air- and missile-defence system (T-LORAMIDS) intended to counter both missiles and aircraft. The project is envisaged to cost some $4 billion, and involves the purchase of about twelve systems.

Presence of foreign forces
Turkey participates in the NATO unified command structure. Personnel participate in the alliance airborne early warning force. During the 1991 and 2003 Iraqi crises, Turkey called upon NATO to provides air and air defence forces to defend its air space. The current NATO air headquarters in Turkey is dubbed Combined Air Operations Center Six, or CAOC 6, which is located in Eskisehir, Turkey.

CAOC Six is a subordinate Command and Control Center of NATO's Allied Air Forces Southern Europe in Naples. It conducts air policing and air defence, and interacts with the Turkish Air Force on behalf of NATO.

Under the command of a Turkish air force lieutenant-general, CAOC Six has the mission of deterring aggression against NATO allies and ensures the security and air space integrity of Allied Command Europe.

The multinational staff of CAOC Six includes about 90 people from six NATO nations, including Turkey, Germany, Greece, Hungary, Italy, Norway, Spain and the USA.

The USA also has several bases in Turkey under national US command. The largest of these is Incirlik airbase. It is currently home to the 39th Air Base Wing and acts as a hub for Boeing KC-135R air refuelling and C-17 Globemaster transport aircraft supporting US operations in Iraq and Afghanistan. The USA has not based combat aircraft in Incirlik since March 2003.

Turkish Army Aviation (Türk Kara Kuvvetleri)
The Turkish land forces operate their own fleet of more than a hundred attack and transport helicopters.

Operational activity
Turkish AH-1W Cobra crews have more than a decade's worth of experience of operations against PKK rebels on the country's eastern borders. They have been supported by the S-70 Blackhawk force.

Aircraft ordnance
The Cobra force has made extensive use of TOW laser-guided missiles, 2.75-inch rockets and 30 mm cannon during their combat operations. The Cirit (Jereed) laser-guided air-to-ground missile, developed by the Turkish company Roketsan for use on AH-1S Cobra attack helicopters, was successfully tested in 2008.

Procurement
The Turkish army has ambitious plans to recapitalise its helicopter fleet. At the heart of these is a joint $2.7 billion programme between TAI and Agusta Westland to produce fifty new attack and tactical reconnaissance (ATAK) helicopters, dubbed the T129, derived from the A129 Mangusta. Work on prototypes is under way and the first of the fifty will be built at TAI's site in Turkey for delivery from 2013. An option exists for a further forty-one helicopters.

Next on the army's priority list is a new multi-purpose helicopter to augment the S-70 fleet and replace many of AB212s. This project has attracted bids from Sikorsky and Agusta Westland. It involves purchase of about 115 helicopters to meet the

Turkey continues to buy F-16s with advanced features and weapon options. *(US DoD)*

Turkey participates in NATO's airborne early warning force, but the country is buying its own national airborne early warning and control force. *(USAF)*

New transport helicopters are being bought for the Turkish armed forces, with Agusta Westland offering its version of the AW149. (*Agusta Westland*)

The Agusta Westland Mengusta is to be Turkey's next attack helicopter. (*Agusta Westland*)

requirements of the army, air force and navy, as well as the GGC, SGK, Ministry of Forestry and General Directorate of Security. The Turkish army has long been interested in a heavy-lift helicopter of the CH-47 or CH-53 class.

The army is also purchasing seventy-six tactical UAVs, and nineteen ground stations produced by the local Turkish company KaleKalip-Baykar were delivered in 2008 to meet internal security requirements. Another tactical unmanned aerial vehicle (UAV) being developed by TAI is due to be delivered in 2010.

Turkish Navy (Türk Deniz Kuvvetleri)

The Turkish naval force has a fleet of ships, embarked helicopters and shore-based fixed maritime patrol aircraft. Its major project is the procurement of ten ATR-72 maritime patrol aircraft.

The navy also maintains the Coast Guard's fleet of aircraft and helicopters.

Paramilitary Police (Türk Jandarma Havaçilik Komutanliği)

This highly trained intervention force has borne the brunt of heavy fighting with Kurdish insurgents in the east of the country. It boasts its own fleet of transport helicopters, including S-70s and Mi-171s.

Assessment

Turkey has one of the most professional air forces in the Middle East. It has modern equipment and an established logistic support network. While Turkish airmen have plenty of experience operating as part of integrated NATO forces, their ability to launch and sustain major independent air campaigns has yet to be put to the test. A key element in maintaining the long term fighting power of the Turkish air force is the ability of the country's economy to support the purchase of next generation aircraft, such as the Joint Strike Fighter.

Turkey is part of the Airbus A400M airlifter project to replace the old C160s and C-130s. (EADS)

CHAPTER FIFTEEN

United Arab Emirates

Population	4.8 million
Military/paramilitary aircraft	555
Air Force personnel	4,500

History

The UAE is a unique political entity, being created as a federation of seven emirates – Abu Dhabi, Ajman, Dubai, Fujairah, Ras al-Khaimah, Sharjah and Umm al-Qaiwain – some thirty-six years ago. These emirates are all ruled by royal families, which had their own armed forces when the UAE was established.

The UAE's geographic position at the southern shore of the Arabian Gulf and its toe-hold on the Indian Ocean, its status as a major oil and natural gas exporter and its growing position as a world trading centre, has meant that the country is increasingly involved in global economy and international political structures.

Within the Gulf region, the UAE continues to dispute Iranian control of the Abu Musa and Greater and Lesser Tunb islands. Tehran's nuclear programme has also raised concern in the UAE government. If any conflict between the USA and Iran resulted in the closure of the strategic Straits of Hormuz, it would cause major economic disruption to the UAE.

Defence procurement is particularly influenced by the contribution that the seven emirates make to the central defence budget, with Abu Dhabi and Dubai having the greatest say in the purchase of new military equipment.

Abu Dhabi, as the UAE's major oil- and natural-gas-producing emirate, makes the largest contribution to defence procurement. It is also home to major shipbuilding and aviation repair companies, and so is keen to attract work to these operations. The UAE central defence budget has been in the region of $2–2.5 billion over the past decade, which meant that major procurement projects had to be spread out over several years to be accommodated. Recent surges in oil and natural gas prices have resulted in significant increases in revenue to the UAE, with one oil industry analyst suggesting that this might be in the region of $50–100 billion over the next decade if prices remain at current levels.

UAE Air Force and Air Defence Force (UAE AF&AD)

Structure

Since the establishment of the UAE, a process of evolution has taken place to bring the armed forces of the individual emirates under the umbrella of the unified UAE

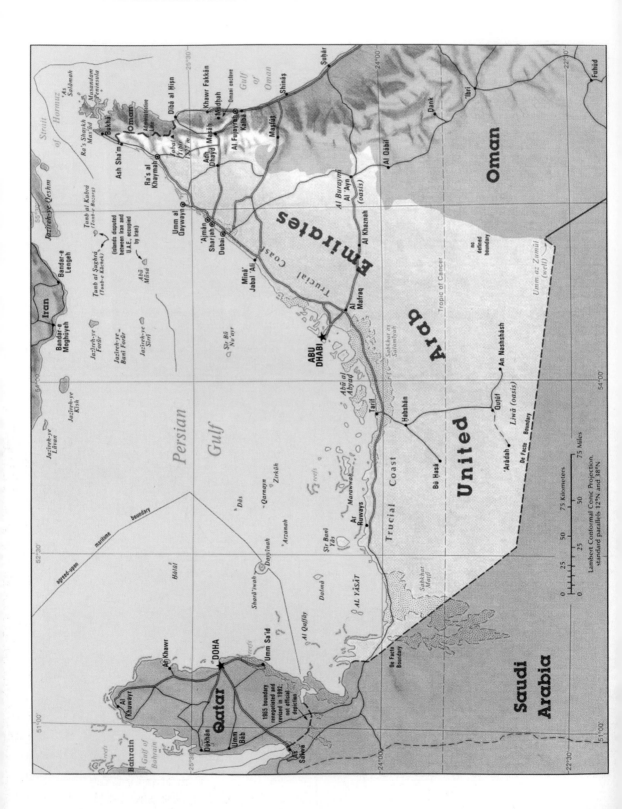

armed forces structure. The last Emiri armed forces joined the unified structure in the mid-1990s.

Although the Abu Dhabi-based UAE Ministry of Defence and General Headquarters have grown in influence, the seven emirates retain influence through the system of regional commands.

A newly formed tri-service Special Forces Command has been established at a purpose-built base on Sas Al Nakheel Island, near to Abu Dhabi city. The command includes land, air and naval forces, which are made available to the command on a task-by-task basis. Its aviation element, dubbed 18 Group, includes a variety of UAE air force and air defence helicopters, including transport, reconnaissance and attack types.

The UAE AF&AD currently operates five batteries of Raytheon I-Hawk SAMs to protect strategic targets. At least three batteries of the missiles are positioned around Abu Dhabi city.

The UAE navy also includes a naval aviation squadron with Eurocopter AS332B/F/M and AS565SB helicopters. The Army Aviation Group has been created by moving the McDonnell Douglas AH-64A Apache attack helicopters over to army control from the UAE AF&AD.

The F-16E/F Desert Falcon is one of the most advanced combat aircraft in the Middle East, and possesses capabilities far in excess of USAF versions of the F-16. (*Lockheed Martin*)

UAE Air Arms Order of Battle as at 1 May 2009.

Airbase	Locations	Wing/Base Designation	Squadon	Aircraft Type	Role	Civil Operator
UAE Air Force and Air Defence						
Western Air Force Command (Abu Dhabi)						
Al Dhafra Air Force Base	24° 14′ N 54° 32′ E		71 Squadron	Mirage 2000-9EAD/DAD	Air defence/Strike	
			76 Squadron	Mirage 2000-9EAD/DAD	Air defence/Strike	
			1 Shaheen Sqn	F-16E/F	Air defence/Strike	
			2 Shaheen Sqn	F-16E/F	Air defence/Strike	
			3 Shaheen Sqn	F-16E/F	Air defence/Strike	
Tuscon, Arizona			Training Cadre	F-16E/F	Air defence/Strike	
Al Safran AB	23° 38′ N 53° 49′ E		86 Squadron	Mirage 2000-9EAD/DAD	Air defence/Strike	
Al Ain Int'l	24° 15′ N 55° 36′ E	Flying Training School	Air College Sqn	Grob G115TA	Training (Basic training/Screening)	
		(Khalif bin Zayed Air College)	2 Sqn	AS350B, SA342L	Liaison/Observation	
				Bell 206B	Helicopter training	Horizon International
			4 Sqn	PC-7	Basic Training	
			Flying Instructor School Sqn	MB339	Instructor training	
			63 Sqn	Hawk T61, Hawk T63, Hawk T63A, Hawk T63C	Advanced training	
Al Ain – Falaj Hazaa	24° 15′ N 55° 36′ E			Cessna 2008B, Twin Otter	Training	
Bateen AFB A43	24° 25′ N 54° 27′ E	Transport Wing	C-130 Sqn	C-130H	Transport	
			Casa Sqn	CN-235M-100	Transport	
			Puma Sqn	SA330C, SA330F, IAR330L	Troop transport	

Airbase	Locations	Wing/Base Designation	Squadon	Aircraft Type	Role	Civil Operator
			6 Sqn	Bell 214, Bell 212, AB412HP/SP	Troop transport	
Sas al Nakheel	24° 26′ N 54° 31′ E	Special Ops Command	18 Group	CH-47C/D, AS365N, AS550C3, AW139, EC1551B, AH-64A, Grand Caravan II, DHC-6-300	Special Forces	

Central Air Force Command (Dubai)
Dubai Int'l A50 25° 15′ N 55° 21′ E

Airbase	Locations	Wing/Base Designation	Squadon	Aircraft Type	Role	Civil Operator
Minhad AFB	25° 01′ N 55° 22′ E		102 Sqn	Hawk Mk102, MB326KD (wfu), MB326LD (wfu)	Training	
			Transport Sqn	2 × C-130H-30, L-100-30, PC-6/ B2-H4, BN-2T, SC7-3M, SD330-UTT	Transport	
??			SAR Det	AW139/ Bell 412ER	SAR	Evergreen Helicopters
??			SAR Det	AW139/ Bell 412ER	SAR	Evergreen Helicopters
??			SAR Det	AW139/ Bell 412ER	SAR	Evergreen Helicopters

UAE Army

Airbase	Locations	Wing/Base Designation	Squadon	Aircraft Type	Role	Civil Operator
Al Dhafra Air Force Base	24° 14′ N 54° 32′ E		10th Army Aviation Brigade	AH-64A. AS550C3 Fennec	Attack/Scout	

UAE Navy

Airbase	Locations	Wing/Base Designation	Squadon	Aircraft Type	Role	Civil Operator
Bateen AFB	24° 25′ N 54° 27′ E		Navy Sqn	AS332B/F/M, AS565SB	Naval support/ ASW	

Airbase	Locations	Wing/Base Designation	Squadon	Aircraft Type	Role	Civil Operator
Police Air Wings						
Dubai Int'l	25° 15′ N 55° 21′ E		Dubai Police Air Element	AB206, AB412, A109K2, Bell 206, Ce172,Ce182N	Observation	
Ras-Al-Khaimah Int'l	25° 36′ N 55° 56′ E		Ras-Al-Khaimah Police Air Element	Mi-2, Sokol W3, Mi-8	Observation	
Sharjah Int'l	25° 19′ N 55° 31′ E		Sharjah Police Air Element	Bo-105, AB212, AB412, Bell 206, BK117B-1	Observation	
VIP Transport Units						
Sharjah Int'l A24	25° 19′ N 55° 31′ E		Ruler Of Sharjah	B737-2W8	VIP transport	
Bateen AFB	24° 25′ N 54° 27′ E		Private Flight Directorate, Amiri Flight	B747-4F6, B747SP-Z5, BAe146-100, Be350, Falcon 900	VIP transport	
Dubai Int'l	25° 15′ N 55° 21′ E		Dubai Air Wing	B737-BBJ, B747-2B4B, B747SP-31, G.1159A, G.1159C	VIP transport	
Ras-Al-Khaimah Int'l	25° 36′ N 55° 56′ E		Ruler Of Ras-Al-Khaimah		VIP transport	Fujairah Aviation
Umm Al Quwain	25° 34′ N 55° 39′ E		Umm Al Quwain Royal Flight		VIP transport	

French-made Mirage 2000s have been in UAE service since the early 1980s and have been progressively upgraded. *(US DoD)*

The first Desert Falcons arrive in the UAE in 2005. *(Lockheed Martin)*

UAE Inventory as at 1 May 2009.

Type	Active	Stored	Ordered	Required
United Arab Emirates Air Force & Air Defence				
ABU DHABI-based elements				
COMBAT AIRCRAFT				
F-16C/D Block 60	54/25			
Mirage 2000-9	61			
Mirage 5A/R/D/E		18		
Mirage III		12		
Rafale				63
ISR/SPECIAL MISSION				
C-295MPA			4	
Super King Air350	3			
AEW aircraft				4 to 6
Dash 8-315 MPA			4	
TANKER				
A330-200 MRT			3	
TRANSPORT				
C-212-200 Aviocar	4			
C-130H	6			
CN-235	7			
DHC-6	1			
Cessna 2008B	7		1	
An-32			5	
C-17A			4	
C-130J-30			12	
COMBAT HELICOPTER				
SA342L Gazelle		3		
AS532UC Cougar	3			
Bell 412SP/HP	3:06			
AB214B	3			
Bell 206		9		
AS565N3/UB/SB Panther	2:06:07			
SA330/IAR330L	0:00	2		
BO105CBS	4			
AW139	2		8	
Bell 412EP	2			
CH-47C			12	
AS350B		30??		
AS352			25?	
UH-60M	3			23
S-70A	5		10	

Type	Active	Stored	Ordered	Required
TRAINING AIRCRAFT/HELICOPTERS				
Hawk Mk63/Mk100	17/13			
PC-7	30			
Grob G115 Acro	12			
AS350B	14			
MB339A	5			
M-346				48
UNMANNED AERIAL VEHICLES				
Camcopter S-100	80			
Dubai-based elements				
TRANSPORT				
C-130H-30/L-100-30	1:01			
SC7 Skyvan	1			
Shorts 330UUT	1			
BN-2T Islander	1			
COMBAT HELICOPTER				
AB412	5			
BO105CBS	3			
TRAINING AIRCRAFT/HELICOPTERS				
MB326KD/MB326LD	3:02			
Hawk Mk61	3	2		
Bell 407	1			
Cessna 172	1			
EC-135	1			
UAE Army				
AS550C-3	12			
AH-64A Apache	30			
AH-64D			30 upgrades	
UAE Navy				
ISR/SPECIAL MISSION				
Learjet	2			
HELICOPTERS				
AS532SC Cougar	4			

Type	Active	Stored	Ordered	Required
Abu Dhabi Amiri Flight				
TRANSPORT				
A300-620	2			
BAe 146-100	1			
Super King Air350	2			
747SP	2			
737	4			
767	1			
Falcon 900/50	2:01			
An-124	1			
HELICOPTER				
AS332L Super Puma	2			
RJ100	1			
Abu Dhabi Police				
HELICOPTERS				
Bell 412	10			
BK-117	1			
AW-139	5		3	
Dubai Royal Flight/Air Wing				
747SP	5			
737	3			
Learjet 60	1			
Gulfstream II/IV	1:01			
Beech 1900D	1			
S-76A	1			
AS365N Dauphin	2		1	
Bell 212/214B	2:-1			
Bell 205	4			
AW139			2	
RJ-85			3	
Dubai Police Air Wing				
HELICOPTERS				
A109	3			
Bell 412	2			
Bell 206	11			
Bell 212	8			
BO105	13			

Type	Active	Stored	Ordered	Required
Ras al Khaimah Royal Flight				
Citation I	1			
PZL W-3A	1			
Commander 114B	1			
Mi-2			2	
Sharjah Royal Flight				
A319-433	1			
Bell 206B	3			
Bell 412	2			
BK-117	4			
Umm al Qaiwan Royal Flight				
Bell 222	1			
Fujariah Ruler's Flight				
Challenger 300	1			

Operational context and activity

Political stability in the Gulf region has long been a high priority for the UAE, and the country has been a major player over the past twenty-six years in efforts by the Gulf Co-operation Council (GCC) to co-ordinate mutual defence activities with Saudi Arabia, Kuwait, Bahrain, Qatar and Oman. This saw the participation of GCC forces in military operations in 1991 to drive Iraqi forces from occupied Kuwait, and until December 2005 the UAE contributed a battalion-sized ground force contingent to the organisation's Peninsula Shield deployment in northern Saudi Arabia. Co-operation has continued on a major project to enhance technical linkages between the GCC countries' air defence networks.

The UAE remains a leading member of the Arab League, and it has contributed significantly to the rebuilding of Lebanon after Israeli air strikes in the summer of 2006. UAE military aircraft also delivered humanitarian aid to Beirut and Syria.

The last decade has seen the UAE become increasingly interested in promoting security and assisting humanitarian relief operations outside the Gulf region, through the United Nations and other international organisations. This began to gain momentum during the 1999 Kosovo crisis, when UAE Aérospatiale Puma helicopters were dispatched to Albania to help UN-led humanitarian relief operations. Subsequently the UAE contributed a mechanised battle group to serve with the NATO-led peacekeeping force in Kosovo, supported by a contingent of six

AH-64A attack helicopters. This force served in the disputed Balkan territory for two years until late 2001.

Airbase infrastructure
The UAE AF&AD has six main operating bases. Al Dhafra and Al Safran airbases are the countries' main fast jet bases, and they are both hardened to allow the UAE AF&AD aircraft to survive a surprise attack. Al Dhafra has some twenty-four hardened shelters. The newest base is Al Safran, some eighty miles to the south-west of Abu Dhabi. The project to build this base has taken several years, and is understood to be costing more than $1 billion. The first Mirage 2000 squadron moved there in early 2007. The base has dual runways, hardened aircraft shelters and underground weapon storage sites. It is expected that the F-16 and Mirage 2000-9 force will move there permanently when the base is complete.

With the exception of Al Ain and Al Safran, the UAE AF&AD's main operating bases are in the coast region, and are beginning to be affected by urban sprawl, which prompted the move to develop Al Safran.

The helicopters assigned to the Special Operations Command are based at the newly constructed airbase at Sas Al Nakheel, near Abu Dhabi city.

Aircraft ordnance
During the mid-1990s, the UAE AF&AD purchased its first advanced precision-guided munition, the GEC Marconi Hakim long-range cruise missile, which had a range of some twenty to fifty kilometres. It is understood that 300 weapons were purchased.

A package of French weapons was purchased in the 1980s to equip Dassault Mirage 2000s and Aérospatiale Gazelle attack helicopters. These included HOT wire-guided anti-tank missile for the Gazelles, AM-39 Exocet anti-ship missiles for the Mirages, along with R-530 MICA semi-active radar air-to-air guided missiles and R-550 Magic heat-seeking guided missiles.

Some 360 Hellfire laser-guided missiles and 4,200 Hydra-70 rockets were purchased for the Apaches in the late 1990s.

To equip the F-16 Desert Falcons, a $2 billion package of arms was ordered from the USA, including 491 AIM-120B advanced medium-range air-to-air missiles (AMRAAM) and twelve AMRAAM training missiles, 267 AIM-9M 1/2 Sidewinder missiles and eighty Sidewinder training missiles, 163 AGM-88 high-speed anti-radiation missiles (HARM) and four HARM training missiles, 1,163 AGM-65D/G Maverick missiles and twenty training missiles, fifty-two AGM-84 Harpoon missiles, and thousands of other bombs, ammunition, and training rounds.

The UAE AF&AD announced in November 2007 that it had ordered CBU-105 sensor-fused weapons from Textron Defense Systems. The contract includes documentation, training and in-country support; deliveries were due to begin in 2008 and there is an option for additional weapons. Company officials at the Dubai Air Show would not disclose the value of the contract or the number of weapons ordered. However, they did state that the weapons were for use on UAE Lockheed Martin F-16 fighter aircraft.

Strategic weapons

The UAE has purchased a number of 'Black Shaheen' cruise missiles, which have a range of 280 kilometres to ensure they remain within the limitations of the US-led Missile Technology Control Regime (MTCR). The first pre-production examples of the missile, which are being deployed on the Mirage 2000-9, were delivered in 2003. To help with the targeting of these weapons, the UAE Ministry of Defence has purchased a satellite ground station to allow access to high-definition commercial satellite imagery.

UAE AF&AD has a strategic reconnaissance capability, via its Space Reconnaissance Centre in Abu Dhabi, which has been in operation for some twenty years to provided access and analysis of the product from Russian, SPOT and Landsat satellites. In late 2000, the UAE established a national ground station with direct reception of IKONOS, IRS and KOMPSAT satellites imagery data. UAE nationals control all stages of data reception, processing, analysis and production. The UAE is also home to the Thuraya Satellite Telecommunications System, which rivals the US-Iridium system.

A strategic air defence requirement emerged in the mid-1990s, but funding issues continue to delay it. UAE interest in the Russian S-300 system was headed off by US government pressure, which claimed the Russian system would not be inter-operable with US-controlled Coalition air defence networks in the Middle East. In 2008, it emerged that the UAE was negotiating with the USA over the purchase of the Theatre High-Altitude Air Defence (THAAD) ballistic missile defence system.

The UAE has been identified as a sales target for the Indian-Russian BrahMos Aerospace long-range cruise missile.

Procurement

The UAE AF&AD has commanded the lion's share of new procurement spending since the late 1990s, with major programmes to buy eighty new F-16E/F Desert Falcon multi-role combat aircraft from the US defence giant Lockheed Martin. This was on the heels of deals with France to buy new Mirage 2000-9 combat jets and upgrade the UAE AF&AD's existing Dassault Mirage 2000 fleet to this new standard. These projects will give the UAE AF&AD long-range precision strike and beyond-visual-range air-to-air combat capabilities, making it one of the advanced air forces in the Middle East. This looks set to continue, with details emerging in early 2009 that the UAE was negotiating with France to buy sixty-three Dassault Rafale multi-role fighters to augment both the Mirage 2000s and F-16s from 2012 onwards.

The Desert Falcon deal was estimated as being worth $6.4 billion, including an associated weapons package from Raytheon, the development of Northrop Grumman Agile Beam Radar (ABR) for improved tracking of multiple targets. Special aircraft equipment for the so-called Block 60 version of the F-16 will include

Aérospatiale SA 330H Puma

The Anglo-French Puma has been widely exported to Middle East countries, serving in a wide-range of roles. UK and French forces have used the Puma extensively in the Middle East. Upgraded versions, including the Super Puma family, feature more powerful engines that are very useful in the 'hot and high' environments found in the Middle East.

Crew: 3
Capacity: 16 passengers
Length: 59 ft 6½ in. (18.15 m)
Rotor diameter: 49 ft 2½ in. (15.00 m)
Max takeoff weight: 7,000 kg (15,430 lb)
Powerplant: Two Turboméca Turmo IVC turboshafts, 1,575 hp (1,175 kW) each
Maximum speed: 138 kts (159 mph, 257 km/h)
Range: 313 nm (360 miles, 580 km)

Armament
   Guns: Coaxial 7.62 mm (0.30 in.) machine-guns, Side-firing 20 mm (0.787 in.) cannon

UAE AH-64A Apaches served on peacekeeping duties in Kosovo from 1999 to 2001. (*Author*)

a new integrated electronic warfare system (IEWS) supplied by Northrop Grumman, which also supplies the internal forward-looking infra-red and targeting system (IFTS) for the aircraft. General Electric has been selected to supply the engines for the aircraft.

Ten F-16E/Fs were delivered to Al Dhafra airbase in May 2005, and Lot 2 deliveries started in 2006. Lot 3 aircraft were scheduled to arrive in 2007, and they will feature a terrain-avoidance system. Integration work has begun on the Al Hakeen stand-off precision-guided missile. This latter weapon was one of the first bespoke products developed specifically for the UAE by the British company, GEC (now part of MBDA), in the 1990s under conditions of great secrecy.

The UAE was the launch customer for the Mirage 2000-9, ordering thirty-two new-build aircraft, including twenty single-seaters and twelve two-seaters as the 'Mirage 2000-9D'. Initial deliveries of the UAE Mirages were in the spring of 2003. Some thirty of the UAE AF&AD older Mirage 2000s were also upgraded to Mirage 2000-9 capability.

The UAE Mirage 2000-9s are well equipped for the strike mission, with the 'Shehab' laser-targeting pod, a variant of the Thales Damocles pod, and the Nahar navigation pod, complementing the air-to-ground modes of the RDY-2 radar. The UAE is also obtaining the 'Black Shahin' cruise missile, a variant of the MBDA APACHE cruise missile. The Mirage III and V fleets were retired in 2003 and are now up for sale after the completion of the Mirage 2000-9 deliveries.

On the heels of these major investments in combat aircraft, the UAE AF&AD is keen to acquire up to sixty lead-in fighter trainer (LIFT) aircraft to replace its current British Aerospace Hawk Mk 102s.

The UAE was a partner with EADS on the ill-fated German Mako project, but this has failed to proceed, and the BAE Systems Hawk Mk 128s, Alenia Aermacchi M-346 or Lockheed Martin/Korean Aerospace T-50 are all now in the running. A new fleet of turboprop-powered trainers is also to be acquired, with the Raytheon T-6 Texan II, Embraer Super Tucano and Pilatus PC-21 competing. The Hawk was dropped from the AJT contest in November 2007. In February 2009, the UAE AF&AD selected the M-346, with some forty-eight aircraft required by 2012 in a deal worth up to $1 billion. Contract negotiations are yet to conclude. The UAE is also looking for a private-sector company to manage its flying training system, based around a new air academy.

UAE pilot training on the F-16E/F began at Tucson Air National Guard Base, Arizona, in September 2004, and the first group of pilots completed their training in April 2005. Additional pilots began F-16 training in Turkey in February 2002. Ten pilots joined the NATO Flying Training in Canada programme in November 2004.

The influx of new advanced fighter aircraft into UAE AF&AD meant it was very keen to ramp up its pilot-training pipeline. Lockheed Martin began negotiating to provide a lead-in fighter-training programme to the UAE AF&AD at the Alliance International Airport at Fort Worth, Texas, in a deal that could have been worth $201 million to the US defence giant and its partner, the Alliance Aviation Center of Excellence.

In the export approval notice that was delivered to the US Congress in July 2007, the project was described as 'enabling the UAE to develop mission-ready and experienced pilots through training by providing a "capstone" course that would take experienced pilots and significantly improves their tactical proficiency'. After completing the introduction to 'fighter fundamentals' on leased ex-Norwegian Northrop Grumman F-5B aircraft, the UAE pilots were to transition to F-16 Block 60-type conversion training at Tucson. In June 2008, the deal collapsed as the UAE moved to accelerate its LIFT purchase.

The UAE AF&AD currently operates a fleet of six C-130 Hercules aircraft, which have been in service for more than thirty years and are in need of service-life extension. An avionics upgrade to some of the aircraft was reportedly under consideration, as is an outright replacement by new tactical airlifters, with the current generation of the Hercules, the C-130J, and the Airbus Military A400M seen as leading contenders.

Next on the agenda are force-multiplying assets to extend the range of the UAE AF&AD strike assets and their ability to participate in networked Coalition operations. Airborne early warning and control (AEW&C) capability is particularly sought after. The UAE AF&AD is still considering buying five Northrop Grumman E-2Cs upgraded to the Hawkeye 2000 standard, and Saab has been proposing its Erieye systems. In a clear sign that the AEW&C programme was moving forward, the US Defense Security Cooperation Agency notified the US Congress in December 2007 of a possible foreign military sale to the United Arab Emirates of upgrades and refurbishments of E-2C aircraft, as well as associated equipment and services. The total value, if all options were exercised, could be as high as $437 million. The request covered refurbished ex-US Navy E-2C Group II Navigation Upgrade configured aircraft. By early 2009, no decision had been made.

A tanker purchase is also anticipated to support long-range F-16 and Mirage operations, with Boeing promoting a 767 variant, EADS offering Airbus A330 and Russian industry trying to sell the Ilyushin Il-78 Midas. The A330-200 was selected in February 2007, and contract negotiations came to a conclusion in February 2008 with an order for three aircraft to be delivered by 2011.

The helicopter force is to be enhanced with a proposed $808 million purchase of twenty-six Sikorsky UH-60M Blackhawks, and the $90 million Puma upgrade project with Romania is progressing, with the first two returned to service in April 2006. This deal involved the upgrade of fifteen original UAE and ten ex-South African Air Force aircraft, which will eventually be brought up to SA330SM standard. Eight AB139s were ordered in February 2005 for $83 million. Everygreen International was contracted in August 2006 to provide SAR coverage with two AW139s and two Bell 412EPs at three locations. In November 2007, the UAE ordered ten S-70As from Sikorsky and export approval from the US government was sought in September 2008 for the purchase of fourteen UH-60Ms valued at $774 million, including a large weapons package of AGM-114 Hellfire missiles and guns.

The UAE's airlift capability was boosted when an An-124 was delivered in February 2004, although it is unclear if this aircraft is operated directly by the country's air force. Five An-32s were ordered from the Ukraine during 2006. The C-130 fleet is receiving defensive equipment. Two PC-6s were sold during 2006. Light tactical transport is to be provided by an order for eight Cessna 200B Caravans.

A significant enhancement to the UAE airlift capability was announced in 2008. It is buying twelve Lockheed Martin C-130J-30 Hercules and four Boeing C-17 Globemasters.

Some of the UAE AF&AD's Bell 206Bs have already been sold to the service's flight training provider, and proposals exist for the service's AS350Bs also to be sold to the same company. The Mirage III and V fleets were retired in 2003 and they are up for sale. Since 2003, the UAE has provided military assistance to the new Iraqi government in Baghdad to rebuild its armed forces, including donating surplus Bell 206 Kiowa light helicopters. In 2006, surplus Gazelles were donated to the Lebanese air force. Further Pumas were donated to Lebanon in 2009.

The UAE AF&AD hopes to replace its BAe Hawks in the training role, and the surplus aircraft could be given to Lebanon. *(BAE Systems)*

A large fleet of Bell 212/214 helicopters is in UAE service. *(Author)*

The Aermacchi M-346 was selected by the UAE in 2009 to replace the Hawks. *(Aermacchi)*

French Rafale combat aircraft are reportedly next on the UAE's shopping list. *(US DoD)*

The agility of the UAE army has been enhanced by the transfer of thirty AH-64As to the newly formed Army Aviation Group, and its capability will be considerably enhanced between 2008 and 2010 by upgrading the helicopters to D-model standard by Boeing and Lockheed Martin under contracts worth more than $300 million signed in January 2007. Some forty micro-UAVs based on a version of the Schiebel S-100 Camcopters, dubbed Al Saber, are on order, which will give the army a close-in intelligence, surveillance, targeting and reconnaissance (ISTAR) capability. These will augment Denel Seeker UAVs, which have been operated by the UAE AF&AD for more than fifteen years.

Central to efforts by the UAE to create more expeditionary armed forces is the recent formation of a Special Operations Command. As well as controlling army special forces units, this tri-service command can also draw on units for the air force and navy. Some twelve CH-47C Chinook support helicopters bought from Libya will be modernised to D standard, with Lycoming T-55-L-7R engines, by Agusta Westland to support the new command. The first examples were undergoing testing in Italy in December 2007.

The UAE has been seeking to acquire four maritime surveillance aircraft since the late 1990s. UAE initially selected the EADS-CASA C-295 at IDEX in March 2001. However, the contract was not finalised, and this led Alenia Aeronautica, a Finnmeccanica company, to submit the ATR-72 ASW aircraft in competition with the C-295. It was reported in November 2005 that Alenia Aeronautica had submitted an altered bid, listing an increased power certification for the aircraft engine and a longer time on station.

In 2007, the UAE bought two surplus de Havilland Dash-8 airliners for conversion into maritime patrol aircraft (MPA), and the aircraft were flown to the Middle East in June 2007. A competition is now under way for the conversion work, with the Canadian company Provincial Aerospace Ltd being known to have submitted a bid for the project. Two additional Dash-8 airframes are also reported to be on order. In late 2008, it emerged that Canada's Provincial Aviation had won a $291 million contract to convert four of the Dash-8Q300s into MPAs.

In December 2007, the US Defense Security Cooperation Agency notified the US Congress of a possible foreign military sale to the UAE of the Patriot Advanced Capability-3 Missile System, as well as associated equipment and services. The total value, if all options are exercised, could be as high as $9 billion. It said the government of the United Arab Emirates had requested a possible sale of an air defence system consisting of 288 Patriot Advanced Capability-3 (PAC-3) missiles, 216 Guidance Enhanced Missiles-T (GEM-T), nine Patriot fire units that include ten phased-array radar sets, ten engagement control stations on trailers and thirty-seven launching stations (four per fire unit). This has since been overtaken by the decision to acquire the THAAD system.

Presence of foreign forces

In response to the Al Qaeda attacks on New York and Washington DC in September 2001, the UAE joined the US-led Global War on Terror and allowed the USAF, including Northrop Grumman RQ-4 Global Hawk unmanned aerial vehicles, Lockheed U-2 Dragon Lady reconnaissance aircraft and McDonnell Douglas KC-10 tanker aircraft supporting the assault on Afghanistan, to use bases in the country. Canada, Italy and other nations contributing forces to the NATO-led International Security Assistance Force (ISAF) have also been allowed to use UAE airbases to provide logistic support to their contingents in Afghanistan.

The UAE's alliance with the United States of America continued during the invasion of Iraq in 2003, and the USAF units based in the country participated in Operation Iraqi Freedom, in reconnaissance and support roles.

The UAE AF&AD has a long tradition of participation in multinational exercises with US and other forces run from the UAE's air warfare centre at Al Dhafra airbase, near Abu Dhabi. The USAF has hinted that it wants to deploy Lockheed Martin F-22 Raptors to the centre to participate in training exercises in the region.

UK RAF Eurofighter Typhoon and Panavia Tornado F3 aircraft visited Al Dhafra in late 2007 for a major air defence exercise with the UAE AF&AD. A similar exercise took place in late 2008.

The UAE has wide foreign policy ambitions in line with the country's growing economic status. It is actively engaged in the UN, Arab League and Gulf Co-operation Council. In 1994, the UAE signed a formal defence pact with the USA. This was followed in 1995 by a defence treaty with France, and the UK signed a defence co-operation agreement in 1996. In January 2008, the French President Nicolas Sarkozy signed an agreement with the UAE to open a military base in Abu Dhabi. Some 500 personnel are to be transferred from the French base in Djibouti to the new facility, which will be predominantly to support naval operations in the Persian Gulf region. In October 2008, the French air force deployed six Mirage 2000-5 jets and a KC-135F tanker to Al Dhafra as part of the new military engagement policy.

Assessment

A decade ago, the UAE AF&D launched a major expansion programme as part of the Emirates' ambitions to create a modern air arm, capable of expeditionary operations.

If plans to buy Dassault Rafale 4th-generation fighters come to fruition, it will put the UAE AF&AD in the front rank of Arab air forces.

Many observers are concerned that the UAE AF&AD's modernisation plans are running ahead of its ability to train suitable manpower to operate its new advanced combat aircraft.

The UAE AF&AD has yet to be tested in a major war or crisis. Only then will the UAE government know if it has made a good investment.

CHAPTER SIXTEEN

Yemen

Population	23 million
Military/paramilitary aircraft	228
Air Force personnel	3,000

al Quwwat al Jawwiya al Yemeniya (Yemen Air and Air Defence Force)

History

Yemen has a complex and bloody history. The south fell under British colonial influence in the nineteenth century, while the interior of the country was part of the Turkish Ottoman Empire until the First World War. In the post-World War Two period it was two states. At various times the two Yemeni states backed different sides in the Cold War. The departure of British forces in 1967 opened the way for the South to drift into the Soviet orbit. The ending of the Cold War saw North and South Yemen merged in 1990. The armed forces, including the air forces, of the two countries were amalgamated. It experienced a civil war in 1994, and sporadic fighting continues.

The country's poor economic position means it has limited revenue to fund military modernisation, and most of its air force equipment dates from the 1970s and 1980s.

Structure

The bulk of the Yemeni air force is based at Sana. Serviceability rates are poor. Yemen's air force employs 3,000 personnel to support 109 combat aircraft and ten armed helicopters. Its main strike force is four strike squadrons, and there are four air defence squadrons. The air force controls Yemen's thirty surface-to-air missile batteries consisting of SA-2s, SA-3s, SA-6s, and SA-9s.

Operational activity

Since 2002, Yemen has allied itself with the USA in the Global War on Terror. In return it has received US military aid.

Government troops, backed by Mi-8 and Mi-24 helicopters, have been engaged in several sweeps in the mountainous regions against rebel tribes and supporters of Islamic fundamentalist clerics.

Helicopters, transport aircraft and ground attack fighters are used regularly to support periodic sweeps against insurgent groups and lawless tribes in the country's interior. The Yemeni air force co-operates with the US Central Intelligence Agency

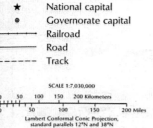

International boundary
★ National capital
⊙ Governorate capital
┼┼┼┼ Railroad
────── Road
------ Track

SCALE 1:7,030,000

0 50 100 150 200 Kilometers
0 50 100 150 200 Miles

Lambert Conformal Conic Projection,
standard parallels 12°N and 38°N

Yemeni Air Arms Order of Battle as at 1 May 2009.

Airbase	Location	Squadron	Aircraft Type	Role
Aden	12° 49′ N 45° 1′ E	128 Sqn Det	Ka-27/28	SAR
Al Anad	13° 10′ N 44° 45′ E	?? Fighter	MiG-21	Air defence
		?? Training	L-39	Training
		128 Sqn Det	Ka-27/28	SAR
Bayhan				
Al Hudaydah	14° 45′ N 42° 58′ E	6 Fighter Sqn	MiG-21	Air defence
		128 Sqn Det	Ka-27/28	SAR
Kamaran Island				
Mukalla/Riyan	14° 39′ N 49° 22′ E	128 Sqn Det	Ka-27/28	SAR
San'a	15° 28′ N 44° 13′ E	9 Sqn	MiG-29	Air defence
		26 Sqn	Su-22	CAS
		121 Sqn	F-5	CAS
		4 Transport	An-26	Transport
		115 Sqn	C-130/L-100, Il-76	Transport
		?? Attack Helicopter	Mi-24	Attack
		3 Sqn	Bell 206	l
		124 Sqn	Bell 214	Liaison
Taiz	13° 41′ N 44° 8′ E	8 Sqn	Mi-8	Troop transport
		9 Sqn	Mi-24	Attack
		128 Sqn Det	Ka-27/28	SAR
		26 Sqn	MiG-21MF	Air Defence
Ataq	14° 33′ N 46° 49′ E			

in making air space available for General Atomics' MQ-1 Predator unmanned aerial vehicle (UAV) operations across the country. One of the US drones carried out a missile strike on suspected al-Qaeda operatives in central Yemen in November 2002.

Mil Mi-17 helicopters supported a military operation against insurgents in the Hauf Sufian Beit Ayanka area in February 2007. One helicopter was lost to hostile fire.

In January 2006, Yemeni combat helicopters are reported to have taken part in operations against insurgents loyal to the late rebel cleric, Hussein Badr Eddin al-Hawthi; further operations followed in the first half of 2006, with rebel forces'

Yemen Inventory as at 15 April 08.

Type	Active	Stored	Ordered	Required
al Quwwat al Jawwiya al Yemeniya (Yemen Air and Air Defence Force)				
COMBAT AIRCRAFT				
Su-27/UB	10:-2			
MiG-23BN/UM		25		
MiG-21MF/bis/UM	18	38/12		
MiG-29SMT/UBT	13		32	
F-5E/F-5B	11:-2			
F-7	6			
Su-22BKL/M-2/U	35			
TRANSPORT				
An-12B	3			
An-2	1			
An-24	5			
An-26	6			
C-130H	2			
Il-76	3			
SC7 Skyvan	2			
COMBAT HELICOPTER				
Mi-24	15			
Mi-8 /17	46			
AB206B JetRanger		6		
AB212/AB212	5:-1			
AB204B	2			
TRAINING AIRCRAFT				
L-39C	12			
Yak-11	18			
Zlin 242L	11			
Government of the Yemen Republic				
Boeing 727	1			
Boeing 747	1			

Saana international airport is the main hub for the Yemeni air force. *(Google Earth)*

hide-outs among targets engaged by armed helicopters. Previously, in mid-2004, Mi-8 assault and Mi-24 gunship helicopters were employed against rebel tribes and supporters of Islamic fundamentalist clerics in mountainous regions.

No contributions have been made to any international peace-support operations.

French Navy Dassault Rafales recently conducted joint training with the Yemeni MiG-29 squadron.

Pilot training in line squadrons is thought to be variable because of a lack of spares from the Yemeni air force's 1970s-era aircraft. When the MiG-29s entered service it was difficult to find suitably qualified pilots who were able to make the leap to the more modern MiG-29. Three of the new aircraft have been lost in crashes that have been attributed to pilot error.

There have also been reports of Iranian involvement with Shia-militant groups, including supplying small unmanned aerial vehicles, one of which has been claimed shot down by government forces.

Airbase infrastructure

Yemen's airbase infrastructure is of very mixed quality. The airbases in the south were renovated by the Soviets during the 1970s and 1980s, but since then have been largely neglected. The most highly developed is Sana, which houses the most modern combat aircraft. Even at this base there are no hardened shelters or other such facilities.

Aircraft ordnance

Little is known about the Yemeni air force's ordnance inventory, but it is thought to include R-13 (AA-2 'Atoll') and AIM-9 Sidewinder heat-seeking guided missiles.

Strategic weapons

The Yemen has a significant force of Scud-class ballistic missiles, a number of which were supplied by North Korea in 2002.

Procurement

In August 2006, a $1.3 billion order was placed for thirty-two more MiG-29SMTs to augment the eighteen previously delivered or upgraded. Ten Su-22s are being overhauled in Belarus under a contract signed in late 2005. Yemen is considering the acquisition of surveillance-configured CN-235s from Indonesian Aerospace to patrol vast desert expanses, which the USA claims are home to al-Qaeda training camps.

Yemen has been seeking to enhance the capabilities of its air and air defence forces through the acquisition of MiG-29 fighter aircraft. Delivery of a batch of at least twenty began in 2002, this number including some two-seaters for training purposes. Subsequently, in September 2006, it was announced that Yemen had signed a protocol of intention with MiG, covering the supply of an additional 32 MiG-29SMT aircraft at a cost of around $1.3 billion; formal contract signature was expected to take place in the first quarter of 2007, and the same announcement also mentioned that MiG had won a tender covering modernisation of sixty-six aircraft supplied earlier. These are almost certainly MiG-21s.

There are few details available as to how effectively the MiG-29 aircraft have been absorbed, but the air force has previous experience of this type, some of which were acquired from Moldova in 1993. The number of aircraft involved was small (perhaps as many as ten, although some sources allude to just four, including a two-seater), and it is doubtful if more than two or three were made airworthy before the 1994 civil war. These machines were eventually returned to Moldova.

Delivery of additional MiG-29s will assist the air force to remedy shortcomings arising from the fact that many of the aircraft in the inventory are aged, obsolete or in storage. Emphasis has recently been placed on enhancing effectiveness of training, with Yemen having received twelve former-Soviet Aero L-39C Albatros twin-seater aircraft for basic and advanced jet training.

Seabird Aviation Jordan (SAJ), part of the King Abdullah II Design and Development Bureau, has reportedly supplied one Seeker SB7L light reconnaissance aircraft.

Presence of foreign forces

The USA and UK have small training teams in Yemen. The US Central Intelligence Agency also has a strong presence in Yemen as part of its effort to monitor Islamic militant groups that might have loyalty to al-Qaeda. During 2008, international naval forces began to use Aden as a logistic hub to support anti-piracy patrols off the Somali coast.

CHAPTER SEVENTEEN

UK Air Power over the Middle East

For the final three years of the Iraq no-fly-zone mission, the RAF presence in the Middle East was fairly constant. The SEPECAT Jaguar force operated from Incirlik in Turkey over northern Iraq. In the south, Tornado GR1/GR4s flew from Kuwait's Ali Al Salem on strike and reconnaissance missions. Saudi Arabian restrictions of strike aircraft meant that the Tornado F3 force operated from Prince Sultan airbase. Each detachment was usually between six and eight aircraft. A pair of Vickers VC-10 tankers supported the southern no-fly zone and a single tanker usually operated from Incirlik to support the Jaguars. A pair of Nimrod MR2 maritime patrol aircraft usually operated from Seeb in Oman or Muharraq in Bahrain to help enforce oil sanctions on Iraq.

The RAF surged aircraft into the Middle East in the first three months of 2003 in preparation for the invasion of Iraq.

The UK's contribution to occupation operations in Iraq between 2003 and 2006 was predominantly an Army responsibility, but the RAF was deployed in strength to provide air support in a variety of ways. An air commodore based at the CAOC in Al Udeid was responsible for ensuring that RAF operations were closely integrated into US air activity in the Middle East.

A detachment of half a dozen Tornado GR4 bomber/reconnaissance aircraft (drawn in rotation from RAF Marham and RAF Lossiemouth) was maintained in the Gulf region until July 2009 in case British troops required close air support. It also contributed to supporting US ground troops throughout Iraq. The detachment was based at Ali Al Salem until it moved to Al Udeid in Qatar in 2004 during major renovation and construction work at the Kuwaiti base. A pair of VC-10 tanker/transports from 101 Squadron were based at Bahrain's Muharraq airport to support RAF and US Navy fighters until 2006, when they moved to Al Udeid.

Two Nimrod maritime patrol aircraft drawn from 120, 201 and 206 Squadrons were forward-based at Seeb in Oman until early 2009 for maritime reconnaissance, and a Nimrod in Basra was used to patrol overland oil pipelines in Iraq to prevent sabotage.

Five Puma helicopters from 33 Squadron and five Chinook helicopters from 18 and 27 Squadrons were based at Basra International airport to provide air mobility for British troops during 2004, along with eight Westland Lynx 7/9s and Gazelle AH.1s of the Army Air Corps. Royal Navy Sea King HC.4s of 845 and 846 Naval

RAF Tornado GR4s bore the brunt of RAF operations over Iraq from 1990 to May 2009, when the UK stood down its air contribution to Coalition operations in that Middle East country. *(USAF)*

Air Squadron replaced the Pumas at the end of 2004. The Sea Kings were equipped with Wescam MX-15 electro-optical video cameras and downlinks to allow senior commanders to watch incidents in real time.

During the spring of 2005, the Chinooks were replaced by Agusta Westland Merlin HC.3s of 28 Squadron to allow the big Boeing helicopters to prepare for their new mission to Afghanistan in 2006. The Gazelles were withdrawn in 2006 because their defensive systems were not up to countering the insurgent threat.

Basra airport was guarded by an RAF Regiment field squadron and Force Protection Wing headquarters from 2003 to 2009.

A number of 7 Squadron Chinook equipped for special forces tasks are also in Iraq, and are known to have operated around Baghdad as part of the Joint Special Forces Aviation Wing detachment. They have been augmented by Pumas and AAC Lynx AH.7s of 657 Squadron. Four Pumas have been lost in accidents.

An HS-125 transport aircraft from 32 (The Royal) Squadron was based in the region to move senior commanders around. Initially they flew from Al Udeid, but relocated to Muharraq in 2006.

Royal Navy Lynx helicopters provided an important maritime airborne surveillance contribution in Middle East waters. *(Author)*

Basra International airport was the hub of UK air operations in Iraq from 2003 to 2009. *(Author)*

Hawker Siddeley Nimrod MR2

The veteran Nimrod is the mainstay of the RAF's maritime patrol force and has operated in the Middle East almost continuously since the mid-1980s, predominantly from Seeb in Oman. After 2001, the Nimrod was enhanced with overland surveillance capabilities, including Wescam MX-15 electro-optical video cameras and real-time downlinks. Nimrods based in Basra supported the UK occupation of Iraq from 2004 onwards.

Crew: 12
Length: 126 ft 9 in. (38.63 m)
Wingspan: 114 ft 10 in. (35.00 m)
Height: 31 ft (9.45 m)
Maximum take-off weight: 192,000 lb (87,090 kg)
Powerplant: Four Rolls-Royce Spey turbofans, 12,160 lbf (54.09 kN) each
Maximum speed: 575 mph (923 km/h)
Cruise speed: 490 mph (787 km/h)
Range: 5,180–5,755 miles (8,340–9,265 km)

BRITISH AIR DEPLOYMENTS
Total 206 aircraft and helicopters
(all squadrons/units RAF except where marked)

Incirlik, Turkey: 4 × Jaguar GR3, 1 × VC10 (10/101 Sqn)

Akrotiri, Cyprus: 1 × VC10 medivac, 8 × C130K/J (LTW)

Iraq, Jordan/Western Iraq: 8 × Harrier GR7 (3 Sqn), 2 × Canberra PR9 (39 Sqn), 8 × Chinook (7 Sqn), 6 × Lynx AH7 (657 Sqn AAC)

Kuwait, Ali al Salem: 18 × Tornado GR4 (II Sqn, 9 Sqn, 31 Sqn, 617 Sqn)

Kuwait, Ahmed al Jaber: 12 × Harrier GR7 (IV Sqn)

Kuwait/Iraq (1 UK Armed Div); 4 × Phoenix UAV launcher and 29 air vehicles (32 Regt RA)

Saudi Arabiam Prince Sultan AB: 14 × Tornado F3 (43, 111 Sqns) 2 HS125 (32 Sqn), 4 E3D AWACS (8/23 Sqn), 4 × Nimrod MR2 120/201/206 Sqn), 7 × VC10 (10/101 Sqn), 1 × Nimrod R1 (51 Sqn)

Bahrain, Muharraq: 4 × Tristar (216 sqn)

Qatar, Al Udeid: 12 × Tornado GR4 (II Sqn, 12 Sqn, 617 Sqn) 1 × HS125 (32 Sqn)

UAE: 4 × C130K/J (LTW) (det. to Camp Coyote, Kuwait)

Oman, Seeb: 2 × Nimrod MR2 (120/201/206 Sqn)

Kuwait, Ali al Salem and Iraq FOB (Joint Helicopter Force): 6 × Chinook (18 Sqn), 7 × Puma (33 Sqn), 12 × Lynx and 10 × Gazelle (3 Regt AAC – Attached 16 Air Assault Brigade)

HMS *Ocean* (Commando Helicopter Force): 10 × Sea King (845 NAS), 6 × Lynx and 6 × Gazelle (847 NAS)

HMS *Ark Royal*: 5 × Chinook (18 Sqn – Joint Helicopter Force), 4 × Sea King AEW7 (849 NAS)

RFA *Fort Victoria*: 4 × Merlin of 814 (NAS)

RFA *Argus*, RFA *Austin* and RFA *Rosalie*: 6 × Sea King Mk 6 (820 NAS) in hack role.

HMS *Liverpool*, HMS *Edinburgh*, HMS *York*, HMS *Marlborough*

HMS *Richmond*, HMS *Chatham* (2 × Lynx), HMS *Cardiff*: Total 9 Lynx HAS3/HMA8 (815 NAS)

During 2003 and 2004, two Hercules C4/5 (J model) transport aircraft from 24 and 30 Squadrons were based at Basra and Al Udeid for inter-theatre transport missions, including flying into Baghdad and Balad to support the British mission at Coalition headquarters in the city. Older Hercules C1/C3 (K model) aircraft of 47 and 70 Squadrons are also tasked for operations in Iraq from bases in the UK, Cyprus and Al Udeid. One C-130 was shot down in 2005 near Baghdad on a special forces mission, and another was blown up by a mine on an improvised landing strip in Maysan province in 2007. VC-10 tanker/transport aircraft from 10 Squadron and C-17 transport aircraft from 99 Squadron provide strategic airlift of troops and supplies direct into Iraq from bases in the UK, or via a regional air transport hub at Al Udeid.

The upsurge in rocket attacks on Basra airport in 2006 and 2007 prompted a major rethink of British basing. The C-130 detachment was pulled back to Al-Udeid in the summer of 2006, and the Nimrod based at Basra followed a year later. The threat of rocket strikes meant it was too dangerous to fly in VC-10s direct, so the C-130 force was increased to four C-130Js, and all troops movements were made on these aircraft, via Al Udeid. The rocket attacks were so intense in 2007 that the Merlins also had to be pulled back to Kuwait, leaving only the AAC Lynx and Sea Kings at Basra. The draw-down of UK forces meant the Royal Navy Sea Kings left Iraq in 2008 and the Lynx force took over the Broadsword mission. Royal Navy Lynx AH.7s of 847 Naval Air Squadron deployed to Iraq in 2006 and 2008. One of the squadron's Lynxes was shot down by a shoulder-launched anti-aircraft missile in Basra city in 2006.

The Nimrod MR 2 detachment at Seeb was committed to support the UK operation in Afghanistan in early 2006, so the Royal Navy in July 2006 deployed six Merlin HM.1 maritime patrol helicopters and fifty personnel of 814 Naval Air Squadron to Seeb in Oman to patrol the Straits of Hormuz to replace the RAF jets. These helicopters were committed to anti-piracy operations off Somalia on 2008, flying from Salalah airport in southern Oman.

The Merlin detachment operated in support of the multinational Combined Task Force 150 (CTF 150), which conducts maritime security operations (MSOs) in the Gulf of Aden, the Gulf of Oman, the Arabian Sea, the Red Sea and the Indian Ocean. The Merlins use their Blue Kestrel surface surveillance radar and Link 11 data-link to help build the Coalition's maritime picture in the key choke-points of the Straits of Hormuz and Horn of Africa. Additional surveillance support to CTF 150 was provided by two Royal Navy Sea King ASaC.7 airborne surveillance and control helicopters from 857 NAS embarked on the afloat support ship RFA *Fort Austin* from February 2007. *Fort Austin* had been conducting operations in the Gulf of Oman, the Gulf of Aden and around the Horn of Africa, operating as part of the UK Operation Kalash.

CHAPTER EIGHTEEN

US Air Power in the Middle East

The United States has been the dominant military force in the Middle East region over the past decade. Since 2003, more than 200,000 US military personnel have been deployed continuously to the region. US air power has been a key component of the US presence in the region throughout this period, with several hundred aircraft and helicopters deployed at any one time. This peaked at more than 2,000 during the invasion of Iraq in March and April 2003, before dropping back to around 700 to 800 during the occupation of Iraq from 2003 to 2009.

US air units deploy to the region from their home bases in the USA, Europe, Japan or South Korea, on temporary deployments of between four months and a year. Almost every air unit from all four US armed services has deployed to the Middle East over the past decade, resulting in the build-up of an unprecedented degree of expertise and experience of flying and fighting in the region.

The USA (as well as the UK) deploys only its best aircraft and weapons systems to the Middle East to ensure they have a combat edge over potential opponents. All US air units arrive in the Middle East fully trained and combat ready after under taking extensive pre-deployment training. This puts them at a considerable advantage compared to local air forces, who have to include a considerable number of personnel under training in their organisation. A considerable number of local air forces' aircraft are also undergoing routine maintenance and overhaul at any point in time.

All US air units in the Middle East are controlled by the US Central Command (US CENTCOM), which has its main headquarters in Tampa, Florida, and a forward headquarters in Qatar. All air operations overland in the region, except for helicopter and tactical unmanned aerial vehicle (UAV) operations flying at low level, are controlled by US CENTCOM's air component headquarters, based in the USAF-run Combined Air and Space Operations Center (CASOC). A USAF three-star general is the air component commander, and most of his staff are air force personnel, although staff officers from other US armed services and allies are also assigned to the CASOC. At the start of the decade this facility was at Prince Sultan airbase (PSAB) in the Kingdom of Saudi Arabia, and it moved to Al Udeid airbase in Qatar in 2003. Even though it was renamed the CASOC in 2007, airmen throughout the region still call it the CAOC, pronounced 'kay-oc'.

Operation Iraqi Freedom

US and UK Order of Battle, March/April 2003
AIRCRAFT TYPE NUMBERS
USAF – Total 805

60 × A-10	48 × F-15E	7 × C-17	33 × KC-10
8 × AC-130	123 × F-117	1 × CN-235	1 × NKC-135
11 × B-1	10 × C-2	1 × DC-130	7 × MQ-1
4 × B-2	3 × C-20	15 × E-3	9 × RC-135
28 × B-52	7 × C-21	7 × E-8	9 × RQ-1
5 × BQM-34	1 × C-32	8 × EC-130	1 × RQ-4
60 × F-16	1× C-40	8 × HC-130	15 × U-2
71 × F-16CJ	5 × C-9	16 × HH-60	
42 × F-15	124 × C-130	149 × KC-135	

USMC – Total 372

60 × F/A-18C/D	58 × AH-1W	67 × CH-46	22 × KC-130T
70 × AV-8B	30 × UH-1	54 × CH-53	10 × EA-6B

US Navy – Total 408

56 × F-14	25 × EA-6B	20 × E-2C	26 × P-3
176 × F/A-18C/E	40 × S-3B	3 × EP-3	4 × SH-3

US Army – Total 700

12 × RC-12	60 × AH-64A	120 × OH-58D
120 × AH-64D	250 × UH-60	170? × CH-47D/UH-1

US Special Operations Forces – Total 972

6 × MC-130	31 × MH-53	18 × MH-60
14 × MH-47	7 × MH-6	1 × PC-6

Australian – Total 22

3 × CH-47D	3 × C-130H/J
14 × F/A-18	2 × P-3

IRAQ (All opened up after US-led troops entered on 21 March 2003)
Tallil airbase – 392 AEW
A-10/AV-8B FARP
8 × HH-60 (301 RQS)

Bashur airfield
86th CRG
6 × MH-53M (21 SOS)

Jallibah airbase
USMC forward operating base/FARP

Al Kut airbase(Blair Field)
USMC forward operating base/FARP

An Numaniyah airbase
USMC forward operating base/FARP

Hantush airfield
USMC forward operating base/FARP

Najaf
US Army forward operating base/FARP

Baghdad International airport
US Army forward operating base/FARP

Umm Qasr docks
UK forward operating base/FARP

Safwan
UK forward operating base/FARP

H-2 airbase
US-UK Aus Special Forces forward operating
  base/FARP

H-1 airbase
US-UK Aus Special Forces forward operating
  base/FARP

KUWAIT
Ali Al Salim airbase – 386 AEW
RQ/MQ-1Predator UAV (15 ERS)
P-3 (VP-1, 40, 46, 47)
5 × RC-12 (US Arny V Corps)
HH-60 (38 RQS)
KC-130 (USMC)
HC-130 (939 RQW, 303 RQS?)
8 × MH-53M (20 SOS)
MC-130 (8 SOS)

Camp Coyote – I MEF/3 MAW
KC-130 (VMGR-234)
RQ-2 (VMU-2)

Ahmed Al Jaber airbase – 322 AEW
18 × F-16CG (524 FS)
48 × A-10 (75, 103, 303, 190, 172 FS)
36 × F/A-18C (VFMA-121, 232, 251)
24 × F/A-18D (VFMA-AW 225, 533)
24 × AV-8B (VMA 214, 542)
4 × HC-130/C-130E (39 RQS)
1 × UC-12 (3 MAW)

Camp Udairi/Iraq – 484 AEW
444 & 447 AEG (3, 4, 18 Air Support Sqns)
FAC Teams with US Army units

Kuwait International airport
UK-US air transport hub

SAUDI ARABIA
Prince Sultan airbase –363 AEW
Combined Air Operations Center(CAOC)
200 US and UK aircraft
F-15C (67 FS)
F-16CJ (77FS, 35 FW)
5 × EA-6B (VMAQ-1)
E-3C AWACS (552 & 513 ACW)
E-8 JSTARS (116 ACW)
RC-135
KC-135 (92 ARW, 70 ARS, 916 ARS?)
2 × U-2 (99 RS)

Ar'ar airport
US SF helicopter base
HH-60H (HCS 5)

QATAR
Doha International airport – 64 AEW
14 × C130 (317 AMW)
3 × C-130H/J (RAAF 36 Sqn)
8 × EC-130H (41 ECS)
6 × EC-130E (193 SOW)

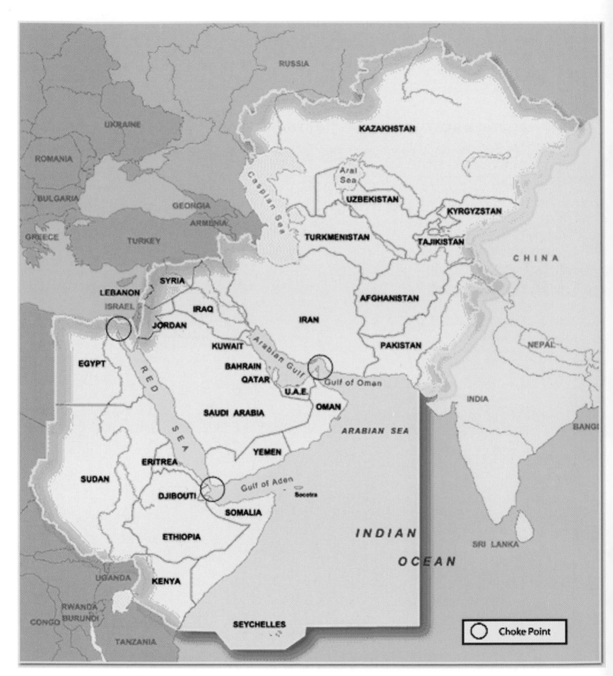

The US Central Command area of responsibility 2009. *(US DoD)*

Al Udeid airbase – 379 AEW
12 × F-117 (8 FS)
48 × F-15E (333/334/336 FS)
F-16CJ (22/23 FS)
F-16C (157FS)
KC-10
KC-135 (911 ARS, 434 ARW)
1 × C40 (1 AS)
14 × F/A-18C (RAAF 75 Sqn)
2 × P-3 (92 Wing, RAAF)

OMAN
Thumrait airbase – 405 AEW
11 × B-1 (34/37 BS)
KC-135 (92nd ARW, 931 ARG)
E-3 AWACS (552 & 513 ACW)

Masirah airbase – 321st AEW/355 AEG
KC-135 (465 ARS, 336 ARS)
C-130 (167 AS)Logistic support for
Afghanistan

Seeb airbase – 320 AEW/AEG
C130 (50, 39/40, 109, 189 AS)

UNITED ARAB EMIRATES
Al Dhafra – 380 AEW
10 × U-2 (99 RS)
1 × RQ-4 Global Hawk UAV (12 RS)
8 × KC-10 (60/305 AMW?)

BAHRAIN
Muharraq airport
3 × EP-3 (VQ-1)
4 × P-3 (VP-1)
6 × CH-53 (HC-4)
3 × C-130 (USN)
4 × SH-3 (HC-2)
6 × C-2A (VRC-30)

Shaikh Isa airbase – 358 AEW?
F-15C (71 FS, 58 FS)
C-130 (105, 130, 139, 142, 165, 180, 185 AS)
KC-130 (VMGR-452)

JORDAN
Azraq airbase – 410 AEW
RQ/MQ-1 UAV (15 RS/46ERS)
18 × A-10 (118, 131 FS)
F-16 (120, 160 FS)
4 × HC-130 (71 RQS)
HH-60 (66 RQS)
8 × AC-130 (4 SOS?)
MC-130 (8 SOS?)
17 × MH-53M (20 SOS?)
3 × CH-47D (5th Avn Regt, Australian Army)

BRITISH INDIAN OCEAN TERRITORY
Diego Garcia – 40 AEW
4 × B-2 (393 BS)
11× B-52 (20 &40BS)
12 × KC-135 (462 AEG/28 ARS)

US EUROPEAN COMMAND

TURKEY
Incirlik airbase
Combined Air Forces North headquarters –
   39 ASEW
50 × US and UK jets
E-3 AWACS(552 & 513 ACW)
16+ × F-16C (55 FS, 113 EFS(ANG))
F-15C(94 FS)
5 × EA-6B (VMAQ-?)
RC-135 (55 RW)
KC-135 (92, 900 ARS)

Konya airbase
5/6 × E-3 AWAC (NATO)

Batman airbase
Forward airbase

Diyarbikar airbase
Forward airbase
US SF helicopter base

Van airbase
Forward airbase

GREECE
NSA Souda Bay, Crete – 398 AEG
RC-135 (55 RW)
1 × NKC-135 (412 Test Wing)
KC-135
3 × EC-130H (43 ECS)
1 × EP-3 (VQ-2)

CYPRUS
RAF Akrotiri – 401 AEW
29 × KC-135 (319th ARW, 163 ARW / 905,
351 153 ARS) U-2 (99 RS)
4 × C-2 A(VRC-40)
2 × E-8 JSTARS (116 ACW / 970 EAACS)
3 × E-3 AWACS(552 & 513 ACW)
5 × MH-53M (21 SOS)
2 × KC-130 (352 SOG)
1 × U-2

UNITED KINGDOM
RAF Fairford – 457 AEG
17 × B-52 (23 & 93 BS)

RAF Mildenhall – 171 AEW
18 × KC-135 KC-135E (171, 134, 190 ARW)
2 × HH-60G (58 RQS)
40 × C-141 (491 AEG / 89, 356, 729, 730, 756 AS)

BULGARIA
Bourgas – 409 AEG
KC-10A (305 & 514 AMW, 507 ARW)

ROMANIA
Constanta – 458th AEG
C-130E (37 AS)
HC-130 (??)
MC-130 (??)
6 × MH-53M (21 SOS) (moved to Bashur /
    Akrotiri)

GERMANY
Rhein Main airbase – 362 AEG
C-17 (8, 14, 17 AS)

US MARINE CORPS HELICOPTER AND AV-8B UNITS
3rd Marine Air Wing
Marine Air Groups 29 (CH-46/53) and 39 (AH-1/UH-1/CH-46)
(forward deployed in Iraq)
HMLA-269, 369 (AH-1W, UH-1N)
HMM-165, 263 (CH-46E)
(Ali Al Salem, Kuwait)
HMM-162, 268, 364, 365 (CH-46E)
HMH-462, 464 (CH-53E)

Amphibious Warfare Ships in Arabian Gulf
AV-8B (elements VMA 211, 223, 231 and 311)
MH-53E (HM-14 & 15) (for minesweeping)
USS *Bataan* (AV-8B)
USS *Bonhommie Richard* (AV-8B VMA-211)
USS *Kearsage* HMH-464 (CH-53E)
USS *Saipan* HM-14, 15 (MH-53E)
USS *Nassau* – 24th MEU (HMM-263, 12 CH-46E, 4 CH-53E, 3 UH-1N, 4 AH-1W, 6 AV-8B)
USS *Tarawa* – 15th MEU(HMM-161, 12 CH-46E, 4 CH-53E, 3 UH-1N, 4 AH-1W, 6 AV-8B)

Amphibious Warfare Ships in Mediterranean Sea (disembarked in mid April by air to Kurdistan)
USS *Iwo Jima* – 26th MEU (HMM-264, 12 CH-46E, 4 CH-53E, 3 UH-1N, 4 AH-1W, 6 AV-8B)

US ARMY HELICOPTER
V Corps
571st Medical Company (UH-60)

11th Aviation Brigade
2nd/6th Cavalry (21 × AH-64D, 6 × UH-60)
6th Squadron, 6th Cavalry Regiment (21 × AH-64A, 6 × UH-60)
1st Battalion, 227th Aviation Regiment (attached from 1st Cav Div) (21 × AH-64D, 6 × UH-60)

12th Aviation Brigade
F Company, 159th Aviation (15 × CH-47D)
5th Battalion, 158th Aviation Regiment (UH-60 and CH-47)
3rd Battalion, 158th Aviation Regiment (UH-60 and CH-47)
D Compay 1-159th Aviation Regiment

2nd Brigade, 82nd Airborne Division
1st Battalion, 82nd Aviation Regiment (OH-58D)\

3rd Infantry Division (Mechanised)
4th Aviation Brigade
1st Battalion, 3rd Aviation Regiment (21 × AH-64D, 6 × UH-60) ,
2st Battalion, 3rd Aviation Regiment (40 × UH-60, 4 × EH-60,
3/7 Cav (16 × OH-58D, 4 × UH-60)

101st Airborne (Air Assault) Division (270 helicopters)
101st Aviation Brigade
2-17 Cav (32× OH-58D)1st Battalion, 101st Aviation Regiment (21 × AH-64D, 6 × UH-60)
2nd Battalion, 101st Aviation Regiment (21 × AH-64D, 6 × UH-60)
3rd Battalion, 101st Aviation Regiment (21 × AH-64A, 6 × UH-60)
6th Battalion, 101st Aviation Regiment (24 × UH-60)

159th Aviation Brigade
4th Battalion, 101st Aviation Regiment (24 × UH-60)
5th Battalion, 101st Aviation Regiment (30 × UH-60)
7th Battalion, 101st Aviation Regiment (48 × CH-47)
9th Battalion, 101st Aviation Regiment (30 × UH-60)

4th Infantry Division (Mechanised)
4th Aviation Brigade
1st Battalion, 4th Aviation Regiment (21 × AH-64D, 6 × UH-60)
2st Battalion, 4th Aviation Regiment (40 × UH-60, 4 × EH-60
1/10th Cav (8 × OH-58d)

The A-10A Warthog brought heavy firepower to Iraqi battlefields. *(USAF)*

Each day, the 700 or so staff officers at the CAOC produce an air tasking order which allocates roles and missions for every aircraft, manned and unmanned, flying in the region, as well as radio frequencies, weapon loads and in some cases targets for the following twenty-four hours of operations. This is disseminated via high-capacity secure internet links to every US and Coalition airbase in the region. It is also the responsibility of the CAOC to secure the necessary diplomatic clearances for US and Coalition aircraft based around the region to enter the airspace of host countries. US forces have treaty rights with the Iraqi government to operate in the country's airspace without consultation, but elsewhere in the Middle East complex approval processes are necessary to allow US aircraft to cross several nations' airspace on combat missions.

US Army and US Marine Corps ground units have control of their own airspace over their local area of responsibility, and can fly their own organic helicopters and UAVs in it without reference to the CAOC. The US Navy also controls air operations over water in the Middle East.

As part of the Global War on Terror the US Central Intelligence Agency and the Pentagon's US Special Operations Command (US SOCOM), also have the ability to conduct military operations in the Middle East independent of US CENTCOM's chain of command. These operations are conducted under conditions of great secrecy, and mainstream US airmen have little visibility beyond being notified of 'no fly' areas where these 'black' operations are under way.

US Air Order of Battle, Iraq Region, June 2004.

IRAQ
Baghdad International airport/Camp Sather
447th Air Expeditionary Group
304th/101st Expeditionary Rescue Squadron (HH-60G)
20th Special Operations Squadron (MH-53M)

Kirkuk airbase
506th Air Expeditionary Group
107th Fighter Squadron (F-16)

Balad airbase
332nd Air Expeditionary Wing
64th Expeditionary Rescue Squadron (HH-60G)
46th Expeditionary Reconnaissance Squadron (RQ/MQ-1 Predator UAV)
USAF air transport hub

Al Asad airbase
3rd Marine Air Wing, 16th Marine Air Group
Marine Medium Helicopter Squadrons 261, 161, 764 (36 x CH-46E)

Marine Heavy Helicopter Squadrons 466, 465 (CH-53E)
Marine Attack Squadrons 542 and 214 (10 x AV-8B)

Al Taqqadum airbase forward operating base
Marine Light/Attack Helicopter Squadrons 167, 775 (36 x AH-1W, 18 x UH-1N)
Marine Unmanned Aerial Vehicle Squadron 2 (RQ-2 UAV)
507th Medical Company (UH-60) (US Army)

Tallil airbase
407th Air Expeditionary Group
332nd Expeditionary Rescue Squadron (HH-60G)

KUWAIT
Ali Al Salem airbase
USAF air transport hub and C-130 operating base
Special Operations Command operating base (AC-130/MC-130/MH-53M)
Marine Aerial Refueler Transport Squadrons 352/234 (KC-130)
71st Rescue Squadron (MC/HC-130P)

Kuwait International airport
USAF air transport hub

QATAR
Al Udeid airbase
Combined Air Operations Center (CAOC)
379th Air Expeditionary Wing
555th Fighter Squadron (F-16CJ)
Detachment 4th Fighter Wing (F-15E)
Detachment B-1B Bombers (4–6 aircraft)
363rd Expeditionary Fighter Squadron (F-15C)
340th Expeditionary Refuelling Squadron (KC-135)
379th Expeditionary Refuelling Squadron (KC-10)
745th Expeditionary Airlift Squadron (C-130)

AFLOAT
USS *George Washington* Carrier Strike Group
Carrier Air Wing 7
Fighter Squadron 11 (10 × F-14B)
Strike Fighter Squadron 82 (12 × F/A-18)
Fighter Squadron 143 (10 × F-14B)
Strike Fighter Squadron 131 (12 × F/A-18)
Strike Fighter Squadron 136 (12 × F/A-18)
Carrier Airborne Early Warning Squadron 121 (4 × E-2C)

Electronic Attack Squadron 140 (4 × EA-6B)

Sea Control Squadron 31 (8 × S-3B)

Fleet Logistics Support 40 Detachment (2 × C-2A)

Helicopter Anti-Submarine Squadron 5 (4 × SH-60F, 2 × HH-60H)

USS *Peleliu*

11th Marine Expeditionary Unit (Special Operations Capable)

166th Marine Medium Helicopter Squadron (reinforced) (AH-1W, CH-46E, CH-53E, AV-8B, UH-1N)

USS *Saipan*

24th Marine Expeditionary Unit (Special Operations Capable)

263rd Marine Medium Helicopter Squadron (reinforced) (AH-1W, CH-46E, CH-53E, AV-8B, UH-1N)

US ARMY HELICOPTER UNITS

III Corps (February 2004 to April 2005)

(III Corps staff replaced V Corps as core of CJTF-7 in February 2004. Multi-National Force – Iraq/Multi-National Corps – Iraq replaced CJTF-7 on 15 May 2004.)

185th Aviation Brigade

1-106th Aviation (UH-60/CH-47D)

1-244th Aviation (UH-60/CH-47D)

1st Infantry Division (Apr 04–Feb 05) – Mosul-Tikrit

4th Aviation Brigade, 1st Infantry Division

1-1st Attack Helicopter Battalion (UH-64D)

2-1st Aviation Battalion (UH-60)

8-229th Aviation

1st Cavalry Division (Apr 04–Feb 05) – Baghdad Region

4h Aviation Brigade

1-227th Attack Helicopter Battalion (AH-64D)

2-227th Attack Helicopter Battalion (AH-64D)

1-25th Attack Battalion (OH-58D)

Combined Joint Special Operations Task Force – Arabian Peninsula (in support of CJTF-7/ MNF-I)

160th Special Operations Aviation Regiment (-) (MH-60, MH-47, MH-6)

USMC 3rd MAW ORDER OF BATTLE, IRAQ NOVEMBER 2004

Al Asad airbase

3rd Marine Air Wing, 16th Marine Air Group

Marine Light/Attack Helicopter Squadrons 169, 367 (36 × AH-1W, 18 × UH-1N)

USAF KC-15R Stratotanker aerial tankers were key force multipliers over Iraq, refuelling Coalition fighters. *(USAF)*

Nose art on a B-1B Lancer at Al Udeid in 2006. *(Author)*

Marine Medium Helicopter Squadrons 365, 268, 774 (36 × CH-46E)
Marine Heavy Helicopter Squadrons 361, (CH-53E)
Marine Attack Squadrons 542 and 214 (10 × AV-8B)
Marine Attack Squadron (All Weather) 242 (12 × F/A-18D)
Marine Aerial Refueler Transport Squadrons 452 (KC-130)

Taqqadum airbase forward operating base
Marine Unmanned Aerial Vehicle Squadron 1 (RQ-1 UAV)
Marine Light/Attack Helicopter Squadrons 169, 367 (36 × AH-1W, 18 × UH-1N)
507th Medical Company (UH-60) (US Army)

KUWAIT
Ali Al Salem airbase
Marine Aerial Refueler Transport Squadrons 352 (KC-130)

US Army Aviation Order of Battle, 1 May 2003

244th Theater Aviation Brigade
1-147th Aviation (Echelon Above Corps Command Aviation) (UH-60)
G/149th Aviation (CH-47)
UH-60 Det/A/1-159th Aviation
1/A/5-159th Aviation (CH-47)
B/5-159th Aviation (CH-47D) (Attached)
UC-35 Det/A/1-214th Aviation
UH-60 Det/C/1-214th Aviation
E/111th Aviation (Air Traffic Service) (-)
C-12 Flight Detachment /Operational Support Airlift Command (Kuwait)

513th Military Intelligence Brigade (-)
B/224th Military Intelligence Bn (Unmanned Aerial Vehicle) (OPCON)

V Corps
4th Brigade, 3rd Infantry Division (-) (Baghdad)
1-3rd Aviation (AH-64D) (-)
Team A/2-3rd Aviation (UH-60) (OPCON)

4th Infantry Division (Taji/Tikrit)
A/15th Military Intelligence Bn (Hunter Unmanned Aerial Vehicle)
Tactical Unmanned Aerial Vehicle Contract Log Support Team

4th Brigade, 4th Infantry Division
1-4th Aviation (AH-64D) (-)

2-4th Aviation (UH-60) (General Support Aviation) (-)
1-10th Cavalry (OH-58D, M3A2)

DREAR/101st Abn Div (Kuwait)
C/3-101st Aviation (AH-64D)

2nd Brigade, 101st Abn Div (Mosul)
2-101st Aviation (AH-64D)
  101st Aviation Brigade (Mosul)
  1-101st Aviation (AH-64D)
  3-101st Aviation (AH-64D)
  6-101st Aviation (UH-60)

  159th Aviation Brigade (Mosul/Tikrit)
  4-101st Aviation (UH-60)
  5-101st Aviation (UH-60)
  7-101st Aviation (CH-47) (-)
  9-101st Aviation (UH-60)

2nd Brigade/82nd Abn Div (Fallujah)
TF 1-82nd Aviation (-)
A/1-82nd Aviation (+) (OH-58D)
A/1-17th Cavalry (OH-58D)

11th Attack Helicopter Regiment (Balad)
2-6th Cavalry (AH-64D)
6-6th Cavalry (AH-64D)
1-227th Aviation (AH-64D), 1st Cavalry Division (Attached)
5-158th Aviation (-) (UH-60)

12th Aviation Brigade
B/158th Aviation (UH-60)
B/159th Aviation (CH-47)
F/159th Aviation (CH-47)
A/5-159th Aviation (CH-47) (-)
2 × Aircraft/1-214th Aviation (CH-47) (-) (Attached)
F/106th Aviation (CH-47)

2nd Armored Cavalry Regiment (Light) (-) (east of Baghdad)
1st Squadron, 2nd Armored Cavalry Regiment (-) (Kuwait)
2nd Squadron, 2nd Armored Cavalry Regiment
3rd Squadron, 2nd Armored Cavalry Regiment (-) (Kuwait)

3rd Armored Cavalry Regiment (western Iraq)
4 × CH-47/12th Aviation Brigade
6 × UH-60 Medical Evacuation Aircraft/30th Medical Brigade

I Marine Expeditionary Force (Reinforced) (south of Baghad) (withdrawn from Iraq by end June 2003)
15th Marine Expeditionary Unit (Special Operations Capable) (MEUSOC)
Marine Medium Helicopter Squadron 161 (Reinforced) (AH-1W, CH-46E, UH-1N)
Detachment/Marine Heavy Helicopter Squadron 361 (-) (CH-53E)
24th Marine Expeditionary Unit (Special Operations Capable) (MEUSOC)
Detachment/Marine Attack Squadron 231 (-) (AV-8B)
Marine Medium Helicopter Squadron 263 (Reinforced) (CH-46E)
Detachment/Marine Light Attack Helicopter Squadron 269 (UH-1N/AH-1W)
Detachment/Marine Heavy Helicopter Squadron 772 (-) (CH-53E)
Detachment/Marine Heavy Helicopter Squadron 461 (CH-53E)

3rd Marine Air Wing (-) (Reinforced)
Marine Air Group 16 (-) (Reinforced)
  Marine Medium Helicopter Squadron 263 (CH-46E)
  Marine Heavy Helicopter Squadron 462 (CH-53E)
  Marine Heavy Helicopter Squadron 465 (CH-53E)
Marine Air Group 29 (-) (Reinforced)
  Marine Medium Helicopter Squadron 162 (CH-46E)
  Marine Medium Helicopter Squadron 365 (-) (CH-46E)
  Marine Heavy Helicopter Squadron 464 (CH-53E)
  Marine Light Attack Helicopter Squadron 269 (-) (AH-1W/UH-1N)
Marine Air Control Group 38 (-) (Reinforced)
  Marine Unmanned Aerial Vehicle Squadron 1 (RQ-2 UAV)
  Marine Unmanned Aerial Vehicle Squadron 2 (RQ-2 UAV)
Marine Air Group 39 (-) (Reinforced)
  Marine Light Attack Helicopter Squadron 169 (AH-1W/UH-1N
  Marine Light Attack Helicopter Squadron 267 (AH-1W/UH-1N
  Marine Medium Helicopter Squadron 268 (CH-46E)
  Marine Medium Helicopter Squadron 364 (CH-46E)
  Marine Light Attack Helicopter Squadron 369 (AH-1W/UH-1N

One area of the Middle East which is outside the normal control of US CENTCOM is Israel. For reasons of political expediency, US links to the Jewish state are co-ordinated by US European Command (US EUCOM) in Stuttgart, Germany. Cyprus and Turkey are also in the US EUCOM area of responsibility, and so operations in the Lebanon that rely on bases in these two countries have to be closely co-ordinated between US CENTCOM and US EUCOM.

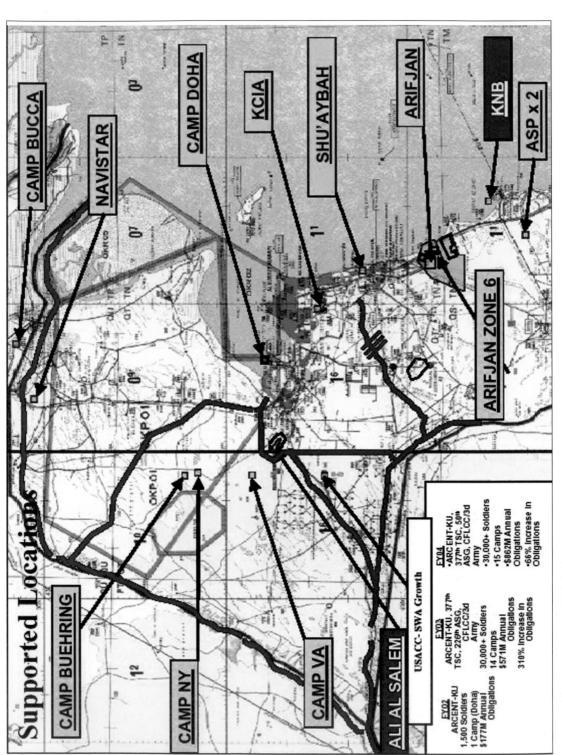

Map 2 US bases in Kuwait. (US DoD)

US Air Force

The USAF has borne the brunt of American air operations in the Middle East since the end of the 1991 Gulf War. Airbases in Turkey, Saudi Arabia, Bahrain and Kuwait were used extensively during the no-fly-zone enforcement operations between 1991 and 2003.

The surge of forces for the Afghanistan operation in 2001 and the Iraqi invasion expanded the footprint of US airbases to Oman, UAE and Jordan.

Air support for US-led occupation forces in Iraq has dominated USAF operations in the Middle East since May 2003. This involved providing the full spectrum of offensive air support, intelligence gathering, strategic and tactical airlift and medical evacuation. The USAF has also had to establish and sustain operations at several air hubs in Iraq and neighbouring countries to allow US Army personnel and equipment to flow in and out of Iraq. This involved setting up bare-base air operations and providing base security. As well as the routine daily movement of people and cargo around the Middle East, the USAF and civilian air lines at twelve-monthly intervals rotated home and replaced the 150,000+ US Army troops serving in Iraq.

From 2004 onwards, the USAF had some 28,000 personnel in the Middle East at any one time.

US Army

The US Army is the next largest operator of US military aircraft and helicopters in the Middle East. The core of US Army aviation operations in Iraq since 2003 have been two or three divisional combat aviation brigades, operating Boeing AH-64D Apache attack helicopters, Sikorsky UH-60M/L Blackhawk utility helicopters, Boeing CH-47D/F Chinook heavy-lift helicopters and Bell OH-58D Kiowa Warrior scout helicopters. These assets are under the direct day-to-day control of US Army divisional commanders to provide surveillance, attack and transport support.

One or two corps-level brigades of UH-60s and CH-47s have also been regularly deployed to Iraq to support the main US headquarters in the country.

The US Army rotates its units through Iraq on a twelve-to-fifteen-month basis, and aviation units take their own helicopters and equipment with them to Iraq for their tours of duty.

From 2003 onwards, the US Army has deployed increasing numbers of UAVs to Iraq, and as with its helicopter forces it has assigned these to be part of specific brigades or divisions on a permanent basis.

Integration of US Army and US Air Force operations is carried out at an air support operations centre in heart of the Green Zone in Baghdad. Here requests for air support are collated and prioritised before being forwarded to the CAOC at Al Udeid. They are then incorporated into the daily air tasking order.

At a tactical level, once aircraft are over Iraq, they are assigned to work with specific joint terminal attack controllers (JTAC) or forward air controllers operating with specific ground units. From 2004 onwards they have been equipped with

US Navy Carrier Deployments to Middle East 2000–2009, Air Wing Composition.

Cruise Dates Type Squadron	Aircraft	John F. Kennedy Sep 99 to Mar 00	Dwight D. Feb to Aug 00	John C. Stennis Eisenhower Jan to Jul 00	Abraham Lincoln Aug 00 to Feb 01	Harry S. Truman Nov 00 to May 01	Enterprise April 01 to Nov 01	Karl Vinson July 01 to Jan 02
Fighter Squadron (VF)	10 × F-14D	102 (F-14B)	143 (F-14B)	211 (F-14A)	31	32 (F-14B)	41 (F-14A)	213
Fighter Squadron (VF)	10 × F-14D		11 (F-14B)				14 (F-14A)	
Strike Fighter Squadron (VFA)	12 × F/A-18F	VFMA-251		314	115	312	15	97 (F/A-18A)
Strike Fighter Squadron (VFA)	12 × F/A-18C	82	136	146	113	37	87	22
Strike Fighter Squadron (VFA)	12 × F/A-18C	86	131	147	23	105		94
Strike Fighter Squadron (VFA)	12 × F/A-18C							
Tactical EW Squadron (VAQ)	4 × EA-6B	137	140	138	139	130	141	135
ASW Squadron (VS)	8 × S-3B	32	31	33	35	22	24	29
AEW Squadron (VAW)	4 × E-2C	123	121	113	113	126	124	117
Helicopter ASW Squadron (HS)	4 × SH-60F, 2 × HH-60H	11	5	8	4	7	3	6
Helicopter ASW Squadron (HSL)	SH-60B							
Logistic Support Squadron (VRC)	2 × C-2	40 Det 2	40 Det 3	40 Det 4	30 Det 1	40 Det 1	40 Det 5	30 Det 3

US Navy Carrier Deployments to Middle East 2000–2009, Air Wing Composition.

Cruise Dates / Type Squadron	Aircraft	Kitty Hawk	Theodore Roosevelt	John C. Stennis	John F. Kennedy	George Washington	Abraham Lincoln	Kitty Hawk
		Oct 01 to Dec 01	Sep 01 to Mar 02	Nov 01 to May 02	Feb to Aug 02	Jun to Dec 02	Jul 02 to May 03	Jan to May 03
Fighter Squadron (VF)	10 × F-14D		102 (F-14B)	211 (F-14A)	143 (F-14B)	103 (F-14B)	31	154 (F-14A)
Strike Fighter Squadron (VFA)	12 × F/A-18F	195	VFMA-251	VFMA-314	136	34	25	195
Strike Fighter Squadron (VFA)	12 × F/A-18C	27	82	146	131	81	113	192
Strike Fighter Squadron (VFA)	12 × F/A-18C	192	86	147		83	115	27
Strike Fighter Squadron (VFA)	12 × F/A-18C							
Tactical EW Squadron (VAQ)	4 × EA-6B		137	138	140	132	139	136
ASW Squadron (VS)	8 × S-3B	21	32	33	31	30	35	27
AEW Squadron (VAW)	4 × E-2C		123	112	121	125	11	115
Helicopter ASW Squadron (HS)	4 × SH-60F, 2 × HH-60H	14	11	8	5	15	4	14
Logistic Support Squadron (VRC)	2 × C-2	30 Det 5	40 Det 2	40 Det 4	40 Det 3	40 Det 4	30 Det 1	30 Det 5

US Navy Carrier Deployments to Middle East 2000–2009, Air Wing Composition.

Cruise Dates / Type Squadron	Aircraft	Constellation Nov 02 to June 02	Theodore Roosevelt Jan to May 03	Harry S. Truman Dec 02 to May 03	Nimitz Mar to Nov 03	Enterprise Oct 03 to Feb 04	George Washington Feb 04 to Jul 04	John F. Kennedy Jun 04 to Dec 04
Fighter Squadron (VF)	10 × F-14D	2	213	32 (F-14B)		211 (F-14A)	143 (F-14B)	103 (F-14B)
Fighter Squadron (VF)	10 × F-14D						11 (F-14B)	
Fighter Squadron (VF)	12 × F/A-18E				14			
Strike Fighter Squadron (VFA)	12 × F/A-18F				41			
Strike Fighter Squadron (VFA)	12 × F/A-18C	137	115	37	94	VFMA-312	136	34
Strike Fighter Squadron (VFA)	12 × F/A-18C	151	87	105	97	82	131	83
Strike Fighter Squadron (VFA)	12 × F/A-18C	VMFA-323	201	115		86		81
Tactical EW Squadron (VAQ)	4 × EA-6B	131	141	130	135	137	140	132
ASW Squadron (VS)	8 × S-3B	38	24	22	29	32	31	30
AEW Squadron (VAW)	4 × E-2C	116	124	126	119	123	121	125
Helicopter ASW Squadron (HS)	4 × SH-60F, 2 × HH-60H	2		7	6	11	5	15
Logistic Support Squadron (VRC)	2 × C-2	30 Det 2	40 Det 5	40 Det 1	30 Det 3	40 Det 2	40 Det 3	40 Det 4

US Navy Carrier Deployments to Middle East 2000–2009, Air Wing Composition.

Type Squadron / Aircraft	Harry S. Truman / Oct 04 to Apr 05	Carl Vinson / Jan to Jul 05	Nimitz / Jun 05 to Sep 05	Theodore Roosevelt / Sep 05 to Mar 06	Ronald Reagan / Jan 06 to Jul 06	John C. Stennis / Feb 06 to May 06	Enterprise / May 06 to Oct 06	Dwight D. Eisenhower / Oct 06 to May 07
Fighter Squadron (VF) — 10 × F-14D	32 (F-14B)			31				
Fighter Squadron (VF) — 10 × F-14D				213				
Fighter Squadron (VF) — 12 × F/A-18E			41		22			143
Strike Fighter Squadron (VFA) — 12 × F/A-18F		154	14	15	115	154	211	103
Strike Fighter Squadron (VFA) — 12 × F/A-18C	VFMA-115 (F/A-18A+)	VMFA-323	VFMA-232	87	113	VFMA-323	VFMA-251	83
Strike Fighter Squadron (VFA) — 12 × F/A-18C	37	146	94		25	146	136	131
Strike Fighter Squadron (VFA) — 12 × F/A-18C	105	147				147	86	
Tactical EW Squadron (VAQ) — 4 × EA-6B	130	138	135	141	139	138	137	140
ASW Squadron (VS) — 8 × S-3B	22	33		24		31	32	
AEW Squadron (VAW) — 4 × E-2C	126	112	117	124	113	112	123	125
Helicopter ASW Squadron (HS) — 4 × SH-60F, 2 × HH-60H	7	8	6	3	4	8	11	5
Logistic Support Squadron (VRC) — 2 × C-2	40 Det 1	30 Det 4	30 Det 3	40 Det 1	30 Det 1	30 Det 4	40 Det 2	40 Det 3

US Navy Carrier Deployments to Middle East 2000–2009, Air Wing Composition.

Cruise Dates / Type Squadron	Aircraft	John C. Stennis — Jan to Aug 07	Nimitz — Apr 07 to Sep 07	Enterprise — Jul 07 to Dec 07	Harry S. Trueman — Nov 07 to May 08	Abraham Lincoln — Mar 08 to Oct 08	Ronald Regan — May 08 to Nov 08	Theodore Roosevelt — Sep 08 to Mar 09	Dwight D. Eisenhower — Feb 09 to ?
Fighter Squadron (VF)	12 x F/A-18E				11				143
Fighter Squadron (VF)	12 x F/A-18E		14		105	137	115	31	
Strike Fighter Squadron (VFA)	12 x F/A-18F	154		211	32	2	22	213	103
Strike Fighter Squadron (VFA)	12 x F/A-18C	VFMA-323	VFMA-232 (F/A-18+)	VFMA-251	37			87 (F/A-18+)	83
Strike Fighter Squadron (VFA)	12 x F/A-18C	146	81	136		151	113	14	131
Strike Fighter Squadron (VFA)	12 x F/A-18C	147		86		34	25		
Tactical EW Squadron (VAQ)	4 x EA-6B	138	135	137	130	131	139	141	140
ASW Squadron (VS)	8 x S-3B	41							
AEW Squadron (VAW)	4 x E-2C	112	117	123	126	116	113	124	125
Helicopter ASW Squadron (HS)	4 x SH-60F, 2 x HH-60H	8	6	11	7	2	4	3	5
Helicopter ASW Squadron (HSL)						47			
Logistic Support Squadron (VRC)	2 x C-2	30 Det 4	30 Det 3	40 Det 4	40 Det 5	30 Det 2	30 Det 1	40 Det 1	40 Det 2

US Air Force, US Army and US Marine Corps, Order of Battle Middle East Region, as at June 2007.

Base and Unit	Squadron	Aircraft Type	Approximate Number
IRAQ			
Baghdad International airport/Camp Sather			
447th Air Expeditionary Group	304/101 ERQS	HH-6G	
Baghdad – Taji Helicopter Base			
4th Aviation Brigade, 1st Cavalry Division (US Army)	1-227th Attack Helicopter Battalion	AH-64D	22
	2-227th Aviation Helicopter Battalion	UH-60, CH-47	12 x CH-47, 42 x UH-60
	1-25th Attack Battalion	UH-60, OH-58	30 x UH-58
COB Speicher, Tikrit + Mosul			
25th Combat Aviation Brigade, 25th Infantry Division (US Army)	2nd Battalion, 25th Aviation Regiment	UH-60, CH-47	12 x CH-47, 42 x UH-60
	3rd Battalion, 25th Aviation Regiment	UH-60, CH-47	12 x CH-47, 42 x UH-60
	2nd Squadron, 6th Cavalry Regiment	AH-64D	22 x AH-64D
	6th Squadron, 17th Cavalry Regiment	OH-58, AH-64D	30 x UH-58, 22 x AH-64D
Kirkuk airbase			
506th Air Expeditionary Group			
Balad airbase			
332nd Air Expeditionary Wing (USAF Air Transport Hub)	6ERQS	HH-6G	8
	?? EFS (USAF active duty)	F-16C/D	12
	?? EFS (USAF active duty)	F-16C/D	12
	?? EFS (USAF Reserve/ ANG)	F-16A/B	12
	46th ERS	MQ/RQ-1	2? 4?
	777th EAS	C-130	
	US Army Mil Int Bn	RC-12	4
160th SOAR	US Army	MH-47E, MH-6, UH-60	
Ali (Tallil) airbase			
407th Air Expeditionary Group	??ERQS	HH-6G	
	??ERS	MQ/RQ-1	2? 4?

Base and Unit	Squadron	Aircraft Type	Approximate Number
Al Asad airbase			
3rd Marine Air Wing (helo FOB	VMA-542 (USMC)	AV-8B	19
Al Habbaniyah/Al Taqaddum)	US Navy Unit	EA-6B	4
	VMFA-115	F-18	?
	VMGR-252 (USMC)	KC-130	5
	HMM-262 (USMC)	CH-46	14
	HMH-362, 364, 361 (USMC)	CH-53	23
	HMLA-167, 773 (USMC)	AH-1/UH-1	15
	VMAQ-2 (USMC)	RQ-2 + other UAV	?
	VMM-263	V-22	
1st Battalion, 52d Aviation		UH-60	
Regiment (US Army)			
438th Expeditionary Air Group	75th EFS	A-10A	12
KUWAIT			
Ali Al Salem airbase			
USAF air transport hub and		C130E/H/	24
C-130 operating base		EC-130	
386th Air Expeditionary Wing		C20(Learjet)	2
	US Army Mil Int Bn	RC-12	3
	US Army	C-23	6
Camp Ubairi	US Army Aviation Brigade	various Helo	31
QATAR			
Al Udeid airbase - 8000 personnel			
Combined Air Operations	Squadron	Aircraft Type	Number
Center (CAOC)			
379th Air Expeditionary Wing	??EFS	F-16C/J	12
	494th EFS	F-15E	12
	34th EBS	B-1B	6
	340th ERS	KC-135	16
	746th EAS (reserve & ANG)	C-130	16
	15th EACCS	E-8C JSTARS	4
	763th ERS	RC-135	4
	US Navy VP	P-3C	6
	VQ-1	EP-3	1
	816th EAS	C-17	4
	Operating Location Alpha	C-21	?
	VMR-1	C-21	1
	?? EAWS	E-3 AWACS	?

RC-135 Rivet Joint intelligence-gathering aircraft provided US commanders with vital insights into insurgent operations. *(USAF)*

The veteran U-2 Dragon Lady remains in demand to collect intelligence over Iraq. *(USAF)*

Base and Unit	Squadron	Aircraft Type	Approximate Number
UNITED ARAB EMIRATES			
Al Dhafra airbase			
380th Air Expeditionary Wing	?? ERS	KC-10	5
	?? ERS	KC-135	10
	?? ERS	U-2	6
	?? ERS	RQ-4	2
OMAN			
Access rights to airbases at Seeb, Messirah and Thumrait airbases			
BAHRAIN			
Muharraq International airport			
US Navy logistic Hub	HSC-26	SH-60	
	VRC-40?	C-2C	
	HC-15	CH-53	
Sheik Isa airbase – access rights to airbase			

remotely operated video-enhanced receiver (ROVER) terminals that allow JTACs to watch in real-time imagery from fast-jet targeting pods or the sensor systems on UAVs. Before and during the 2003 invasion, the CAOC had the authority to clear aircraft to attack ground targets in large areas of Iraq, but since then clearance for air strikes generally has to be given by a JTAC. In some circumstances, pilots can request clearance-drop weapons in Iraq, but only if there are no friendly ground troops present. High-ranking officers in the CAOC need to authorise such missions, after taking legal advice.

The US Army also has responsibility for theatre and tactical air defence. Up to the 2003 invasion of Iraq, the US Army deployed five batteries of Raytheon Patriot anti-missile batteries to Saudi Arabia and Kuwait as part of a missile defence task force. This was expanded considerably during the 2003 invasion to thirty-four batteries in Kuwait, Turkey, Israel, Jordan, Saudi Arabia, Bahrain and Qatar. Patriot batteries also moved into Iraq with advancing ground troops to protect them from Iraqi short-range ballistic missiles. The ballistic missile defence mission involves close co-operation with the CAOC to de-conflict air space and to ensure that the real-time recognised air picture, showing all aircraft movements in the Middle East, is piped into each Patriot missile battery control centre.

In the aftermath of the invasion, the US Army Air Defense Artillery (ADA) force was scaled back considerably, and all the batteries returned home. The ADA units left the region, but a considerable amount of Patriot equipment was left behind in pre-positioned equipment warehouses in Kuwait and Qatar. The US Army ADA force returned to the Middle East in early 2007 when one battalion of Patriots was deployed from Fort Hood in Texas to Qatar and Kuwait to provide protection against Iranian ballistic missiles.

US Marine Corps

As the US military's expeditionary force, the US Marine Corps has been in the forefront of all major US operations in the Middle East. Like the US Army, the USMC controls all its own helicopters and tactical UAVs, but also has its own fast-jet attack jet squadrons and air refuelling tankers. The USMC and USAF have come to a gentleman's agreement to include USMC fixed-wing aircraft on the daily air tasking order, but USMC units in Iraq have first call on their use.

The USMC contributed a full division of troops, backed by a complete air wing, for the invasion of Iraq in 2003, but by the summer they had all been withdrawn. As the situation in Iraq deteriorated in the winter of 2003, plans were put in place for a USMC division, and an air group returned to western Iraq in the spring of 2004.

The Marine Corps bore the brunt of the heavy fighting in Anbar province in 2004 to 2007, but by 2009 was beginning to draw down its forces. In a major development the USMC combat débuted the Bell-Boeing V-22 Osprey in Iraq in the summer of 2007, when ten of the tilt-rotor craft deployed to Al Asad as part of VMA26.

US Navy

The US Navy has maintained a carrier strike group in the Gulf region continuously since the start of operations in Afghanistan in October 2001. On a daily basis the Gulf carrier commits aircraft to both Iraq and Afghanistan, flying offensive and combat support missions. In a typical six-month Gulf cruise, a carrier's air wing will launch some 650 combat sorties 'over the beach'.

During the past decade, the organisation of US Navy carrier air wings has undergone considerable evolution, with the Grumman F-14 Tomcat and Lockheed S-3 Viking both being phased out of front-line service. By the end of the decade, carrier air wings boasted two squadrons of McDonnell Douglas F/A-18C/D Hornets and two of Boeing F/A-18E/F Super Hornets.

The most 'in demand' US Navy carrier-borne assets are Northrop Grumman E-2C Hawkeyes and EA-6B Prowlers, to monitor airspace and intercept suspicious communications broadcasts respectively. The E-2Cs are particularly valued because the USAF pulled all its Boeing E-3 Sentry AWACS force back to its home base until 2007.

In 2007, the US Navy 'surged' two carriers in the Gulf to allow continuous air support for both Iraq and Afghanistan. It also became common for US Navy squadrons to disembark from carriers and deploy to Al Asad airbase in Iraq to increase their time on station over conflict zones.

USAF Special Operations MH-53M Pave Lows served in Iraq until 2008, when the veteran helicopters were retired from service. *(USAF)*

US Army OH-58D Kiowa Warriors are very popular with ground commanders in Baghdad because of their speed, armament and low noise. *(USAF)*

The AH-1W Cobra provides the US Marine Corps with awesome airborne firepower. *(USMC)*

The V-22 Osprey received its combat debut in Iraq in 2008. *(USMC)*

As well as its ship-born aviation assets, the US Navy maintained considerable shore-based capabilities in the region. Lockheed P-3C Orion aircraft were forward-based at Muharraq International airport in Bahrain, close to the US Navy's Middle East headquarters, until 2005. Muharraq is also home to logistic support squadrons of Sikorsky UH-3A Sea King, SH-60 and CH-53E Sea Stallion helicopters that supply US Navy ships in Middle Eastern waters. The Orions regularly patrol Middle Eastern waters looking for suspicious maritime activity, and they occasionally detach aircraft to Masirah in Oman and Djibouti to extend their endurance. Pakistani Navy Dassault Atlantique crews visited Bahrain to co-ordinate joint patrols with their US maritime patrol colleagues. Overland surveillance missions are also flown over Iraq and Afghanistan, from Ali Al Salem and Bagram respectively.

Expansion of the civilian side of Muharraq airport led the US Navy to relocate its P-3C and EP-3 hub to Al Udeid in Qatar in 2005. Maritime patrol aircraft are allocated on a daily basis to the three US Navy combined task forces (CTF) operating in Middle East waters.

- CTF 150 operates in the Gulf of Aden, the Gulf of Oman, the Arabian Sea, the Red Sea and the Indian Ocean
- CTF 151 operates in the Gulf of Aden and off the Somali coast
- CTF 152 operates in the Arabian Gulf.

Since January 2007, CTF 151 has received an increasing amount of support from the P-3C force as US operations against al-Qaeda supporting groups have escalated.

In 2007, usually around a squadron-and-a-half's worth of P-3Cs were based at Al Udeid at any one time, supported by some 400 sailors, on six-month tours of duty. They were designated Task Group 57.2 when operating in the Middle East.

Central Intelligence Agency

The CIA has played a major part in the US-led Global War on Terror since September 2001, operating across the Middle East. The Agency's Special Activities Division runs its own air force of transport aircraft, intelligence-gathering aircraft and missile-armed UAVs.

CIA paramilitary and US SOCOM operate closely together and often conduct joint operations ahead of the deployment of conventional US military forces. CIA air units have been identified operating in Afghanistan and Iraq. They are suspected of conducting UAV missile strikes in Pakistan and Yemen, as well as running a large-scale covert operation in Somalia against the Islamic Courts regime in Mogadishu in 2007.

CIA operatives have their own 'air force' of Russian-made Mil Mi-17 helicopters. (UK Media Pool)

Logistic support for US Navy ships in the Middle East relied on Bahrain-based SH-60s. *(Author)*

The P-3C Orion proved a most flexible intelligence and surveillance asset in the Middle East. *(US Navy)*

CHAPTER NINETEEN

Coalition Air Forces in Iraq

Australia

After the UK, Australia has been the USA's longest-serving ally in Iraq. Fourteen McDonnell Douglas F/A-18C Hornets of 75 Squadron and half a dozen Lockheed C-130 Hercules of 36 Squadron of the Royal Australian Air Force operated from Qatar to support the invasion of Iraq in 2003. The Hornets flew from Al Udeid and the Hercules served with a USAF C-130 wing at Doha International airport. Special Force Army Aviation Boeing CH-47D Chinooks operated in Jordan and western Iraq.

Maritime patrol aircraft from Australia, France, Germany, Spain and the UK joined Operation Enduring Freedom in 2001. Here an RAAF AP-3C takes off from the UAE on a mission. *(RAAF)*

Baghdad International airport control tower was operated by Australians during the first days of the Coalition occupation. *(RAAF)*

Subsequently the RAAF maintained a small C-130 detachment at Al Udeid to support the contingent of Australian troops in Iraq. RAAF air traffic controllers ran the control tower at Baghdad International during the latter half of 2003.

A pair of RAAF Lockheed AP-3C Orions deployed to Minhad airbase in the United Arab Emirates in the aftermath of the September 2001 attacks on New York. A detachment of the aircraft have remained in the Middle East since then, supporting maritime patrol tasks and overland surveillance missions to Afghanistan.

Denmark
The Danish air force deployed a detachment of four Eurocopter AS350 Squirrel helicopters to Basra airbase in southern Iraq in June 2007 to work alongside the UK's Joint Helicopter Force. It conducted liaison and surveillance missions until December 2007, when Denmark ended its military involvement in southern Iraq.

Italy
During 2003 the Italian government deployed a brigade of some 3,000 troops to garrison the southern Iraqi city of Nasiraiya. It was supported by a contingent of ten Agusta Bell 212 utility helicopters operating from Tallil or Ali airbase. After an increase in attacks on Italian forces the garrison was augmented in April 2005 by a detachment of Agusta Westland A-129 Mangusta attack helicopters from the 25th Airmobile Brigade. The Italian air force also deployed a detachment of its General Atomics RQ-1 Predator unmanned aerial vehicles, and one was lost in May 2006. Italian forces withdrew from Iraq at the end of 2006.

Netherlands
The Royal Netherlands Air Force deployed four Boeing CH-47Ds and a similar number of Boeing AH-64D Apaches to Samawah in southern Iraq between 2003 and 2005.

Poland
The Polish Army deployed to Iraq in the summer of 2003 to lead the Multinational Division (Centre) which was responsible for the region of Iraq south of Baghdad. An army aviation air group, equipped initially with four Mil Mi-8T transport and eight W-3SA Sokol utility helicopters, was deployed to Iraq to support it, and was involved in heavy fighting in the spring and summer of 2004 against Iraqi insurgents. The aviation contingent was based at Diwaniyah. It was augmented by Mil Mi-24D attack helicopters in 2004. One Sokol was lost in December 2004. The Polish contingent returned home in October 2008.

Boeing C-17A Globemaster III

The giant C-17 has been the workhorse of the USAF and RAF in operations throughout the Middle East over the past decade. Its large capacity and ability to operate from austere air strips has made the C-17 invaluable. During the 2003 Iraq invasion, the USAF even used the C-17 to conduct a combat parachute drop. Qatar and the UAE are in the process of buying C-17s to enhance their expeditionary warfare capabilities.

Crew: 3 (2 pilots, 1 loadmaster)
Capacity: 102 troops with standard centre-line seats, or 134 troops with palletised seats, or 36 litter and 54 ambulatory patients
Payload: 170,900 lb (77,519 kg) of cargo distributed at maximum over 18 463L master pallets or a mix of palletised cargo and vehicles
Length: 174 ft (53 m)
Wingspan: 169.8 ft (51.75 m)
Height: 55.1 ft (16.8 m)
Maximum take-off weight: 585,000 lb (265,350 kg)
Powerplant: Four Pratt & Whitney F117-PW-100 turbofans, 40,440 lbf (180 kN) each
Cruise speed: Mach 0.76 (450 kts, 515 mph, 830 km/h)
Range: 2,420 nm [89] (2,785 miles, 4,482 km)

RAAF F/A-18 Hornets were the only non-US and non-UK fast-jet units to participate in operations over Iraq. *(RAAF)*

Grumman F-14 D Tomcat

Iran is the last user of the famous Tomcat after the US Navy retired its last F-14 in 2006. The Iranian aerospace industry has managed to reverse-enginer most components of the Tomcat, and the country's air force expects to use the aircraft for the foreseeable future.

Crew: 2 (pilot and radar intercept officer)
Length: 62 ft 9 in. (19.1 m)

Wingspan
Spread: 64 ft (19.55 m)
Swept: 38 ft (11.58 m)
Height: 16 ft (4.88 m)
Maximum take-off weight: 74,350 lb (33,720 kg)
Powerplant: Two General Electric F110-GE-400 afterburning turbofans
Maximum speed: Mach 2.34 (1,544 mph, 2,485 km/h) at high altitude
Combat radius: 500 nm (575 miles, 926 km)

Armament
Guns: One 20 mm (0.787 in) M61 Vulcan Gatling gun, with 675 rounds
Hardpoints: Ten total: six under fuselage, two under nacelles and two on wing gloves [46] with a capacity of 14,500 lb (6,600 kg) of ordnance and fuel tanks [47]

Missiles
Air-to-air missiles: AIM-54 Phoenix, AIM-7 Sparrow, AIM-9 Sidewinder

Bombs
JDAM precision-guided munitions (PGMs)
Paveway series of laser-guided bombs
Mk 80 series of unguided iron bombs
Mk 20 Rockeye II
Others: LITENING targeting pod, or two 267 gal (US) drop-tanks for extended range/loitering time

CHAPTER TWENTY

The Middle East Aerospace Industry

A s befits a region with a fast-growing economy, the Middle East boasts a vibrant and expanding aerospace industry. Middle East airlines, such as Gulf Air, Emirates and Qatar Airlines, are world-famous brands. The region's military aerospace industry is less well known, but it boasts some important capabilities that have significant implications for Middle East air forces.

Some nations, such as Israel and Iran, put great stress on using their aerospace industries to reduce their reliance on foreign imports. Other nations, including Turkey, Saudi Arabia and the UAE, see the creation and expansion of domestic military aerospace industries as a means to attract foreign investment and to create jobs for growing populations.

The Eurofighter Typhoon is set to become a familiar sight around the Middle East, with several countries in the region likely to buy the European aircraft. *(BAE Systems)*

Saudi Arabia's deal with the UK to set up an assembly facility for the Eurofighter Typhoon with the kingdom is of huge regional significance and shows that Middle East nations are no longer just purchasers of military hardware but want to have access to advanced Western military technology.

Egypt

Up to 1990, Egypt's aerospace industry benefited from considerable foreign investment, but since then it has languished in the doldrums, conducting limited amounts of repair and overhaul work.

Egypt did not manufacture its own aircraft, but it assembled Tucano primary trainers from Brazil, Chenyang fighters from China, and Alpha Jet trainers designed in France and West Germany, as well as Sea King helicopters from the UK. Egyptian technicians had also reverse-engineered and modified two Soviet SAMs – the Ayn as Saqr (a version of the SA-7) and the Tayir as Sabah (a version of the SA-2).

The Arab Organisation for Industrialisation (AOI) supervises nine military factories, which were originally set up to be the powerhouse of the Arab world's future defence industry. These ambitions never came to fruition. Initially the owners of AOI were Egypt, Saudi Arabia and the United Arab Emirates. During the 1980s, the AOI did a booming trade selling arms to Saddam Hussein's government in Iraq as it waged a bloody war with Iran. When the Iraqi arms market collapsed after the invasion of Kuwait in 1990, AOI found itself owed huge amounts by Baghdad, with little prospect of being paid back because of international sanctions. Saudi Arabia and the Emirates gave back their shares in AOI in 1993, which were valued at $1.8 billion, to Egypt. AOI now is entirely owned by the government of Egypt. AOI has about 19,000 employees, of whom 1,250 are engineers. AOI fully owns six factories and shares in three joint ventures, beside the Arab Institute for Advanced Technology.

AOI was established in 1975, with the aim of building an advanced technological industrial base. Egypt, Qatar, Saudi Arabia, and the United Arab Emirates capitalised the AOI with more than US$1 billion. These countries set up the AOI to establish an Arab defence industry by combining Egypt's managerial ability and industrial labour force with the Gulf states' oil money and foreign technology. The bulk of the arms manufacturing was intended to take place in Egypt.

The AOI stalled before it could become a major arms producer because most Gulf states broke relations with Egypt over President Anwar Sadat's peace initiatives with Israel. Egypt kept the AOI functioning in spite of a 1979 proclamation by Saudi Arabia dissolving the body. Some of the AOI's members have renewed military contacts with Egypt, but the AOI was not been restored to its original status.

The Egyptian AOI plants did manufacture missiles, rockets, aircraft engine parts, armoured personnel carriers, electronics, radar, communications gear and assembled aircraft. The Arab British Helicopters Company was a joint venture with the UK to set up the Hulwan Factory in Cairo in the 1980s, to produce Lynx helicopters and overhaul their engines. The project ended in an acrimonious court case that resulted in the Egyptians paying Westland Helicopters more than $300 million in compensation.

A separate company on the same site successfully conducted aircraft assembly, including French Dassault Mirage 2000 fighter aircraft and the Brazilian Tucano trainer. Its most recent project has been the assembly of forty Hongdu JL-8 trainers from components supplied by China.

Egypt's military aircraft industry has never fulfilled its potential because the country's own economy has not been able to generate sufficient funds to support it.

Iran

In the aftermath of its Islamic revolution in 1979, Iran found itself isolated from the global aviation industry, but the needs of the war with Iraq during the 1980s forced it to look to innovative ways to keep its large fleet of US-sourced aircraft and helicopters airworthy. Initially the Iranians turned to the international black market, but soon they started to establish the capability to reverse-engineer spare parts. The Iran Aircraft Industries (IACI) and Iran Helicopter Support and Renewal Company (IHSRC) have since begun to re-engineer complete aircraft and helicopters, as well as developing their own derivatives.

IACI's main sites are at Mehrabad and Shahin Shahr Esfahan, while IHSRC's major site is at Esfahan. The two companies have reverse-engineered a number of US products, including:

* The Simorgh, a Northrop F-5A to F-5B conversion by IAMI at Shahin Shahr Esfahan
* Parastu (*Swallow*), a reverse-engineered Beech F33 Bonanza
* Azarakhsh (*Lightning*), a reverse-engineered F-5E, powered by two RD-33s and believed to have a local development of the Phazotron Topaz radar. The first example is believed to have flown in August 2007
* Shahed 274, a locally designed light helicopter with a combination of components of several helicopter types, mainly the Bell 206
* Shavabiz 75, a reverse-engineered Bell 214C
* Project 2061, a reverse-engineered Bell 206
* Project 2091, an upgrade programme for the AH-1J

The exact number of these aircraft and helicopters to actually enter service is unclear, but it is not thought to be a large number.

During the 1990s, co-operation was opened with the Russian and Ukrainian aircraft industries. Major projects included the Iran-140, a licence-built Antonov An-140 in co-operation with its Ukrainian designers. Both civil and military applications are to be built, including transport and maritime patrol versions to replace the P-3. By early 2009, production was under way in Iran, and first examples had been delivered to Iranian government agencies.

The fate of the Shafagh project, a two-seat advanced training and attack aircraft that is allegedly based on the Russian-Iranian 'Project Integral', is uncertain. Plans exist to produce three versions of the Shafagh, including a two-seat trainer/light strike version and one-seat fighter-bomber versions. They will be fitted with Russian ejection seats.

It is also unclear if the JT2-2 Tazarv, the third prototype of the jet-powered Dorna (Lark) light trainer, has moved forward to production.

Russia and Iran have discussed purchases including Ka-52 attack and Ka-60 transport helicopters. Discussions on licence-building Klimov RD-33 engines for MiG-29s – which Iran has operated since 1990 – have taken place. It has also started development of the Azarakhsh to replace F-5s and is developing the Tazarve jet trainer. Little is known about the former aircraft.

IACI has launched a major upgrade and overhaul programme to keep the F-14 Tomcats in service. This work is under way at Mehrabad, and at least twenty aircraft had been refurbished by early 2009.

A reverse-engineered twin-tailed F-5 variant, dubbed the Saeghe, is now the focus of IACI's efforts, and it reportedly entered IRIAF service in 2007, although few details are available outside Iran.

Israel

The Israeli defence industry is by the far the most advanced in the region and it is a major player on the global stage. During the 1980s, the Israeli government had ambitions to design and build supersonic fighters, but the costs of the Lavi project proved beyond the country's means. US military aid is tied to strict rules that it must be used to purchase products of American companies. This limits considerably the amount Israel's Ministry of Defence can spend on home-produced hardware. To compensate for this the state-owned Israeli defence companies have developed export markets. Also, the Israeli military has concentrated its limited local purchasing power on a few specific niche areas, such as unmanned aerial vehicles, air-launched weapons, electronic warfare equipment, airborne early warning aircraft and intelligence-gathering equipment.

The Israeli defence industry has its roots in the 1950s, when the Jewish state's armed forces found they had to rapidly develop electronic intelligence-gathering equipment to counter advanced hardware supplied by the Soviet Union to Israel's Arab neighbours.

In the aerospace sector, the Israel Aircraft Industries (IAI), is now the Israel Aerospace Industry. The company was first established in 1953 as Bedek Aviation Company, five years after the establishment of the State of Israel. In 2007, it had some 16,000 employees working on military and civil projects.

IAI's Military Aircraft Group is the core of the company's support to the Israeli air force, carrying out upgrade work on fast-jet combat aircraft.

Support to large military aircraft is carried out by the Bedek Aviation Group on a complex at Ben Gurion civilian airport. It handle conversions, modification,

Israel's aerospace industry builds and installs many of the advanced features on the country's US-built F-16s. *(IAI)*

upgrading and total-maintenance packages for all types of large commercial and military aircraft. This unit has contracts to carry out maintenance on Israel Air and Space Force large transport and reconnaissance aircraft.

Work on helicopters is carried out at IAI Mata division's site near Jerusalem.

A major part of the IAI is ELTA, the defence systems house. It is based on electromagnetic sensors (radar, electronic warfare and communication) and on information technology. ELTA Systems' products are designed for intelligence, surveillance, target acquisition and reconnaissance (ISTAR), early warning and control, homeland security (HLS), self-protection and self-defence, and fire-control applications. It is playing a key role in the project to provide the Israel Air and Space Force with new airborne early warning and intelligence-gathering aircraft based on the Gulfstream G550 airframe.

IAI's MALAT division is a world leader in the development of unmanned aerial vehicles, including the newly developed Heron (or Eitan) long-range system that uses satellite communications to control its operations.

IAI's Systems Missiles and Space Group initiates, designs, develops and delivers a variety of solutions, systems and products in the area of missile systems, space

The disastrous Lavi in the 1980s was cancelled, and Israel has since relied on the USA to provide fast-jet airframes. *(IDF Spokesman)*

Israel has a successful radar industry that has produced airborne early warning aircraft such as the Phalcon, which has been sold to Chile. *(IAI)*

and information technology. It co-operates with the US Ballistic Missile Defence System in the production of the Arrow missile defence system.

The Rafael Armaments Authority was set up by the Israeli government in the 1950s to develop advanced missile systems, including long-range Jericho missiles to carry the Jewish state's first nuclear warheads. It has now been rebranded the Rafael Advanced Defence System Ltd, headquartered in Haifa, and markets a wide range of products, including unmanned aerial vehicles, air-to-air missiles, electro-optical sensors, network communications equipment, warheads and missile defence systems. The company currently has some 5,000 staff, working at several development, production and test sites.

The third major state-owned Israeli defence company, Israel Military Industries, concentrates on land-sector business.

As well as the state-owned enterprises, Israel's defence industrial base comprises some 120 private-sector companies of various sizes. The largest of these is Elbit

Systems, which employs 8,000 people. Its most famous aerospace product is the Hermes 450 UAV, and it is co-operating with France's Thales to sell a derivative, the Watchkeeper, to the British Army.

The Israeli Air and Space Force has a sophisticated equipment procurement organisation, headed by its Material Group. This unit has the ability to project manage the development and procurement of complex air warfare systems.

The air force also has it own in-house capabilities to overhaul and upgrade aircraft, helicopters and missiles. This organization, known as the Air Maintenance Unit, is based at Tel Nof airbase.

Jordan

Jordan has long had extensive army and air force workshops providing specialised sub-systems and maintenance of equipment. It has also been seeking to build up its fledgling defence industry. In this regard, a major development was the establishment by royal decree, in August 1999, of the King Abdullah II Design and Development Bureau (KADDB). The bureau has been structured as an independent, government-owned, military-civilian agency existing within the Jordan Armed Forces (JAF). The bureau reports directly to King Abdullah and is responsible for consolidating military research and development efforts within Jordan, with a view to creating a sustainable industrial base. It is part of the role of the KADDB to provide an indigenous capability for the supply of independent, high-quality, efficient and cost-effective scientific and technical services to JAF. In order to commercially exploit KADDB projects, the kingdom announced that it was setting up the National Industrialisation Commission (NIC), reporting to the country's prime minister.

In seeking to build up the defence industry, King Abdullah is following the example of his late father, King Hussein, who in 1997 established the National Resources Development Company (NRDC) to spearhead the development of an indigenous defence industry.

The Royal Jordanian Air Force Industry has been involved in recent years in the manufacture of navigation and test equipment. The first C-130 Hercules to be given a major overhaul at Marka airbase in association with Marshalls of Cambridge was handed back to the Royal Jordanian Air Force in 2001. Others, including those operated by international agencies, have since followed.

In 1999, the RJAF set up Jordan Aeronautical Systems (JAS) to carry out aircraft repair and maintenance at Marka airbase near Amman. It has some fifty employees involved in work on C-130s, UH-1Hs and 737s. Its clients include Iraq, Sri Lanka and the RJAF.

It was announced in September 2003 that the KADDB and Australia's Seabird Aviation had established a joint venture covering the supply of the latter's Seeker SB7L-360 low-level observation and surveillance aircraft. It was stated that the joint-venture company, called Seabird Aviation Jordan, would target the aircraft initially at Iraq's requirement for patrol aircraft to protect its expansive and increasingly vulnerable oil fields and pipelines. It was planned that the aircraft would be assembled at the Marka airbase, with production from 2006 shifting to new facilities at Queen Alia International airport, when output was expected to rise to some sixty units a year.

It was announced in August 2004 that the KADDB had formed a partnership with the private company Jordan Aerospace Industries (JAI), to jointly produce surveillance and target unmanned aerial vehicles (UAVs). This joint venture is dubbed Jordan Advanced Remote Systems (JARS). Its first remotely piloted vehicle (RPV) system was expected to be demonstrated in Ghana in June 2008 and the first production order for the system was expected to be placed on behalf of the Jordan armed forces in mid-2008. It comprises two types of unmanned aerial vehicle (UAV) that have common wings (span 3.1 m), tail units and fuselages (length 1.9 m), and use a common ground-control station and autopilot. The lighter of the two, Silent Eye, is powered by an electric motor, with a maximum speed of 120 km/h; a 10 km line-of-sight radius of action; a ceiling of 1,000 m; a flight duration of 1 hour; and a payload of 1.5 kg. The Jordan Falcon version is heavier (14 kg) and is powered by a two-stroke piston engine that gives a maximum speed of 180 km/h; a ceiling of 3,000 m; an operations radius of 30 km; and an endurance of 4 hours. Its payload capacity is 5.5 kg. Both types are launched from a ramp attached to a KADDB Desert Iris high-mobility 4×4 vehicle. This also now integrates a new directional link added for extended-range video downlink capability (30 km in bad weather, 50 km in good).

Saudi Arabia

Saudi Arabia boasts the largest air force on the Arabian Peninsula, and is in the process of launching a major procurement effort to modernise its inventory of combat aircraft and helicopters. Deals to purchase Eurofighter Typhoon combat aircraft, Airbus A330 Multi-Role Tanker Transports and an array of new helicopters are all under way.

Hand-in-hand with these new procurement projects, the Saudi armed forces are taking a close interest in developing their locally based logistic support capacity. This is a continuation of a process begun almost twenty years ago, and it has been gathering momentum since the late 1990s.

At the heart of these efforts is the Alsalam Aircraft Company, a joint-venture company established in 1988 under the auspices of the Kingdom of Saudi Arabia's Ministry of Defence and Aviation Economic Offset Programme. The company states its shareholdings originally consisted of 50% Boeing Industrial Technology Group (BITG), 25% Saudi Arabian Airlines (25%), 10% Saudi Advanced Industries Company, 10% Gulf Investment Company, and 5% National Industrialisation Company. In 2006 Boeing announced that it had taken control of an additional 10% shareholding.

From its main operations centre at the industrial park at the King Khalid International airport north of Riyadh, the capital of Saudi Arabia, the company

Saudi Arabia's Alsalam aircraft company is playing an important role in sustaining the RSAF's Tornado fleet. *(BAE Systems)*

says it now employs 2,500 people working on a wide range of military and civil aviation maintenance projects. This site has three climate-controlled, wide-body hangars, each capable of housing Boeing 747-400-sized aircraft, dedicated military hangars and a wide range of support capabilities, including a composite repair shop.

Alsalam is now the major provider of maintenance support to the aviation arms of the Saudi Arabian military, and it says that 1,800 personnel – three-quarters of its workforce – are employed on these programmes. It currently has contracts with the USAF, BAE Systems and the Saudi Ministry of Defence to support Royal Saudi Air

Force (RSAF) and Royal Saudi Land Forces Aviation Command (RSLFAC) aircraft and helicopters. The company has become the main vehicle for 'Saudisation' of the military and civil aviation industry in the kingdom, under which the Saudi government aims to displace expatriates and push local employment in this sector above 50%.

Alsalam operates as three distinct business units – a civil maintenance unit, a technical services support unit and a programmed depot maintenance unit. The civil maintenance business unit began operations in 1993 and performs a full range of heavy maintenance and modifications on both wide-body and narrow-body aircraft, such as Boeing 747s, 737s, 727s, 707s and Lockheed Tristars. It is also capable of servicing Airbus A300s, A320s and a variety of business-jet-class aircraft.

The programmed depot maintenance (PDM) business unit performs depot-level, or 'deep', scheduled maintenance and modifications on military aircraft. During PDM each aircraft is dismantled, including the removal of wings, fuel tanks and gears, and then inspected, repaired or upgraded as necessary before being reassembled. After a functional check flight the jet is given a new coat of paint and prepared for its return to its home base. Alsalam's entry into this highly specialised field gained prominence in 1996 with the launching of the RSAF Tornado PDM project under a contract with BAE Systems. Further PDM contracts with the RSAF, covering Boeing E-3A Sentry AWACS and KE-3A, followed.

Under a contract with the United States Air Force the company carries out PDM on RSAF Boeing F-15 Eagle aircraft. The F-15 PDM project employs over 200 multinational personnel. Its involvement in the F-15 programme began in May of 1997 when the company became a subcontractor to McDonnell Douglas Services, now Boeing, which was the prime contractor for this US government-administered foreign military sale programme since the mid-1980s, when the 'Peace Sun' project was launched.

The Tornado PDM effort involves both types in RSAF service – the IDS and the ADV variants. It was the first PDM project to be undertaken in the kingdom with the involvement of the Saudi Arabian Economic Offset Program Company. The contract was awarded by British Aerospace, now BAE Systems, in August 1996, and by July 1997 the first aircraft had arrived at the company's Riyadh site. Previously this work had been undertaken in the UK. After six years of Tornado PDM, Alsalam has built a great deal of experience on the aircraft, and some 125 employees work on this project.

Alsalam performs PDM on RSAF AWACS and air-refuelling aircraft every six years. The company is also closely linked with the RSAF C-130 PDM and technical support for all types of C-130s (VIP, hospital, tanker and logistic variants). Alsalam involvement in the RSAF C-130 PDM began in 1993, with a subcontract from Lockheed Martin Middle East Services (LMMES), which at the time was the prime contractor for this programme. Since then, Alsalam says it has steadily increased

A Typhoon assembly line could eventually open in Saudi Arabia, closely modelled on the BAE Systems site at Warton in the UK. *(BAE Systems)*

its maintenance capability on these aircraft and has acquired the experience to carry out major repair on C-130s, including the RSAF fleet Structure Maintenance Programme.

The technical support programme (TSP) business unit provides flight-line aircraft maintenance support to the military at airbases throughout the Kingdom of Saudi Arabia. The first commercial business started in 1989 with Alsalam, when it was appointed a subcontractor to Boeing for the maintenance of the RSAF fleet of E-3A AWACS and KE-3 tankers. Alsalam is currently the prime contractor on the RSAF F-15 TSP, the RSLFAC maintenance programme for its fleet of Apache AH-64A and Black Hawk UH-60 helicopters and for the remainder of the RSAF helicopter fleet.

Under the technical support programme (TSP), Alsalam provides fully qualified manpower to advise, augment and assist RSAF personnel, provide training and performing functions that are not typically available within the current RSAF force

English Electric Lightning fighters were the first complex aircraft to be repaired and over-hauled in Saudi Arabia in the 1960s. *(BAE Systems)*

structure. The primary focus of this support is related to flight-line maintenance, as well as technical system and component support on the F-15 C/D and F-15S aircraft. The company is also responsible for the operation and maintenance of RSAF Learjets, G4 Gulfstream aircraft and RSAF local procurement. While the F-15 TSP work is managed and administered from Riyadh, company employees work at nine different RSAF installations throughout the kingdom.

The current direct commercial contract between Alsalam and Saudi Arabia's Ministry of Defence and Aviation for the F-15 TSP began on 1 October 2001 and ended in September 2004. Alsalam was then notified that a follow-on three-year contract would begin in October 2004.

Alsalam supports the RSLFAC through the provision of Contractors and Directed Manning Augmentees. This insures that the personnel and the support services, including the repair and return, helicopter components are in place to support the

RSLFAC fleet of AH-64A Apache attack, UH-60A/L Blackhawk transport and Bell 406 Combat Scout reconnaissance helicopters. In March 2002, Alsalam was selected by the RSAF to provide helicopter technical support at several of its airbases. The range of helicopters to be supported includes Bell 412, 212 and 206, as well as the Sikorsky ASH-3D (VIP). Its involvement in the AWACS and KE-3 programme began in 1989 when the company was awarded a subcontract by Boeing Middle East (BME), which was the prime contractor for the 'Peace Sentinel' technical support programme. Under the programme, Alsalam provided fully qualified manpower, including a variety of personnel to support aircraft operations, including planners, technicians, and ground support operations personnel.

Although the final shape of Saudi Arabia's next round of defence procurement is a closely guarded secret, many industry sources in the Middle East have suggested that Alsalam will play a key role in these plans, particularly in two prospective deals with the UK, via BAE Systems.

Development work on the Tornado sustainment programme to bring the RSAF's IDS aircraft up to a similar configuration as the RAF Tornado GR4s began at BAE Systems' site at Warton in the UK. Once this phase is completed, Alsalam will complete the conversion of the RSAF Tornado IDS fleet to the enhanced standard.

Saudi Arabia is keen to expand further the scope and size of its aviation industry, and wants to move from aircraft maintenance into aircraft upgrade and airframe final assembly and check-out. At the heart of these ambitions are plans to assemble Eurofighter Typhoon aircraft in the kingdom under the banner of Project Salam, and again Alsalam would seem the ideal vehicle to undertake this work.

Given the size and scope of such a project, it would suggest that a purpose-built facility in addition to the company's current Riyadh site would be needed to assemble Typhoon aircraft. It is also likely that the shareholding structure of the company would be altered as a result of Project Salem, with BAE Systems possibly becoming a shareholder.

Press reports in the Middle East say that the Saudis hope to employ 15,000 people in their future aviation industry, which would suggest that investment in human resources will play a vital part in this ambitious project. The experience the Alsalam Aircraft Company has gained to date is clearly going to be in great demand if the Kingdom of Saudi Arabia's aviation industry is going to achieve its full potential.

Turkey

The state-owned Turkish Aircraft Industries (TASUS) was set up in 1984 to be the commercial vehicle for the local assembly of the General Dynamics (now Lockheed Martin) F-16 Fighting Falcon combat aircraft. On the back of this deal, the company has established its presence in international military and civil markets. It has considerable influence in the Middle East region, assembling F-16s for Egypt, upgrading F-16s for Jordan and engaging in co-operative projects with Israeli companies.

The Turkish aerospace industry has played an important role in upgrading the country's F-4Es. *(IAI)*

During the 'Share Purchase Agreement' signing ceremony held at TAI facilities on 12 January 2005, the Lockheed Martin of Turkey, Inc. (42%) and General Electric International, Inc. (7%) transfered all the shares it had owned of TASUS, which in turn became Turkish Aerospace Industries. The company is owned by the Turkish Armed Forces Strengthening Foundation (TSKGV), Undersecretariat for Defense Industries (SSM) and Turkish Aeronautical Association (THK).

Located in Ankara, Turkey's capital, TAI facilities cover an area of 5 million square metres, with a roofed industrial facility of 150,000 square metres. The company has a modern aircraft facility furnished with high-technology machinery and equipment that provides extensive manufacturing capabilities ranging from parts manufacturing to aircraft assembly, flight tests and delivery. The TAI aircraft manufacture and overhaul facility at Akinci was formerly known as Mürted.

The Airbus-led A400M consortium includes a strong Turkish element. *(EADS)*

TAI's experience includes co-production of F-16 Fighting Falcon jets, CN-235 light transport/maritime patrol/surveillance aircraft, SF-260 trainers, Cougar AS-532 search and rescue (SAR), combat search and rescue (CSAR) and utility helicopters, as well as design and development of unmanned aerial vehicles (UAV), target drones and agricultural aircraft.

TAI's core business also includes modernisation, modification and systems integration programmes, and after-sales support of both fixed and rotary-wing military and commercial aircraft that are in the inventory of Turkey and friendly countries.

Its major programmes have included:

- Electronic warfare retrofit and structural modifications on Turkish air force F-16s
- MLU, Falcon-Up and Falcon Star modifications on Royal Jordanian Air Force F-16s
- Modification of the S-2E Tracker maritime patrol aircraft into fire-fighting aircraft

- CN-235 and Black Hawk modifications for special forces
- Modification of CN-235 platforms for MPA/MSA missions for the Turkish navy and coast guard
- Modification and modernisation of the Cougar AS-532
- Glass cockpit retrofit of S-70 helicopters
- Conversion of Boeing 737-700 aircraft into AEW&C aircraft
- Avionics modernisation of C-130 aircraft for the Turkish air force
- Design and development of primary and basic trainer (Hurkus) aircraft
- Avionics modernisation of T-38 aircraft for the Turkish air force
- Possible design, development and production of the attack helicopter for the Turkish armed forces (TAF)
- TAI is engaged in manufacturing aerostructures for fixed and rotary-wing, military and commercial aircraft for worldwide customers. The company's experience in the aircraft and aerostructures manufacturing business makes it a uniquely qualified partner of Agusta, Alenia Aeronautica, Airbus, Boeing, CASA, Eurocopter, IAI, Lockheed Martin, Northrop Grumman, MDHI, Sikorsky, Sonaca and many more.

The company's most high-profile international programme is the production of the centre fuselage of the US Joint Strike Fighter (JSF) F-35 aircraft. It is also a partner of the Airbus Military Company in the design and development activities of the Airbus A400M programme with Airbus (France, Germany, Spain and UK), EADS CASA (Spain) and FLABEL (Belgium).

As part of the Göktürk electro-optical surveillance satellite project, a satellite assembly and test centre, which will serve all satellites produced in Turkey in the long term, will be set up at the facilities of the Turkish aerospace firm TAI so as to boost domestic capabilities.

United Arab Emirates

The UAE's purchase of F-16 Desert Falcon aircraft from the USA was a major development for the country's aerospace industry. Under the deal the UAE agreed to fund the development of capabilities that were not in service with the USAF. This resulted in the UAE paying Lockheed Martin to develop these capabilities, and the US government gave the company access to test ranges to prove them. A significant amount of technology, particularly software codes, involved in these projects now resides in the UAE. This is the first such technology transfer that has been undertaken with an Arab country.

The Abu Dhabi-based Gulf Aircraft Maintenance Company (GAMCO) has extensive business in the civil aviation sector, but has recently established a new division in order to handle expanding military business.

It was appointed by Lockheed Martin to be a C-130 authorised service centre in January 2002, covering more than sixteen countries in the Middle East, Africa and Asia. The company has been the depot-level maintenance base for UAE C-130s for

GAMCO technicians work on a UAE AF&AD Eurocopter Squirrel helicopter. *(GAMCO)*

more than fourteen years, and it is expanding its operations to provide maintenance for more recent types of aircraft to enter UAE AF&AD service, including the CASA CN-235, Mirage 2000 and F-16E/F. It also carries out engine overhaul and repairs and has been selected by UAE AF&AD to conduct depot-level maintenance on the General Electric GE F110-132 turbofan engines of the F-16E/Fs. This follows on from work on UAE AF&AD T700-701C engines of the service's Apache helicopter and CT7-9C engines of its CN-235 aircraft. GAMCO already repairs the UAE AF&AD's Hawks, and it is expected to play a large part in the future training aircraft procurement projects, including possibly local assembly.

The new military hangar was approved in April 2002 to accommodate military C-130s, CN-235 aircraft, fighters and helicopters. GAMCO is also contracted to provide depot-level maintenance on the UK's Lockheed Tristar transport and airlift fleet. Specific components and limited overhaul support is being provided for a wide range of aircraft owned and operated by UAE AF&AD, Dubai Air Wing (DAW), Ministry of the Interior Air Wings and other military customers in the region. In-house capability also exists for the Gazelle helicopter. GAMCO has completed the installation of a state-of-the-art cockpit avionics upgrade system on DAW L100-30 aircraft in full co-ordination with CMC Canada as system provider and integrator.

In 2004, the UAE military established a UAV research and technology centre under the guidance of its air force. The centre, located in Abu Dhabi, is the first of its kind in the Gulf region. The UAE has launched a number of new projects to locally produce UAVs, including the 'Al Sber,' which is a version of the Schiebel S-100. The second programme – the Apid 55, a smaller, multi-purpose UAV – is being developed in conjunction with CybAero, a Swedish company. The UAV centre is also working with GAMCO to develop the GRS 100 Falcon 1 UAV as an anti-submarine-warfare platform carrying a miniature magnetic anomaly detection system in a pod beneath the air wing.

The Abu Dhabi-based ADCOM Group has been developing unmanned systems for use as targets for thirteen years. Its SAT-400 medium-speed target system is in operation in Canada and the UAE military. ADCOM has just developed the double-delta-wing Yabhon-M UAV, which has a range of 6,000 km.

DynCorp, the US technical services firm, holds contracts with the UAE Ministry of Defence to provide maintenance services for the UAE AF&AD's fleet of F-16s and King Air 350s. The US$62 million contract for F-16 support was signed in February 2007. Raytheon has support contracts for its I-HAWK SAMs in service in the UAE.

It emerged in November 2007 that GAMCO was planning to move out of military work and had renamed itself Abu Dhabi Aircraft Technologies (ADAT) after a strategic investment by the state-owned investment group, Mubadala Development Company. The company signed a memorandum of understanding with Lockheed Martin, Boeing and Northrop Grumman in November 2007, with a view to spinning off GAMCO/ADAT's military business into a new defence-focused maintenance repair and overhaul joint venture. Thales, EADS and Finnmechanica are also involved in these discussions. Finnmechanica's involvement is reportedly linked to the purchase by the UAE AF&AD of Aermacchi training jets. The new entity will be able to provide in-country logistic support to the UAE's F-16 fighters, AH-64 helicopters and other aircraft and helicopters of US and French origin. This mirrors Mubadala Development Company's joint venture with Dynco in the land sector.

Assessment

The fast-growing and dynamic nature of the Middle East's aerospace industry clearly has major implications for the region's air forces. The industry has been strong in repair and overhaul for several years, but it is developing expertise in areas that for a long time were the preserve of the Western powers, such as systems integration and final assembly of complex advanced combat aircraft.

The Saudi deal to assemble and support Eurofighter Typhoon aircraft within their kingdom is of major significance. Likewise the UAE's purchase of a unique version of the F-16, with capabilities in advance of those used on USAF versions of the aircraft are potentially 'game changing'. Turkey is a key industry player in the region and is emerging as a supplier of important military aerospace services and aircraft final assembly. The Israelis remain strong in the field of UAVs, missile defence, airborne weapons and space.

The Middle East is not ready to be independent of outside suppliers for its defence needs, but the region can no longer be treated simply as a consumer of hand-me-down military hardware.

PART THREE

Middle East Air Campaigns

CHAPTER TWENTY-ONE

No-Fly-Zone Operations,
2000–2003

In the heady days after US-led troops drove the Iraqi occupation force from
Kuwait in February 1991, the idea that Western forces would have still been
confronting Saddam Hussein's government for another decade would have
seemed ludicrous. The Iraqi president, however, proved more resilient that many
imagined, and his armed forces were soon locked in a war of attrition against
American and British aircraft that made daily forays into Iraqi air space to enforce
no-fly zones.

At the turn of the century, American and British airmen serving in the Middle
East could be forgiven for thinking they were serving in a secondary theatre of
operations. Only a few months before, more than a 1,000 NATO aircraft had been
locked in a three-month air war against Serbia. The Balkans seemed to be the centre
of global attention, and enforcement of no-fly zones over Iraq was increasingly seen
as an exercise in diminishing returns. Turkey, Kuwait, Bahrain and Saudi Arabia

Map 1: The southern and northern no-fly-zones. *(US DoD)*

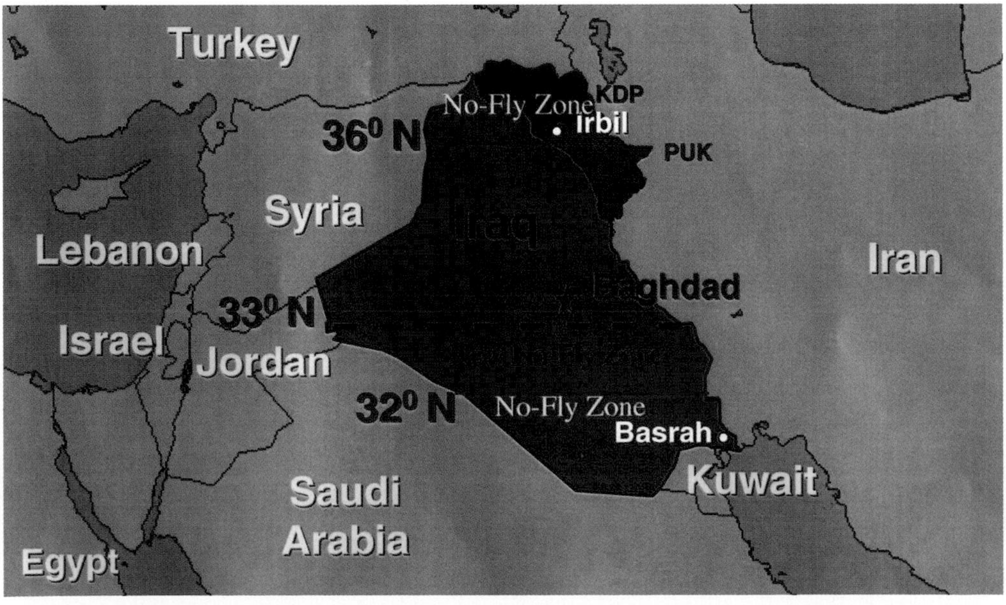

USAF F-15Cs dominated the no-fly-zones over Iraq from 1991 to 2003. *(USAF)*

refused to allow media visits to the bases used by British and US air force units engaged in no-fly-zone operations, adding to the feeling that the mission in the Middle East was a 'forgotten war'. This war was costing the US tax payer some $1 billion a year.

At airbases across the Middle East, the tempo of operations did not let up. During 2000 and into 2001, US-led air task forces in Saudi Arabia and Turkey made daily forays into Iraqi air space. The process was directed from the Combined Air Operations Centre (CAOC) at Prince Sultan airbase (PSAB) in Saudi Arabia and the command post of Combined Task Force Northern Watch at Incirlik airbase in southern Turkey.

Ground-based radar and USAF Boeing E-3 Sentry AWACS aircraft provided round-the-clock coverage of the northern and southern no-fly zones to watch for unusual Iraqi air activity. USAF F-16s and F-15s were held on ground alert to be scrambled to counter any attempts by the Iraqis to launch major air operations. US Navy F-14s and F/A-18s on aircraft carriers also took turns to stand ready to react to Iraqi provocations. These, however, proved very rare, and it was almost unheard of for the ground alert aircraft to be scrambled in the twelve-year-long no-fly-zone operation.

The 'normal' routine was for a large package of aircraft to be flown on a daily basis into southern and northern no-fly zones. They would then patrol over Iraq for

McDonnell Douglas F-15C Eagle

The Eagle has been dominating skies over the Middle East since the 1980s, when Israeli and Saudi F-15s fought and won a series of dog fights respectively with Syrian and Iranian opponents. USAF F-15Cs swept the Iraqi air force from the skies in Operation Desert Storm, and then became the mainstay of no-fly-zone combat air patrols until 2003.

Crew: 1
Length: 63 ft 9 in. (19.43 m)
Wingspan: 42 ft 10 in. (13.05 m)
Height: 18 ft 6 in. (5.63 m)
Maximum take-off weight: 68,000 lb (30,845 kg)
Powerplant: Two Pratt & Whitney F100-100, -220 or -229 afterburning turbofans
Maximum speed: High altitude, Mach 2.5+ (1,650+ mph, 2,660+ km/h)
    Low altitude, Mach 1.2 (900 mph, 1,450 km/h)
Combat radius: 1,061 nm (1,222 miles, 1,967 km) for interdiction mission

Armament
Guns: One internally mounted 20 mm (0.787 in.) M61A1 Gatling gun, 940 rounds
Hardpoints: four wing, four fuselage, two wing stations, centre-line station, optional fuselage pylons with a capacity of 16,000 lb (7,300 kg)
Missiles: AIM-7F Sparrows, AIM-120 AMRAAMs, AIM-9 Sidewinders

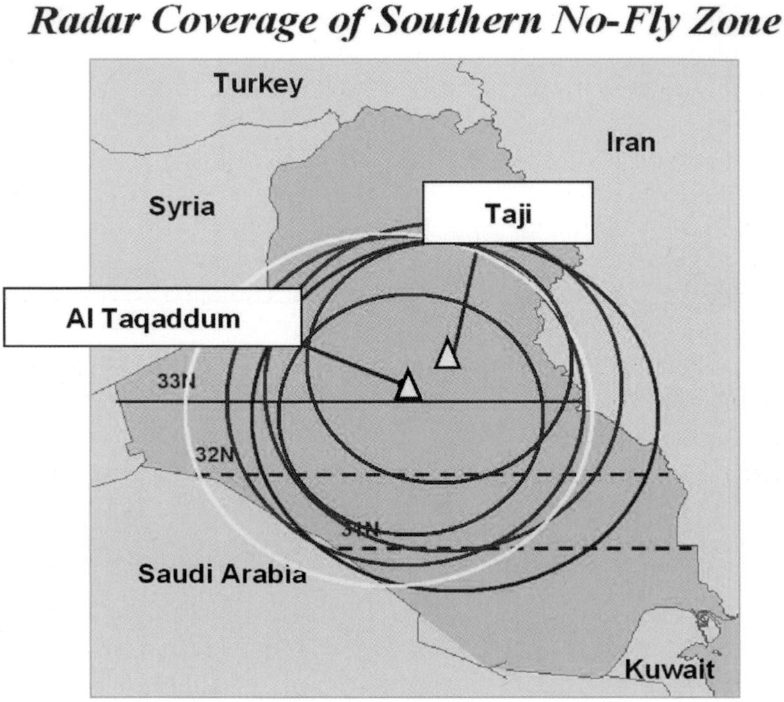

Radar Coverage of Southern No-Fly Zone

Map 2: Iraqi air defence radar coverage. *(US DoD)*

a couple of hours before returning to base. The timings and routes were staggered to keep the Iraqis guessing and make it more difficult for them to position anti-aircraft missiles to engage US and British aircraft.

Operations in the south were more complex because the aircraft needed to form packages were spread over several bases in a number of countries. Each host country imposed different restrictions on the type of aircraft, weapons and rules of engagement operating from their bases. The Saudis refused to allow bombs to be carried by aircraft based at PSAB, but did allow air-to-air and anti-radiation missiles because they were 'defensive' weapons. Only the Kuwaitis allowed bombers on their bases, so the USAF and RAF had to base their offensive strike aircraft at either Ali Al Salem or Ahmed Al Jaber airbases, while Bahrain only allowed tanker and other support aircraft at its bases. The restrictions on land-based strike aircraft across the Middle East meant the US Navy was called upon to provide carrier strike aircraft for more than two dozen days a month to support the no-fly-zone mission.

A typical Operation Southern Watch package usually consisted of a USAF E-3 and RC-135 Rivet Joint or RAF Nimrod R.1 electronic-intelligence-gathering aircraft, which monitored Iraqi air space and alerted the fast jets of attempts by the Iraqi air force or air defence to engage the package. US Navy EA-6B Prowler jammers would also be on station to frustrate Iraqi radar surveillance.

Once surveillance coverage was in place, a combat air patrol of fighter aircraft would be established high over southern Iraq, and then a pair of anti-radiation-missile-equipped jets would swing into Iraqi air space to react when missile control radars came up to engage the jets. The final element of the package would be a pair of bomb-armed jets, usually RAF Tornado GR1/4s, USAF F-15E Strike Eagles or US Navy Hornets, which would be ready to execute a 'response option' if the Iraqis were foolish enough to try to engage the package. These included firing anti-radiation missiles at Iraqi radars that illuminated the package, bombing missile or gun batteries that open fired or bombing Iraqi command posts controlling the engagement.

The RAF and US Navy jets were also usually equipped with photographic reconnaissance pods to take pictures of Iraqi airbases and air defence sites to monitor any unusual activity or build-ups.

The decision to execute a response option was usually left to pilots and controllers in the E-3s. They had to run through a rules-of-engagement check-list to ensure they had confirmation that the Iraqis had lit up their radars or fired weapons.

These incursions usually ran for up to two hours or so before the US and British aircraft would return to base. This process was repeated in the northern no-fly zone, but with some difference. The Turks were very sensitive about Kurdish rebel activity in their eastern provinces, and wanted to keep a close leash on the US and British operations, which were aimed at protecting the Kurdish 'safe area' in northern Iraq. For this reason, the Turks insisted on one of their air force generals being present in the Operation Northern Watch command post at Incirlik when the daily package made its foray into Iraqi air space. This officer monitored the mission and had a veto, or 'red card', over the execution of response options if the package was engaged by the Iraqis.

The composition of the northern package was slightly smaller that in the south, and it had less air space to manoeuvre in. Its operations were more predictable because it could only enter Iraqi airspace across the Turkish border zone, making it easier for the Iraqis to plan SAM ambushes. This meant the northern package carried a higher number of anti-radiation missiles and put a great deal of effort into photographic reconnaissance of Iraqi air defence sites to ensure there were no surprises. RAF Jaguar jets bore the brunt of this element of the mission.

The Iraqis played a cat-and-mouse game with the USAF and RAF pilots, regularly moving their air defence missiles and radars around to try to spring SAM ambushes on the daily package. Although engagements ebbed and flowed, on average some sort of incident occurred every week in the southern no-fly zone. It was also common for the Iraqis to claim that the US and British aircraft had caused civilian casualties in their airstrikes. Iraqi air defence crews in the no-fly zones clearly knew that every time they opened fire they risked being on the receiving end of precision-guided munitions dropped from a British or American bomber. Yet on at least 1,100 occasions, or on average thirty-six times a month, after December 1998 they chose to open fire. By late 2002, the Iraqi government claimed US and British bombing

Iraqi missile crews scramble to engage a Coalition reconnaissance flight after being caught by surprise. *(Vinten)*

had killed 1,477 people and injured 1,358 since the no-fly zones were imposed by London and Washington. The vast majority of these casualties were probably not civilians but personnel of the Air Defence Command who had been caught in American and British airstrikes on their command posts, and missile and gun batteries. Saddam, however, had provided his air defence forces with incentives to fight the Americans and British, offering a cash reward of $5,000 to the air defence unit that shot down a US or British aircraft, and a $2,500 bonus to the individual who captured a downed flier.

The Iraqi Air Defence Command built a fibre optic cable network to give it a small tactical advantage. This allowed the Iraqis to detect and track targets with their area surveillance radars based outside the no-fly zones and rapidly pass the information to forward-based SAM batteries. This meant they did not have to use their organic radar systems until the very last minute before missile launch, giving them a degree of surprise. The US command then deployed a squadron of General Atomic RQ-1 Predator unmanned aerial vehicles to Kuwait to fly surveillance missions in high-risk areas of Iraq. Three were lost to Iraqi fire during the second half of 2001, and another was shot down by a MiG-25 in December 2002.

This tempo of operation meant that by 2000 almost every member of the USAF's Air Combat Command and the RAF Tornado and Jaguar forces spent long periods of duty in the Middle East. American airmen called the Middle East the 'Sand Box' because they spent months at a time in remote desert airbases with little to do but fly missions over Iraq.

The change of administration in the USA in January 2001 did not immediately lead to a major change in operations over the no-fly zones, but the events of 11 September 2001 would dramatically transform US and British air operations over the Middle East. The command and airbase infrastructure established for the no-fly-zone mission would soon be very useful in the launching of offensive operations against Afghanistan in October 2001.

The US military cited more than 110 separate incidents of Iraqi surface-to-air missile and anti-aircraft artillery fire directed against Coalition aircraft between January and early August 2002 alone. In mid-May 2002, Iraqi attacks against US and UK jets began to escalate considerably, prompting an increase in retaliatory bombing.

CHAPTER TWENTY-TWO

The Second Intifada, 2000–2003 and Beyond

In the first decade of the twenty-first century the Israeli Air and Space Force (IASF) has been preoccupied with involvement in operations against Palestinian insurgent groups in the occupied territories of Gaza and the West Bank, as well as against the Lebanese militia group Hizbullah. To the Palestinians, these were known as Intifadas, or uprisings. For the Israeli military the campaigns in the occupied terroritories were highly complex and difficult operations because they involved fighting in built-up areas containing large civilian populations.

High-intensity Israeli combat operations almost always resulted in heavy civilian casualties among the Palestinians, which inflamed international opinion and more ominously prompted a wave of Palestinian suicide bombings against civilians inside Israel.

At one point or another, all IASF units were involved in these operations in the occupied territories or Lebanon.

Second Intifada, also known as the al-Aqsa Intifada, 2000 to 2003

The Oslo peace process in the 1990s dramatically reduced violence in the occupied territories, but conflict between the Palestinian insurgent groups and the IDF never really ceased. Several hundred people were killed in violence during the 1990s.

US President Bill Clinton tried to bring the Oslo process to a conclusion during 2000 and secure a final peace settlement between the Israeli government and the Palestinian Authority (PA), led by the veteran Palestine Liberation Organisation chief, Yasser Arafat. This peace drive ended in failure in July, prompting the outbreak of low-level violence across the West Bank and Gaza.

On 28 September 2000, the former Israeli general and leader of the Likud party, Ariel Sharon, made a high-profile visit to the Temple Mount in Jerusalem. This area contains holy sites sacred to both Jews and Muslims, prompting protests from Palestinian leaders. The next day a large Palestinian demonstration was held in Jerusalem against Sharon which resulted in Israeli riot police storming Temple Mount, killing four Palestinians and injuring some 200. Over the following days every Palestinian town and city in the occupied territories was engulfed in rioting. IDF troops were brought in to put down what was now being called a full-scale Intifada.

The first AH-64As were delivered to Israel in the early 1990s, and have since been used extensively in Lebanon and the occupied territories. *(IDF Spokesman)*

Israeli Heron unmanned aerial vehicles are used as part of a 24/7 intelligence-gathering operation against Palestinian insurgents in the occupied territories. *(IDF Spokesman)*

On 12 October, two Israeli reservists who entered Ramallah were arrested by the PA police. Believing them to be Mossad intelligence agents, an agitated Palestinian mob stormed the police station, beat the soldiers to death, and threw their mutilated bodies into the street from a second-floor window. The killings were captured on video by an Italian TV crew and broadcast on television.

In response, Israel launched a series of retaliatory airstrikes against the Palestinian Authority buildings with AH-1 Cobra gunships. Tension and violence across the occupied territories continued into 2001, and intensified after Sharon was appointed Israeli Prime Minister in February 2001.

On 18 May 2001, Israel for the first time since 1967 used warplanes to attack targets in the territories, hitting PA security force bases. Airstrikes on Gaza airport destroyed the PA's handful of Mil Mi-8 helicopters and devastated its facilities. Later, IDF troops bulldozed the runway. Prior to that, air attacks on the occupied territories had only been carried out by helicopter gunships. Violence continued to escalate during the rest of 2001, and Palestinian insurgency groups struck into the heart of Israel, killing hundreds of civilians in suicide bombings.

In response to these attacks, Sharon announced that the IDF would launch Operation Defensive Shield to take back control of all main Palestinian cities in the West Bank, with the exception of Hebron and Jericho. In April 2002, IDF tank columns encircled Bethlehem, Jenin, Nablus and Ramallah. Strike forces, backed by attack helicopters, pushed deep into these towns to try to destroy the Palestinian militants holding them. Two weeks of fighting culminated in the capture of the Palestinian cities and refugee towns. The strongest resistance was in Jenin, and most of the centre of the town's refugee camp was flattened by Israeli artillery fire, airstrikes and bulldozers. Hundreds of Palestinian civilians were killed in the fighting. In Ramallah, Arafat was besieged in his compound for several weeks until the fighting died down.

Israeli air power was used to support all phases of these operations, including surveillance by UAVs, attack helicopters and fixed-wing airstrikes, as well as troop transport and casualty evacuation. UAV operations came into their own, allowing IDF ground commanders to keep Palestinian-controlled areas under constant surveillance without exposing their troops to danger. Reports emerged from Palestinian sources of missile strikes by Israeli UAVs, although the IDF would not confirm the use of armed UAVs.

One of the most controversial aspects of IASF operations in the occupied territories has been the tactic known as 'targeted assassination' of Palestinian leaders. In the first years of the Intifada, the Israelis used a combination of informers inside occupied territories, UAV and attack helicopters to set up the strikes on Palestinian leaders. Once a target was identified by the Israeli internal security agency, the Shin Bet, a UAV would be tasked to maintain constant surveillance from a discreet distance. By flying daily UAV patrols over the occupied territories the IASF 'conditioned' the population not to pay any attention to them. When a suitable opportunity emerged to engage the target, an AH-64 or an AH-1 would be tasked to engage it with an anti-tank guided missile or cannon fire. This process was simplified when a modified version of the Rafael Spike anti-tank missile was integrated onto Hermes 450 UAVs.

From 2000 to the end of 2006, some 339 Palestinians were killed in targeted assassinations, but only 210 were the intended targets, the rest being passers-by or the target's wives and children. This latter aspect led to international criticism of the Israeli tactic. There was also concern that it actually backfired on the Israelis. By mid-2006, almost all of the political leadership of the Islamic group Hamas had been killed by helicopter or UAV strikes. This led the survivors to become expert at avoiding Israeli surveillance, and made them more implacable opponents of the Jewish state. This would plague the ability of the Israelis to resolve the crisis in Gaza in 2008 and 2009.

For the Israeli air force, the major issue was sustaining a high tempo of operations by its helicopters and UAV units over many months and years. These in-demand units had to be reinforced regularly by reservists. Private contractors were also hired to help fly UAV missions.

By the summer of 2003, the Intifada had run its course. The heavy-handed IDF reoccupation of the West Bank in 2002 defeated the main Palestinian insurgent groups. Thousands of suspected insurgents were arrested by the Israeli authorities. The construction of the controversial Separation Wall also made it almost impossible for Palestinian suicide bombers to cross from the West Bank into Israel proper.

Gaza Conflict 2004 to 2008

In 2004, Sharon announced that all Israeli civilian settlements and troops would be withdrawn from Gaza by the following August. It was hoped that Israeli casualties would be reduced by pulling the settlers back into Israel proper. The pull-back also made the IDF ever more reliant on IASF UAVs to maintain intelligence coverage on what was happening inside Gaza.

The Israeli withdrawal from Gaza set in train an internal feud between the mainstream Palestinian group Fatah, which was loyal to the Ramallah-based Palestinian President Abbas, and the hardline Islamic Palestinian group Hamas. This culminated in the June 2007 election victory for Hamas in Gaza, and weeks later they launched a military offensive to drive out security forces loyal to Fatah. Israel immediately stepped up its air, land and sea blockade of the Gaza Strip.

Palestinian insurgent groups in Gaza had long been some of the most hardline and effective fighters among resistance groups to Israeli occupation. They had also developed a strong interest and expertise in the development, manufacture and use of rockets and other improvised stand-off weapons. They smuggled Iranian rockets into Gaza and then mass-produced their own copies. The first rocket strikes occurred in 2001 when seven Qassam missiles were fired into Israel. By 2004, the annual rate of fire had risen to 234.

After it seized power, Hamas soon set about escalating its military confrontation with Israel. Tunnels were dug under the closed border with Egypt to allow weapons

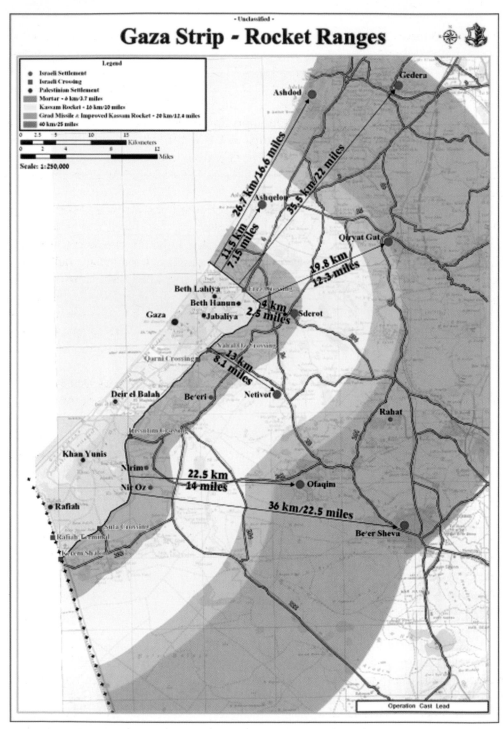

Hamas rocket teams in Gaza were the main target of Israeli air strikes in the 2008/9 offensive against the territory. *(IDF Spokesman)*

to be brought into the Gaza Strip, and production of Qassam rockets and improvised mortars was stepped up. According to Israel, between the Hamas takeover of the Gaza Strip and the end of January 2008, 697 rockets and 822 mortar bombs were fired at Israeli towns. In response, Israel targeted home-made Qassam launchers and military targets with artillery and helicopter gunship strikes.

In May 2004, the IDF launched Operation Rainbow to raid tunnels near Rafha with strong support from Apache gunships, with the IASF claiming they accounted for thirty-seven per cent of Palestinian insurgent casualties. The Apache played a key role in Operation Days of Atonement in Gaza in October 2005, killing fifty-five per cent of insurgents killed by Israeli forces.

On 25 June 2006, Hamas staged an audacious attack on an IDF position along the border of the Gaza Strip. Fighters tunnelled under the Israeli border wall and ambushed an IDF position, capturing one Israeli soldier. In retaliation, the IDF launched Operation Summer Rains over the night of 27/28 June. Attack helicopters destroyed Gaza's main power transformer, and three bridges were dropped by air strikes. IASF jets buzzed the Strip and set off sonic booms to unsettle the population. Several IDF columns mounted ground raids. Hamas refused to release the captured soldier and the Israeli government refused to talk to the government of Gaza, declaring it a 'terrorist organisation'. The low-level war between Hamas and the IDF would continue.

Although the tempo of offensive operations ebbed and flowed over the following months, the IASF maintained almost continuous UAV surveillance of Gaza to monitor Hamas activity.

Hamas rocket fire escalated considerably in January and February 2008. On 29 February, the IDF launched Operation Hot Winter, which included a strong air element. IASF F-16Is, Apaches and AH-1s surged their operations against Palestinian rocket factories, anti-aircraft positions and Hamas leaders. The IASF attack helicopters were forward-deployed to temporary bases on the edge of Gaza to maintain the tempo of operations.

An IDF ground force also conducted a major raid into Gaza. The IDF lost three dead, and some 119 Palestinians were killed. The brief upsurge in violence did result in a tacit truce between the two sides, though this did not totally end armed clashes, which included the damaging of an Israeli helicopter gunship by anti-aircraft gunfire on 14 March. A calm of sorts settled in June after Egypt brokered a cease-fire.

New Year War

Hamas ambitions to copy the tactics and strategy of Lebanon's Hizbullah militia was clearly a great worry for the Israeli military. For the remainder of 2008, the Israeli defence minister Ehud Barak and the IDF high command began planning a major operation against Hamas to deal a major blow to the group's military capability. The lessons of the ill-fated Lebanon were in the forefront of the minds of the planners for a new incursion into Gaza.

Hamas rocket teams in Gaza were the main target of Israeli air strikes in the 2008/9 offensive against the territory. *(IDF Spokesman)*

The Egyptian cease-fire started to fray badly in November 2008 after Israeli troops launched a raid into Gaza to destroy a tunnel which the IDF said was being prepared for another Hamas foray into Israel. Hamas responded by ramping up rocket attacks to pre-cease-fire levels, with up to eighty-seven rocket strikes a day inside Israel. Prime Minister Ehud Olmert and Defence Minister Ehud Barak decided the time was ripe to strike a major blow against Hamas's military infrastructure, particularly its rocket units. The close proximity of civilian population centres to Hamas military sites meant that any Israeli incursion was bound to result in heavy civilian casualities, which would inflame international opinion against Israel. For this reason Olmert was keen to get the insurection over and done before US President George Bush left office on 20 January 2009. The Israeli government had no idea how the new US adminstration would react to television coverage of the inevitable civilian caualties.

Preparations for Operation Case Lead were meticulous. To achieve surprise, the Israelis even opened border crossings for humanitarian aid convoys on the day before the offensive began on 27 December 2008.

During that evening, IASF jets launched a concerted bombing campaign across the Gaza Strip. Over 170 targets were hit with precision-guided munitions from

The veteran AH-1 Cobra remains a mainstay of the IASF's attack helicopter force and they have been progressively upgraded. *(IDF Spokesman)*

some fifty F-16s, F-15s and AH-64Ds. These included Hamas paramilitary bases, training camps, and underground Kassam launchers. The airstrikes also hit Hamas headquarters, government offices and police stations, killing around 140 Hamas policemen, including the chief of police, Tawfiq Jabber. The Israelis made use of the Boeing GBU-39 small-diameter bomb for the first time after deliveries had started from the USA a month earlier. A concerted effort was made to locate and kill senior Hamas leaders in an extended targeted assassination effort.

Hamas responded by ramping up rocket attacks on Israeli border towns, with some 700 being fired on 27 December. They kept up returning fire on Israel until the end of the operation in late January.

The Israeli offensive now rolled out in a similar pattern for more than a week. Day after day, round the clock, Israeli aircraft and attack helicopters systematically worked through a list of Hamas targets. Continous UAV surveillance of Gaza meant that emerging targets were also engaged by aircraft, helicopters or in some cases missile-armed Elbit Hermes 450 UAVs. Close attention was given to striking the entrances to tunnels under the border fence with Egypt to try to stop arms smuggling into Gaza. The Israelis were very worried that Hamas would be able to gain access to the long-range Iranian rockets used by Hizbullah to bombard northern Israel in 2006. It set up a major intelligence-gathering operation to monitor the sea around Gaza and off the Egyptian coast. This paid dividends in early January when the Israelis detected an Iranian ship in the Red Sea delivering long-range rockets to Sudanese smugglers who were being paid to deliver them to Hamas in Gaza. Reports are unclear as to whether fixed-wing aircraft or armed IAI Eitan UAVs were used in the subsequent airstrike that destroyed the smugglers' convoy as it drove north towards the Sudan–Egypt border.

The use of 1,000 lb and 2,000 lb bombs in populated areas caused tremendous amounts of damage. Whole houses and apartment blocks were knocked down in the strikes, and dozens of civilians were killed and hundreds injured each day of the offensive.

Israeli government leaders decided to up the ante on 3 January 2009, when IDF tank columns were sent into Gaza to cut the Strip into distinct sections, to prevent Hamas fighters moving around. The presence of IDF ground troops limited the IASF's room to strike, and the weight of air support shifted to the attack helicopter and UAV forces. IASF strikes were now reduced to between ten and twenty targets a day, and most of these were so-called 'emerging targets' identified by UAVs or ground troops, such as Hamas mortar and rocket teams.

With the inauguration of US President Barack Obama fast approaching, the Israeli government declared the IDF military operation had achieved all its objects on 19 January. By 21 January, all IDF ground troops had pulled out of the Gaza Strip. Hamas also declared its own unilateral cease-fire to bring Operation Case Lead to a very messy end.

Once the dust cleared, the devastation in Gaza was seen to be on a scale that was even worse than in Lebanon two-and-a-half years earlier. Just over 900 Palestinian civilians were killed, along with nearly 480 Palestinian insurgents and security personnel. Humanitarian agencies reported that the damage to Gaza's infrastructure was enormous, in the range of nearly $2 billion in assets, including 4,000 homes and 600–700 factories, small industries and workshops and business enterprises destroyed.

Israel has stated that thirteen Israelis were killed during the conflict, including three civilians and ten IDF soldiers. Out of those figures, five were killed engaging Hamas combatants, four were killed by friendly fire, and one was killed when Hamas rockets hit a military base inside Israel. Some 300 Israeli soldiers were wounded.

The stand-off between Hamas and Israel was far from over. Incidents occurred on a daily basis during the first months of 2009. These occasionally escalated to involve IASF air power, including an airstrike on a Hizbullah leader on 4 March. Tunnel entrances were bombed on 11 and 12 March, and a gathering of Hamas fighters was attacked by IASF jets on 19 March. Hamas fighters continued to respond to IDF actions with rocket fire into Israel.

The results of Operation Case Lead were again mixed for the Israeli government and military. Hamas's military organisation, and particularly its rocket infrastructure, was badly damaged by the Israeli onslaught. It returned to action after 20 January, but at a significantly reduced level. Unlike Hizbullah, it was unable to immediately rebuild its forces, because of the Israeli blockade.

For Israeli airmen, the assault on Gaza was very straightforward. Hamas had no meaningful air defences, so the IASF could operate with impunity. Its main challenge was finding targets in a confused urban battlefield, while avoiding hitting civilians and IDF ground troops. The IASF's large UAV force came into its own during the Gaza battles.

The internatational standing of Israel after the extent of the damage inflicted on Gaza emerged will be more difficult for the Israeli government to rebuild.

CHAPTER TWENTY-THREE

Afghanistan, 2001–2002

Phase 1, 2001–2002

The attacks by Osama Bin Laden's al-Qaeda network on New York and Washington DC on 11 September 2001 prompted US President George Bush to order an immediate military response. These attacks killed more than 3,000 American civilians, and the US military was soon planning to strike at bin Laden's bases in Afghanistan.

Although Afghanistan is far removed from the Middle East, US and British forces already in the region on no-fly-zone duty and participating in exercises in Egypt, Jordan and Oman were soon assigned to support the new mission, dubbed Operation Enduring Freedom.

The Combined Air Operations Centre (CAOC) at Prince Sultan airbase (PSAB) in Saudi Arabia was at the heart of this initial planning as US Central Command's (CENTCOM) only major headquarters in the Middle East region. USAF Lt Gen Chuck Wald commanded the no-fly-zone mission from the CAOC, but in theory also had responsibility for air operations across the CENTCOM area of responsibility (AOR), which stretched from the Horn of Africa into Central Asia.

The famous B-2 Stealth bomber spearheaded the US air offensive against Afghanistan in October 2001. *(USAF)*

However, General Wald would soon find that his staff would not lead the war-planning for the coming operation in Afghanistan because the US Defense Secretary Donald Rumsfeld was determined to keep a close hold on the Afghan War, and directed that the CENTCOM chief, General Tommy Franks, should run most of the war from his headquarters in Tampa, Florida. Other complicating factors were the involvement of the Central Intelligence Agency's (CIA) covert paramilitary air force, including General Atomics MQ-1 Predator unmanned aerial vehicles in the war. These were controlled direct from CIA headquarters in Langley, Virginia, in co-ordination with CENTCOM in Tampa. US Special Operations Command, which did not like taking orders from 'blue suit' air force officers at the CAOC, also sent a strong contingent of its 'black', or covert, helicopter and aircraft units to Afghanistan. Then the Saudis refused to allow the CAOC staff to be augmented with hundreds of extra staff to help run the Afghan War. The initial phases of the Afghan War would therefore be run directly from Tampa and Washington, to a large degree bypassing the CAOC.

Middle East airbases would play a key role in the US-led assault on Afghanistan. Many governments in the region were not keen to be publicly identified with the US campaign in Afghanistan because of a fear of a backlash from their populations, which contained large anti-American elements. Saudi Arabia refused to allow any of its bases to be used in the campaign, and the UAE, Qatar and Oman ordered media blackouts on their assistance to the US and British forces. The Saudi decision was a major blow to campaign planners, and key reconnaissance assets, such as Boeing RC-135 Rivet Joint and Lockheed U-2S Dragon Lady aircraft, had initially to be based at Seeb in Oman for the first phase of the Afghan War, before a more permanent base could be found at Al Dhafra in the UAE. The Saudis stuck to their hardline position for the remainder of the year, including on one occasion refusing permission for a U-2 to divert to PSAB after Al Dhafra was closed because of bad weather. The U-2 crew were low on fuel and could not reach an alternative airfield, and so landed anyway, creating a major diplomatic incident with the Saudis.

The Qataris allowed the US to move into Al Udeid airbase to establish a base for tanker aircraft that were essential to allow bombers and strike aircraft to hit targets in Afghanistan from aircraft carriers or the giant airbase on the British Indian Ocean Territory of Diego Garcia.

Oman's role proved critical to the Afghan campaign. It opened the airbase on Masirah island to US forces, allowing them to activate pre-positioned tents, command post and aircraft ground handling equipment. Masirah became the forward headquarters for US special forces heading into southern Afghanistan. Lockheed AC-130 Spectre gunships, MC-130 Combat Talon deep-penetration transports and HC-130 Combat Shadow tankers, as well as MH-53 Pave Low helicopters, soon arrived to prepare for the Afghan mission.

For several years, UK forces had been planning a major exercise, dubbed Saif Sareea II, in Oman during September and October 2001, and so when the Afghan crisis erupted the RAF was well positioned to participate in emerging operations.

USAF F-15E Strike Eagles based in Kuwait flew some of the longest 'fighter missions' in history to support US troops fighting in Afghanistan in early 2002. *(USAF)*

Boeing B-52H Stratrofortress

The USAF's veteran nuclear bomber saw action with conventional weapons against Iraqi targets in 1991 and 2003. During the latter confict, it employed long-range cruise missiles and satellite-guided joint direct attack munitions against a range of targets.

Crew: 5 (pilot, co-pilot, radar navigator (bombardier), navigator, and electronic warfare officer)
Length: 159 ft 4 in. (48.5 m)
Wingspan: 185 ft (56.4 m)
Height: 40 ft 8 in. (12.4 m)
Maximum take-off weight: 488,000 lb (220,000 kg)
Powerplant: Eight Pratt & Whitney TF33-P-3/103 turbofans, 17,000 lbf (76 kN) each
Maximum speed: 560 kt (650 mph, 1,000 km/h [6])
Combat radius: 4,480 miles (3,890 nm, 7,210 km)

Armament
Guns: One 20 mm M61 Vulcan cannon in a remote-controlled tail turret now decommissioned and removed from all operational aircraft
Bombs: Approximately 70,000 lb (31,500 kg) mixed ordnance – bombs, mines, missiles, in various configurations

Senior RAF officers, led by Air Marshal Jock Stirrup, were sent to CENTOM in Tampa to integrate UK operations with their US counterparts. In Oman, the bulk of the RAF force, including Tornado GR1, Tornado F3 and Harrier GR7 fast jets, VC-10 tankers, C-130 Hercules and E-3D Sentry aircraft, was concentrated at Thumrait airbase in the south of the country. Other support aircraft staged through Seeb, on Oman's northern coast.

USAF and US Navy commanders were keen to get British air support because as well as launching the Afghan operation, they were having to maintain combat air patrols over US cities to guard against any hijackings of civilian airliners. RAF VC-10s and Tristars were in high demand because they could refuel US Navy probe-equipped fighters to allow them to operate over Afghanistan from carriers in the Arabian Sea. Additional tankers were deployed to Oman in late September 2001 in preparation for the start of the US offensive. The USAF E-3 AWACS fleet was also heavily committed to operations in Iraq and over the USA, so the RAF enhanced its Sentry detachment in Oman to allow a continuous orbit to be maintained over Afghanistan to control complex air operations by US aircraft. Operation Veritas, as the UK mission was codenamed, also led to the RAF Canberra PR9 unit, 39 Squadron, deploying to Seeb to fly photographic missions over Afghanistan. Seeb also played host to RAF Nimrod MR2 patrol aircraft and Nimrod R1 signals intelligence aircraft for the Afghan mission. The RAF Special Force Hercules unit, 47 Squadron, was already in Oman for Saif Sareea II, and soon found itself working side by side with its US counterparts on Masirah.

Strike operations began against Afghan targets on 7 October. Once the war was under way the US and UK support units in the Middle East found themselves heavily involved. The collapse of the Taliban regime in November led the US and British special forces to move into Afghanistan in strength, via forward bases in Pakistan.

Reinforcements to the USAF presence in the Middle East included the first ever combat deployment of the Northrop Grumman RQ-4 Global Hawk unmanned aerial vehicle. Flying from Al Dhafra, along with the U-2s, the Global Hawks flew long-endurance missions over Afghanistan, even though they were still in the experimental development stage. One was lost in a crash in the UAE desert while returning to base later in 2001.

The diversion of the US Navy aircraft carriers committed to no-fly-zone support to the Arabian Sea to support the Afghan mission did lead the Pentagon to beef up its presence in Kuwait to deter any Iraqi attempt to exploit the crisis. Additional USAF F-15E Strike Eagles of the 366th Wing were deployed to Al Jaber airbase in Kuwait, and a battalion of US Army AH-64A Apache attack helicopters was also sent to the Gulf state. The F-15Es were eventually committed to the Afghan mission in early 2002, flying long-endurance close air support missions to assist US Army troops engaging al-Qaeda fighters during Operation Anaconda in March 2002.

US Navy commanders were ordered to beef up their patrols in Middle Eastern waters during the Afghan campaign to intercept any al-Qaeda operatives who might try to escape by sea and to prevent any attacks on civilian shipping. Additional US Navy P-3C Orion maritime patrol aircraft were sent to Bahrain, Masirah and Djibouti to patrol the region's seas. Masirah-based P-3Cs and British Nimrods also flew overland surveillance missions into Afghanistan at this time.

Canada, Australia, Spain, Germany and France sent patrol aircraft to the region to support the enhanced maritime surveillance mission, using bases in Djibouti, UAE and Qatar.

Phase 2 – ISAF Mission starts 2002

In December 2001, an international conference in Bonn on the future of Afghanistan set in train events that led to the deployment of the NATO-led International Security Assistance Force (ISAF) to the Afghan capital Kabul to help in the formation of a new government in the war-ravaged country.

Land routes into Afghanistan were almost non-existent, so NATO nations had to rely on air transport to move their troops into the country. The CAOC in PSAB now had a greater influence on air operations over Afghanistan, and was responsible for organising this airlift, allocating slots to land transport aircraft at the US-controlled Bagram airbase and the ISAF-controlled Kabul International airport.

As lead-nation for the ISAF, the UK was in the forefront of this effort, using its C-17 Globemasters and C-130s. The UK forward air mounting centre was set up at Thumrait in Oman. Other nations made their own arrangements, with Canada and Italy, for example, operating from the UAE.

CHAPTER TWENTY-FOUR

The Iraq Invasion, 2003

In the wake of the 1991 Gulf war, US Central Command (CENTCOM) developed contingency plans to attack and defeat Iraq. They were revised annually during the years of the Clinton Administration, but this was a routine exercise as there was little appetite in the White House between 1992 and 2000 for a major war in the Middle East.

This changed with the arrival of the Bush administration in January 2001, and the installation of Donald Rumsfeld as Defense Secretary and Paul Wolfowitz as his deputy. In the aftermath of the 11 September 2001 attacks on New York and Washington, the political climate in the USA changed fundamentally, and an attack on Iraq climbed up the agenda, even if it would have to wait until the situation in Afghanistan stabilised during the spring and summer of 2002 for planning to go forward.

Examination of detailed contingency planning for an attack of Iraq now began in earnest. Debates raged within the administration throughout the summer of 2002 over the wisdom of attacking Iraq and how it would be done. The decision to go ahead with an attack on Iraq was made in September 2002. It was decided to try one last round of UN inspections at the behest of the the British Prime Minister, Tony Blair. Crucially the US President, George Bush, secured political top cover for his Iraq strategy from both houses of the US Congress, which passed a war powers resolution in October.

The military planning process began in parallel to the political one, with President Bush requesting the Joint Chiefs of Staff to begin preparing contingency plans. They in turn, tasked General Tommy Franks, the commander of CENTCOM, which had responsibility for all American military operations in the Middle East, to begin detailed planning.

Throughout the late summer and into the autumn of 2002, arguments raged between Franks, Rumsfeld and the White House over the Iraq invasion plan. In the end a compromise was agreed, which was soon dubbed the 'rolling start'. This envisaged starting the attack with a 'medium-sized' force of three corps-sized ground formations, backed by massive air power, but a further 100,000 troops would be held back in reserve until the war started and it became clear whether they were needed. Their equipment would be loaded on ships heading to the region, but the troops themselves would remain at their home bases waiting to fly out to the Middle East.

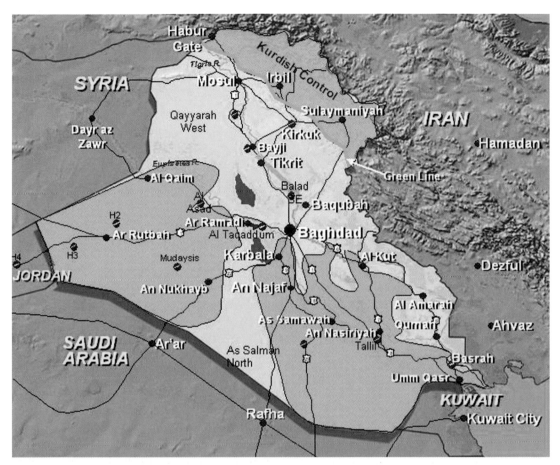

The battle situation on 3 April 2003 as US troops closed in on Baghdad. *(US DoD)*

Fundamental to the US war planning was the assessment that the Iraqis would 'fold' early because of poor morale and opposition to the government of Saddam Hussein among large segments of the population. Iraq's government was defined as 'brittle', and certain to crack open as soon as a strong force of US troops arrived in Baghdad.

President Bush's political directive set several operational objectives for Franks' planners to achieve during any military campaign, including to:

- end the regime of Saddam Hussein
- identify, isolate and eliminate Iraq's weapons of mass destruction
- search for, capture and drive out terrorists from Iraq
- collect intelligence related to terrorist networks
- collect intelligence related to the global network of illicit weapons of mass destruction

- deliver humanitarian support to the displaced and needy Iraqi citizens
- secure Iraq's oilfields and resources
- create conditions for a transition to a representative self-government in Iraq.

The planning process then entered a new phase as Franks allocated tasks to his main air, land, sea and special-operations forces component commanders. During the last three months of 2002, these officers and their staffs examined the details of what was required of them, and began what was known as the 'force generation' process. These assessments were honed during a series of command post exercises held in the Gulf region during November and December 2002, under the banner of Exercise Internal Look. This in turn honed the exact requirements for troops and equipment needed for any war, as well as the diplomatic clearances for basing and over-flight rights in countries neighbouring Iraq. Long-term logistic support measures, including the moving of some pre-positioned equipment from stores in Qatar and Diego Garcia, had already begun. The main bulk of the troops began moving early in January, and the deployment rolled out over the next two months.

Franks also began reorganising his headquarters staff to allow CENTCOM to fight Iraq while still conducting anti-terrorist operations in Afghanistan and the Horn of Africa. Regional headquarters in Afghanistan and Djibouti were beefed up to take the pressure off the main CENTCOM staff. An alternative combined air operations centre (CAOC) was activated at the massive Al Udeid airbase in Qatar to conduct Afghan and Horn of Africa air operations. The main CAOC to Prince Sultan airbase (PSAB) remained focused entirely on Iraq no-fly-zone operations and war planning. The main CENTCOM staff was also split, with a 'forward' headquarters being established at Camp As Saliyah under Franks' deputy, Lieutenant General John Abizaid, specially to run any Iraq operation.

One requirement that was identified early in the planning process was the need to prevent any pre-emptive Iraqi strikes to disrupt the deployment of US troops in Kuwait. The Americans had long based ground troops in Kuwait, and they had been reinforced late in 2001 when US carrier air power was diverted from the Middle East to support the Afghan campaign.

At the heart of the US battle plan was the need to bring the main bulk of the Republican Guard Forces Command into battle and destroy them. These supposed élite troops were seen as one of the Iraqi government's main 'centres of gravity', and their destruction was seen as a way to engender 'psychological fracture' in the ruling circle. Once they were gone, the rapid advance of US troops into the heart of Baghdad would be possible, to allow the *coup de grâce* to be delivered to Saddam Hussein. The assessment was that once the government was seen to be defeated, the population and the mass of the Regular Army would lose heart and give up the fight. To do this job, Franks requested the US Army's V Corps and the 1 Marine Expeditionary Force (I MEF), with some 150,000 combat troops. The only realistic basing option was in Kuwait, because of its friendly government and extensive port facilities. The southern desert was also largely undefended, so US planners believed their main land force would have a relatively free run to the Baghdad region where the Republican Guard Forces Command was based, or US air power would destroy them if they moved south to join battle with the invaders.

In the early US planning it became clear that a corps-sized land force was needed to strike into northern Iraq from Turkey, to pin the three Iraqi corps holding the front lines opposite the Kurdish safe haven, preventing them swinging south to held to defend Baghdad. The force would then move to secure Tikrit, Saddam Hussein's home town.

While Franks was very successful in winning basing rights from Jordan, Saudi Arabia and the Gulf states for his forces, the 'northern front' ran into trouble during January and February, culminating in the Ankara parliament rejecting the US request to move 60,000 ground troops across Turkish territory. To try to maintain the threat of a northern front, Franks kept the ships carrying the equipment for the 4th Infantry Division in the Mediterranean until the war had started.

The other main pillar of the US plan was a strategic air campaign, backed by special-operations forces, aimed at neutralising and possibly killing senior members of the Iraqi government. Unlike in 1991, when the strategic air campaign had focused heavily on infrastructure targets, such as bridges, oil refineries and power stations, this time only presidential palaces, government ministries, command bunkers, air defence sites and locations associated with the weapons of mass destruction programme were to be attacked.

Fundamental to the planning was the need for concentric air, land and sea-borne attacks from north, south and west to rapidly overwhelm Iraq's defences. The aim was not to physically destroy Iraq's armed forces, but to neutralise them to open the way for US-led forces to attack and kill leading members of the government. In military jargon, this was to be an effects-based campaign.

Special emphasis was put on giving the US-led air forces the capability of attacking high-value targets, such as Saddam Hussein and his immediate circle, on the basis of fleeting intelligence. A cell to manage attacks against so-called 'time-sensitive targets' was set up inside the US air headquarters in Saudi Arabia.

The nerve centre of US air operations in the Middle East was the CAOC where General Franks' air commander, USAF Lieutenant General Michael 'Buzz' Moseley, had his headquarters. The CAOC was classed as a 'weapon system' in its own right, and its computerised communications links allowed the rapid collection of intelligence on targets in Iraq and the dissemination of attack orders to strike aircraft.

Prior to the war, the CAOC had a staff of 672 US, British and Australian staff officers attached, but as conflict neared, the number of personnel had risen to 1,966. The core of their work was the production of a daily air tasking order, which included all the targeting, routes and communications detail needed for every aircraft and cruise missile sent into Iraqi air space. This centralised system allowed air power to be concentrated at specific targets and ensured that hundreds of friendly aircraft did not endanger each other.

The USS *Abraham Lincoln* (CVN 72) had three squadrons of F/A-18 Hornets embarked, VFA-25 and 113 with the F/A-18C and VFA-115 with the F/A-18E Super Hornet. The ship is operating in the Northern Arabian Gulf in November 2002 while supporting Operation Southern Watch. (*Author*)

The CAOC was a true joint-service effort, for example controlling all the US Navy and British Royal Navy BGM-109 Tomahawk land attack missiles (TLAMs) launched from ships and submarines against Iraqi targets, and all the US Army's Patriot missile defence units in the Middle East.

While the planning for the air offensive against Iraq gathered momentum during 2002, it was not until January 2003 that the flow of additional aircraft to execute the attack began in earnest. This was eased by more than a decade of no-fly-zone operations, which meant that most of the communications and logistic infrastructure needed to support the extra aircraft and personnel was already in place at bases around the Middle East.

By the time the war got under way on 19 March 2003, some 466,985 US personnel were in the Middle East, with 233,342 coming from the US Army, 74,405 from the US Marine Corps, 61,296 from the US Navy. The US Air Force provided 54,995, of whom 2,084 came from the Air Force Reserve and 7,207 from the Air National Guard. Britain was the largest provider of non-US forces, with 40,905 personnel in the Middle East, alongside 2,050 Australians.

Out of some 1,801 aircraft deployed, some 1,477 were fixed wing and 186 helicopters. The largest number of these were provided by the USAF, which dispatched some 863 aircraft to bases in the Middle East and Europe for the operation, including 293 fighters, 51 bombers, 22 command and control, 182 tankers, 60 intelligence, surveillance and reconnaissance, 73 special operations and 58 rescue, 111 airlift and 13 other aircraft. The Air National Guard provided 236 of these aircraft and the Air Force Reserve 70. The US Navy managed to muster some 232 fighters, 20 command and control, 52 tanker, 29 intelligence, surveillance and reconnaissance, 5 airlift and 70 other types of aircraft. The US Marine Corps dispatched some 130 fighters, 22 tankers and 220 other aircraft, mostly helicopters. The British armed forces provided some 200 aircraft and helicopters, and the Australians sent 22 airframes. The US Army deployed some 700 attack, scout and transport helicopters.

Many of these aircraft headed for airbases already in use for Operation Southern Watch missions over the southern no-fly zone or supporting Operation Enduring Freedom in Afghanistan. Other bases had to be activated from pre-positioning equipment and stores maintained at them. Many of the host governments were very sensitive to their public opinion, which was almost universally opposed to any war against Iraq, and deployments had to take place under conditions of great secrecy. Saudi Arabia, Bahrain and the United Arab Emirates banned offensive strike aircraft from operating on their territory and banned media access to their airbases. Qatar, Oman and Jordan all allowed offensive aircraft, but imposed draconian secrecy on US and British deployments to their airbases. The exception to this was Kuwait, which embraced the US war plans with enthusiasm, and allowed the US and British forces use of all their main airbases. When these became full of helicopters and other aircraft, field air strips and helicopter landing pads were constructed in the northern deserts close to the Iraqi border.

As soon as fighter and strike squadrons arrived at bases in the Middle East, planners in the CAOC began to use them for Operation Southern Watch to give the crews experience of countering Iraqi air defences and the procedures for flying in Iraqi air space.

General Moseley had also been making efforts to 'prepare the battlefield' for several months, so when his forces were sent into action to support the land invasions they would have destroyed key elements of the Iraqi air defence systems. This effort was dubbed Southern Focus, and it concentrated on destroying key surface-to-air missile batteries and fibre optic communications nodes. This took advantage of a change in the rules of engagement that allowed Iraqi command posts and communications sites to be attacked in response to firings on US and British jets patrolling the no-fly zones. These static targets also had the advantage of being far easier to locate than mobile missile launchers or gun batteries. From June 2002 to early 2003, some 21,736 sorties were flown and 345 targets attacked as part of this effort, which effectively put out of action the air defences in the south and west of Iraq by mid-March 2003.

As the UN political process failed to produce the results to the liking of the Bush administration during February, it became more determined to go ahead with the attack, come what may. Rumsfeld and his senior CENTCOM military commanders began pressing for efforts to 'prepare the battlefield' to be stepped up. They wanted to give their air power freedom to attack Iraqi surface-to-surface missile launchers and artillery batteries in southern Iraq. The senior British officers in the Middle East now played their 'red card' and objected. They claimed that this had no legality and had not been approved by the British government. The issue bounced up to the senior levels in both governments. Blair, who was still trying to win approval for a second UN resolution to placate increasing anti-war feeling in his party and cabinet, backed his military men. Rumsfeld was told his pilots could only attack Iraqi weapons that could be proved to be 'threatening' US and British troops in Kuwait and inside the Kurdish 'safe haven' in northern Iraq. Five strikes did occur against Iraqi missile launchers that were located moving outside their barracks.

Opening attack
US President George Bush's 17 March 2003 deadline for Saddam Hussein and his two sons to leave Iraq set the clock ticking for war. US-led forces in the Middle East increased their readiness, reducing their notice-to-move time to four hours.

General Tommy Franks was ordered to be ready to launch his troops into action as soon as the ultimatum ran out. During 19 March, intelligence emerged from Baghdad that Saddam Hussein and his sons where meeting at Al-Dura Farm on the southern outskirts of the Iraqi capital.

A series of high-level video conferences between Washington and US Central Command (CENTCOM) in Qatar was held, and eventually President Bush agreed to an attack being made to kill Saddam Hussein. It seems the prospect of killing the Iraqi president was considered just too good an opportunity to miss, even if the other elements of the main attack force were not quite ready. General Franks had presented President Bush with the attack option, and he signed it off, allowing the US Middle East commander to give the 'go-command'.

Planning for time-sensitive targeting had been under way for a long time, with a pair of Lockheed F-117 Nighthawks of the 8th Fighter Squadron being held on alert at the giant US airbase at Al Udeid in Qatar. The F-117 pilots were given four hours until dawn broke to prepare the mission and fly to Baghdad. The aircraft were each armed with Raytheon EGBU-27 bombs, which could be guided by both lasers and satellite guidance systems.

Although famous for its radar invisibility, one F-117 was shot down during the Kosovo war, so an air defence suppression package was sent up to make sure that no Iraqi air defence crews were as lucky. Grumman EA-6B Prowler jamming and Lockheed F-16CJ Fighting Falcons suppression-of-enemy-air-defence (SEAD) aircraft also helped ease the way to Baghdad for the F-117s. A barrage of some forty Tomahawk cruise missiles was also launched against Al-Dura Farm from four US Navy warships, the USS *Milius*, *Donald Cook*, *Bunker Hill* and *Cowpens*, and two nuclear submarines, the USS *Montpilier* and *Cheyenne*, in the Arabian Gulf and Red Sea. Although the strike was mounted with great rapidly, it seems that the Iraqi president and his sons escaped unharmed.

As the strike against Baghdad was under way, more waves of airstrikes on Iraqi troop positions around Basra knocked out four radar and communications sites. Other US airstrikes hit Iraqi troop positions along the Kuwaiti border, including long-range artillery near Az Zubayr, GHN-45 and 155 mm long-range artillery on the Al Faw peninsula and a surface-to-surface missile system near Basra, to neutralise the threat to US and British troops in Kuwait.

In an apparent rerun of the 1991 Gulf War, the opening morning of Operation Iraqi Freedom saw a duel between Iraqi missiles and US Patriot anti-ballistic missile batteries. Two Ababil 100 or Al Samoud battlefield ballistic missiles were intercepted over northern Kuwait by Patriots defending US and British airfields, ports and troop concentrations in the Gulf emirate.

At least half a dozen Patriot batteries had been deployed to Kuwait for just such an eventuality. They were equipped with the latest PAC-3 version of the Scud, which uses so-called 'hit-to-kill' technology very different from the old Patriots that were used in Operation Desert Storm.

Tension within the US military was not eased by reports from the Central Intelligence Agency (CIA) that a column of ninety Iraqi tanks was heading towards the Kuwaiti border. A flight of USAF McDonnell Douglas F-15E Strike Eagles was sent to intercept the column, which turned out not to exist, but this was not before the 1st Marine Division had hurriedly reorganised its attack plan.

These attacks and intelligence that the Iraqis were about to commit acts of sabotage to destroy oilfields around Basra led General Franks to consider moving forward the start of the land invasion to the evening of 20 March. This was twenty-four hours ahead of when the air forces would be ready to strike Baghdad, but the need

Bell AH-1W Super Cobra

The US Marine Corps light attack helicopter squadron makes extensive use of the Super Cobra, although it often dubs it the Whiskey Cobra. Its robust and simple design makes it ideal for the extreme environments found in the Middle East. The Turkish army has also used it against Kurdish rebels.

Crew: 2 (pilot, co-pilot/gunner)
Length: 44 ft 7 in. (13.6 m)
Rotor diameter: 48 ft (14.6 m)
Height: 13 ft 5 in. (4.1 m)
Disc area: 530.83 ft² (168.1 m²)
Maximum take-off weight: 14,750 lb (6,690 kg)
Powerplant: Two General Electric T700 turboshafts, 1,680 shp (1,300 kW) each
Maximum speed: 190 knots (218 mph, 352 km/h)
Range: 317 nm (365 miles, 587 km)

Armament
M197 3-barrelled 20 mm 'Gatling-style' cannon in the A/A49E-7 turret (750 rounds ammo capacity), 2.75 in. (70 mm) Hydra 70 rockets, mounted in LAU-68C/A (7-shot) or LAU-61D/A (19-shot) launchers, 5 in. (127 mm) Zuni rockets – eight rockets in two 4-round LAU-10D/A launchers, TOW missiles: up to 8 missiles mounted in two-missile launchers on each hardpoint, AGM-114 Hellfire missiles: up to 8 missiles mounted in two 4-round M272 missile launchers, one on each outboard hardpoint, AIM-9 Sidewinder anti-aircraft missiles: one mounted on each outboard hardpoint (total of two)

Patriot missile launchers, of Battery C, 2nd Battalion, 1st Air Defense Artillery Regiment, deployed to Kuwait to defend against Iraqi missile attacks, were equipped with the new PAC-3 version of the weapon. *(US Central Command)*

The Combined Air Operation Center (CAOC) at Prince Sultan airbase in Saudi Arabia was the nerve centre for all US, British and Australian air activity over Iraq. *(USAF)*

to prevent what was dubbed environmental terrorism led General Franks to re-sequence his attack plan.

US and British ground troops started advancing into southern Iraq during the evening of 20 March, capturing the Al Faw peninsula, driving to the gates of Basra and punching 200 miles up the Euphrates valley towards Baghdad.

Helicopters played a key role in the first of these operations, lifting assault troops of the British 3 Commando Brigade into landing zones near to the oil facilities on the Al Faw oilfields. US special-forces troops landed by USAF Sikorsky MH-53M Pave Lows preceded the main landings to secure the oil facilities in *coup de main* operations. The British Joint Helicopter Force used a force of RAF Chinooks and Pumas, Royal Navy Sea King HC4s, Army Air Corps Lynx AH7s and AH1s, supported by US Marine Corps CH-53E Sea Stallions, CH-46E Sea Knights and AH-1W Super Cobras to move the assault force. Royal Navy Sea King AEW7s and Merlin HM1s flew top cover, co-ordinating the scores of helicopters flying in the congested air space over the northern Gulf. Tragedy struck during these operations when a USMC CH-46E carrying British Royal Marines into action crashed, killing all twelve people on board. These landings were the first phase of British operations to secure Basra, Iraq's second city.

At the same time the 1st US Marine Division advanced north into the Rumaila oilfields, under air cover provided by the 3rd Marine Air Wing.

The US Army's V Corps was now pushing directly towards Baghdad with the aim of destroying the Republican Guard forces defending the southern approaches to the Iraqi capital. Bell OH-58D Kiowa Warrior scout helicopters of the 7th Cavalry ranged ahead of the 3rd Infantry Division as it pushed past Nasiriyah, seized Talill airbase on 22 March and then pressed on to Najaf, only 100 miles from Baghdad. V Corps began massing around Najaf, with work beginning on forward bases for attack helicopters and Patriot anti-missile batteries being brought up. A runway for Hunter unmanned aerial vehicles was also built near Najaf to allow them to find targets for 11th Aviation Brigade's Boeing AH-64D Longbow Apaches.

Following up behind V Corps, the 1st Marine Division reached Nasiriyah during 23 March, and soon found itself locked into a series of ambushes and skirmishes. Bell AH-1W Super Cobras were called up to provide close air support, but the fighting was so intense that fixed-wing aircraft were called in. Tragedy struck when a USAF Fairchild A-10A Warthog hit a Marine convoy by accident and nine Americans died. The casualties during the battle were heavy, with fifteen Marines dying and more than a hundred being wounded. This overwhelmed the Marines' casualty-evacuation systems, and there were not enough Bell UH-1N Hueys or CH-46Es to fly out the wounded.

US, British and Australian air forces provided extensive air support for these operations, but there were few military targets of any significance in southern Iraq. The regular Iraqi army seemed to melt away into the cities, and paramilitary forces provided the main opposition to the US-led forces.

Apart from the US Marines' CH-46E, the only aircraft lost so far were two Westland Sea King AEW7s which collided over the northern Gulf, killing all seven crewmen, and an RAF Panavia Tornado GR4 which was shot down accidentally by a US Patriot missile battery in Kuwait, with the loss of two crewmen.

Strategic air campaign
The next phase of the US-led onslaught on Iraq was the strategic air campaign, which began to unfold around Baghdad from the evening of 21 March.

The aim of the strike was to cripple the Iraqi government in a series of huge air and missile strikes. In the space of a few hours the majority of Saddam Hussein's palaces, security operations, intelligence services and Ba'ath party buildings in Baghdad were to be hit.

These targets were concentrated in the centre of downtown Baghdad in an area within view of the international media's camera positions on the roof of the Iraqi Ministry of Information. The dramatic footage was broadcast live around the world, and the evening became immortalised as the 'shock and awe' night.

The concentration of targets was deliberate, and it was hoped the attack would dramatically 'decapitate' the Iraqi government by killing its senior leadership. If they could not be killed then it was hoped the attack would severely disrupt their ability to co-ordinate resistance, and scare Saddam Hussein and his top lieutenants into fleeing the capital.

The USA was also sending a 'message' to the Iraqi population and military, in the hope they would change sides and stop supporting the government.

'We wanted to make it clear to the Iraqi people that we were attacking regime targets', said USAF Colonel Mace Carpenter, chief strategist at the CAOC. 'We wanted them to see that we were clearly targeting those people who had been repressing them.'

To achieve the desired effect, hundreds of strike aircraft were to be employed in the 'shock and awe' effort that would last for seventy-two hours, which would see the employment of some 2,500 individual bombs and cruise missiles. Stealth Lockheed F-117 Nighthawks and Northrop Grumman B-2 Spirits led the air assault into Baghdad, along with hundreds of stand-off weapons, including Raytheon BGM-109 Tomahawk land attack missiles (TLAM), Boeing AGM-86C/D conventional air-launched cruise missiles (CALCM), MBDA Storm Shadows and Raytheon AGM-154 Joint Stand-off Weapons (JSOW).

To fight through the air defences around Baghdad, hundreds more suppression-of-enemy-air-defence (SEAD) aircraft were launched against surface-to-air missile (SAM) batteries, radar sites, communications nodes and command bunkers of Iraqi Air Defence Command. The predominantly US SEAD force was backed up by British Tornado GR4 aircraft firing the new Storm Shadow cruise missile fitted with BROACH penetrating warheads, which were used to destroy hardened air defence command bunkers. US Navy BGM-34 Firebee drones were launched over Baghdad to drop chaff corridors to confuse Iraqi radars. Scores of AGM-141 tactical air-launched decoys (TALDs) were fired to try to force the Iraqis to switch on radars to allow them to be targeted by US Raytheon AGM-88 high-speed anti-radiation missiles and British BAe Dynamics' ALARM missiles.

Supporting this huge air armada would require a major effort by US and British air refuelling tankers to ensure all the strike jets reached their targets with a full weapon load.

Many of the targets in and around Baghdad were studied extensively prior to the war, but the CAOC staff kept them constantly under review and incorporated new targets as they emerged or old ones were found to be invalid. This process continued even as the attack was under way, in co-operation with the CAOC's time-sensitive targeting cell. Out of some 2,124 'regime leadership' targets nominated for attack, only some 1,779 were eventually bombed by the end of the war.

The first 'shock and awe' strikes went off with no US or British air losses after the Iraqi 'super missile engagement zone' (MEZ) failed to live up to expectations. 'We had been led to believe that venturing into the 'super MEZ' meant certain death', commented one British pilot.

Even as CAOC officers watched television broadcasts live from Baghdad on 'shock and

USAF General 'Buzz' Moseley master-minded the air offensive against Iraq. (USAF)

awe' night, their attention had moved to rolling out further air strikes against Iraqi strategic targets.

For the remainder of the war, strike aircraft and missiles were used to hit leadership targets in Baghdad and elsewhere in Iraq. This also required a constant effort to hunt down and destroy what remained of the Iraqi Air Defence Command. This resulted in a 'cat and mouse' game between US and British SEAD forces and the Iraqi missile crews, as the latter tried to hide their diminishing assets from detection.

During night time, fixed-wing strike aircraft made forays into the Baghdad 'super MEZ' to hit targets such as palaces, telephone exchanges and security headquarters. Cruise missiles took up the strain during daytime. These strikes remained a mix of pre-planned raids and missions against targets of opportunity revealed by intelligence. Eventually some fifty time-sensitive leadership targets were attacked, along with 102 associated with weapons of mass destruction and four designated 'terrorist' related.

RAF Tornado GR4s were massed at Ali Al Salem airbase in Kuwait ahead of the air war. *(Author)*

An F-117 Nighthawk of the 8th Expeditionary Fighter Squadron based at Al Udeid airbase in Qatar dropped the first bombs of Operation Iraqi Freedom in the early hours of 20 March. *(USAF)*

Iraqi resistance to US and British air offensives was at first furious, as hundreds of SAMs and thousands of anti-aircraft artillery (AAA) pieces were fired at the attacking aircraft. After the first few days of the air offensive against Baghdad, the level of resistance began to diminish until the commander of the Iraqi Air Defence Command was sacked and his replacement re-energised his forces. In total during the war, the Iraqis fired some 1,660 SAMs, with 1,224 'AAA events' and 436 radar illuminations being recorded by US, British and Australian airmen. Although there were some close shaves, the Iraqi Air Defence Command failed to shoot down a single US, British or Australian aircraft with any of its radar-guided SAMs.

The Iraqi air force proved equally ineffective at putting up resistance to the US-led airborne onslaught. No Iraqi fighters took to the skies during the war. It seems that the Iraqi Air Force commanders before the war ordered their squadrons to disperse into the countryside to hide their aircraft from US surveillance efforts. Iraqi aircraft were towed off airbases and hidden in palm groves, industrial complexes and residential areas. Some aircraft were even buried in sand.

The exact reasons for this strategy are unclear. It could either have been an effort to preserve their assets until after the war was over or that US attacks on the Iraqi communications systems prevented counter-attack orders getting through to front-line pilots. Given the 'top-down' nature of the Baghdad regime, initiative, not surprisingly, was not in large supply among Iraq's airmen.

The strategic air campaign proved to be remarkably limited in scope and intensity compared to Operation Desert Storm, with just under 1,500 regime leadership targets being attacked. Efforts to neutralise the Iraqi air force and air defences were also limited, with 1,441 'air supremacy' targets being attacked. Unlike in the 1991 conflict, there was no systematic effort to destroy the Iraqi airbase infrastructure of hardened aircraft shelters, beyond the cratering of a number of runways. A further 832 strikes were made against targets that were believed to be associated with weapons of mass destruction.

The civilian infrastructure of Iraq was also not attacked, and up to the point that US ground troops approached the capital, Baghdad's power and water remained on. The buzzword among US and British air planners was 'effects-based warfare'. This emphasised the effect of an air attack, rather than just physical destruction. The chaotic and disorganised nature of Iraqi resistance to US-led ground offensives is seen by US and British commanders as proof that its strategic air campaign effectively paralysed the ability of the Iraqis to fight back. Until insiders from Saddam Hussein's inner circle give their side of the war it will be difficult to truly judge the success of the air campaign against Baghdad.

The enablers

The air campaign against Iraq was only possible because of an array of specialist support aircraft – command and control, reconnaissance, surveillance, air refuelling and airlift.

While the 'strikers' or 'bomb-dropping' aircraft may have stole the limelight during Operation Iraqi Freedom, more than two-thirds of all participating aircraft were specialist support machines, or 'enablers'.

In the 1991 Gulf War, intelligence, surveillance and reconnaissance (ISR) aircraft had limited ability to transmit any intelligence they had collected to ground-based command posts and strike aircraft. By 2003, the Americans and British had installed high-capacity data-links on their ISR platforms to allow intelligence to be downloaded 'live', or in real time. Out of the 41,404 sorties flown during the war, some 1,683 were by ISR aircraft.

The aim was to provide commanders in the CAOC with real-time intelligence on what was happening in air and on the ground throughout Iraq and neighbouring countries. The fusion of this information into air, land and sea 'pictures' projected onto computer screens was the key to allowing senior US commanders to make rapid decisions about the tasking of strike aircraft. The world's largest-ever tactical data-link network then ensured that every user – in the air, on the ground or at sea – connected to the network could view these 'pictures'.

At the heart of generating the 'air picture' was the Boeing E-3 Sentry AWACS radar aircraft. The USAF's fifteen E-3Cs and the RAF's four E-3Ds in the Middle East were airborne '24/7' over Iraq and neighbouring airspace in a series of orbits to ensure total coverage of the operational theatre. There radar returns were downloaded in real time to CAOC and other command posts in the Middle East to allow commanders to watch the air war unfold. Icons on the air-picture display showed the position of every friendly and Iraqi aircraft, as well as civilian traffic. An airborne 'battle staff' was also embarked on each E-3 to allow controllers to finesse the final execution of the hundreds of US, British and Australian aircraft flying into Iraqi air space. Controllers on the AWACS were also a key link with the ground forces, allocating individual strike aircraft to attack close air support targets nominated by forward air controllers.

The US Navy's twenty carrier-borne Northrop Grumman E-2C Hawkeyes added to the air picture, and also filled in gaps in AWACs coverage, flying some 442 missions during the war.

The job of monitoring Iraqi air defence activity and communications traffic was the job of the USAF Boeing RC-135 River Joint, RAF BAe Nimrod R.1 and US Navy Lockheed EP-3 Aries III. These 'hovered' Iraqi radar signals and communications traffic, and in real time downloaded it to the CAOC and AWACS. Fusion technology then displayed the information as threat icons on the air picture.

To give the ground force commanders the same level of situational awareness as their air force counterparts, seven Northrop Grumman E-8C Joint STARS ground surveillance aircraft were used extensively during the Iraq War. They maintained continuous orbits over Iraq to provide total coverage of the battlefield, and used the moving target indicator (MTI) radar to identify the movement of Iraqi tanks, missile launchers and other military equipment in all weathers or at night. Ground commanders then merged the JSTARS radar returns with the Blue Forces Tracking

A US Marine Corps CH-46 Sea Knight flies over the crowded streets of Nasiriyah, where US troops ran into serious resistance on the opening weekend of the war. *(USMC)*

Three CH-47D Chinook helicopters of the Australian Army's 5th Aviation Regiment flew to Azraq in Jordan to support the country's Special Air Service Regiment, which fought alongside their British and American counterparts in western Iraq. *(Australian DoD)*

McDonnell Douglas AH-64A/D Apache

US Army attack aviation units have used the Apache extensively in the Middle East. Early A-model helicopters proved themselves in the 1991 war, and both A and D models saw action during the 2003 invasion of Iraq. The upgraded D model, which has advanced avionics and computer systems, has been progressively introduced, and by the end of the decade it was the mainstay of US Army aviation units in Iraq. The Israeli Air and Space Force has used both A and D models in action in the West Bank, Gaza and Lebanon. The UAE Air Force and Air Defence has deployed its AH-64As on peacekeeping duties to the Balkans.

Crew: 2 (pilot, co-pilot/gunner)
Length: 58.17 ft (17.73 m) (with both rotors turning)
Rotor diameter: 48 ft (14.63 m)
Height: 12.7 ft (3.87 m)
Maximum take-off weight: 21,000 lb (9,500 kg)
Powerplant: Two General Electric T700-GE-701s, later upgraded to T700-GE-701C (1990–present) and T700-GE-701D (AH-64D block III) turboshafts, -701: 1,690 shp, -701C: 1,890 shp, -701D: 2,000 shp (-701: 1,260 kW, -701C: 1,490 kW) each
Fuselage length: 49 ft 5 in. (15.06 m)
Maximum speed: 158 knots (182 mph, 293 km/h)
Cruise speed: 143 knots (165 mph, 265 km/h)
Combat radius: 260 nm (300 miles, 480 km)

Armament
Guns: One 30x113 mm (1.18x4.45 in.) M230 cannon, 1,200 rounds
Rockets: Hydra 70 FFARs
Missiles: combination of AGM-114 Hellfires, AIM-92 Stingers, and AIM-9 Sidewinders

satellite-based location system fitted to all US and British vehicles to produce the 'land picture'. When sandstorms engulfed the advance on Baghdad, JSTARS was the only way US ground commanders could ensure the Iraqis did not use the bad weather to move forces to counter-attack. Some 1,700 hours of MTI radar coverage were recorded during the war.

The USAF E-3C and E-8D fleet flew some 432 missions during the war, along with 112 missions by RAF E-3Ds. To support them, US Marine Corps Lockheed KC-130 (DASC-A) airborne-command-post aircraft flew some seventy-five missions co-ordinating the efforts of 3rd Marine Air Wing strike aircraft.

While the platforms that contributed the air, land and naval pictures provided the means for senior commanders to manage the battle, the information they gathered was often not in itself good enough to allow air attacks to be launched because of the need to avoid civilian casualties or confirm target identification. This was the job of specific intelligence collection platforms, particularly imagery intelligence aircraft. These collected information needed to plan future strike missions or to confirm targets' time-sensitive attack. Still imagery was the primary means of providing the former type of intelligence, and video imagery predominated in time-sensitive targeting. The level of effort aimed towards collecting imagery intelligence can be gauged from the fact the US, British and Australian ISR aircraft collected some 42,000 still battlefield images and 3,200 hours of video imagery during the war.

USAF Lockheed U-2S Dragon Lady and RAF English Electric Canberra PR9 were the main strategic still-imagery collection platforms, and they were used to maintain orbits over western, northern and southern Iraq throughout the war. They could also download imagery in real time to CAOC if necessary. A single Northrop Grumman RQ-4 Global Hawk unmanned aerial vehicle (UAV) was also used in the strategic reconnaissance role, maintaining an orbit over Baghdad and central Iraq for much of the war.

These strategic platforms were augmented extensively in the collection of still imagery by British, US Marine Corps and US Navy tactical reconnaissance (tact recce) aircraft. These BAe Tornado GR4s, BAe Harrier GR7s, McDonnell Douglas F/A-18D Hornets and Grumman F-14 Tomcats all used pod systems to photograph Iraqi targets, often going to low level to achieve tactical surprise.

Moving video imagery was the preserve of four main platforms – the USAF General Atomics RQ-1 Predator UAVs, US Army IAI/TRW RQ5 Hunter UAVs, US Marine Corps IAI/TRW RQ-2B Pioneer UAVs and US Navy Lockheed P-3C (AIP) Orions. These had real-time data-links to allow their imagery to be downloaded into the CAOC or ground forces command post. This capability was highly prized and allowed time-sensitive targeting to be undertaken in a way that dramatically affected ground operations.

The P-3s were particularly popular with ground commanders because their large size, long endurance and extensive communications meant senior ground forces officers could be carried to hasten the co-ordination of airstrikes against targets identified by Orion's electro-optical vision systems. Both the British and Australians used the BAe Nimrod MR2 and Orions in similar roles to support ground forces operations, but because they lacked the ability to download video in real time they had to rely on verbal reporting over radio links.

Uniquely among the UAVs employed in the Iraq war, the Predator could be armed with either AGM-114 Hellfire laser-guided missiles or Raytheon AIM-9 Sidewinder air-to-air missiles. This allowed it to rapidly engage any targets discovered, and made it the weapon of choice for time-sensitive targeting.

All senior air commanders involved in the Iraq war reported that the most important aircraft for their ability to conduct high-tempo operations were the 268 air-to-air refuelling tankers in the Middle East. Without the tankers no tactical aircraft or bombers would have been able to reach targets deep in Iraq, and the ISR fleet would have been limited to fleeting missions over hostile territory. The tankers were constantly used to fill orbits around Iraq's borders so that 'inbound' strike aircraft could top off their tanks before heading for their targets. When the advance on Baghdad reached its climax in early April, a tanker orbit was set up over the Iraqi capital so that close air support aircraft could remain constantly on station ready to protect US troops. Even though the tanker fleet passed more than 417 million litres of fuel, there were never enough tankers to go round, and battle staff in the CAOC or on AWACS aircraft were constantly finessing the operations of the tankers, often at the last minute, to ensure aircraft assigned to high-priority missions had the fuel they needed. This was particularly demanding when time-sensitive targets emerged and jets attacking them needed fuel at short notice.

The tankers also supported the airlift fleet, refuelling aircraft flying direct from continental USA or Europe with high-priority cargos. The air-drop missions into Iraq by Boeing C-17 Globemasters were also only possible thanks to air refuelling.

Airlift was a key element of the US invasion plan, and the USAF, RAF and RAAF deployed more than 120 Lockheed C-130 aircraft to the Middle East to support the movement and resupply of ground troops. The USAF and RAF also moved scores of C-17s to bases in southern and central Europe to support the war.

As US ground troops advanced into Iraq, following up behind were specialist teams who rapidly opened up abandoned Iraqi airfields and turned them into forward operating bases (FOB) for close air support aircraft, airlifters and helicopters. The USAF used its contingency response groups for this task, and US Marine Corps aviation support units were also used for this mission. Many of these FOBs were within range of Iraqi artillery, so air operations had to be conducted largely at night to ensure the protection of slow-flying airlifters landing at them.

During the war some 7,413 airlift sorties were flown by USAF C-130s and C-17s, which when compared to the 8,828 fighter missions flown by the USAF illustrates the level of activity of the airlift force. Some 9,962 passengers were moved by the USAF airlifters alone, and more than 12,000 tons of cargo were carried.

Operation Iraqi Freedom showed yet again the vital role played by 'enabling' aircraft. Not only did they play a key role in finding targets and co-ordinating strike

McDonnel Douglas F/A-18C/D Hornet

The Hornet has been the mainstay of US Navy carrier-borne aviation since the mid-1980s, and has seen extensive service in the Middle East. Kuwait is the sole export customer of the aircraft in the region.

Crew: 1 (C model), 2 (D model)
Length: 56 ft (16.8 m)
Height: 15 ft 4 in. (4.6 m)
Wingspan: 40 ft 5 in. (13.5 m)
Weight: Maximum take-off gross weight 51,900 lb (23,537 kg)
Airspeed: Mach 1.7+
Propulsion: Two F404-GE-402 enhanced performance turbofan engines. 17,700 lb static thrust per engine
Range: Combat, 1,089 nm (1,252.4 miles, 2,003 km), clean plus two AIM-9s
Ferry: 1,546 nm (1,777.9 miles, 2,844 km), two AIM-9s plus three 330 gal tanks

Armament
One M61A1/A2 Vulcan 20 mm cannon; AIM 9 Sidewinder, AIM 7 Sparrow, AIM-120 AMRAAM, Harpoon, Harm, SLAM, SLAM-ER, Maverick missiles; joint stand-off weapon (JSOW); joint direct attack munition (JDAM); various general-purpose bombs, mines and rockets.

A B-1 Lancer assigned to the 405th Air Expeditionary Wing based in Oman flew missions to support US troops advancing into southern Iraq. (USAF)

F-16CJs assigned to the 379th Air Expeditionary Wing weather a sandstorm at Al Udeid during the second week of the war. The storm engulfed most of the Arabian peninsula and severely inhibited air operations. (USAF)

missions, but refuelling and airlift efforts ensured that the pace and tempo of US-led onslaught was unrelenting.

Special forces

Western Iraq is a barren desert region, thinly populated by Arab tribes who make a living from herding cattle. The region, however, is one of the most strategic in the Middle East because it is the only part of Iraq from where Scud ballistic missiles could be launched at Israel. The dual-carriageway road from Baghdad to the Jordanian capital Amman, which runs through the region, was also the main route to the outside world for the sanction-busting trade by the Iraqis.

Neutralising a repeat of Iraqi Scud missile attacks on Israel was a high priority for General Franks, and he made preparations to neutralise the threat as he developed his war plans. Attention quickly focused on Jordan, which was identified as a key base to mount raids into western Iraq to prevent the region being used as a missile launch pad. This task was assigned to US Central Command's special-operations component and its commander, Brigadier General Gary Harrell, who made several visits to Jordan during the autumn of 2002 to tie up details of basing rights for US commando units, helicopters and attack jets, including F-16s and A-10s.

Preparations were also made to deploy US Patriot anti-missile batteries to Jordanian bases to enhance the missile defences around Israel. British special forces and the Royal Air Force Harrier squadrons were closely involved in these efforts, and they began training to operate from Jordan during October 2002. US special forces and British Special Air Service (SAS) and advance teams then visited Jordan under the cover of 'exercises'. Some reports suggested they crossed into Iraq at this time to observe targets.

These preparations and subsequent deployment of troops to the Hashemite Kingdom had to be cloaked under intensive secrecy because of widespread pro-Iraqi feeling among Jordan's population. King Abdullah was taking a major gamble by joining the US-led war and reversing the policy of his father, King Hussein, of being neutral in the conflicts between the USA and Iraq.

The build-up of US, British and Australian troops gained momentum during January and February 2003, when Azraq airbase in north-eastern Jordan was activated as General Harrell's forward headquarters. Eventually some 10,000 Western troops were to be based in Jordan, with Azraq as the main base for fighter and reconnaissance aircraft, along with special forces' helicopters. The US Army's 5th Special Forces Group provided the main assault force, backed by Ranger battalions. Britain's 22nd Special Air Service Regiment and its Australian counterpart also moved to Jordan, and the British Royal Marines 45 Commando was assigned to support the SAS.

The USAF dispatched Lockheed F-16 Fighting Falcons and Fairchild A-10 Warthog squadrons of the Air National Guard, supported by combat search and rescue (CSAR) units with Sikorsky HH-60 Rescue Hawk helicopters and Lockheed HC-130P tankers. They were grouped under the 410th Air Expeditionary Wing. Eight

RAF BAe Harrier GR7 strike jets and two English Electric Canberra PR9 surveillance aircraft were also deployed to Azraq. Jordanian basing was particularly important for these units because they were not reliant on air-to-air refuelling to hit targets in western Iraq, which considerably reduced the pressure on the thinly stretched USAF tanker fleet.

The US Army's 160th Special Operations Aviation Regiment (Airborne) (SOAR(A)) provided the bulk of the assault helicopters with eighteen Sikorsky MH-60 Pave Hawks, seven Hughes MH-6 Little Birds and fourteen Boeing MH-47 Chinooks. Attached to the 160th Regiment were eight British Boeing Chinook HC2s of the RAF's 7 Squadron and six Westland Lynx AH7s of the Army Air Corps 657 Squadron. The Australian Army's 5th Aviation Regiment completed the force, with three Boeing Chinook CH-47Ds.

As US, British and Australian troops moved into Jordan, a smaller-scale deployment was taking place to the south, in Saudi Arabia, under conditions of even greater secrecy. 'Black', or covert, units of the US Delta Force set up a highly secret base in north-western Saudi Arabia. Sikorsky HH-60H Rescue Hawks of the US Navy's Helicopter Combat Support Squadron 5 set up a forward base at Ar'ar on the kingdom's northern border with Iraq, to provide CSAR coverage to the south of Baghdad.

Combat operations against western Iraq began even before President Bush's ultimatum expired in the early hours of 20 March. Reconnaissance teams were inserted into western Iraq, while no-fly-zone air patrols had carried out several air strikes against key communications links and air defence radar sites.

In the early hours of the 20th, Little Bird gunships mounted simultaneous raids against Iraqi border posts to open up corridors for special forces ground convoys to push across the border. The first targets were the airfield complexes at H-2 and H-3, which were the centre of Iraqi defences in the west and the most likely storage site of any Scud missiles. Ground and helicopter-borne troops quickly overcame the defences, with strong air support from the Jordan-based F-16s, A-10s and Harriers. These two captured airfields were quickly converted into forward operating bases for US, British and Australian forces.

Over the next two weeks, the special forces teams began steadily moving towards the Euphrates valley, with US Rangers capturing H1 airfield in a daring night-time parachute drop from Lockheed MC-130 Combat Talons on 25 March. Apart from their small forward operating bases, which were being guarded by Royal Marines and US Rangers, the special forces teams did not try to occupy ground, but moved fast to keep the small Iraqi garrisons in the region off guard. Travellers on the road from Baghdad to the Jordanian border reported few signs of the Western troops apart from occasional vehicle check-points, suggesting they were moved largely at night, away from populated areas.

The main opposition to the special forces came from Iraqi commando units who were attempting to keep the main roads to Jordan and Syria open to allow key members of the regime to travel abroad and potentially escape if Baghdad should

Two CH-46Es from HMM-268 taxi to get refuelled at Jalibah airbase in southern Iraq before heading north to support the US Marine Corps' advance on Baghdad. *(USMC)*

A US Army AH-64 Apache sets off for a night-time mission during the advance on Baghdad. *(US Army)*

Sikorsky CH-53E Super Stallion

Sikorsky's heavy-lift helicopter has been used by the US Marine Corps for battlefield transport roles and the US Navy for logistic support of ships at sea and mine sweeping. A variant, the MH-53M Pave Low, was used by US Air Force Special Operations Command until 2008 on covert missions around the Middle East.

Crew: 5 (2 pilots, 1 crew chief/right gunner, 1 left gunner, 1 tail gunner (combat crew))
Capacity: 37 troops (55 with centre-line seats installed)
Payload: internal: 30,000 lb or 13,600 kg (external: 32,000 lb or 14,500 kg)
Length: 99 ft ½ in. (30.2 m)
Rotor diameter: 79 ft (24 m)
Height: 27 ft 9 in. (8.46 m)
Maximum take-off weight: 73,500 lb (33,300 kg)
Powerplant: Three General Electric T64-GE-416 turboshafts, 4,380 shp (3,270 kW) each
Maximum speed: 170 knots (196 mph, 315 km/h)
Range: 540 nm (621 miles, 1,000 km)
Ferry range: 990 nm (1,139 miles, 1,833 km)

Armament
Guns: Two 0.50 BMG (12.7 × 99 mm) window-mounted XM218 machine-guns. One 0.50 BMG (12.7 × 99 mm) ramp-mounted weapons system, GAU-21 (M3M-mounted machine-gun)
Other: Chaff and flare dispensers

fall. When the Iraqis tried to rally resistance to US forces at their headquarters prison in the dusty town of Ar Rutbah, special forces directed an airstrike onto the building during the early morning of 30 March.

Australian officers have given one of the few insights into the work of their Special Air Service patrols, which had been operating closely with their British and US counterparts, in long-range reconnaissance and 'direct action' against various targets 'deep inside Iraq'. 'Our SAS task force has had a number of contacts, some initiated by the enemy, some by us', said a senior Australian officer. 'In some cases Iraqi troops were killed, military positions and equipment destroyed. In one incident special forces medics stopped to render medical assistance to two wounded soldiers before moving on.'

By the third week of the war, US British and Australian special forces teams were operating well beyond the Euphrates valley. A vehicle patrol of the British Special Boat Service was ambushed by Iraqi troops in the desert to the west of Mosul on 1 April. The troops managed to break contact and move to a rendezvous point to be recovered by RAF Chinook helicopters. USAF F-16s provided top cover for the trapped British troops, but in the confusion one soldier was left behind. He later successfully escaped to safety in Syria.

On 2 April, 160th SOAR conducted its most audacious raid of the war against Tharthar Palace, north-west of Baghdad. Little Bird gunships shot up Iraqi anti-aircraft guns to allow MH-47s to drop Rangers into the palace complex.

In three weeks of war, the special forces task forces had pushed from Jordan to deep into central Iraq, and swept all before them. Their mission had been to deny the Baghdad regime the use of western Iraq as a launch pad for missile attacks on Israel.

On the southern flank in Kuwait, USAF special forces aviation units were deployed to support the activities of the highly secret Task Force 20 (TF-20), which included elements of Delta Force's commando unit, US Navy SEALs and Central Intelligence Agency paramilitary teams. These included Lockheed AC-130U Spook gunships and Sikorsky MH-53Ms of the 16th Special Operations Wing based at Ali Al Salem in Kuwait.

TF-20 reported direct to General Franks at Central Command's forward headquarters in Qatar, and was only used for strategic missions, such as locating weapons of mass destruction and regime leadership targets. The first mission of Task Force 20 was the securing of Iraqi oil installations around Basra to prevent their sabotage. As in the west, reconnaissance teams were inserted inside Iraq well before the start of the war. During one of these missions on 19 March, a MH-53M had to put down inside Iraq due to mechanical problems and was later destroyed by a US airstrike. The 20th Special Operations Squadron then led the assault on the oil facilities on the Al Faw peninsula during the early hours of 21 March.

Over the next two weeks, TF-20 helicopters were used to shuttle special forces teams deep into Iraq, and to help these efforts began operating from the US forward operating base at Tallil in southern Iraq. The most high-profile mission was the airlifting of the recovery force to Nasiriyah civilian hospital on 1 April to secure the US Army prisoner of war, Private Jessica Lynch.

The AC-130s found themselves in great demand during the US Army and US Marine Corps sieges of southern Iraqi cities, where they proved their worth targeting buildings containing paramilitaries in highly populated urban areas.

Special forces aviation units may not have provided the most high-profile contribution to the war, but their impact may have been out of all proportion to their size.

Missile war

In the run-up to the start of the US invasion on 20 March 2003, the Iraqi surface-to-surface (SSM) forces were systematically deployed out of their peacetime barracks. The Americans kept them under intense surveillance because of the possibility they might be used as chemical or biological delivery systems. These procedures had been regularly practised by the Iraqis, who became expert at using the terrain and local buildings as cover. US military commanders were very vigilant, and when they appeared to threaten their forces, airstrikes were launched. A Seersucker launcher was hit in September 2002 on the Al Faw peninsula, and on 18 February 2003 two Ababil-100s and ASTROs were bombed near Basra. Three FROG-7s were bombed near Mosul later in February 2003.

After the US aircraft and cruise missiles launched a pre-emptive strike on Baghdad in the early hours of 20 March 2003, the missile forces in the south were the first Iraqi units to respond. The 225th Brigade's Ababil-100 battery set up firing positions in date palm groves north of Basra and near Al Zubayr. Each battery fired a missile on the morning of 20 March at US bases in northern Kuwait, and another two were fired later that evening. The Iraqi coastal defence battery also managed to fire off a Seersucker into northern Kuwait on that day.

The Ababil-100 battery north of Basra managed to fire off two missiles on 21 March, the day that major US and British ground forces swept north over the Kuwaiti border. For almost a week, the Iraqis were able to fire at least one missile a day at northern Kuwait. The terrain north of Basra was ideal for hiding the tractor erector launchers (TELs) of the 225th Brigade. By 23 March, Al Samoud II launchers had arrived south of Al Amara from around Baghdad, and fired two missiles over the next two days. A FROG-7 was fired on 29 March to conclude the Iraqi ballistic missile barrage against Kuwait.

The 225th Brigade was the subject of an intense surveillance effort by US-led forces, and five airstrikes were conducted against its missile launchers. Perhaps the most imaginative Iraqi missile crews were those of the coastal defence battery, who managed to set up a firing position on the Al Faw peninsula on 28 March and fire two Seersucker missiles at Kuwait right under the noses of British Royal Marines who had occupied the peninsula a week earlier. Three days later they managed to fire off two missiles from a position north of Basra. When British troops occupied Al Zubayr heliport, the Seersucker barrage eventually subsided. It seems clear that

Boeing F-18E Super Hornet

The latest derivatives of the US Navy Hornet first saw service in the Middle East in 2002 from the deck of the USS *Abraham Lincoln*. Since then the US Navy has embarked two F-18E squadrons on each of its aircraft carriers, replacing the Grumman F-14 Tomcat.

Crew: 1
Length: 60.3 ft (18.5 m)
Height: 16 ft (4.87 m)
Wingspan: 44.9 ft (13.68 m)
Weight: Maximum take-Off gross weight is 66,000 pounds (29,932 kg).
Airspeed: Mach 1.8+
Propulsion: Two F414-GE-400 turbofan engines, 22,000 pounds (9,977 kg) static thrust per engine
Range: Combat, 1,275 nm (2,346 km), clean plus two AIM-9s Ferry, 1,660 nautical miles (3,054 kilometers), two AIM-9s, three 480 gallon tanks retained.

Armament

One M61A1/A2 Vulcan 20 mm cannon; AIM 9 Sidewinder, AIM-9X (projected), AIM 7 Sparrow, AIM-120 AMRAAM, Harpoon, Harm, SLAM, SLAM-ER (projected), Maverick missiles; joint stand-off weapon (JSOW); joint direct attack munition (JDAM); Data-Link pod; Paveway laser-guided bomb; various general-purpose bombs, mines and rockets.

Four squadrons of A-10A Warthog 'tankbuster' aircraft were based at Ahmed Al Jaber airbase in Kuwait, which was the largest concentration of A-10s since the 1991 Gulf War. *(Author)*

B52 Stratofortress bombers armed with JDAM satellite-guided weapons provided close air support for US forces, repeating tactics perfected in Afghanistan. *(US DoD/JCC(D))*

McDonnell Douglas F-15E Strike Eagle

The Strike Eagle is the attack variant of the F-15C air supremacy fighter and has been in the forefront of all USAF strike operations in the Middle East since the 1991 war with Iraq. Its long range and heavy payload make it ideal for deep-penetration strike missions. Since 2003, these capabilities have been adapted to enable the F-15E to be used extensively in close air support operations. The Israeli F-15I and Saudi F-15S variants have similar capabilities to the Strike Eagle.

Crew: 2
Length: 63.8 ft (19.4 m)
Wingspan: 42.8 ft (13.05 m)
Height: 18.5 ft (5.63 m)
Maximum take-off weight: 81,000 lb (36,700 kg)
Powerplant: Two Pratt & Whitney F100-229 afterburning turbofans, 29,000 lbf (129 kN) each
Maximum speed: Mach 2.5+ (1,650+ mph, 2,660+ km/h)
Ferry range: 2,400 miles (2,100 nm, 3,900 km) with conformal fuel tank and three external fuel tanks

Armament
Guns: One 20 mm (0.787 in.) M61 Vulcan Gatling gun, 510 rounds of either M-56 or PGU-28 ammunition
Hardpoints: Two wing pylons, fuselage pylons, bomb racks on CFTs with a capacity of 24,250 lb (11,000 kg) external fuel and ordnance
Air-to-air missiles: Two AIM-9M Sidewinders or two AIM-120 AMRAAMs, and four AIM-7M Sparrows or additional four AIM-120 AMRAAMs
Air-to-surface missiles: Six AGM-65 Mavericks, AGM-130s, AGM-84 Harpoons, AGM-84K SLAM-ER, AGM-154 JSOW, AGM-158 JASSM, B61 nuclear bomb, Mark 82 bomb, Mark 84 bomb, CBU-87 combined-effects munition, CBU-89 Gator, CBU-97 sensor-fuzed weapon, CBU-103 CEM, CBU-104 Gator, CBU-105 SFW, GBU-10 Paveway II, GBU-12 Paveway II, GBU-15, GBU-24 Paveway III, GBU-27 Paveway III, GBU-28, GBU-31 JDAM, GBU-38 JDAM, GBU-39 small-diameter bomb, GBU-54 Laser JDAM

the US-led forces never quite managed to track down all the Seersucker missiles during the war. The missile crews apparently melted away during the fall of Basra. One Seersucker launcher was even discovered by British troops in the search of an industrial site near Basra in late 2003.

Perhaps the most ineffective missile brigade was the unit in Mosul. It only managed to fire a single missile during the war, to very little effect. Some eight US airstrikes were directed against the 224th Brigade's missile batteries.

In central Iraq, the missile battalions supporting the RGFC attempted to stall the US final assault on Baghdad. One Al Samoud II was fired on 1 April, and three FROG-7s were launched in what appeared to be a co-ordinated barrage in the early hours of 2 April. A rocket from an unidentified multiple-launch rocket system did hit a brigade command post of the US Army's 3rd Infantry Division on 7 April, killing two soldiers and two journalists.

Out of the twenty-three Iraqi ballistic and cruise missiles fired during the war, only a limited number got anywhere near a valid target. Nine were intercepted by US and Kuwaiti Patriots. Eight were not engaged by US-led anti-missile defences because they were deemed not to be threatening any friendly forces. The missile fired at the Kurdish enclave could not be engaged because the Americans were not able to deploy any Patriots there. Four Seersucker missiles did not land near any valid target, and one hit a shopping mall in Kuwait city, causing a moderate amount of damage. While the Iraqi missile crews showed plenty of determination to keep firing under conditions of total US air supremacy, it is clear they were severely hampered by a lack of up-to-date target intelligence. The missile crews proved one of the most determined elements of the Iraqi armed forces during the war, indicating that Saddam Hussein's efforts to ensure their loyalty had had some impact.

US Army experts spent five months after the war running an accounting exercise to locate the remnants of Iraq's SSM forces. Eleven of the fifteen Ababil-100 launchers were judged to have been destroyed by combat action during the war, and a further four were secured by US troops after the capture of Baghdad. Seven Al Samoud II missile launchers were destroyed in combat and four were located after the war. Of the most numerous missiles, the FROG-7, some twenty-eight were destroyed in the war and seventeen were located later. One was judged to remain unaccounted for by September 2003.

Sixty-one US and British air strikes and special forces attacks were mounted against Iraqi theatre ballistic missile strikes during the war. Apparently some thirty attacks were launched as a result of trajectory data gathered by US early warning radars and space sensors. The remainder were detected by unmanned aerial vehicles, special forces teams or E-8 Joint-STARS radar aircraft. The US Army claims that seventy-six per cent of Iraq's missile launchers were destroyed in the US counter-theatre ballistic missile campaign.

One element of the Iraqi missile campaign that caused US and British intelligence officers much puzzlement was the non-appearance of the supposedly hidden Scud/

Bomb artwork on a Paveway laser-guided bomb on the wing of an F-16CG Fighting Falcon of 524th Fighter Squadron at Ahmed Al Jaber airbase, Kuwait. *(Author)*

US Marine Corps AV-8B Harriers forward deployed to Ahmed Al Jaber airbase in Kuwait, as well as operating from amphibious warfare ships of the coast of the emirate. *(Author)*

A US Marine Corps AH-1A Cobra lands at Forward Arming Refuelling Point in Tikrit run by Marine Wing Support Squadron 373 during the final advance to capture the home town of Saddam Hussein. *(USMC/ Lance Cpl Nicholous Radloff)*

Abandoned and destroyed military equipment, such as this T-55, littered the roads leading to Baghdad. *(Staff Sgt Bryan P. Reed)*

Al Hussein missile force. Even though US and British propaganda in the first days of the war described the missiles fired at Kuwait as 'Scuds', this later proved not to be the case, and the Coalition press spokesman had to backtrack with considerable loss of credibility. Only three Al Samoud II, ten Ababil-100, four FROG-7 and one unidentified ballistic missiles were fired during the war. No Scuds or Al Husseins were fired.

The Scud threat was taken very seriously by the USA. Some eighty per cent of the US Army's Patriot force was deployed around the Middle East to protect US bases in Turkey, Israel, Jordan, Saudi Arabia, Qatar, Bahrain and Kuwait, as well as US manoeuvre units advancing on Baghdad. A major special forces and air campaign was launched against western Iraq from Jordan to neutralise the Scud threat.

British officers who fought in western Iraq reported finding no real Scuds, but a number of wooden missile and missile launcher mock-ups. This would suggest the US and British fell victim to an Iraqi deception campaign to make them think the threat posed by the Scuds was greater than it really was. The Iraq Survey Group has also not been able to find any Scuds or Scud debris, which supports this thesis.

In the end the strategic impact of the Iraqi SSM force was negligible. It was not able to inflict serious damage on the US-led invasion force. It did tie down a huge number of US troops and Patriot missile batteries. The inability of the US anti-missile defences to detect and destroy the Iraqi Seersuckers was a major capability gap and one that future opponents of the USA are no doubt taking on board.

Drive on Baghdad

A week into Operation Iraqi Freedom, the US-led invasion of Iraq seemed to be stalled. Heavy sand storms and surprise guerrilla resistance in southern Iraq combined to slow the advance on Baghdad.

For US Army and Marine Corps commanders battling in the sand and high winds against the Iraqis and supply problems, the need was to regain momentum and prevent the Baghdad government from building a coherent defensive line south of its capital.

Early on the morning of 24 March, the US Army's V Corps had launched its 11th Aviation Brigade into action on a night-time 'deep-strike' raid to hit the Republican Guard's Medina mechanised division. Its Boeing AH-64D Longbow Apache attack helicopter flew into a hornet's nest of anti-aircraft fire. One of the 11th Brigade's Apaches was shot down, another crashed in a dust cloud on take-off and thirty-three were hit by heavy Iraqi anti-aircraft artillery fire in the attack. Only seven of the brigade's Apaches were ready for action a week later, although eleven were reported to be under repair. Two captured Apache crewmen were later paraded on Baghdad TV, although the Pentagon denied that the $50 million helicopter had been shot down by an Iraqi farmer. Sandstorms now engulfed the battlefield, and further attack-helicopter strikes were not possible. Now was the time for US, British and Australian airmen to step up their game to help clear the way for the ground forces.

The commander of the US Third Army, Lieutenant General. David McKiernan, and his senior US Air Force adviser, Major General Dan Leaf, set their staffs to work to ramp up the level of air support for US troops fighting towards Baghdad.

On call was an impressive force of aircraft and helicopters, optimised for attacking enemy ground forces. The US Army's V Corps had more than a hundred Boeing AH-64D Apache Longbow attack helicopters, assigned to the 3rd Infantry and 101st Airborne Divisions, as well as the 11th Aviation Brigade.

Supporting the US Marines Corps I Marine Expeditionary Force (I MEF) were the 400 aircraft and helicopters of the 3rd Marine Air Wing (MAW), including McDonnell Douglas AV-8B and F/A-18C/D Hornet strike jets, and Bell AH-1W Super Cobra helicopter gunships.

USAF support included a force of four squadrons of Fairchild A-10A Warthog 'tank busters', backed up by several squadrons of Lockheed Martin F-16C Fighting Falcons and McDonnell Douglas F-15E Strike Eagles. Twenty-eight Boeing B-52H Stratofortress and eleven Rockwell B-1B Lancer heavy bombers were also on call to aid the close air support effort with dumb bombs or satellite-guided joint direct attack munitions (JDAMs). Hornet and Grumman F-14 Tomcat strike aircraft on the three US Navy carriers in the Gulf were also primarily tasked to support the attack effort.

Contributing to this effort were British RAF Panavia Tornado GR4 and BAe Harrier GR7 aircraft, and Royal Australian Air Force Hornets.

In total more than 800 strike aircraft and attack helicopters were available to support General McKiernan's troops, and for the next week more than 600 attack sorties a day were flown. General Leaf's staff began generating a 'direct support air tasking order' to co-ordinate all these aircraft into a single integrated attack plan.

Even before US-led forces crossed the border into Iraq on 20 March, the Iraqi leader Saddam Hussein had deployed his defences in the south of Iraq. Holding the border with Kuwait, Basra and Nasiriyah was the job of three regular army divisions backed up by Ba'ath Party militia troops and Saddam Fedayeen fighters. Although outnumbered and outgunned, for the first two weeks of the war these rag-tag troops caused the US and British forces major headaches after they launched a guerrilla campaign in southern Iraq.

To hold the southern approaches to Baghdad, Saddam Hussein posted six divisions of his supposedly élite Republican Guard Forces Command (RGFC). The first defence was set up along a line between the towns of Karbala and Al Kut, with the Median armoured division in the west, the Al Nida armoured division in the centre and the Baghdad mechanised division out to the east. Elements of the Nebuchadnezzar and Hammurabi mechanised divisions were deployed just south of Baghdad, as a second line of defence.

The task given to the US-led air forces was to render these units combat ineffective before the main elements of the ground forces were committed to action.

General Leaf and his direct boss, the USAF commander in the Middle East, General Moseley, turned to tried and tested tactics to do the job. Targets behind the

Incirlik airbase in Turkey was the home to USAF and other aircraft patrolling the northern no-fly zone from April 1991 to March 2003. F-16 Fighting Falcons and KC-135 Stratotankers were the core of the force operating from Turkey. *(USAF/JCC(D))*

After dropping off pallets of food and equipment, a C-130 Hercules of the 37th Airlift Squadron takes off from Bashur airfield in northern Iraq for its return flight to Romania. *(USAF/Master Sgt Keith Reed)*

front line were the responsibility of air commanders to destroy, and a system of 'kill boxes' was set up over the main Iraqi troop positions. The location of targets within the 'kill boxes' was the job of fast-jet 'forward air controllers – airborne' (FAC-A) who circled above them for hours at a time. Also known as Strike Co-ordinating Armed Reconnaissance (SCAR), these were usually two-seat Hornets, Strike Eagles and Tomcats. They required special qualifications and were much in demand to ensure that constant coverage was maintained over the Iraqi battlefield to maintain the tempo of 'kill box' close air support or Kick-CAS.

Iraqi troops in direct battle or 'contact' with US troops were dealt with by close air support, directed by forward air controllers riding in armoured vehicles with the tank spearheads. Air controllers in Boeing E-3 Sentry AWACS were responsible for the minute-by-minute massaging of these fire-control measures to ensure the maximum damage was inflicted on the Iraqis and friendly fire was kept to the minimum.

Lieutenant General William Wallace, commander of V Corps, put his main effort into destroying the Medina division around Karbala. For a week up to 2 April, he pounded the Medina division with artillery and rocket launchers, while fixed aircraft joined in the battle, striking both close air support and kill box or interdiction targets around the clock. Apache gunships were also able to join the battle now that the sandstorms had lifted.

The Iraqi deployment perplexed many US and British pilots, who night after night flew over the battlefield looking at targets through their thermal imaging night-vision systems. They reported seeing hundreds of 'cold' tanks and artillery pieces parked up in central Iraq. 'It looked like they had been abandoned', said one RAF Harrier pilot. 'Intelligence told us that the Republican Guards who wanted to fight had gone south to fight. The ones left behind didn't have much fight and just went home rather than sitting around to be blown up by us.'

Strike aircraft systematically worked over the kill boxes, using laser- or GPS-guided munitions to destroy or 'plink' individual Iraqi vehicles. 'Each aircraft would fly into a kill box with four weapons and come out without any weapons', said an A-10 pilot. US and British pilots reported very little Iraqi troop movements under this relentless bombardment, so they had little need to employ 'area' weapons such as cluster bombs or B-52 'carpet bombing'. 'We saw hardly any massing of Iraqi tanks, so could rely almost totally on precision-guided munitions', said an RAF pilot.

As the interdiction effort gained momentum, strike pilots started to run out of valid targets, as the only Iraqi tanks and artillery surviving were positioned close to civilian areas, making them off limits due to collateral damage constraints. An increasing number of aircraft started to return to base with their bombs unused, so they began to be given secondary fixed targets to strike, such as Iraqi military barracks and ammunition dumps. Some 234 of these targets were hit during the war.

Over to the east, I MEF was fighting a similar battle against the Baghdad division to the south of Al Kut. Its infantry regimental combat teams were fighting against dogged Iraqi resistance in Nasiriyah, Qat al Sakkar, Ash Shatrah and Ad Diwaniyah, requiring constant close air support from Marine Cobras and Harriers. Meanwhile, Marine Hornets and Harriers joined the effort to hit kill boxes around Al Kut as part of a deep-strike effort, co-ordinated with artillery fire.

In the early hours of 2 April, both V Corps and I MEF rolled forward to crush what was left of the Republican Guard. The 3rd Infantry bypassed Karbala and raced north towards the Euphrates with Apache gunships flying top cover. A few Iraqi tanks tried to resist the advance, but the Medina division had ceased to exist as a fighting formation. Those Republican Guards who wanted to fight retreated into Karbala to make a last stand. The 3rd Infantry's own aviation brigade and the 11th Brigade flew extensive flank protection operations during this advance. To avoid the problems encountered during the previous week, these missions were fully integrated with air force suppression of enemy air defence (SEAD) and artillery support.

It was a similar picture in the east, where the 1st Marine Division met negligible resistance from the Baghdad division, as they seized a crossing over the Tigris. Marine Hornets and Harriers then shifted their emphasis to hitting the Iraqi IV Corps around Amara, near the Iranian border, to prevent it striking into I MEF's flank as it drove north towards Baghdad. Using information from IAI/TRW RQ-2 Pioneer unmanned aerial vehicles, 3rd MAW aircraft hit the only Iraqi armoured column that tried to move to engage the 1st Marine troops, inflicting heavy casualties.

Two days later, the US Army and US Marines were at the gates of Baghdad, with the 3rd Infantry in control of the city's airport and the 1st Marines pushing into the eastern suburbs. Task Force 20 special-forces troops were already operating inside Baghdad and were waiting at Baghdad International airport for the 3rd Infantry.

At the same time as the drive on Baghdad was under way, US and British troops were mopping up towns along the Euphrates that had become centres of resistance. Najaf, Karbala and Hillah were all swept by troops of the 101st Airborne Division, who flew by helicopter to secure them. Shayka Mazhar airfield was also captured in a division-sized air assault operation.

Further south, the 2nd Brigade of the 82nd Airborne was securing Al Samawah with the help of Lockheed AC-130 Spectre gunships, and British troops were sweeping into Basra. US Marines of the 24th Marine Expeditionary Unit and British paratroopers of 16 Air Assault Brigade rolled up Iraqi troops around Al Amara in a series of helicopter-borne moves.

With Iraqi resistance apparently crumbling, General McKiernan now decided to push his troops forward into the heart of Baghdad to complete the 'psychological fracture' of Saddam Hussein's government. It was hoped that the sudden appearance of US tanks in the heart of Baghdad would bring the Iraqi government crashing down. This was a high-risk strategy. 'This was the time to take risks', said General Leaf. 'We lost an A-10. There was a need to be aggressive, to take risks.'

To provide the close air support for the advancing soldiers and marines, a huge 'CAS stack' was created over Baghdad, which contained scores of strike aircraft armed with every type of ordnance in the US and British inventory. Aircraft were cycled through the stack on a twenty-four-hour basis, to allow forward air controllers on the ground to instantly call aircraft into action with the necessary ordnance. General Moseley moved his tanker orbits deep over Iraq so that the close air support aircraft had easy access to fuel and could remain on station for long periods. The world's media caught much of this action live, broadcasting dramatic imagery of A-10s blasting an Iraqi ministry with its 30 mm cannon. The RAF débuted its so-called inert, or concrete, bombs during this period, allowing targets to be hit with reduced blast effects in order to minimise collateral damage.

Co-ordinated Iraqi resistance had all but collapsed, allowing the US Army engineers to clear debris from the runways and taxi-ways of Baghdad airport unhindered by artillery fire. This allowed USAF Lockheed C-130 Hercules transports to fly in on 6 April. A battalion of the 101st Airborne Division was flown into the airport by Boeing CH-46D Chinooks and Sikorsky UH-60 Blackhawks to bolster its defence.

As the US troops and Marines fought the remnants of the Iraqi army, intelligence emerged that Saddam Hussein might be meeting his two sons in a Baghdad restaurant. In some forty-seven minutes a B-1B was diverted to hit the location with four JDAMs. The Iraqi leader and his two sons escaped and the body of a child was dug out of the ruins.

By the afternoon of Wednesday 9 April, US troops were in the centre of the Iraqi capital and the leaders of the Iraqi regime were nowhere to be seen. Sporadic fighting continued around the city, with US Army Apaches and US Marine Cobras seeing action to support ground troops in action. The final close air support mission in the city was flown the following day when US Marines were sent to seize a mosque where Saddam Hussein was said to be hiding. When they met fierce resistance, an A-10 was called from the CAS Stack to bomb a position near the mosque.

The securing of Baghdad did not mean the end of the ground war. Over the next five days, units of I MEF raced north to seize Saddam Hussein's home town of Tikrit. The kill box system remained in place as the Republican Guard Adnan mechanised division based around Tikrit was pounded relentlessly. Marine forward arming and refuelling teams were pushed forward with the spearhead units to ensure Cobra gunships were always on hand to provide close air support. Iraqi resistance did result in one F-15E being shot down on 7 April over Tikrit.

By late in the evening of 13 April, US Marine armoured vehicles were on the outskirts of Tikrit, and it appeared that the Adnan division had melted away. Organised resistance to the US military had ceased.

Air support for the ground forces was the top priority for US, British and Australian airmen from the second week of the war, making up just over 50% of air sorties compared to 9.8% against regime leadership, or 10.2% against weapons of mass destruction and 14.2% to maintain air supremacy. The remainder of sorties were flown in support of special forces in the west and north. Out of some 25,240

Panavia Tornado GR.4

The RAF's primary strike aircraft has seen extensive service in the Middle East since 1990. Upgraded GR.4 variants, which incorporated major computer enhancements to allow an increased number of 'smart' precision-guided munitions to be employed, were first deployed to the Middle East in 2002. The Royal Saudi Air Force is bringing its Tornado IDS variants up to a similar standard as the RAF's GR.4 under the Tornado Capability Sustainment (TSP) programme.

Crew: 2
Length: 54 ft 10 in. (16.72 m)
Wingspan: 45.6 ft at 25° wing sweep, 28.2 ft at 67° wing sweep (13.91 m/8.60 m)
Height: 19.5 ft (5.95 m)
Maximum take-off weight: 61,700 lb (28,000 kg)
Powerplant: Two Turbo-Union RB199-34R Mk 103 afterburning turbofans
Dry thrust: 9,850 lbf (43.8 kN) each
Maximum speed: Mach 2.34 (1,511 mph, 2,417.6 km/h)
Range: 870 miles (1,390 km) typical combat

Armament
Guns: Single 27 mm Mauser BK-27 cannon with 180 rounds
Hardpoints: Four fuselage pylons and four swivelling underwing pylons with a capacity of a maximum of 19,800 lb(9,000 kg) of weapons, fuel, and ECM pods, inner wing pylons have shoulder rails for two AIM-9 Sidewinder, IRIS-T or AIM-132 ASRAAM air-to-air self-defence missiles. A wide variety of air-to-ground weapons can be carried . RAPTOR Reconnaissance pod, TIALD or Litening laser designator

An F/A-18 Hornet of VFA-37 heads towards targets in northern Iraq, armed with laser-guided bombs. *(US Navy/Paul Farley)*

An aerial gunner on an MH-53M Pavelow IV helicopter from the 21st Special Operations Squadron scans northern Iraq as the helicopter approaches Bashur airfield. *(USAF/Staff Sgt Jerry Morrison)*

Aviano AB in Italy was used as the launch pad for the parachute drop by the US Army's 173rd Airborne Brigade into northern Iraq on 26 March. *(USAF/Tech. Sgt Stephen Faulisi)*

individual aiming points for air-delivered munitions identified by air planners before the invasion, some 12,983 were land targets, but in the end 15,593 land-force targets were identified and attacked, representing 79% of all targets attacked.

Northern front

US war plans for the attack on Iraq had originally called for simultaneous assaults by air, sea and land from the north, west and south, with the aim of rapidly overwhelming Baghdad's defences.

While US Central Command was responsible for providing the forces attacking from Kuwait, Jordan, Saudi Arabia and other Gulf states, marshalling the forces for the northern front from Turkey was the job of US European Command. US and British aircraft were already based in Turkey to patrol the no-fly zone over Kurdish regions of Iraq, and it was envisaged that these forces would form the core of the northern front.

Combined Task Force Northern Watch based at Incirlik airbase in southern Turkey had evolved from the forces that had moved into Iraq in the spring of 1991 under the banner of Operation Provide Comfort to protect Kurds from Baghdad's troops. Up to March 2003, the force of some fifty fighter, strike, reconnaissance, tanker and rescue aircraft had mounted daily patrols over the Kurdish 'safe haven' in northern Iraq, occasionally attracting anti-aircraft and surface-to-air missile (SAM) fire. The Iraqis, however, had generally kept out of the safe area, leaving the Kurds to run their own affairs under the leadership of the PUK and KDP groups.

Turkey had always been suspicious of the task force's operations because of an ongoing rebellion by its own Kurdish minority. It regularly mounted raids into the safe area to destroy bases of the rebel PKK group. As a result the Turks placed tight restrictions on US and British air patrols, and Turkish officers insisted on having joint command of them.

So when the US government began to approach the Turks in late 2002 to propose basing 60,000 troops for the northern front in their country, they received a far from positive response. The idea was that the 1st and 4th Infantry Divisions, supported by British armoured units, would attack into northern Iraq from Turkey, supported by more than 200 USAF strike aircraft based at Incirlik and other Turkish bases, or embarked on two US Navy aircraft carriers. These aircraft were being provided by the main USAF units in Europe, including McDonnell Douglas F-15E Strike Eagles, Lockheed F-16 Fighting Falcons and Fairchild A-10 Warthogs. Special forces, reconnaissance and transport aircraft would support the Turkey-based air armada. A strong contingent of RAF aircraft, including SEPECAT Jaguar GR3 aircraft, were also supposed to support the northern front.

The diplomatic tension and confusion was increased when NATO plans to deploy Boeing E-3A Sentry AWACS and Dutch Raytheon Patriot missile defence batteries were vetoed by the French at alliance headquarters in Brussels. Eventually this was resolved, and the NATO defensive forces deployed to Turkey during late February.

The Turkish General Staff backed the US plans, but the newly elected government was lukewarm and insisted that the Ankara parliament should vote on the issue. Turkish public opinion was overwhelmingly opposed to the US plans, despite the offer of some $30 billion in loan guarantees, and a further $6 billion in direct aid. This waving of financial aid failed to win over the Turks, and their parliament voted down the proposal on 1 March.

In anticipation of a positive vote, the US military had already begun making preparatory moves for its deployment, and American logistic troops were already on the ground in Turkey, opening ports and setting up forward air bases. Advance elements of the USAF 352nd Special Operations Group had set up a forward staging area at Constanta in Romania, along with 37th Airlift Squadron Lockheed C-130E Hercules tactical airlifters. McDonnell Douglas KC-10A Extender tankers had arrived at Bourgas in Bulgaria to support missions by 13 Boeing B-52 Stratofortresses that had just arrived at RAF Fairford in the UK. Further Boeing KC-135 Stratotankers mustered at RAF Mildenhall to support the British-based B-52 force. A force of some

Post-strike bomb damage assessment imagery of an Iraqi ballistic missile factory near Mosul. *(US DoD)*

30 Boeing C-17 Globemaster airlifters also deployed to Rhein-Main in Germany ready to support the movement of troops into northern Iraq.

The US Navy had also began moving two carriers, the USS *Theodore Roosevelt* and USS *Harry S. Truman*, into the eastern Mediterranean, and to support their missions to Iraq the RAF opened its base at Akrotiri on Cyprus to USAF KC-135s and other support aircraft. The Greeks also opened Souda Bay on Crete for use by USAF tankers and reconnaissance aircraft.

Despite the Turkish parliament's decision, the US government still hoped to at least get Ankara to open its airspace and airbases to US aircraft so that they could support the special-forces troops operating with Kurdish rebels in northern Iraq. Negotiations soon got bogged down, and as the first US attack on Baghdad began in the early morning of 20 March, no agreement had been reached. This meant that the air groups of the *Truman* and *Roosevelt* had to be diverted southwards over Egypt and Saudi Arabia to participate in the 'shock and awe' strikes on Baghdad. These strikes had to be organised at short notice, and the two carriers had to be moved south, close to the Egyptian coast. Uncertainty about overflight rights led the US Navy also to move eight warships and five nuclear-attack submarines from the Mediterranean into the Red Sea in the week before the outbreak of the war, to enable them to fire Raytheon BGM-109 Tomahawk land attack missiles (TLAM) over Saudi Arabia into Iraq.

MH-53M Pavelow IV helicopter from the 21st Special Operations Squadron on a mission into northern Iraq to support US special forces troops working with Kurdish rebel groups. (US DoD/JCC(D))

A B-52 Stratofortress from the 457th Air Expeditionary Group takes off for its 100th combat mission from RAF Fairford on 11 April. Aircrews from the British base flew more than 1,200 hours and dropped more than 2,400 bombs during the war. (US DoD/JCC(D))

Late on 20 March, the Turkish parliament at last agree to over-flight rights, but it banned any aircraft participating in the raids from using Turkish airfields. This limitation meant US air commanders had to put in train a major reorganisation of their plans to operate without the USAF and British aircraft at Incirlik. The *Truman* and *Roosevelt* were called back to the Turkish coast in preparation for launching sorties into northern Iraq. Special-forces Sikorsky MH-53M Pave Lows and Lockheed MC-130P Combat Shadow tankers were forward deployed to RAF Akrotiri, ready to move ground troops into northern Iraq.

To help ease the diplomatic tensions with the Turks concerning over-flight rights, the USAF now dispatched Lieutenant General Glen W. Moorhead, the peacetime commander of the 16th Air Force at Aviano airbase in Italy, to head a special team of 180 staff officers at Incirlik, dubbed Coalition Air Forces North.

By 24 March, the air offensive on the northern front opened in earnest, with strike packages being launched around the clock from the *Truman* and *Roosevelt*. US forward air controller teams from the 10th Special Forces Group working with the Kurds began to step up the pressure on 150,000 Iraq troops around Mosul and Kirkuk. If the Americans could not take the offensive on the ground then it was hoped to use air power to keep the Iraqis pinned down and prevent them moving south to join the defence of Baghdad.

Although Kurds had prepared airstrips in their territory for use by fixed-wing aircraft for the first days of the war, the MH-53Ms and MC-130s of the 352nd Group were the main way of moving troops and supplies to the special-forces teams in northern Iraq. The wing aircraft and helicopters flew some 4,300 personnel and 375 million pounds of cargo into two forward operating locations in Kurdistan.

This situation changed on 26 March, when 1,000 US Army paratroopers of the 173rd Airborne Brigade mounted a combat parachute drop to secure Bashur airstrip in northern Iraq. A fleet of C-17s was launched from Aviano airbase in Italy carrying the paratroopers, and it was protected by three waves of attack aircraft launched from the two US Navy carriers in the Mediterranean. They attacked Iraqi headquarters and artillery positions within range of Bashur. In the event, the US airborne landing was unopposed, and within hours, technicians from the USAF 86th Contingency Response Group began preparing the airstrip to receive further follow-up flights of C-17s and C-130s.

For almost three weeks of continuous operations, the *Truman* and *Roosevelt*'s air wing kept up a round-the-clock air presence over northern Iraq. The *Truman* flew mainly day operations, and *Roosevelt* concentrated on night missions. The 400-mile flight from the eastern Mediterranean meant US Navy fliers often spent between five and six hours in their cockpits during these missions. TLAMs could also now be used to hit targets in northern Iraq, and they were used on 28 March to blast at the mountain base of the Ansar al-Islam group before Kurdish Peshmerga fighters, backed by American special-forces troops, stormed the base.

This 'long-distance' war had many similarities with the Afghanistan campaign of 2001. On the ground, small special-forces teams were working hand-in-glove with Kurdish rebels, and were applying precise aerial firepower carried by US Navy aircraft to break the morale of Iraqi defenders. B-52s from RAF Fairford joined this effort on a daily basis, and their large bomb loads resulted in Iraqi positions being saturated with joint direct attack munitions (JDAMs). As in Afghanistan, the B-52s were able to orbit over Iraqi positions for several hours at a time, waiting to be directed by special-forces teams to drop individual bombs against pin-point targets, or putting in 'area' attacks against larger targets. The Fairford B-52s also débuted the Rafael/Northrop Grumman Litening 2 laser-designating pod to direct laser-guided bombs against a target on the northern front.

Iraqi resistance to this aerial onslaught was furious at first, and some eighty Raytheon AGM-88 HARM anti-radar missiles were fired against air defence sites in northern Iraq.

As US troops surged into Baghdad during the first week of April, the northern front was also beginning to unravel. To boost their ground forces, the US Army flew in M1A1 Abrams tanks of the 1st Infantry Division into Bashur from Germany. The US Marine Corps 26th Marine Expeditionary Unit also overflew Turkey in its Sikorsky CH-53E Sea Stallions and Boeing Vertol CH-46E Sea Knight helicopters from the USS *Iwo Jima* to join the battle in northern Iraq.

By 10 April, Kurdish forces were surging forward and had taken Kirkuk. The following day, Iraqi commanders in Mosul surrendered and their troops started deserting *en masse*. From the south, US Marines of Task Force Tripoli were racing north from Baghdad to capture Tikrit, Saddam Hussein's birthplace. The task force of three Light Armoured Reconnaissance battalions received massive air support from both the north and the south, so there was little organised resistance when it entered Tikrit on 13 April. Some 800 close air support sorties were tasked against targets around Tikrit, and 200 munitions were dropped. By this point *Truman*'s air wing alone had flown 1,946 sorties and dropped 1,198 munitions, of which more than ninety per cent were precision-guided weapons. The *Roosevelt*'s aircraft flew to similar level of intensity, while RAF Fairford's B-52s flew 120 missions and dropped 2,700 munitions.

In the course of almost three weeks, sustained aerial bombardment had broken the back of Iraq's northern defences. The combination of special forces on the ground, US Navy strike forces and USAF shore-based support assets had proved effective and turned General Franks' concept of a northern front into a deadly reality.

Occupation

When President George Bush declared on 1 May 2003 that major combat operations in Iraq had ended, it did not mean that the US-led air activity ceased.

US Central Command quickly authorised a drawdown in the fixed-wing strike aircraft and specialist support aircraft that had been at the forefront of the air campaign against Baghdad. The decision by the US and British governments to occupy Iraqi with a 150,000-strong garrison of troops meant there was a need for continued air support, but in a very different form.

The attack helicopters of the main US Army and US Marine Corps divisions took on most of the responsibility for close air support for troops carrying out internal security and humanitarian aid operations in Iraq.

USAF participation in the occupation effort was extensive, and centred on four large former Iraqi airbases that were being converted into forward operating bases. Baghdad International airport became the main transport hub for US military traffic supporting the garrison in the capital and the Coalition Provisional Authority. Tallil in the south, Kirkuk in the north and H-12 in the west were transformed into forward operating bases, complete with detachments of USAF Fairchild A-10A Warthog close air support aircraft, General Atomic RQ-1 Predators and Sirkorsky HH-60 Pave Hawk helicopters.

Further afield in the Middle East, operations were wound down at PSAB in Saudi Arabia and at many of the other bases in the region. Al Udeid airbase in Qatar became the new home of the CAOC, as well as units of USAF F-16 fighters. Ahmed Al Jaber airbase in Kuwait emptied of the hundreds of USAF, RAF and US Marine Corps fighters that had supported the advance on Baghdad, but the RAF retained a small detachment of GR4 Tornados at Ali Al Salem airbase in the Emirate to support the British division in Basra. From having several hundred fast jets and bombers available at the start of the war, US and British air commanders now required only a few score fast jets. The US Navy continued to maintain a carrier strike group in Middle East waters.

Logistic support for the US troops was a top priority, and the USAF fleet of Boeing C-17 Globemasters and Lockheed C-130 Hercules found itself heavily tasked.

Assessment

Operation Iraqi Freedom saw extensive use of air power as part of a joint air, land and sea campaign to overthrow the government of Iraq. In the space of just under a month, US-led forces easily achieved their tactical and operational-level objectives.

Air power was instrumental in almost every aspect of this campaign, from strategic reconnaissance, strike missions in Baghdad, air support for ground forces and air transport of vital supplies and personnel.

Apart from the gunners and missile crews of the Iraqi Air Defence Command, US, British and Australian airmen faced no organised resistance. Iraq's air force stayed on the ground for reasons that as yet are unclear. The number of aircraft shot down by hostile fire can be counted on one hand, and more US and British airmen died as a result of 'friendly fire' or in accidents than due to enemy fire.

On best estimates some 5,000 to 7,000 Iraqi military personnel and civilians died and 20,000 were wounded during the war. Only a few hundred of these were civilians. Given the number of munitions employed, some 28,000, this was a relatively small number, but it demonstrates that there is no such thing as a 'casualty-free' war. The casualty figures were also low because the US-led Coalition avoided targeting bridges, power stations and other infrastructure targets positioned in civilian areas. It was recognised that these would be needed during the occupation phase of the campaign.

The impact of air power was overwhelmingly psychological. The Iraqis were just over-awed, and their military folded after putting up very limited resistance. This phase of the campaign could be described as the high point of 'effects-based warfare'.

CHAPTER TWENTY-FIVE

Lebanon, 2006

Israel's war against Lebanon between 12 July and 14 August 2006 saw extensive use of air power to hit targets along the Israel-Lebanon border and on deep-strike missions against targets in Beirut and along the Lebanese–Syrian border. This has been described as the IASF's first strategic air campaign.

The results were far from encouraging for the IASF leadership. Although the IASF flew some 15,500 sorties during the Lebanon conflict, including 10,000 by fast jets, 2,000 by attack helicopters, 1,000 by utility helicopters, 1,200 by cargo aircraft and 1,300 by UAVs, it was unable to achieve strategic success by itself. The IDF was unable to prevent the guerrilla group firing several thousand rockets into northern Israel throughout the conflict, while the Hizbullah leadership and the Lebanese government refused to heed Israeli demands to release two captured IDF soldiers. Ultimately, the IDF had to launch a major ground operation to clear Hizbullah fighters from the Lebanese border region.

Hizbullah raid

Israel's northern border with Lebanon remained a source of continuing tension, even though the IDF withdrew its ground troops from the security zone inside the country in 2000. Militia fighters from the Hizbullah militia continued to launch hit-and-run strikes on the Israeli border defences. On 12 July 2006, they launched a raid into Israel with the aim of capturing some IDF soldiers whom they could use as bargaining chips to secure the release of Hizbullah fighters held in Israel. This deadly attack led to two IDF soldiers being seized.

This caught the Israeli government by surprise, and it took them a couple of days to formulate a response. In the meantime IASF aircraft launched a series of strikes across Lebanon against suspected Hizbullah targets.

Israeli Prime Minister Ehud Olmert and his cabinet, on the advice of IDF Chief of Staff Lieutenant General Dan Halutz, decided to launch a strategic air campaign against high-profile targets across Lebanon. The aim of Operation Change of Direction was to inflict so much 'pain' on the Lebanese government and population that they would force Hizbullah to give up their captives. Halutz told Israel's Channel 10, 'If the soldiers are not returned, we will turn Lebanon's clock back twenty years.' As the first air force commander to rise to be IDF Chief of Staff, Halutz was putting great faith in the Jewish state's air power.

Strike operations by IASF were ramped up dramatically. The runway of Beirut International airport and radars were cut by laser-guided bombs. Bridges, roads, electrical power stations, fuel storage sites and industrial facilities were all attacked. Hizbullah command centres and military sites deep in Lebanon, including areas of downtown Beirut, were all hit by the IASF as well.

The IDF had expected Hizbullah to retaliate with Katyusha and other short-range rockets, and so had prepared defensive operations along the border. This included intensive UAV surveillance of suspected rocket launch sites. Imagery was downloaded into targeting centres co-located with artillery batteries to allow rapid fire to be brought to bear against any Hizbullah rocket teams that broke cover to fire into Israel. Fixed-wing strike aircraft and attack helicopters were also on call to attack the rocket teams.

However, Hizbullah had been preparing for conflict with Israel for several years, and had built a formidable network of concealed rocket-storage sites across southern Lebanon. Within hours of the first Israeli airstrikes, Hizbullah rocket teams were firing into Israel, hitting border towns and cities further south, including Haifa. Scores of Israeli civilians were killed and injured.

The rocket fire was soon a major complicating factor for the IASF strategic air campaign. Israeli UAV and radar surveillance could not cope with the large number of rocket strikes. It took too long to bring down counter-battery fire, and the Hizbullah rocket teams were long gone by the time IDF artillery shells were landing. In the first nine days of the war, some 505 rockets landed in Israel. On 2 August alone, more than 200 rockets were fired on Israel. This unfolding drama was caught by international television teams, and Israel's civilian population was becoming increasingly unhappy at the slow progress of the campaign.

Israeli over-confidence was dramatically illustrated when a Hizbullah missile team targeted and hit an Israeli warship on patrol off Beirut. On 14 July, Hizbollah attacked the INS *Hanit*, an Israeli navy Sa'ar 5-class corvette enforcing a naval blockade of the Lebanese coast, with what was believed to be a radar-guided C-802 anti-ship missile. The Hizbullah missile crew had taken over a Lebanese civilian maritime radar site to monitor the Israeli warship in the hours before the attack. Four sailors were killed and the warship was severely damaged. It subsequently emerged that the captain had not expected any Hizbullah attack and had not activated defensive systems.

In the face of these setbacks, pressure grew for the IDF to launch a ground incursion into Lebanon to clear out the Hizbullah rocket teams once and for all. The mobilisation of the three divisions of reservists needed for the large ground invasion would take time, so the IASF had to continue to pound Lebanon. In the meantime a series of smaller raids into Lebanon by IDF tank columns met heavy resistance from heavily dug-in Hizbullah fighters armed with the latest generation of Russian-made anti-tank missiles. Some fifty heavily armoured Israeli Merkevas were hit and significantly damaged by Hizbullah missile teams. IASF Apache and Cobra gunships repeated close air support missions to protect isolated Israeli troops.

By early August, the IASF fast-jet force was flying more than 250 sorties a day, striking deep into Lebanon. The newly arrived Gulfstream Compact Airborne Early Warning (CAEW) aircraft was pressed into service to try to monitor Syrian airspace. The regime in Damascus, however, was not tempted to join the fight. Hizbullah

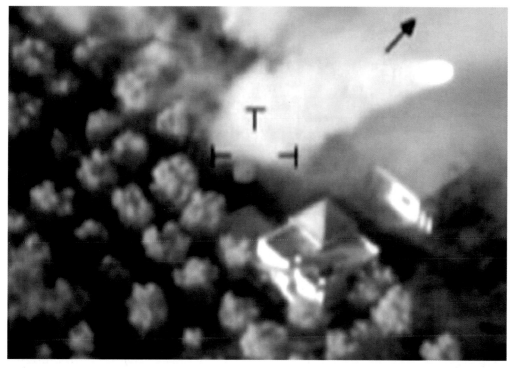

Hizbullah rocket teams severely challenged the Israeli surveillance effort and kept up their barrage against the Jewish state throughout the conflict. *(IDF Spokesman)*

seemed to be snaring the Israelis with little help. Israel and the USA repeatedly accused the Syrians of allowing Iranian weapons to be shipped across its territory to resupply Hizbullah rocket teams. In an attempt to interdict these supply columns, Israeli jets repeatedly bombed bridges and roads along the Lebanese–Syrian border. Strikes were launched on suspected Hizbullah weapon stores in the Beka'a valley to the east of Beirut. This effort also included a helicopter-borne raid by Israeli special-forces commandos on Baalbek in the heart of Beka'a on 1 August. The raid was reportedly intended to capture a senior Hizbullah commander to hold as a bargaining chip against the release of the two IDF soldiers captured at the start of the war, but the attackers returned home empty handed.

The intensity of the air campaign was starting to eat into the IASF's stock of precision-guided munitions, particularly satellite-guided JDAMs and GBU-28 'penetrator' warhead weapons. This prompted the Israelis to ask the US government to speed up the delivery of an arms package agreed in 2007. Some six resupply flights by chartered Airbus A310s and Boeing 747s were routed through the UK. They at first landed at Prestwick civilian airport to refuel, but then were diverted to RAF Mildenhall and Brize Norton.

On 11 August, some 30,000 recently mobilised IDF troops surged into southern Lebanon. For three days heavy fighting raged across the area as the IDF tried to drive Hizbullah from key terrain dominating the border region. IDF commanders

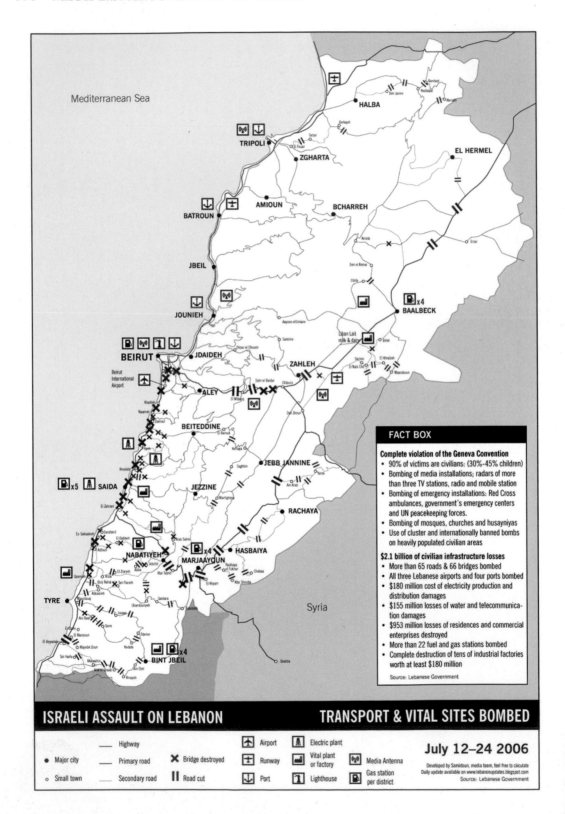

ISRAELI ASSAULT ON LEBANON

TRANSPORT & VITAL SITES BOMBED

Mediterranean Sea

HALBA

TRIPOLI
ZGHARTA
EL HERMEL

AMIOUN
BATROUN
BCHARREH

JBEIL

JOUNIEH
BAALBECK x4

BEIRUT
JDAIDEH
ZAHLEH
Beirut International Airport
ALEY

BEITEDDINE

JEBB JANNINE

SAIDA x5
JEZZINE

RACHAYA

NABATIYEH x4
MARJAAYOUN
HASBAIYA

TYRE
Syria

BINT JBEIL x4

FACT BOX

Complete violation of the Geneva Convention
- 90% of victims are civilians: (30%–45% children)
- Bombing of media installations; radars of more than three TV stations, radio and mobile station
- Bombing of emergency installations: Red Cross ambulances, government's emergency centers and UN peacekeeping forces.
- Bombing of mosques, churches and husayniyas
- Use of cluster and internationally banned bombs on heavily populated civilian areas

$2.1 billion of civilian infrastructure losses
- More than 65 roads & 66 bridges bombed
- All three Lebanese airports and four ports bombed
- $180 million cost of electricity production and distribution damages
- $155 million losses of water and telecommunication damages
- $953 million losses of residences and commercial enterprises destroyed
- More than 22 fuel and gas stations bombed
- Complete destruction of tens of industrial factories worth at least $180 million

Source: Lebanese Government

July 12–24 2006

Developed by Samidoun, media team, feel free to circulate
Daily update available on www.lebanonupdates.blogspot.com
Source: Lebanese Government

Legend:
- ● Major city
- ○ Small town
- —— Highway
- —— Primary road
- —— Secondary road
- ✕ Bridge destroyed
- ‖ Road cut
- ✈ Airport
- ⊞ Runway
- ⊥ Port
- ⚡ Electric plant
- 🏭 Vital plant or factory
- 🗼 Lighthouse
- Media Antenna
- Gas station per district

Israel's new F-16Is received their combat debut in the 2006 Lebanon War. *(IDF spokesman)*

Heavy airstrikes against strategic targets were meant to force the Lebanese government and population to turn against Hizbullah; it did not work out like that. *(IDF Spokesman)*

called in heavy air support and used extensive helicopter support to drop troops behind Hizbullah positions. An IASF CH-53 transport helicopter was shot down in the Maryamein valley near the village of Yater, and other helicopters scrambled to the area to try to rescue the crew, but all five soldiers on board were killed. C-130s were also called upon to drop supplies to front-line IDF troops.

This was the fourth helicopter to be lost since Operation Change of Direction was launched on 12 July. Two Apaches collided and crashed, and a third crashed separately in northern Israel early on in the fighting.

After thirty-four days of intensive Israeli air, land and naval operations against Lebanon, Hizbullah had not relented. The two IDF soldiers were still in Hizbullah captivity, although some reports suggested they might have been killed in the initial attack on 12 July and their bodies seized by the militia group. Perhaps of more concern to the Israeli government, there was no let-up in the daily rocket barrage of the northern third of the Jewish state. More than a million people were forced to take cover in their cellars and bomb shelters during the rocket attacks. The inability of the Israeli military to develop an effective response to Hizbullah put tremendous pressure on Prime Minister Olmert to bring the war to an end. In a humiliating climbdown, he turned to the United Nations to broker a ceasefire with Hizbullah and get the militia groups to agree to the deployment of an expanded international peacekeeping mission in southern Lebanon. The ceasefire came into effect on 14 August. Hizbullah declared the first-ever Arab victory over the Jewish state.

The war devastated large parts of Lebanon, causing billions of dollars of damage to its infrastructure. During the campaign, Israel's air force flew more than 12,000 combat missions, its navy fired 2,500 shells, and its army fired over 100,000 shells. Large parts of the Lebanese civilian infrastructure were destroyed, including 400 miles (640 km) of roads, 73 bridges, and 31 other targets, such as Beirut's Rafic Hariri International airport, ports, water and sewage treatment plants, electrical facilities, 25 fuel stations, 900 commercial structures, up to 350 schools and two hospitals, and 15,000 homes. Some 130,000 more homes were damaged.

Lebanese government officials put the death toll at 1,123, including 37 soldiers and police officers. Around 500 Hizbullah fighters were also reported to have been killed. Total Israeli military casualties were 121 dead and 628 wounded. Some 43 Israeli civilians were killed and 4,262 civilians were injured.

For Israel's air force, Operation Change of Direction was not a happy experience. On a tactical level, UAVs got high marks from Israeli commanders, and armed UAVs conducted strikes against guerrilla targets. IASF F-16s shot down three Hizbullah UAVs, including the début of the Python 4/5 air-to-air missile shooting down of one of these UAVs. IASF losses included one CH-53 shot down, while three Apache gunships and an F-16I were lost due to technical problems or accidents.

The ambitions of Lieutenant General Halutz were thwarted, and within a few weeks of the end of the war he stood down as the IDF's Chief of Staff. This was an unprecedented move for Israel's senior military officer, and a sign of his unpopularity. An official board of inquiry subsequently severely criticised the performance of the IDF, particularly its poor organisation and planning of the land invasion. Halutz had banked everything on air power, and his strategy came up wanting.

CHAPTER TWENTY-SIX

Lebanon, 2006 – International Involvement

Political instability in the eastern Mediterranean region had long been a concern of the UK and USA. The strategic importance of the region meant that the UK continued to maintain two large airbases, Akrotiri and Episkopi, on the island of Cyprus, along with a major intelligence-gathering site. These bases were ideally placed to monitor events in Lebanon when fighting broke out between Israeli and Hizbullah forces in July 2006. The Americans had also kept a close interest in the region, and had based a pair of USAF Lockheed U-2 Dragon Lady reconnaissance aircraft at RAF Akrotiri continuously since the 1970s. US Army transport helicopters were also regularly stationed at the British base to fly shuttle missions to the US Embassy in the Lebanese capital, Beirut, in time of tension. Given Lebanon's long history, both the UK and USA maintained contingency plans to evacuate their citizens from Lebanon via Cyprus.

The 2006 War

As Israeli warplanes started to strike at targets in Beirut on 12 July 2006, foreign embassies in Beirut began activating plans to evacuate their citizens. When Israeli warplanes cratered the main runway at Beirut airport and then started to drop the bridges on all the roads from the Lebanese capital to Syria, several nations activated plans to use military forces to get their citizens to safety.

The US military activated Joint Task Force Lebanon to oversee its evacuation operation to bring 14,000 Americans to safety. The core of its rescue force was the amphibious warfare ship, USS *Iwo Jima*, with Sikorsky CH-46E Sea Kinght and CH-53E Sea Stallion helicopters of the 24th Marine Expeditionary Unit (Special Operations Capable) (MEU (SOC)) embarked. US Army CH-47D helicopters from Germany were deployed to RAF Akrotiri to join the rescue mission. USAF Sikorsky MH-53M Pave Lows and Lockheed HC-130P Combat Shadows, of the 352nd Special Operations Group, also joined Task Force Lebanon at Akrotiri.

The next-largest military force, some 2,500 personnel, was deployed by the UK under the codename Operation Highbrow. Royal Navy Sea King Mk 4 Helicopters of 846 Naval Air Squadron and three RAF Boeing Chinook HC2s of 27 Squadron self-deployed from the UK to RAF Akrotiri to allow a helicopter airbridge to be opened to Cyprus.

Both the UK and USA also deployed strong naval task forces of frigates and destroyers to support the evacuation. The UK's naval task force was commanded

A US door gunner watches Beirut during the early phase of the evacuation. *(US Navy)*

by the aircraft carrier HMS *Illustrious*. Several other nations also deployed vessels, including ships from the Indian navy.

The USA flew its first evacuation flight on 17 July, when USMC CH-53E brought forty-two Americans out of the US Embassy in Beirut. Britain began its evacuation the same day, with Chinooks flying evacuees from a landing zone in Beirut harbour. The RAF helicopters also became involved in flying the European Union diplomat Dr Solana from Cyprus to Beirut.

The following day the big Chinooks and Sea Stallions ramped up their shuttle effort between Cyprus and Beirut. They also started dropping evacuees on ships off the coast.

The air flow was managed by Royal Navy Westland Sea King Airborne Surveillance and Control (ASAC) Mk 7s flying off HMS *Illustrious*. These helcopters also kept a close watch on the Israeli air force and Hizbullah missile teams to ensure the rescue operation could proceed safely.

Although the evacuation had got under way using helicopters, the number of people – more than 30,000 – needing to moved out of Lebanon was beyond the capacity of the available helicopters alone. The decision was taken to start running ships into Lebanese ports to bring out thousands.

The first ships ventured into Lebanon on 18 July, and they continued to shuttle evacuees out over the next week. This allowed the helicopters to move over to concentrate on evacuating civilians in need of medical assistance and carrying international diplomats in and out of the city.

Sikorsky UH-60L Blackhawk

The Blackhawk is the workhorse of US Army aviation, and so has seen extensive service in the Middle East, in troop transport, medical evacuation, electronic warfare, command and control roles. The US Navy uses a variant for anti-submarine, surface surveillance and utility roles, and the USAF uses a variant for combat search and rescue. The Israeli and Turkish military have also used the helicopter in combat operations over the past decade.

Crew: 2 pilots (flight crew)
Capacity: 2,640 lb of cargo internally, including 14 troops or 6 stretchers, or 8,000 lb (UH-60A) or 9,000 lb (UH-60L) of cargo externally
Length: 64 ft 10 in. (19.76 m)
Fuselage width: 7 ft 9 in. (2.36 m)
Rotor diameter: 53 ft 8 in. (16.36 m)
Height: 16 ft 10 in. (5.13 m)
Max takeoff weight: 23,500 lb (10,660 kg)
Powerplant: Two General Electric T700-GE-701C turboshafts, 1,890 hp (1,410 kW) each
Maximum speed: 159 kt (183 mph, 295 km/h)
Combat radius: 368 miles (320 nm, 592 km)

Armament
Guns: 2 7.62 mm (0.30 in.) M240H machine-guns or M134 miniguns. Can be equipped with 2 GAU-19 0.50 in. (12.7 mm) Gatling guns.

Once in Cyprus, a huge logistic operation was put into place by several nations to move their citizens back to their home countries. Most governments chartered civilian airliners, but some, including the UK, Greece and Australia, used C-130s and other military aircraft.

On 22 July, the UK completed its evacuation of 3,500 British citizens, and the USA finished its evacuation on 26 July, after moving 14,000 Americans from Lebanon. The rescue forces started to return home, but residual forces were kept on hand to support diplomatic efforts to resolve the conflict. For example, the UK kept its Sea Kings on Cyprus to support the movement of diplomats to Cyprus.

UN mission

The diplomatic effort to broker a cease-fire came to fruition on 14 August, and immediately it came into effect, European nations began to deploy troops to beef-up the United Nations Interim Force in Lebanon (UNIFIL) along the Israeli border. The first troops ashore were French from an amphibious task force, supported by Aérospatiale Super Puma helicopters. They joined Italian Bell AB212 helicopters already serving with UNIFIL.

Offshore a large naval task force continued to gather to form the UN Maritime Task Force to patrol Lebanon's coast and prevent Hizbullah rearming.

The arrival of the UN reinforcements brought peace to southern Lebanon, but tension remained high in the border region. On several occasions UN troops and naval forces reported repeated incidents when Israeli aircraft buzzed their positions and ships.

USAF MH-53Ms along with their US Navy and Marine Corps counterparts were the core of the US evacuation helicopter fleet. *(US Navy)*

CHAPTER TWENTY-SEVEN

Air Power and the Iraq Insurgency, 2003–2009

The arrival of US troops in the Iraqi capital in early April 2003 seemed to herald the end of resistance from the forces loyal to President Saddam Hussein. Iraq's uniformed armed forces had put up half-hearted resistance and melted away as US tanks powered north from Kuwait. However, guerrilla attacks and suicide bombings against US troops in several Iraqi towns during the brief land war were a portent of things to come.

When President George W. Bush made his dramatic deck landing on the USS *Abraham Lincoln* off California in a Lockheed S-3B Viking on 1 May 2003 to declare 'the end of major combat operations' in Iraq, his troops in the Middle Eastern country were already beginning to detect the first signs of the insurgency that by April 2009 would cost the lives of more than 4,100 US troops and result in 30,000 being wounded, on top of tens of thousands of Iraqis dead. More than 100,000 Iraqis would die in this insurgency, and over two million would flee the country to find safety.

The first shots of the insurgency were fired on 28 April in the town of Fallujah, when US Paratroopers of the 82nd Airborne Division were drawn into a confrontation with local people, which resulted in eighteen civilians being killed and seventy-eight injured. Within weeks, combat would be raging in several Iraqi towns and cities.

In the first eighteen months of the insurgency, air power played a key role supporting US and Coalition troops in action against rebel fighters, providing vital logistic support and assisting the delivery of humanitarian aid. While the air power was operating in a support role to the land forces, the desert geography and extreme climate of Iraq meant it offered US commanders unique capabilities that would be exploited to their maximum potential. This first phase of the Iraq insurgency would see US air power employ significant amounts of 'kinetic effects'. This situation would be reversed in 2006 when the US command in Iraq adopted a new counter-insurgency strategy.

Occupation duty
In the wake of the defeat of President Saddam Hussein's government, the Americans, British and Australians dramatically scaled back their air power in the region from some 1,800 aircraft of all types to fewer than a quarter of that number. The focus of

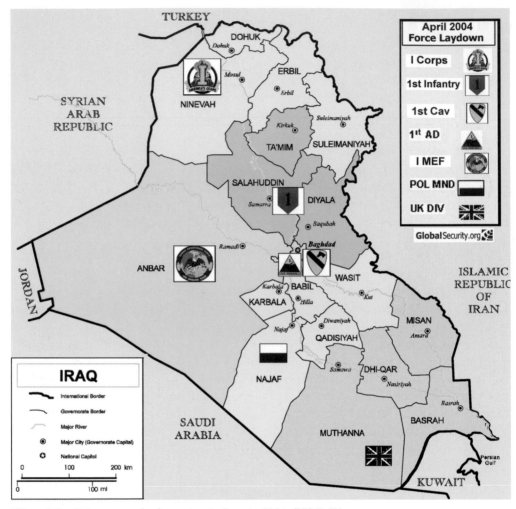

US and Coalition troop deployments in Iraq in 2004. *(US DoD)*

air operations became support for the 150,000 Coalition troops and the rebuilding of the devastated country. Not surprisingly, the air transport of troops and supplies and the tactical movement of troops by helicopter came to the fore.

Combat aircraft were rapidly pulled back from bases in countries surrounding Iraq, and a major effort was put into opening airports inside Iraq to support and sustain the occupation forces. Perhaps the most significant example of this was the withdrawal of all US air power from Saudi Arabia and the relocation of the US Combined Air Operations Center (CAOC) to Al Udeid airbase in Qatar. The hi-tech CAOC was packed with computers and communications equipment to give air commanders real-time control of all US and Coalition aircraft operating over Iraq, Afghanistan and other parts of the Middle East and the Horn of Africa.

US troops arrived in Al Udeid airbase in late 2001 to support air operations in Afghanistan, which have been steadily expanded since then. In the run-up to the March 2003 attack on Iraq, a sub-CAOC at Al Udeid took over the running of air operations over Afghanistan and the Horn of Africa as part of the US-led Global War on Terror. The CAOC at Prince Sultan airbase in Saudi Arabia was the nerve centre of the Operation Iraqi Freedom air campaign. During the early summer of 2003, some 400 airlift and 100 close air support sorties were being co-ordinated and flown each day by the CAOC at Al Udeid.

Al Udeid also became the only airbase in the Gulf region to host a USAF combat wing, with a mix of Lockheed F-16 Fighting Falcon multi-role jets, McDonnell Douglas F-15C air supremacy aircraft and F-15E Strike Eagles in residence. At any one time in 2003 and 2004, a squadron of each type of aircraft was deployed to the base, along with a dozen or so Boeing KC-135 Stratotankers. The Al Udeid wing was also to be ready to support ongoing US operations in Afghanistan. A northern transport and tanker base was established at Incirlik airbase in Turkey to support fighter operations over northern Iraq and high-priority transport aircraft flying direct from continental USA heading for Iraq, which needed to be refuelled in flight over the eastern Mediterranean. McDonnell Douglas KC-10A Extender air refuelling aircraft continued to be based at Al Dhafra in the UAE.

Within Iraq, two squadrons of Fairchild A-10A Warthog close air support jets were deployed to forward operating bases at Tallil in the south of the country and Kirkuk in the north. These were subsequently replaced in late 2003 by a squadron of F-16s in Kirkuk. These aircraft were to assist US Army troops that might need close air support. Additional air support could be provided by US Navy jets from the aircraft carrier that was kept on station in the Arabian Gulf.

Humanitarian aid

The three-week-long American blitzkrieg assault on Iraq came to a climax on 4 April when US Army tanks stormed Baghdad airport and were filmed driving past the burnt-out remains of Iraqi Airways aircraft. Within days the government of Saddam Hussein had collapsed. Even before the final fall of the Iraqi government, US Army engineers had repaired the bomb craters in the runway, and USAF Lockheed C-130 Hercules transports were landing to help the military build-up for the final assault on the capital. Further south, British Army Challenger tanks were crashing through the perimeter fence at Basra airport, and had soon turned the largely undamaged terminal building into the British headquarters in southern Iraq.

In the immediate aftermath of the fall of the old government, US, British and Australian forces moved to establish control of Iraq's main airports to allow them to support their occupation effort and allow the delivery of military supplies and humanitarian aid.

Immediately behind the combat troops came units specially trained and equipped to get 'austere' airfields up and running. The USAF's 447th Air Expeditionary Wing took over the now renamed Baghdad International airport, to turn it into a major transport hub to support the thousands of US troops trying to bring law and order to the Iraqi capital. Construction teams from the 1st Expeditionary Red Horse Group and the Civil Engineer Maintenance, Inspection and Repair Team made good repairs to the runway and established an airport lighting system. A constant stream of Hercules, Boeing C-17 Globemaster and Lockheed C-5 Galaxy aircraft were now landing at the airport, along with the first flights of aircraft chartered by non-governmental organisations and aid agencies. Royal Australian Air Force air controllers took over running the air traffic control for the airport.

Other USAF units opened up airfields at Tallil in the south, Mosul and Kirkuk in the north and several remote sites in the western desert. These latter airfields were predominantly used by military aircraft. At Basra a 500-strong team of RAF personnel set up a Deployed Operating Base (DOB) to run the airport as a transport hub for British forces in the Middle East. Soon between twenty and fifty fixed-wing and fifty helicopter flights a day were using the airport. The majority of these were military, but they also included a large number of charter flights carrying troops and humanitarian aid flights. This latter category included a high-profile visit by the flamboyant Virgin Atlantic boss, Sir Richard Branson, in one of his Boeing 747s.

The US and British military quickly moved to set up a system of navigation aids at the airports they controlled, and also installed ground radar there to provide limited approach coverage. There was no countrywide radar coverage, and all air traffic was controlled procedurally by the Regional Air Movements Control Centre (RAMCC) inside the CAOC at Al Udeid airbase in Qatar. The RAMCC staff issued 'time slots' and transponder codes for aircraft aiming to land at Iraqi airfields. The RAMCC negotiated over-flight procedures for entering Iraqi airspace from Kuwait, Jordan, Syria and Turkey.

While the main terminal and other facilities at both Baghdad and Basra airports were largely undamaged in the war, the collapse of Iraq's power grid, telephone and sewage systems meant that the military had to bring in almost every resource they needed to run flight operations. US and British officers who inspected the airports after the end of the war commented that their main problems stemmed from more than a decade without maintenance due to UN sanctions rather than war damage. The collapse of law and order resulted in hundreds of troops having to be diverted to guard these airports to prevent them being looted by desperate civilians trying to scrape an existence. Drastic security measures, including ground surveillance radars and machine-gun positions, were established around the airports.

Civil control

To fill the power vacuum in Iraq, early in the summer the US and British governments eventually formed the Coalition Provisional Authority (CPA), headed by Ambassador Paul Bremer, to run the country. Using his almost unlimited powers, Bremer set up teams of foreign experts to run each Iraqi ministry and government agency until Iraq regained its sovereignty in June 2004, ahead of the election of a democratic government some time in the future.

The CPA found itself responsible for all of Iraq's aviation infrastructure, its aviation administration and its state-owned airline. To get Iraq's airport open, the CPA was able to draw on some $150 million allocated to the Ministry of Transport to fund emergency repair work. As part of its multi-billion infrastructure contract the US construction giant Bechtel was contracted, via the US Agency for International Development, to begin emergency projects at both Baghdad and Basra airports. The work at Baghdad included installation of a five-megawatt emergency power generation, refurbishment of Terminal C, restoration of sewage and water supplies, installation of security check-points, passenger-handling facilities, air conditioning and refurbishment of the air traffic control tower and fire station.

A similar programme of works was contracted for Basra, including renewing the power supply, heating, air conditioning and sewerage, and painting new runway markings.

In May 2003, the CPA contracted the airport facilities management company, Skylink Air and Logistic Support Incorporated, to assess and the manage the running of civil aviation at five airports in Iraq.

Offensive operations

Insurgent attacks began to escalate during the summer of 2003, and US C-130s operating out of Baghdad airport were soon fired at by guerilla fighters armed with shoulder-launched man-portable surface-to-air missiles, or manpads. Commercial operators all got cold feet about open routes into Baghdad after the US military issued security warnings. DHL and the Jordanian carrier Royal Wings were the only airlines to continue offering civilian flights into Baghdad, but they suspended their services in November after a DHL Airbus 330 cargo aircraft was hit by a manpad missile and only just managed to turn around and land at Baghdad. No crew were injured, but it highlighted the threat to aircraft operating into the Iraqi capital's airport.

In the first six months of the occupation, US Army troops' first port of call for air support was their division's organic aviation brigades. These had some 140 Boeing AH-64D Longbow Apache attack helicopters, 90 Bell OH-54D Kiowa Warrior armed scout helicopters, 300 Sikorsky UH-60D Black Hawk transport helicopters and 80 Boeing CH-47D Chinooks heavy-lift helicopters forward deployed with the occupation troops, and they could be overhead trouble spots in a few minutes. During the summer and autumn of 2003, the US Army mounted a series of helicopter-borne search and destroy operations into the heart of the infamous Sunni Triangle in a bid to track down supporters of the growing insurgency against the occupation.

The first of these operations was mounted in June 2003 around Tikrit and Mosul, against the heartland of the old regime. Dubbed Operation Peninsula Strike, it involved Chinook heavy-lift helicopters of the 159th Aviation Regiment, backed

The USAF F-16 Fighting Falcon and A-10A Warthogs were in the forefront of the service's close air support effort during the Iraq occupation. *(USAF)*

US-led Coalition ground troops found themselves locked in a bloody counter-insurgency from the summer of 2003 onwards. *(USAF)*

Boeing CH-47D Chinook

Boeing's heavy-lift helicopter has proved to be invaluable to the US Army in the Middle East because of its power and cargo-carrying capability in 'hot and high' environments. The RAF also made extensive use of the Chinook in Iraq during 2003–2005. Egypt is the major user in the Middle East region, and the UAE Special Forces are in the process of acquiring refurbished Libyan Chinooks. Turkey is keen to acquire Chinooks to support combat operations against Kurdish rebels in its mountainous east.

Crew: 3 (pilot, co-pilot, flight engineer)
Capacity: 33–55 troops or 24 litters and 3 attendants, 28,000 lb (12,700 kg) cargo
Length: 98 ft 10 in. (30.1 m)
Rotor diameter: 60 ft (18.3 m)
Height: 18 ft 11 in. (5.7 m)
Max takeoff weight: 50,000 lb (22,680 kg)
Powerplant: 2 Lycoming T55-GA-712 turboshafts, 3,750 hp (2,796 kW) each
Maximum speed: 170 kts (196 mph, 315 km/h)
Range: 400 nm (450 miles, 741 km)

Armament
M134 7.62 mm (0.308 in.) minigun, M240 7.62 mm (0.308 in.) machine-gun

up by Apache gunships and other support helicopters. The first combat loss was a 101st Airborne Division's AH-64D shot down on 12 June 2003 in western Iraq, the first known incident linking Iraqi insurgents to the loss of a US helicopter. British troops were also in action in June in Maysan province, south of Al Amara, when a patrol of Royal Military Policemen was attached and the six soldiers killed. A Royal Air Force Chinook came under fire during a rescue mission to pick up wounded British soldiers.

Perhaps the high point for US Army helicopter crews in July 2003 was the raid in the northern city of Mosul that resulted in the deaths of Saddam Hussein's two sons, Uday and Qusay. OH-58D of the 101st Airborne Division's aviation brigade participated in the assault on the villa were the two men were hiding, blasting the building with 2.75-inch free-flight rockets.

The insurgents in turn began targeting the US Army helicopters with small-arms fire, rocket-propelled grenades and manpads. In a 21-day period beginning on 25 October 2003, Iraqi insurgents are believed to have shot down six US Army helicopters, including four UH-60, one Boeing CH-47D Chinook and one AH-64. Five of the attacks involved rocket-propelled grenades (RPG). On 2 November, a US Army National Guard Chinook carrying forty-two troops was shot down near Fallujah by insurgents with man-portable surface-to-air missiles, perhaps an SA-7 or SA-14, killing sixteen people and injuring a further twenty-six. Five more US army helicopters were brought down in a month, with the loss of forty-one US personnel killed and more than two dozen wounded. In response the US Army launched a major effort to re-equip its helicopters in Iraq with new defensive systems.

US Army sources were very critical of the predictable flight profiles flown by its helicopter pilots, which made it easy for insurgents to position themselves near US bases and wait for helicopters to fly by. In December 2003, changes in tactics were introduced that considerably inhibited the ability of the insurgents to attack US Army helicopters.

In response to the escalating insurgency, the US Army commander in Iraq, Lieutenant General Richardo Sanchez, ordered a series of integrated offensive operations to be launched around Baghdad, dubbed Operation Iron Hammer, which involved the use of fixed-wing aircraft dropping bombs for the first time since the end of the 'war' in April.

On 12 November 2003 the 1st Armoured Division's 3rd Brigade began its assault on the city of Baghdad, targeting Saddam loyalists and other insurgents. Many of the targeted buildings, including an abandoned dye factory, were suspected of being used as staging grounds by insurgents, and were deemed named areas of interest. Advanced munitions such as 2,000 lb satellite-guided bombs were dropped on suspected improvised bomb-making camps, and 1,000 lb bombs were dropped on a target in Kirkuk. Co-ordinated US strikes also included the use of Lockheed AC-130 gunships. Other targets in Tikrit, Baqouba and Fallujah were attacked by heavy artillery, battle tanks, attack helicopters, F-16 fighter-bombers and gunships. This was followed up by Operation Ivy Cyclone II, which saw air support being flown by aircraft of Carrier Air Wing 1 off the USS *Enterprise* in the Arabian Gulf.

Even the capture of Saddam Hussein in December 2003 did not seem to put a lid on the insurgency that was now spreading throughout the country, with bombings and gun attacks on Coalition troops now a daily occurrence.

The shift from war fighting to post-war stabilisation tasks meant a major change took place in the control of air support in May 2003. During the war, senior USAF officers in the CAOC were allocated large areas of Iraq where they could strike at will. After 1 May 2003, almost every airstrike would have to be conducted under the positive control of a forward air controller (FAC) operating with US or Coalition troops on the ground inside Iraq or airborne in an army helicopter. An air support operations centre inside the US ground forces headquarters in Baghdad made requests for air support to the CAOC and then handed off in-bound strike aircraft to FACs near the scene of any action to conclude the final phase of the air attack. Only when the FAC was happy that the attacking aircraft had correctly identified the target would he be allowed to clear the pilot to drop his ordnance. Each US Army division was assigned USAF tactical air control parties from Air Support Operations Squadrons manned by fully qualified FACs or Joint Terminal Attack Controllers (JTAC), who worked closely with their army counterparts and were usually in the thick of any action.

The use of fixed-wing close air support was still a very rare occurrence until April 2004, when the fighting rose to a new intensity. In the early part of 2004, the USAF and US Navy were flying some thirty to forty fixed combat sorties each day, but these were almost all combat air patrols that were not usually called into action. The usual tempo of air activity at this time was between 135 and 140 airlift and tanker sorties each day, supported by ten to fifteen reconnaissance sorties flown mainly by General Atomic RQ/MQ-1 Predator unmanned aerial vehicles based inside Iraq.

Airlift

The insurgents continued to mount manpad missile attacks on military and civil aircraft using Baghdad international airport. To counter these threats, increasing use was made of the cover of night to protect flights, but attacks continued. In December 2003, guerrillas hit a US Air Force C-17 transport plane with a surface-to-air missile shortly after it took off from Baghdad, causing one engine to explode. The plane returned to the airport and landed safely, with only one of the sixteen people aboard slightly injured. On 8 January 2004, a USAF C-5 transport plane with sixty-three passengers and crew limped safely back to Baghdad's airport after being hit by fire from insurgents.

In early 2004, the USAF began a major airlift effort to replace the 130,000 US troops in Iraq were with 110,000 fresh soldiers, requiring more than 3,000 flights into Ali Al Salem airbase and Kuwait International airport. The troops were then moved into Iraq by truck or C-130 flights. Airlift efforts intensified over the summer as

Air strikes on insurgent strongholds, such as Fallujah, were eventually seen by senior US Army generals as part of the problem, not the solution, to defeating the insurgency. *(USAF)*

Baghdad International airport became the hub for aid flights into the Iraqi capital during 2003. *(USAF)*

insurgent ambushes on US supply convoys made the US military rely more heavily on airlifts to get troops and supplies into Iraq.

By late 2004 the CAOC's air mobility division was typically organising more than 140 intra-theatre C-130 sorties a day, and more than thirty Boeing KC-135 Stratotanker and McDonnell Douglas KC-10 Extender air refuelling sorties a day – offloading close to 1.3 million pounds of fuel a day to our receivers. US air mobility assets also moved on average more than 1,700 passengers a day.

The Marines arrive

As part of the rotation of troops, the US Marine Corps was drafted in to replace US Army troops based around the hot-spot towns of Fallujah and Raamdi, as well as taking over responsibility for patrolling the western desert out to the Jordanian and Syrian borders, where foreign fighters were suspected of having infiltration routes.

The 25,000-strong I Marine Expeditionary Force (I MEF) was configured for its Iraqi mission as a Marine Air Ground Task Force (MAGTF), with the 3rd Marine Air Wing (3 MAW) providing the air support element to the combat troops of the 1st Marine Division. Many of these troops were veterans of the 2003 invasion of Iraq.

The main air element of 3 MAW was provided by the 16th Marine Air Group, which had two squadrons of Sikorsky CH-53E Sea Stallions for heavy lift, two squadrons of Boeing CH-46E Sea Knights for troop transport and a light attack squadron with AH-1Ws and Bell UH-1N Hueys. Although the I MEF relied at first on the USAF to provide fixed-wing combat support, it provided its own FAC teams and co-ordination elements at major ground headquarters to ensure close air support arrived on time and in the right place.

The bulk of 3 MAW bedded down at Al Asad airbase in north-west Iraq, and a major effort began to improve the infrastructure at Al Taqqadum airbase, including repairing the runway to allow Lockheed KC-130 Hercules. This was a few miles from Fallujah and allowed detachments of AH-1Ws to be forward deployed to provide close air support for Marines patrolling the dangerous town.

Two squadrons of KC-130Ts were deployed with 3 MAW to provide a link to I MEF's main logistic bases in Kuwait, as well as providing air-to-air refuelling support for fixed-wing combat aircraft.

A major job of I MEF was to prevent infiltration of foreign fighters from Iraq and air patrol of key roads and border crossing-points as a top priority for 3 MAW. Cobra and Huey patrols were augmented by IAI/AAI RQ-2 Pioneers from the Marine Unmanned Aerial Vehicle Squadron, which relayed back real-time imagery of locations of interest to I MEF headquarters.

The US Marines were in the forefront of the response to the deaths of four American private security contractors in Fallujah on 31 March. A mob mutilated their bodies and paraded them for television cameras. President Bush ordered a major assault on the city, and I MEF moved thousands of troops to surround it. The aim was to capture the city and crush the insurrection, under the codename Operation Vigilant Response.

When the First Battle for Fallujah was at its height in April and early May, AH-1Ws were airborne around the clock to support front-line Marines, using 20 mm cannon fire and AGM-114 Hellfire missiles. Marine FACs were also up with the front-line troops, directing USAF F-16s, F-15Es, AC-130U/H gunships and US Navy McDonnell Douglas F/A-18C Hornets onto targets. The shooting down of a USAF Special Operations Command MH-53M Pave Low special helicopter outside Fallujah during the battle briefly lifted a veil on the role of special-forces operations in central Iraq by the mysterious Task Force 21.

On 8 April, one F/A-18 Hornet from Strike Fighter Squadron (VFA) 131 flying from the nuclear-powered aircraft carrier USS *George Washington* (CVN 73) in the Arabian Gulf even conducted a strafing run against an insurgent position with its 20 mm cannon.

At noon on 9 April, Marines and Coalition forces unilaterally suspended combat in Fallujah in order to hold meetings between members of the Governing Council, the Fallujah leadership and the leadership of the anti-Coalition forces, to allow the delivery of additional supplies by the relevant departments of the Iraqi government and to allow residents of Fallujah to tend to their wounded and dead. This, however, proved to be only a temporary truce, and the US Marines were soon trading fire with insurgents inside the city. A mutiny by Iraqi troops meant the Americans never had enough troops to push home their attack, so Fallujah remained an insurgent stronghold for the following six months.

The First Battle of Fallujah resulted in 3 MAW calling up additional reinforcements that arrived in early May, including an additional squadron of CH-46Es and AH-1Ws. They were later followed by two squadrons of AV-8B Harriers. At the same time two Marine Expeditionary Units (MEUs) were ordered to Iraq to boost the US garrison in the country.

Sadr's rebellion

As Fallujah was going critical in mid-April, Shia militia fighters loyal to the radical cleric Moqtada Sadr began uprisings against the US-led occupation in several cities and in Shia districts of Baghdad.

The US Army's 1st Armoured Division was in the process of handing over responsibility for security of the greater Baghdad region to troops of the 1st Cavalry Division when the Sadr revolt broke out. Helicopter units of both divisions' aviation brigades were involved in the subsequent fighting, with Apaches being used to launch missile attacks on Sadr militia positions in eastern Baghdad.

Sadr fighters seized several police stations and government buildings in Baghdad, prompting the US military command to order troops to take them back. AH-64Ds were used to support these efforts, and they launched several Hellfire missile attacks on buildings occupied by Sadr supporters. One AH-64D of the 1st Cavalry was lost on 11 April during fighting near Baghdad airport, with the loss of two crew. An OH-58D had been lost four days earlier but the crew survived.

To the south of Baghdad, the Polish-led Multinational Division (Central South) found itself under attack by Sadr militia troops in Al Kut, Karbala and Najaf. The 1st Armoured Division, 1st Infantry Division and 2nd Armoured Cavalry Regiment were sent to restore the situation and help the Poles. Aviation elements of these divisions were closely involved in these operations, flying attack, reconnaissance, transport and medical-evacuation missions.

By early May, US troops were positioned on the outskirts of the holy Shia cities of Najaf and Karbala, and they soon began operations to undermine Sadr's control of them. Armoured raids supported by AH-64Ds and OH-58Ds hit police stations and other positions controlled by Sadr's fighters. The OH-58Ds of the 2nd Cavalry were in the thick of this action, trying to locate Sadr fighters hiding near the holy shrines, which were very sensitive and off-limits to US forces. To try to undermine support among the population for Sadr, leaflet drops were conducted by US UH-60s and Polish PZL Swindnik W-3 Sokol helicopters.

Shia militiamen were targeted by gunships in the airstrikes on Al Amara on 8 May, during the largest air support operation for British troops since the occupation of Basra in April 2003 during the US-led invasion of Iraq. AC-130s were used to support the initial amphibious assault on the Al Faw peninsula by 3 Commando Brigade the previous March, but this new operation was the first time the British Army had made such extensive use of the AC-130.

Operation Waterloo involved the use of the AC-130 gunships to strike at targets inside the city of Al Amara. In media interviews, Major-General Andrew Stewart, the commander of British forces in south-eastern Iraq, said the AC-130s were employed because of their ability to hit targets with great accuracy, so as to minimise the risk of civilian casualties. The AC-130 strikes involved the use of 'thousands of rounds' of 40 mm and 105 mm cannon fire, according to the general.

RAF involvement in Operation Waterloo included BAE Systems Nimrod MR2 maritime patrol aircraft, from the RAF Kinloss wing, and Panavia Tornado GR4 aircraft. The Nimrods used a Wescam MX-15 electro-optical sensor pod to detect targets for the AC-130s and co-ordinate low passes by Tornados to disperse concentrations of rebels.

New Iraq

At the end of June, the US-led Coalition officially handed over sovereignty to an interim Iraqi government, but it did little to quell the violence, and it was now clear that international military troops would have to remain in the war-torn country for many years to counter instability. Even the departure of Ambassador Bremer from Baghdad airport in a USAF aircraft did not stem the violence. A US Air Force C-130 transport plane was hit by small-arms fire after taking off from Baghdad International airport the day before the handover of sovereignty, resulting in an unknown number of wounded, US officials said. The aircraft was hit west of the airport. It returned to Baghdad airport and landed safely.

Northrop Grumman RQ-4A Global Hawk

The Global Hawk is intended to replace the iconic Lockheed U-2 Dragon Lady as the USAF's main strategic reconnaissance platform. From its forward operating airbase at Al Dhafra in the United Arab Emirates, the USAF's Global Hawks have seen action in Afghanistan and Iraq since 2001. The unmanned aerial vehicle features electro-optical video cameras, synthetic aperture radars and electronic listening devices.

Length: 44 ft 5 in. (13.5 m)
Wingspan: 116 ft 2 in. (35.4 m)
Height: 15 ft 2 in. (4.6 m)
Gross weight: 22,900 lb (10,400 kg)
Powerplant: One Allison Rolls-Royce AE3007H turbofan engine, 7,050 lbf (31.4 kN)
Cruise speed: 404 mph (650 km/h)
Endurance: 36 hours
Service ceiling: 65,000 ft (20,000 m)

USAF C-5 Galaxy airlifters flew missions into the heart of Baghdad during 2003. *(USAF)*

US Army AH-64 Apaches were the core of the service's offensive aviation effort in Iraq. *(US Army)*

Casualty evacuation UH-60s were in constant demand as fighting intensified. *(USAF)*

US Navy aircraft carriers were always on hand in the Arabian Gulf to augment land-based air power. *(US Navy)*

USAF C-5 Galaxy airlifters flew missions into the heart of Baghdad during 2003. *(USAF)*

US Army AH-64 Apaches were the core of the service's offensive aviation effort in Iraq. *(US Army)*

The Pentagon said in May that it planned to keep about 138,000 US troops in Iraq until the end of 2005 at least. The USAF was to retain control of four main airbases, at Kirkuk, Tallil and Balad and Al Asad. Balad airfield was to be the primary air transport hub because of the need to eventually hand Baghdad International airport over to civilian control.

By July, the US command in Iraq had developed a co-ordinated plan to neutralise Sunni and Shia rebels in Iraq. The first phase would concentrate on neutralising Sadr's militia, in order to free forces for a major showdown with the Sunni insurgents in the autumn.

It was to be the job of the 11th Marine Expeditionary Unit to spearhead the effort to wrest control of Najaf from Sadr's forces. A gradual process of chipping away at territory controlled by the rebel militia was begun, backed up by heavy air support from the unit's own AH-1W Cobras and a battalion of AH-64Ds and OH-58Ds from the 1st Cavalry Division. Fixed-wing air support from the USAF was also called upon, including laser- and satellite-guided bomb strikes from F-15Es. One strike involved the Marines calling down bombs from an F-15E within a few metres of the Imam Ali Shrine without damaging the holy shrine. There were also nightly AC-130 attacks.

It took until the end of August to finally wear down Sadr's men, and their morale was broken after a political deal was brokered with a rival Shia leader to take over control of Najaf's holy shrine.

Further east, in Al Amara, British troops were engaged in a series of running battles with Sadr's militia troops throughout August. These nightly fire-fights often escalated into major battles. On one occasion an RAF Regiment forward air controller in Al Amara called in USAF F-16s to bomb rebel positions with laser-guided bombs.

Crushing Fallujah

With the Shia rebellion in the south and Baghdad's Sadr City neutralised by early September, the US command in Iraq rolled out its plans to deal once and for all with the rebel city of Fallujah, and other rebel strongholds in the Sunni Triangle. USAF Predator, USMC Hunter, US Army Hunter and Shadow UAVs led a major reconnaissance effort to pinpoint rebel bases and head off ambushes against US troops. AC-130s and fixed-wing jets conducted nightly strikes into the heart of Fallujah in a attempt to 'decapitate' leadership of the insurgency by killing rebel commanders detected by the UAVs and other intelligence sources.

For most of the summer and into the autumn, Fallujah was the focus of 3 MAW air operations, with the Cobras and Hueys forward deploying to Al Taqqadum airbase to provide on-call close air support for Marine fighting in the streets of the city. A squadron of McDonnell Douglas F/A-18Ds was dispatched to Al Asad to reinforce 3 MAW for the coming offensive.

The Harriers and Hornets were in demand to drop laser- and satellite-guided weapons, as well as flying top cover for road convoys, using their forward-looking infra-red targeting pods to detect insurgent ambushes. By the end of the year, the 3rd MAW had flown some 200,000 sorties out of Al Asad.

The final battle for Fallujah unfolded in the middle of November, with a major division-level assault involving up to 20,000 US, British and Iraqi troops. USMC Cobras and US Army Apaches of the 1st Cavalry were on call to support the attack, with two AH-1Ws being lost to hostile fire. During the height of operations, Carrier Air Wing-17 aircraft from the USS *John F. Kennedy* flew an average of thirty-eight missions a day in support of ground troops.

I MEF first mounted a major operation to establish a tight cordon around Fallujah to stop any rebels escaping. This involved the British Army redeploying an armoured infantry battlegroup to Camp Dogwood, south-east of Fallujah, to work with US Marines of the 24th MEU. A detachment of RAF Westland Puma HC1s of 1563 Flight and Army Air Corps Lynx AH.7 helicopters deployed to support the soldiers of the Black Watch Regiment. They flew liaison missions and inserted patrols near suspected rebel bases. One Lynx was hit by ground fire on 10 November and a crewman was badly injured.

Within two weeks, Fallujah had been swept clear of rebel fighters, with the US Marines claiming an estimated 1,200 insurgents killed. Thirty-eight US troops, five British and six Iraqi soldiers were killed. Three of the US fatalities were non-battle-related injuries. A total of 275 US troops were also wounded in the battle.

While US and Coalition ground troops have borne the greatest burden in the increasing guerrilla war, their aviator comrades were also heavily involved in almost every major combat operation. The most highly praised aviators were the medical evacuation helicopter crews, who time and time again flew into the heart of danger to lift wounded soldiers and civilians out of danger.

Although elections scheduled for the end of January 2005 produced a record turn-out, they did not produce political, religious or ethnic reconciliation. The Shia parties won a majority of seats in parliament and formed a government. For the Sunni population in the region to the west of Baghdad, dubbed the 'Sunni Triangle' this was confirmation that they needed to continue with their insurgency. By the end of 2005, Iraq remained locked in a conflict. Insurgent forces continued to kill US and Iraqi forces on a daily basis.

For the US and British airmen, the war in Iraq had now settled into an almost routine tempo of operations. Each day hundreds of jets loaded with precision-guided munitions would be launched to fly combat air patrols over the main troop positions in Iraq, waiting for calls for action from ground troops. Hundreds of attack helicopters flew continuous patrols to support ground troops. Thousands of unmanned aerial vehicles, ranging from small hand-launched to the giant Desert Hawk, were on continuous patrol over Iraq. To protect troops from insurgents' roadside improvised explosive devices (IEDs), the air transport force was used to set up a shuttle between the main US bases in Iraq.

During 2005 and 2006, the Iraqi insurgency was a daily grind of small-scale battles and incidents that sometimes attracted air support. Occasionally high-

Casualty evacuation UH-60s were in constant demand as fighting intensified. *(USAF)*

US Navy aircraft carriers were always on hand in the Arabian Gulf to augment land-based air power. *(US Navy)*

profile incidents attracted media interest, such as the shooting-down of an RAF C-130 Hercules near Baghdad in January 2005, but more often than not US and Coalition air forces were in the background. Almost every USAF active-duty and reserve component squadron pulled duty over Iraq between 2003 and 2009. This was the service's main effort.

This changed on 9 June 2006, when US intelligence pinpointed the base of the leader of the al-Qaeda in Iraq group, Abu Musab al-Zarqawi, who was said by the US to be the mastermind of numerous attacks on Coalition forces. Within minutes, a USAF F-16 on patrol nearby was diverted by the CAOC to attack the location, and dropped two 500 lb satellite JDAMs. The target was devastated and al-Zarqawi was later confirmed dead by DNA analysis. The attack was lauded by President Bush in a White House press conference, but on the ground in Iraq the insurgency continued unabated.

Running the air war

In late 2006, the US Central Command's (CENTCOM) air component commander was USAF Lieutenant General Gary North. His peacetime job was commander of the US 9th Air Force at Shaw AFB in South Carolina, but he spent the vast majority of his time at his forward headquarters at Al Udeid airbase in Qatar or other bases in the Middle East. His mission was to support land forces in Iraq and Afghanistan with the full range of air power. Until March 2008, CENTCOM's air component was designated US Central Command Air Forces (CENTAF), but was renamed US Air Forces Central (USAFCENT).

Throughout 2006 and 2007, the USAF and US Navy deployed some 500 fixed-wing combat and support aircraft, including bombers, reconnaissance, tankers and airlift, to the Middle East to support the conflicts in Iraq and Afghanistan. Although it was rare for fast jets to be 'swung' between theatres, the combat support forces were used to support both wars, especially the strategic bombers, reconnaissance and air-to-air refuelling assets.

For this reason, the USAF insisted on remaining in centralised control of all air power deployed to both theatres. It has resisted attempts to establish separate air headquarters in Iraq and Afghanistan, and retained its Combined Air and Space Operations Centre (CASOC), until 2007 the Combined Air Operations Centre (CAOC), at Al Udeid to direct all air operations across the CENTCOM area of responsibility.

During the combat phase in Afghanistan in 2001 and in Iraq in 2003, senior commanders in CAOC could direct airstrikes on targets within certain rules of engagement (ROE) restrictions. As US-led ground forces moved into both countries and fighting with insurgents intensified, the ROE were tightened up considerably, and air commanders lost almost all of their ability to authorise air strikes, without specific authorisation from ground commanders. In military jargon, the land headquarters in Iraq and Afghanistan become the CENTCOM 'main effort' and designated the 'supported' headquarters. While the CENTAF commander could offer his advice to the commander of CENTCOM on air power issues, in the last resort it was the land commander whose views had pre-eminence.

In 2006, US Air Force Secretary Michael Wynne described the Al Udeid CAOC as possessing 'jaw-dropping capabilities', and said it 'showcased' his service's shift from scheduled air offensive against massed enemies and fixed sites to on-call strikes against time-sensitive fleeting targets on fluid and asymmetric battlefields.

By 2006, the CAOC staff were focused on the strategic direction of air operations across the US Central Command area of responsibility (AOR) rather than micro-managing the release of individual weapons by individual aircraft. 'We look at the big picture, the strategic picture here', said a senior air planner in late 2006. 'We are fighting two separate wars, and within those theatres, each army division is fighting its own little war.'

Although almost all weapon-release authority had now been delegated to Joint Terminal Attack Controllers (JTACs) or forward air controllers on the ground with army units in Iraq and Afghanistan, the strategic direction of air power was needed to ensure the efficient allocation of resources – particularly scarce tanker, airlift and intelligence, surveillance and reconnaissance (ISR) assets – across the AOR, said the planner. 'We deal with ground-alert aircraft, tanker support and rules of engagement, that sort of thing.'

The CAOC itself was divided into a number of distinct sections, which all operated on a twenty-four-hour basis. On a raised deck above the main floor of CAOC was a separate section dubbed the Battle Cab, where the CAOC director, a USAF two-star general, his senior staff and ground forces representatives monitored the progress of air operations. 'The offensive co-ordination guys are on the floor and they feed up here things that need decisions from the general or the duty lawyer', said the officer.

The main CAOC floor was dimly lit and was dominated by large projected screens showing the real-time air picture in both Iraq and Afghanistan, giving the position of all military and civil air traffic. On either side of these maps were live feeds from General Atomics MQ/RQ-1/9 Predator/Reaper unmanned aerial vehicles flying over Iraq and Afghanistan, as well as CNN television news broadcasts. Next to the main CAOC building was the ISR Division, or ISRD, where intelligence feeds from airborne sensors and collection platforms were monitored. In old-style CAOCs, full-motion-video imagery from Predators and other ISR platforms could not be shared with ground units, resulting in high-level decision makers tending to monopolise its use. CAOC staff say the development of Remote Operations Video Enhanced Receiver, or ROVER, technology, meant that suitably equipped JTACs could now receive Predator imagery, and this had allowed authority for weapon release from the UAVs to be delegated to troops on the ground. Aircraft equipped with Litening AT and Sniper targeting pods are also be able to download imagery to ROVER-equipped JTACs.

On the main CAOC floor the director of combat operations controlled ongoing activity, assisted by several rows of specialist staff who represented the main air

An airstrike on an insurgent target as seen through a US pilot's night vision system. *(USAF)*

units in theatre. The director post was shared by three lieutenant colonels, including one RAF officer. It was the director's job to choreograph the execution of the daily air tasking order (ATO), or air plan. This was the daily plan, which in late 2006 saw fifty strike aircraft a day being flown over Iraq, in six-hour time blocks.

'Things start with scheduling, the air operations support centre (ASOC) in the ground component headquarters in Kabul and Baghdad prioritise ranking of requests for air support', said a CAOC staffer. 'The operations team here then generates the ATO. We put our say in at that stage, saying if the task is appropriate to our assets.'

The dynamic nature of the battlefields in both Iraq and Afghanistan meant few targets could now be pre-planned. When army units reported that they had troops in contact, or TIC, the CAOC staff had to begin to juggle their assets. At this point aircraft had to be allocated to JTACs who could then authorise weapon release. The CAOC staff would then scramble ground-alert strike aircraft to provide additional fire power, divert tankers to keep fuel on hand and move ISTAR assets to provide coverage of incidents.

Surprisingly, the CAOC floor was very quiet, with almost all activity co-ordinated over internet-style chat rooms. Many staff officers had multiple computer screens to show all the messages that were transmitted over secure computer networks

General Atomics RQ/MQ-1B Predator

The Predator was the primary USAF unmanned/manned aerial vehicle (UAV) for much of the past decade. The RQ-1 is the unmanned variant and the MQ-1 is the armed variant, which entered service at the start of the US intervention in Afghanistan in October 2001. USAF and RAF personnel have jointly operated Predators supporting Coalition forces in Iraq and Afghanistan since 2004, via satellite links from Creech Air Force Base in Nevada. The Central Intelligence Agency operates its own Predator force, which has seen action in Afghanistan, Somalia and Yemen.

Length: 27 ft (8.22 m)
Wingspan: 48.7 ft (14.8 m (dependent on block of aircraft))
Height: 6.9 ft (2.1 m)
Loaded weight: 2,250 lb (1,020 kg)
Maximum take-off weight: 2,250 lb [44] (1,020 kg)
Powerplant: One Rotax 914F turbocharged four-cylinder engine, 115 hp [44] (86 kW)
Maximum speed: 135 mph (117 knots, 217 km/h)
Range: >2,000 nm [45] (3,704 km, 2,302 miles)
Service ceiling: 25,000 ft [44] (7,620 m)

Armament
2 hard points
2 AGM-114 Hellfires (MQ-1B) or 2 AIM-92 Stingers (unknown number) (MQ-1B)

RAF Tornado GR4s provided the UK's fast-jet contribution to the Coalition effort, and they regularly flew missions over Baghdad and other Iraqi 'hot spots'. (USAF)

US Marine Corps Pioneers were some of the first unmanned aerial vehicles to be used to find insurgent targets. (USMC)

or data-links to airborne aircraft and ships at sea. High-priority messages, such as requests for close air support for TIC incidents, were highlighted and logged in red, as well as being projected onto the large CAOC maps, to aid decision making.

A large sign outside the CAOC building proclaims its mission is to 'enable the kill chain', and an air planner said their work is 'all about supporting the land campaign and the ISRD is no different – the air campaign is for the ground commander.'

Stalemate, 2005/6

Senior US and allied commanders were now openly refering to the situation in Iraq as being a counter-insurgency (COIN) campaign, in which their troops and locally recruited forces were fighting insurgents in a guerrilla-war scenario. Unlike in 2001 and 2003, when US-led forces faced uniformed Afghan Taliban and Iraqi government armies in stand-up conventional warfare, by 2006 the enemy were elusive, small groups of insurgents who took shelter among the civilian population and who only rarely gathered in large groups to strike at US-led forces. The enemy's chosen methods of attack were improvised explosive devises, small ambushes, suicide bomb attacks on civilians and targeted assassination of the supporters of the pro-US government in Iraq. This was a war for the 'hearts and minds' of Iraq's population, in which victory and defeat were very difficult to define.

For the US military, the experience of Vietnam in the 1960s was a sobering lesson in the unsuitability of employing conventional forces and strategies in COIN battles. The initial phase of the US occupation of Iraq saw the USA making many of the same mistakes as were made in Vietnam. Reconstruction work had ground to a halt. The country's main ethnic groups were fighting a brutal civil war and Iraq's government was barely functioning. The US-led military force in Iraq seemed to have little influence on events and was under daily attack by insurgents. US military tactics, including heavy-handed use of air power, artillery and other heavy weapons, was alienating large sections of the population. By autumn 2006 it seemed as if the war to defeat the insurgency in the Middle East country was lost. The monthly body count of Iraqi civilian deaths was running at over 3,000, and around a hundred US military personnel were being killed each month, with nearly 1,000 being wounded.

The heavy-handed all-out US assault on the insurgent-occupied town of Fallujah in 2004, continuing shortages of electricity and the Abu Ghraib prison torture scandal dramatically boosted support for the insurgents among Iraq's Sunni Muslim population. At the same time, the country's majority Shia population had splintered into rival factions, fighting for political dominance.

The surge

To try to turn around this desperate situation, President Bush appointed General David Petraeus to head the Multinational Force – Iraq (MNF–I), and 30,000 extra troops were 'surged' into the country in early 2007 to try to put more 'boots on the ground' at street level in Baghdad and other Iraqi cities. Hand-in-hand with the surge of ground troops, extra air power was deployed to the region to provide extra support. The US Navy surged two extra carrier deployments during 2007, and so at any one time two carriers were in the Middle East and one each was always on station off Iraq and Afghanistan. Additional tankers were also needed because air-to-air refuelling was the only way to allow strike aircraft based on US Navy aircraft carriers in the Arabian Gulf or at Al Udeid to operate over Iraq. For the aircrew the distances involved meant that if they operated over Baghdad they would have to spend between six and eight hours in their cockpits.

As well as fixed-wing air power, the US Army and US Marine Corps already maintained fleets of several hundred battlefield helicopters within Iraq. These included the full range of attack, scout, liaison and transport helicopters. By being forward based in-country they had rapid-response capabilities, but their bases were vulnerable to insurgent indirect fire weapons, such as rockets and mortars.

Petraeus had just finished being commander of the US Army's Combined Arms Centre at Fort Levenworth, and while a student at Princeton he had written a PhD dissertation entitled 'The American Military and the Lessons of Vietnam'. He had strong views on the role of air power in COIN operations, and many of these were not to the liking of the senior leadership of the USAF, particularly Petraeus's views that air power should be under the tight control of ground-force commanders.

Before heading to Iraq, Petraeus and his US Marine Corps counterpart, Lt Gen James F. Amos, had rewritten US Army and US Marine Corps COIN doctrine, and they would import most of these ideas into Iraq to revamp the war against the insurgents.

Petraeus and Amos said air and space power's greatest contributions in the COIN operations were that they offered 'asymmetric advantages' over the enemy, allowing immediate movement of 'land forces where they are needed,' especially in rough terrain. Airlift could also 'quickly deliver humanitarian assistance,' especially in isolated areas, and this built great credibility and favour with the local population. Offensive air strikes were useful if the insurgents 'assembled a conventional force' and huddled together for easy air attack. 'However, commanders [should] exercise exceptional care when using air power in the strike role', they said. The doctrine asserted that errant bombs causing civilian casualties and destruction of civil facilities 'provides insurgents with a major propaganda victory'. Even when such attacks were justified, media coverage of such attacks 'works to the insurgents' benefit'. The new doctrine portrayed the decision to call in air strikes as one requiring heavy deliberation, as commanders must 'weigh collateral damage against the unintended consequences of taking no action'. Inappropriate or indiscriminate use of air strikes could erode popular support and fuel insurgent propaganda. For these reasons, commanders should consider the use of air strikes carefully during COIN operations, they said.

Air power offered advantages in collecting intelligence, surveillance and reconnaissance, and signals intelligence, for spotting and tracking insurgents and pinpointing their positions. 'Helicopters are especially useful in providing overwatch, fire support, alternate communications, and medevac support', the doctrine said. Air assets should be at the disposal of the ground commander: 'At the tactical level, air support requires a decentralized command and control system

F-15E Strike Eagles stand ground alert at Al Udeid airbase in Qatar. They were some of the first aircraft to use the new small-diameter bomb, which boasted low collateral damage, in Iraq in late 2006. *(Author)*

The US Army drafted its veteran C-23 Sherpa aircraft into service in Iraq to reduce reliance on road convoys, which were vulnerable to insurgent attack. *(US Army)*

Lockheed Martin's Sniper pod was integrated on B-1B Lancer bombers to allow them to guide precision weapons and download video imagery to ground troops. *(USAF)*

The Combined Air Operations Centre at Al Udeid airbase in Qatar was the nerve centre of US-led air operations in the Middle East. *(USAF)*

that gives supported units immediate access to available combat air assets and to information collected by air reconnaissance and support assets.' During COIN operations, the air force should work as fast as it could to help the host nation build up its air capabilities. Those should focus on mobility and surveillance.

Some eighteen months on from the start of the 'surge', the situation in Iraq seemed to have dramatically improved, with civilian deaths dropping towards 500 a month and US military deaths dropping below fifty a month. While his COIN doctrine appeared to have been vindicated, Petraeus was still not the flavour of the month with some senior USAF officers. The solutions adopted by the USAF and US Army to fight the war in Iraq suggest a major advance in the employment of air power in COIN operations have taken place.

General Petraeus dramatically overhauled US strategy and tactics in Iraq. No longer were kinetic operations or the employment of lethal force considered decisive. All US operations were focused on improving the daily lives of ordinary Iraqis by posting troops to local neighbourhoods to deter attacks on civilians, collect intelligence on insurgents and allow economic regeneration to take place. Air power's role in this classic counter-insurgency war was now very much in the support sphere.

US troops were moved out of their large bases on the edges of Iraq's cities and placed into every neighbourhood of Baghdad to directly protect the population from insurgent attacks. It meant small contingents of US troops set up forward operating bases in urban areas. This allowed them to pick up better intelligence on the insurgent groups and to build up contacts among the local population. Almost immediately it became more difficult for the insurgents to launch successful improvised-explosive attacks on US troops, which up to then had been the main cause of US casualties.

The insurgents, however, clearly saw the threat the new US deployments posed, and began to step up their attacks to drive the US forces out of their new bases. One of the most audacious insurgent attacks was on a US Army company base in Tarmiyah, north-east of Baghdad in February 2007. A huge truck bomb was driven into the wall of the outpost, and then dozens of al-Qaeda in Iraq insurgents tried to storm the base. The surviving US troops desperately tried to fight off the insurgents, and called up US Army Apache gunships to strafe the attackers, and they drove many of them off. UAVs were directed over the base and began streaming video to US headquarters. Medical-evacuation helicopters and reinforcement troops were sent to the post, and soon the insurgents were on the run. Almost every US soldier in the base was wounded, but it held out and the reputation of the US Army rose among the local population, which up to then had been left alone without any protection.

The focus of fast-jet operations became what was termed non-traditional intelligence, surveillance and reconnaissance (NTISR) tactics during missions to support US bases around Baghdad. The aim was to have jets overhead around the clock, using their electro-optical targeting pods to improve situational awareness for ground troops and detect insurgent threats before they developed into major incidents. Non-kinetic effects were to the fore rather than dropping bombs, according to RAF and US aircrew involved in flying missions over Iraq.

USAF, US Marine Corps, US Navy and RAF aircraft were now equipped with direct data-links to allow the downloading of imagery from their targeting pod direct to ground controllers. RAF officers said NTISR tactics were aimed at countering guerrilla mortar attacks on Coalition bases and improvised-explosive-devices (IED) attacks on Coalition road convoys in 'asymmetric warfare situations where combatants are not clearly defined'.

'We can look on the roofs of houses to see if people are on them or ahead of convoys. Doing NTISR you have to interpret the situation on the ground for army commanders', the RAF pilot said. He described the move to third-generation pods, such as the Litening III and Sniper, as a 'quantum leap forward' because they allow US and UK aircrews to identify specific weapon types being carried by insurgents or IEDs.

'We desperately need it to track people and vehicles and send information direct to the ground controller', said the pilot. 'These pods and terminals give us connectivity to Joint Terminal Attack Controllers.'

Although the RAF and US fast jets usually flew with Paveway satellite/laser-guided bombs for their missions over Iraq, pilots said it became increasingly rare for them to employ their weapons. The crews had an escalatory ladder of weapon employment, starting with low-level shows of force with loud jet noise, to the internal cannon and then bombs. 'It is very rare that we go up the ladder', said an RAF pilot. 'If you drop bombs you have lost [in counter-insurgency warfare]. Bombs are very destructive; we look to achieve low collateral damage.'

The employment of air-dropped weapons could only be carried out with the specific approval of a ground controller. This strict rule of engagement means that air support was always operating in direct support of ground commanders in Iraq.

An equally important element of air support to the land forces in Iraq in 2007 was intelligence, surveillance, targeting and reconnaissance (ISTAR) activity. As with close air support, the needs of those on the ground were paramount in ISTAR operations. Procedures had been established to allow ground commanders to bid for support for airborne ISTAR assets, ranging from RC-135 Rivet Joint electronic-surveillance aircraft, P-3C AIP Orion multi-mission aircraft, MQ/RQ-1 Predator, MQ-9 Reaper and RQ-4 Global Hawk unmanned aerial vehicles. These UAVs were used to establish five near-permanent orbits over central Iraq and then train their sensors on targets of interest, as requested by ground commanders. Ground-force commanders were then allocated sensor coverage for specific periods according to their requirements and the relative importance of their operations. Each US Army brigade in Iraq had its own RQ-7 Shadow tactical UAV system that worked only in its specific area of operations. By 2009, there were more than 5,000 UAVs operating over Iraq.

In much the same way that close air support was now directed by front-line troops, ISTAR support was moved down the same decentralised operations route. Old-style intelligence systems or stovepipes, which resulted in intelligence 'product' collected by airborne sensors being analysed in centralised headquarters before being distributed back out to front-line troops, have largely been rendered obsolete by technological developments.

General Atomics MQ-9A Reaper

The Reaper is the next evolution of the Predator family of unmanned aerial vehicles, which entered service in 2007. It features a more powerful engine and greater fuel capacity, giving it the ability to get on station more quickly and stay on station for far longer than the smaller Predator. USAF and RAF jointly operate Reapers, supporting Coalition forces in Iraq and Afghanistan via satellite links from Creech Air Force Base in Nevada.

Powerplant: Honeywell TP331-10T turboprop engine, 950 SHP (712 kW)
Fuel capacity: 4,000 lb (1,815 kg)
Length: 36 ft (11 m)
Wingspan: 66 ft (20 m)
Height: 12.5 ft (3.8 m)
Maximum take-off weight: 10,500 lb (4760 kg) [45]
Service ceiling: 50,000 ft (15 km)
Endurance: 14–28 hours (14 hours fully loaded)
Range: 3,200 nm (3,682 miles, 5,926 km)
Payload: 3,750 lb (1,700 kg)
Maximum speed: 260 kts (300 mph, 482 km/h), AN/APY-8 Lynx II radar, AN/DAS-1 MTS-B Multi-Spectral Targeting System, 6 Hardpoints, 1,500 lb (680 kg) on the two inboard weapons stations, 500–600 lb (230–270 kg) on the two middle stations, 150–200 lb (68–91 kg) on the outboard stations. Up to fourteen AGM-114 Hellfire air-to-ground missiles can be carried, or four Hellfire missiles and two 500 lb (230 kg) GBU-12 Paveway II laser-guided bombs. The ability to carry the JDAM in the future is also possible, as well as the AIM-9 Sidewinder.

Moving civilians by air was a vital element in winning hearts and minds in Iraq. *(USAF)*

MQ-9 Reaper armed unmanned aerial vehicles took on an increasing role in Iraq as ground commanders demanded real-time video imagery of the complex battlefield. *(USAF)*

The RAF Merlin HC.3 was the workhorse of British helicopter forces in southern Iraq from 2005 onwards. *(Agusta Westland)*

US Marines were able to use the new V-22 Osprey tilt rotor from 2008 onwards to replace their ageing CH-46E Sea Knight helicopters. *(USMC)*

Moving civilians by air was a vital element in winning hearts and minds in Iraq. *(USAF)*

MQ-9 Reaper armed unmanned aerial vehicles took on an increasing role in Iraq as ground commanders demanded real-time video imagery of the complex battlefield. *(USAF)*

In 2007, US and British troops in Iraq had large numbers of hand-held Remote Operations Video-Enhanced Receiver, or ROVER, terminals that allowed them to download in real-time imagery from any suitably equipped UAV or targeting pod on a fast jet within range. This technology put intelligence information and imagery directly into the hands of front-line troops, eliminating several layers of military bureaucracy. The troops reported that it had dramatically increased the number of occasions they had called up air support.

The Iraq conflict has seen the widespread use of armed UAVs, but as with manned attack aircraft, any authorisation for the employment of ordnance has to gained from ground controllers. The use of ROVER terminals speeded up this procedure.

The presence of the jets, attack helicopters and UAVs over the US bases in Baghdad provided them with reassurance that if something went wrong then they could get help very quickly. Through the summer of 2007, the effect of the surge and the new US tactics began to transform the situation on the ground. The emphasis on protection of the population, rather than kinetic, or 'shoot first and ask questions later', types of operation made it increasingly less likely that US troops would have to call for air support. But the presence of air power overhead meant US troops had the confidence to take risks and reduce their use of firepower. This created a 'virtuous circle' of improving security during 2007. Attacks on US troops and the civilian population dropped considerably. The number of US troops killed in Iraq in May 2007 was 126, but by July 2007 this had dropped to fifty-five, and then to just fourteen in December. More importantly, the number of civilian casualties also dropped dramatically. Car bombs killed 253 civilians in Baghdad in February 2007, but only twelve in December. This drop in violence meant that air support rarely involved escalation to the use of live weapons during the latter half of 2007.

US casualties from IEDs also dropped because US and allied airlift forces were used extensively to move personnel around Iraq to avoid using vulnerable roads. These aircraft are used to fly a network of shuttle services between bases in Iraq and the USAF's main regional transport hubs at Ali Al Salem airbase in Kuwait, Al Udeid in Qatar and Balad inside Iraq. During major troop rotations, thousands of troops were flown from the bases in continental USA or Europe to the hubs by charter aircraft before being shuttled to their deployed locations by C-130s or US Army CH-47 Chinooks. On a daily basis, other C-130s flew circular shuttles around the main airbases in central Iraq to pick up and drop off personnel who needed to move between locations. Another major activity of the C-130 fleet was the air-dropping of supplies to remote detachments of troops. These airlift efforts were credited with saving hundreds of lives simply by reducing the number of US personnel who had to drive around Iraq, so reducing their exposure to attack.

One area where the US forces became more aggressive was in the hunt for the hard-core insurgent group known as the al-Qaeda in Iraq. The US special forces deployed Task Force Black of Delta Force and Rangers troops to Balad airbase, north of Baghdad, supported by MH-6, UH-60 and MH-47 helicopters of the 160th Special Operations Aviation Regiment. They launched raids on al-Qaeda in Iraq bases after employing a special US Army aerial reconnaissance unit, entitled Task Force

Odin, equipped with Hawker Beechcraft King Air RC-12 aircraft fitted with night-vision systems, signals-intelligence sensors and real-time down-links, and the new General Atomics MQ-1C Warrior-armed variant of the Predator. Intelligence from these aircraft and signals intelligence was shared instantly with the strike units, to allow raids to be launched within a few minutes of insurgent bases being detected. Task Forces Black and Odin were credited with the killing of 3,000 insurgents. British special forces contributed to Task Force Black, including on occasions RAF Puma HC.1s of 33 and 230 Squadrons, RAF Chinook HC.2s of 7 Squadron and Army Air Corps Lynx AH.7s of 657 Squadron.

The US land headquarters in Iraq and the senior USAF leadership at the CASOC worked hard to smooth the procedures and tactics for synchronising air and land operations in Iraq as a result of lessons learnt during the surge. During 2008, they held three air synchronisation conferences at Al-Faw Palace in Baghdad's heavily fortified 'Green Zone'. The last one took place in early March 2008, and brought together ground operators and planners from the US Army-led Multinational Corps – Iraq and its subordinate units, as well as air power experts from CASOC and the 18th Expeditionary Air Support Operations Group. Most discussion fell into one or more of three key focus areas: streamlining the kill chain, optimising intelligence, surveillance and reconnaissance, and force protection. 'This was truly a joint effort ... from the planning stages through to execution', said Lt Col Matt Isler, a USAF air liaison officer in Iraq.

Charge of the Knights

In March 2008, Iraqi forces launched a major offensive, dubbed Operation Charge of the Knights, in the southern city of Basra, which dealt a deadly blow to pro-Iranian Shia militia groups that had seized control after British troops pulled out of their bases in the centre of the city in the autumn of 2007. Iraq's government ordered reinforcements from Baghdad to enhance the garrison of the city ahead of the offensive. The initial advance was undertaken without co-ordination with US and UK forces based at Basra airbase, in the desert outside the city. It appeared as if the offensive had stalled, and General Petraeus ordered the USAF to assist in the deployment of extra reinforcements to be flown south to Basra from Baghdad in C-17s and C-130s.

The street battles between militia forces loyal to the rogue cleric Moqtada Sadr and Iraqi troops directed personally by Prime Minister Nouri al-Maliki, who had flown down to Basra, pulled in US and UK forces to provide specialist intelligence, surveillance, targeting and reconnaissance (ISTAR), and air support for the government side.

USAF MQ-1B Predator and British Army Elbit Hermes 450 UAVs operated over the city continuously during the battle. US and UK special-forces detachments working alongside the Iraqi military command in Basra were able to view imagery of militia activity from the UAVs on ROVER III terminals. US special forces' JTAC teams working with front-line government troops also used the terminals to direct a series of missile strikes from Predators on militia positions.

The RAF Merlin HC.3 was the workhorse of British helicopter forces in southern Iraq from 2005 onwards. *(Agusta Westland)*

US Marines were able to use the new V-22 Osprey tilt rotor from 2008 onwards to replace their ageing CH-46E Sea Knight helicopters. *(USMC)*

The OH-58D Kiowa Warrior was the natural stable-mate of the bigger AH-64 Apache over Iraqi battlefields. *(USAF)*

Throughout the battle US and UK fast jets were overhead to provide shows of force to deter militia fighters. RAF Tornado GR4s from 13 Squadron conducted a strafing attack with their 27 mm cannon against militia fighters in Basra on the opening day of the battle. On 27 March, US Navy Boeing F/A-18C Hornets and F/A-18E Super Hornets flying from the USS *Harry S. Truman* carried out more strafing attacks in Basra. A day later a USAF MQ-1B destroyed a militia mortar emplacement with a Lockheed Martin AGM-114 Hellfire missile.

A day later, a US JTAC working with Iraqi special-operations forces troops in street battles in Basra called down an airstrike that killed sixteen militia fighters. The fighting continued on 30 March when US Air Force F-16s and US Navy F/A-18Es dropped Boeing GBU-38 joint direct attack munitions (JDAMs) on militia mortar teams, machine-gun emplacements and occupied buildings. Although militia commanders called a cease-fire in Basra on 31 March, US and UK air operations continued, with a Predator strike on a militia road block on that day. The next day an RAF Tornado dropped a Raytheon Enhanced Paveway II 1,000 lb GPS-guided bomb on a militia rocket launcher.

The offensive was a major success for the Iraqi government and its army. The militia were driven from Basra and the Iraqi army seemed to thrive on its new-found confidence. This crowned the success of General Pretreaus's surge. By the summer of 2008, the US military was confident that the security situation was now stable enough for it to begin to draw down its forces to pre-surge levels. In February 2009, the newly inaugurated US President, Barack Odama, announced a plan to pull all US combat troops out of Iraq by the middle of 2010, with all US forces leaving by 2011. America's longest war of the modern era appeared to be coming to an end.

Assessment

Over the first eight years of the US occupation of Iraq, the nature of air operations changed dramatically. The era of centrally controlled air power, with air commanders sitting in the CAOC directing individual airstrikes, appears to be largely a thing of the past.

Technology devolved much of the tactical decision-making function to troops on the ground, often within rifle-range of the enemy.

By 2009, air commanders concentrated on the 'big picture' to make sure that the right forces were in the air at the right time, over the right place, ready to respond to the call for help from troops in contact with the enemy. For some air power purists this development was not welcome and undermined the case for air as the decisive force in its own right. But the change in tactics worked, and US-led air power made an important contribution to the eventual success of the 'surge' that brought the Iraq insurgency under control.

The nature of counter-insurgency warfare in Iraq meant that the centralised concept for the use of air power was rendered largely obsolete. If airmen had not adapted to the needs to the ground forces they would have faced serious criticism, and the long-term future of this service would have been called into doubt.

US Navy F/A-18 Hornets flew almost daily missions over Iraq from 2003 onwards as the service committed carriers almost full time to support the US effort. *(US Navy)*

Monitoring the Iraqi battlefield in real time was the job of the USAF E-8 Joint STARS fleet, which provided wide-area and synthetic-aperture radar coverage. The latter system was much in demand because it could find targets in bad weather, which could blind electro-optical sensors. *(USAF)*

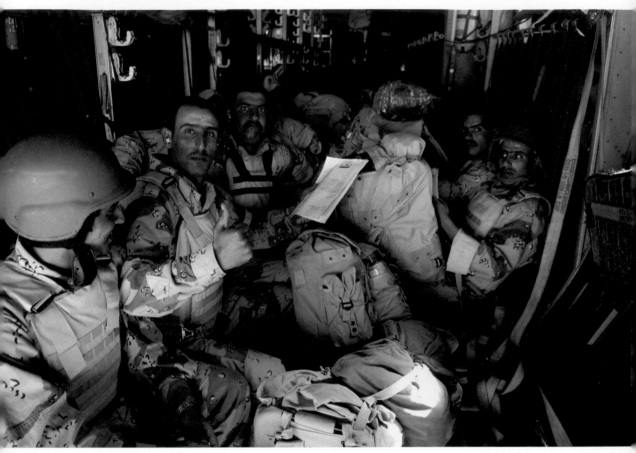

USAF C-17s moved thousands of Iraqi troops from Baghdad to Basra during Operation Charge of the Knights, which is credited with ending militia rule in the southern city. *(USAF)*

Specially modified US Army King Air surveillance aircraft were drafted into Task Force Odin, which was instrumental in tracking down key insurgent leaders during the US 'surge' in 2007 and 2008. *(US Army)*

Afghanistan, 2006–2009

Phase 3 – ISAF, 2006–2009

From 2002 to 2006, ISAF had a limited role in Kabul and the north of Afghanistan with US-led Coalition forces' operations in the rest of the central Asian country. US troops relied almost exclusively on air power based in Afghanistan, central Asia or Diego Garcia during this period. Occasionally reconnaissance assets in the Middle East could be called upon, but the war in Iraq meant there was little capacity to spare from 2003 onwards. The CAOC, which had now relocated from PSAB to Al Udeid in Qatar, still had an important role co-ordinating air transport operations into Afghanistan, but by this point land routes had been opened up, taking much of the logistic burden off NATO's airlift assets.

In 2005, NATO nations agreed that ISAF would take on a greater burden and expand its responsibility to cover all the country during 2006. This resulted in a major shake-up of air support operations in Afghanistan, and assets based in the Middle East became increasingly involved. The role of the CAOC changed, with NATO liaison staff being posted to co-ordinate requests for air support from ISAF ground-force headquarters in Kabul and Kandahar.

US Navy aircraft carriers were on station in the Arabian Sea throughout 2006 and 2007 to support NATO's Afghan mission. *(US Navy)*

USAF B-1B Lancer bombers were able to stay on station for up to ten hours, and provide 'on-call' close air support for NATO troops under attack in Afghanistan. *(USAF)*

CHAPTER TWENTY-EIGHT

Afghanistan, 2006–2009

Phase 3 – ISAF, 2006–2009

From 2002 to 2006, ISAF had a limited role in Kabul and the north of Afghanistan with US-led Coalition forces' operations in the rest of the central Asian country. US troops relied almost exclusively on air power based in Afghanistan, central Asia or Diego Garcia during this period. Occasionally reconnaissance assets in the Middle East could be called upon, but the war in Iraq meant there was little capacity to spare from 2003 onwards. The CAOC, which had now relocated from PSAB to Al Udeid in Qatar, still had an important role co-ordinating air transport operations into Afghanistan, but by this point land routes had been opened up, taking much of the logistic burden off NATO's airlift assets.

In 2005, NATO nations agreed that ISAF would take on a greater burden and expand its responsibility to cover all the country during 2006. This resulted in a major shake-up of air support operations in Afghanistan, and assets based in the Middle East became increasingly involved. The role of the CAOC changed, with NATO liaison staff being posted to co-ordinate requests for air support from ISAF ground-force headquarters in Kabul and Kandahar.

US Navy aircraft carriers were on station in the Arabian Sea throughout 2006 and 2007 to support NATO's Afghan mission. (*US Navy*)

Offensive air assets based in Afghanistan, such as RAF Harrier GR7s, were switched to support NATO, but until heavy fighting broke out in southern Afghanistan in the summer of 2006 it was not envisaged that Middle East-based Coalition assets would participate in operations in support of the country.

The upsurge in fighting with Taliban insurgents in June 2006 led US and UK air commanders in the CAOC being swamped with requests for additional air support. To improve heavy bomber coverage, the USAF moved its B-1B Lancer detachment from Diego Garcia to Al Udeid in Qatar. A major shortfall was in reconnaissance and surveillance, so USAF E-8 JSTARS ground-surveillance-radar aircraft, USAF RC-135s and US Navy P-3Cs at Al Udeid all began to fly more missions over Afghanistan. The Global Hawk force at Al Dhafra similarly began devoting more effort to Afghan operations.

More RAF reconnaissance aircraft were also diverted to support the Afghan mission. The 39 Squadron Canberra PR9 detachment had returned to Seeb in early 2006 to support the deployment of IASF troops to southern Afghanistan, only to be withdrawn in June as the veteran aircraft were retired from service as a cost-saving measure. To fill the gap, the RAF deployed an additional Nimrod MR2 to Seeb to fly a mission over Afghanistan to hunt out Taliban targets with its Wescam MX-15 electro-optical cameras. Two Tristar tankers of 216 Squadron were also sent to Seeb to refuel the Nimrods and US Navy strike aircraft heading to Afghanistan. Tragedy struck the RAF Nimrod detachment in September 2006 when a fire caused one of the aircraft to crash near Kandahar with the loss of all on board.

Afghan operations continued at this high tempo over the next three years as fighting with the Taliban remained intense. The CAOC continued its co-ordinating role, but as the airbase infrastructure inside Afghanistan was enhanced, the use of air assets based in the Middle East region gradually reduced. Air support operations peaked in the summer of 2007 when the US Navy dispatched extra aircraft carriers to the Middle East to allow one carrier to be continuously on station off both Iraq and Afghanistan, providing offensive support.

RQ-4 Global Hawk unmanned aerial vehicles monitored Afghanistan 24/7 during missions flown from the USAF base in the United Arab Emirates. (USAF)

Rockwell B-1B Lancer

Affectionately known as 'the Bone' by its USAF crews, the B-1B has proved a potent weapon during campaigns in the Middle East over the past decade. It has been progressively enhanced with precision-guided weapons, and most recently has had Litening advanced targeting pods integrated to allow B-1B crews to pinpoint and attack very small targets, such as individual insurgents in complex urban environments. B-1Bs operated from Diego Garcia against Afghanistan and Iraq until moving forward to Al Udeid in Qatar to allow greater endurance over the area of operations.

Crew: 4 (aircraft commander, co-pilot, offensive systems officer and defensive systems officer)
Length: 146 ft (44.5 m)
Wingspan: Extended, 137 ft (41.8 m); Swept, 79 ft (24.1 m)
Height: 34 ft (10.4 m)
Max take-off weight: 477,000 lb (216,400 kg)
Powerplant: Four General Electric F101-GE-102 augmented turbofans
Maximum speed: At altitude, Mach 1.25 (830 mph, 1,330 km/h)
  At low level, Mach 0.92 (700 mph, 1,130 km/h)
Range: 6,478 nm (7,456 miles, 11,998 km)
Combat radius: 2,993 nm (3,445 miles, 5,543 km)

Armament
Hardpoints: Six external hardpoints for 59,000 lb (27,000 kg) of ordnance (use for weapons currently restricted by START I treaty [42]), and three internal bomb bays for 75,000 lb (34,000 kg) of ordnance.
Bombs: 84 Mk-82 AIR inflatable retarder general-purpose bombs, or 81 Mk-82 low-drag general-purpose bombs, or 84 Mk-62 Quickstrike sea mines, or 24 Mk-65 naval mines, or 30 CBU-87/89/CBU-97 cluster bomb units (CBU), or 30 CBU-103/104/105 wind-corrected munitions dispenser, or 24 GBU-31 JDAM GPS-guided bombs, or 15 GBU-38 JDAM GPS-guided bombs (Mk-82 general-purpose warhead), or 24 Mk 84 general-purpose bombs, or 12 AGM-154 joint standoff weapons, or 96 or 144 GBU-39 small-diameter bomb GPS-guided bombs (not fielded on B-1 yet), or 24 AGM-158 JASSMs, or 24 B61 thermonuclear variable-yield gravity bombs, or 24 B83 nuclear bombs.

USAF B-1B Lancer bombers were able to stay on station for up to ten hours, and provide 'on-call' close air support for NATO troops under attack in Afghanistan. *(USAF)*

CHAPTER TWENTY-NINE

Israel and Syria Confrontation, 2000–2009

Israel and Syria remain officially at war. Tension remains high, and each country's air force continues to probe in the other's air space.

On occasions this 'cold war' has turned hot. The potential for conflict was shown on 28 June 2006,when, in response to a Hamas attack on IDF troops in Gaza, the IASF was ordered to buzz the Syrian presidential palace in the Latakiya suburb of Damascus. Rattling the windows of the Syrian President, Bashar al-Assad, was an easy mission for the IASF F-16I force.

Israeli F-15s reportedly led the strike on Syria's nuclear reactor in 2007. (*Author*)

Commercial satellite imagery shows the Deir ez-Zor site before the Israeli air strike in 2007. *(Google Earth)*

A far more difficult challenge emerged after intelligence reports indicated that Syria was trying to build a nuclear reactor in co-operation with North Korea. The site, near the city of Dir A-Zur in north-east Syria, was far from the Israeli border and would require any strike force to penetrate through or around several Syrian surface-to-air missile (SAM) engagement zones.

The Israeli government and IASF have never confirmed their participation in the raid on 27 September 2007. But when the White House in Washington released a dossier about the raid, including intelligence photos taken inside the reactor site, the role of Israeli bombers in its destruction became difficult to hide.

The first indication that something had happened was when the Syrians released reports that their air defence had fired at 'enemy aircraft' and forced them to flee Syrian air space. Then Turkey confirmed that it had found aircraft drop-tanks close to the Syrian border.

This seemed to suggest that Israeli aircraft had flown out over the eastern Mediterranean Sea, then skirted along the Turkish border before turning south to strike their target. The ranges involved would point to the conformal-fuel-tank-equipped F-16I or F-15I aircraft being involved, possibly supported by the new Gulfstream G550 Compact Airborne Early Warning Aircraft.

The results of the strike were difficult to judge. The Syrians immediately bulldozed the site of the reactor, so commercial satellite imagery of it tells little about the raid.

The political impact was more impressive. The Syrians distanced themselves from the nuclear project and denied any ambitions to build a nuclear weapon.

CHAPTER THIRTY

Somalia Strikes, 2007–2009

Senior US military commanders and Central Intelligence Agency (CIA) officials in the Middle East have long suspected that Somalia was a haven for supporters of Osama bin Laden. The anarchic, lawless situation in Somalia was a great worry for the Bush administration, which feared it would eventually require military intervention. The troubled history of US interventions in Somalia, as well as over-commitment of US forces in Iraq and Afghanistan, meant it would be difficult to dispatch a large force of ground troops to the country.

In this situation, the USA would rely on air power to monitor what was happening in Somalia and react to any events. In late 2001 and early 2002, US, British and German aircraft were dispatched to East Africa to monitor Somalia and the seas

USAF AC-130U Spectre gunships were sent to hit Islamic fundamentalists in Somalia in January 2009. *(USAF)*

An unidentified light aircraft parachuted a $3 million dollar ransom to pirates holding the Saudi-owned oil tanker *Sirius Star* in January 2009. *(US Navy)*

Royal Navy Merlin HM.1 maritime helicopters have been used to support Coalition anti-piracy patrols off Somalia, using their radar and data links to identify threats to civilian shipping. *(Author)*

Lockheed P-3C Orion

The US Navy's primary maritime patrol aircraft has been a common sight in the Middle East for more than forty years. Almost permanent detachments have been sustained in Bahrain, Al Udeid and Masirah Island since 1990 to support embargo enforcement against Iraq. The aircraft currently deployed in the region are P-3C Anti-surface-warfare Improvement Programme (AIP) variants equipped for overland surveillance, with real-time video imagery download capabilities.

Crew: 11
Length: 116 ft 10 in. (35.6 m)
Wingspan: 99 ft 8 in. (30.4 m)
Height: 33 ft 8.5 in. (10.3 m)
Max take-off weight: 142,000 lb (64,400 kg)
Powerplant: 4 Allison T56-A-14 turboprops,
    4,600 shp (3,700 kW) each

Performance
Maximum speed: 405 knots (750 km/h)
Range: 5,600 miles ferry (9,000 km)

Armament
Bombs: 20,000 lb (9,000 kg)
Missiles: AGM-84 Harpoon, the Standoff Land Attack Missile, AGM-65 Maverick
Sonobuoys: 48 pre-loaded, 50+ deployable from inside
Other: Mk 46, Mk 50 and MU90 Impact torpedoes, mines, depth charges

around the country. In October 2002, US Central Command set up Combined Joint Task Force – Horn of Africa (CJTF-HOA) in Djibouti. This small headquarters team was tasked with monitoring al-Qaeda activity in the Horn of Africa, in co-operation with the CIA.

The rise to power in 2006 of the Islamic Courts regime in the Somali capital of Mogadishu led to the USA organising military intervention. In January 2007, the US provided military and political support to an operation by Ethiopian troops to seize Mogadishu and depose the Islamic Courts.

US intervention was co-ordinated by CJTF-HOA, and US Special Operations Command AC-130U Spectre gunships were deployed to support the Ethiopians. A detachment of MQ-1 Predator-armed UAVs, believed to be operated by the CIA, supported the mission, and US Navy P-3Cs also monitored the Somali coast. The basing for these forces is unclear, but Djibouti, Mombasa in Kenya and Masirah Island off Oman are strong candidates.

The USS *Dwight D. Eisenhower* carrier battlegroup was also diverted from the Arabian Sea to provide more air support, including airborne command and control, combat search and rescue and surveillance.

During the three-week-long crisis, AC-130 strikes occurred on 8 January, when a group of suspected al-Qaeda leaders were attacked south of Mogadishu. At least three more AC-130 strikes occurred. US special-forces troops also made a number of small-scale incursions into Somalia to help in targeting and to conduct bomb-damage assessment after attacks. These operations all took place in a media vacuum, with no coverage or film footage of US operations appearing.

The US forces pulled back after the Ethiopians took Mogadishu, and since then surveillance efforts have continued with considerable intensity.

The upsurge in Somali piracy in 2008 has also attracted serious attention from US forces. The seizure of the US cargo ship MV *Maersk Alabama* in April 2008 resulted in the US Navy P-3C force providing continuous surveillance coverage of the incident. US Navy SEAL commandos parachuted to the USS *Bainbridge* before rescuing the captain of the cargo ship. Scan Eagle UAVs launched from the amphibious-warfare vessel USS *Boxer* joined the surveillance effort over the *Maersk-Alabama*.

CHAPTER THIRTY-ONE

The Future of Air Power in the Middle East

Analysing Middle East air power is a far-from-easy subject. Fielding effective air power is akin to grooming a winning Formula One racing-car team: it involves being ahead of the technological curve, moulding a highly motivated team and training it to a higher level than your opponents. A winning team one season can easily slip behind if it neglects even the smallest thing, is denied funding or loses key personnel.

Over the past sixty years, the Middle East has seen the combat capability of air forces rise and fall with great regularity. Israel has consistently been number one, but it is not given that this situation will remain for ever, in the wake of the country's economic difficulties and reduction, in real terms, of US financial aid.

Unmanned air vehicles, such as the BAE Systems' Teranis, look set to play an increasing role in Middle East conflicts. (*BAE Systems*)

Gaining access to technology and design information, as the UAE did with their Desert Falcon project, will rise up the agenda of Middle Eastern countries. *(Lockheed Martin)*

The USAF's prestigious F-22 Raptor air dominance fighter could soon be heading to the Middle East to take part in training exercises. *(USAF)*

Turkey and Israel look set to be the first Middle East nations to buy the US-made F-35 Joint Strike Fighter. *(Lockheed Martin)*

Table 18. Comparison of Middle East Air Power in 2009.

	Number/% 3/4th Generation Combat Aircraft	BVR Active AAM	Long-Range PGM	AAR	UAV	High-Level Pilot Training
Bahrain	33/100%	x				
Egypt	222/63%				x	
Iran	115/54%			x	x	
Israel	425/94%	x		x	x	x
Jordan	94/78%	x				
Kuwait	39/100%					
Oman	45/100%	x				
Qatar	12/100%					
Saudi Arabia	245/100%	x	x	x		
Syria	250/41%					
Turkey	227/51%	x	x	x	x	
UAE	140/100%	x	x	x	x	
Yemen	13/12.5%					
USAF	72/100%	x	x	x	x	x
USN	54/100%	x	x	x		x
USMC	24/100%	x				
RAF	8/100%	x	x		x	x
French	6/100%	x	x		x	

Jordan in the 1960s and 1970s had a powerful and well-trained air force, but it is now only a shadow of its former glory. Likewise, Egypt has not managed to keep up with Israel, in spite of its procurement of large numbers of Western aircraft. Turkey, thanks to its NATO heritage, is now coming on strongly. The UAE is also investing heavily in modern air warfare technology. Saudi Arabia has set the standard for its regional rivals by ordering the Eurofighter Typhoon for delivery from mid-2009, making it the first air force in the region to acquire true 4th-generation combat aircraft.

The dark horses are Syria and Iran. The Syrian armed forces inflicted some nasty surprises on the Israelis in the 1982 Lebanon War, and they could be expected to put up a strong show, even if their technology is now somewhat dated.

Iran's air force modernisation programme continues at a steady but slow pace, purchases of new equipment have been slowed, and resources seem to have been concentrated on training and ordnance upgrades. Aircrew training has taken place in China, Russia and Pakistan, and an increasing number of new weapons are being seen on Iranian combat aircraft.

Iraq's air force was dealt a deadly blow in 2003, driving the war with the USA, and is only just beginning to acquire modern aircraft and equipment in sizeable quantities.

Implications of current equipment programmes and requirements

In spite of the downturn in Middle East economies in 2009 due to a drop in crude oil prices, the states of the region continue to purchase large quantities of advanced air warfare hardware. Table 19 is based on known requirements, orders or aspirations.

The second decade of the twenty-first century will see a dramatic evolution in the military balance with the introduction of a number of new capabilities to the region.

Will the air power balance change?

The air warfare capabilities being sought by Middle Eastern armed forces, if accompanied by improvements in personnel and training, will threaten considerably the current superiority of the Western and Israeli air forces.

Political and economic imperatives mean it is unlikely that European, Chinese and Russian governments, or even the United States, will be able to resist the demands of Middle Eastern countries to acquire the latest and best air warfare technology.

Modern airframes have always been very numerous in the Middle East. What is new is the interest being shown in the technologies and capabilities that allow air power to be used in a hard-hitting, high-tempo, offensive air campaign. For most of the second half of the twentieth century only Israel boasted what could be called a 'full-spectrum' air force. In the second decade of the twenty-first century, Saudi Arabia, Turkey and the UAE will be near to acquiring full-spectrum capabilities.

Table 19. Middle East air power requirements by 2015.

	4th Generation Combat Aircraft	BVR Active AAM	Long-Range PGM	AAR	UAV	High-Level Pilot Training
Bahrain	x	x				x
Egypt	x	x	x	x	x	x
Iran	x		x	x		x
Iraq	x	x	x		x	x
Israel	x	x	x	x	x	x
Jordan	x					
Kuwait	x					
Oman	x	x				x
Qatar						
Saudi Arabia	x	x	x	x		
Syria	x	x		x		x
Turkey	x		x		x	x
UAE	x	x	x	x	x	x
Yemen						

Note: C3I is command, communications and intelligence gathering systems, such as satellite communications, electronic warfare and reconnaissance systems.

Things such as air-to-air refuelling, electronic warfare and precision-guided munitions were once a preserve of Western air forces, but these capabilities are now becoming widely available.

It is also relatively easy for any nation with a basic aviation, engineering and computer software industry, such as Turkey, Iran, India or Israel, to produce reasonably advanced weaponry domestically. The West's monopoly of 'hi-technology' has been well and truly broken. It is only a matter of time before this technology for air warfare weapons is used against the West.

There are a number of key decision points approaching which will indicate if the Middle East air power race will be ratcheted up a major notch.

- The sale of 4th-generation agile combat aircraft such as the Su-35, Rafale, Eurofighter Typhoon and F-22 Raptor to air forces in the region.
- The fielding of active radar-guided, beyond-visual-range, air-to-air missiles, such as the American AIM-120 and Russian R-77 AAM-EE in the Middle East, which will provide the users with a significant and possibly decisive advantage in air combat.
- Large-scale deliveries of advanced precision-guided munitions such as the MBDA Apache/Storm Shadow and Boeing AGM-84 SLAM or their Russian/Chinese equivalents.
- The fielding of ballistic missile defence systems, which will increase pressure to field more advanced combat aircraft and longer-range precision-guided munitions.
- Widespread availability of commercial satellite communications and remote sensing (reconnaissance) systems, which will provide Middle Eastern countries with unprecedented 'battlefield awareness' and at a stroke remove one of the West's (and Israel's) major advantages. These systems when combined with long-range PGM will make key targets highly vulnerable.

While arms control may seem like the obvious route to take to restrict the spreading of destabilising air warfare capabilities to the Middle East, these technologies are now openly available on the world defence market, and some countries now have indigenous aviation defence industries capable of producing them. The genie is now out of the bottle. Only an unlikely outbreak of 'peace and harmony' or a major collapse in the crude oil price is likely to prevent the Middle East air power race continuing at its current rapid pace.

Future Middle East air wars
The underlying sources of tension and conflict in the Middle East look unlikely to be resolved in the near future. It is therefore highly likely that air power will be involved in conflict in the region at some point. State-on-state conflict is currently the least likely in the range of possible scenarios, so the focus of future air campaigns is probably going to be asymmetric warfare.

The experiences of Iraq, Gaza and Lebanon are very relevant, and show the potential and limitations of air power against opponents who want to hide their forces in urban areas and civilian populations. The comparison of the USA in Iraq and Israel in Lebanon shows that mastery of technology and tactics of air warfare do not compensate for failures in overall political and strategic direction. The USA was able to built a coherent political and military strategy in Iraq that turned around the war in Iraq in 2007/8, but Israel's flawed strategy in Lebanon in 2006 meant its war was doomed to fail.

Just as the US and Israeli air forces learnt from their experiences in asymmetric campaigns, insurgent and paramilitary groups are undoubtedly learning lessons. Future asymmetric campaigns will therefore be very different from recent battles, and air power involvement will likewise be very different. The upsurge in piracy attacks off the coast of Somalia and the US-led response show the dynamic nature of air warfare in the Middle East.

The proliferation of modern aircraft around the Middle East mean that any state-on-state war in the region will be likely to involve the employment of advanced air warfare equipment. Saudi Arabia, UAE, Turkey and Egypt are all near to acquiring air warfare capabilities on a par with Israeli, British, French and US air forces.

If any of the major air forces of the Middle East is ever allowed to use its modern weaponry in a major war, this conflict will be unlike anything that has been seen before in the region. The world is used to seeing media coverage of US and British air power, but Middle Eastern air forces now, or soon will, have similar capabilities, and have the ability to inflict considerable damage on opponents in high-tempo air campaigns.

A major Middle Eastern war will look very different from the asymmetric wars we have seen over the past decade. Precision air strikes on strategic targets, such as oil and energy infrastructure, communications hubs, military bases and weapons of mass destruction sites, will be the norm in these wars.

Given the fragile nature of many societies in the Middle East, this type of warfare will have lasting political impacts, leading to the collapse of regimes, insurrections, environmental and humanitarian disasters. Modern air power gives Middle Eastern states unprecedented abilities to inflict death and destruction on their opponents.

Even though the Middle East's air forces are rapidly improving their equipment and capabilities, it is unlikely that the current dominance of US air power in the region will be successfully challenged. The USA is likely to retain the ability to 'take down' any Middle Eastern state, as it did to Iraq in 2003, if it is able to summon the political will to do so. The role of US air power in any future 'rapid decisive operation' in the Middle East will be instrumental to its success.

Air power will continue to dominate Middle East battlefields for many years to come.

Sources

To compile the inventories, a wide range of published sources have been consulted, including a number of editions of the following:

Magazines
Airforces Monthly
Air Force
Air Force, Army, Navy Times
Air International
Aviation & Space Technology Week
Code One Magazine
Defence News
Flight Daily News
Flight International
Jane's All the World's Aircraft
Jane's Defence Weekly
Jane's International Defence Review
Jane's Intelligence Review
Jane's Sentinel
RUSI Journal
Strategic Assessments (National Defence University)
The Hook
World Air Power Journal/International Air Power Journal

Books
CIA World Fact Book
Cordesman, Anthony, *Iran & Iraq: The Threat from the Northern Gulf*, Westview
The Conduct of the Persian Gulf War, US DoD
The IISS Military Balance (annual)

Corporate
A number of international companies have provided details of their products sold to the Middle East, including EADS, Boeing Compaby, BAE Systems, Israeli Aircraft Industries, Lockheed Martin, Matra BAe Dynamics/MBDA, MiG-MAPO, Raytheon, Sukhoi OKB.

Internet
www.earth.google.com
www.globesecurity.org
www.scramble.nl

This study is by its very nature a 'snap shot' of Middle East Airpower at the end of the first decade of the 21st Century. If readers have additional information that could be used to update future editions please direct it to the author via the publisher.